To Dave,

Another book written by your son-in-law! I give credit to the Lord for providing me the wisdom and commitment to write and inspire others.

Enjoy!

May You and Annie have a great year ahead of 2004!

R. Barri & H. Loraine ☺

MALE CRIME AND DEVIANCE

MALE CRIME AND DEVIANCE

Exploring Its Causes, Dynamics, and Nature

By

R. BARRI FLOWERS

CHARLES C THOMAS • PUBLISHER, LTD.
Springfield • Illinois • U.S.A.

Published and Distributed Throughout the World by

CHARLES C THOMAS • PUBLISHER, LTD.
2600 South First Street
Springfield, Illinois 62704

©*2003 by* CHARLES C THOMAS • PUBLISHER, LTD.

ISBN 0-398-07400-3 (hard)
ISBN 0-398-07401-1 (paper)

Library of Congress Catalog Card Number: 2003040179

With THOMAS BOOKS *careful attention is given to all details of manufacturing
and design. It is the Publisher's desire to present books that are satisfactory as to their
physical qualities and artistic possibilities and appropriate for their particular use.*
THOMAS BOOKS *will be true to those laws of quality that assure a good name
and good will.*

Printed in the United States of America
SR-*R*-3

Library of Congress Cataloging-in-Publication Data

Flowers, Ronald B.
 Male crime and deviance : exploring its causes, dynamics, and nature / by R. Barri Flowers.
   p. cm.
 Includes bibliographical references and index.
 ISBN 0-398-07400-3 (hard) -- ISBN 0-398-07401-1 (pbk.)
 1. Criminal behavior. 2. Violence in men. 3. Crime--United States. I. Title.

HV6080F56 2003
364′.081′0973--dc21

2003040179

To the future study of crime, criminals, and victims.

And to my parents,
Johnnie Sr. and Marjah Al,
along with my partner in life, love, and happiness,
H. Loraine.

PREFACE

Serious and violent crime has seen a recent rise in this country. This is attributed to, among other things, a depressed economy, the release of more prisoners back into society, access to firearms, and the growth in the teenage population–typically the age group responsible for much of the crime. A number of highly publicized intrafamilial homicides, mass murders, terrorist attacks, and school shootings have further put the focus squarely on crime and violence, prevention, ways to identify offenders, and tough new laws in getting criminals off the street.

Males are primarily responsible for the vast majority of serious crimes. This is reflected in arrest and prisoner data, self-report surveys, and studies on patterns and prevalence of criminal activity. The much greater criminality of males over females for most violent, property, and drug offenses is believed by many criminologists to be due to a variety of sociological and cultural factors and influences. The role of masculinity has been examined in relation to male crime and violence. Some blame biological and psychological variables for male crime and violence. In particular, testosterone has been related in a number of studies to male aggression and violent behavior. Current criminological research often takes a multidisciplinary approach in combining biological, psychological, sociological, and cultural perspectives in the study of criminality.

Male Crime and Deviance: Exploring Its Causes, Dynamics, and Nature seeks to explore in-depth the types of offenses most identified with and committed by males, dynamics of male crime, characteristics of male offenders, how male criminality and delinquency compare with and differ from female delinquent and criminal behavior, explanations for male crime, and efforts at combating crime in this country.

The book is written for undergraduate and graduate level students for coursework in criminal justice, criminology, male aggression, violent behavior, homicide, youth studies, gang studies, delinquency, law, law enforcement, sociology, social science, psychology, biology, and related areas of study. Further, it is intended for general reading by academians, social scientists, psychologists, law officers, medical workers, and laypersons with a vested interest in antisocial behavior and its implications on society.

I offer my thanks to Charles C Thomas for their consistent and excellent contribution to the body of criminology textbooks, including two of my previous works to that effect. *Male Crime and Deviance* will continue that tradition and, no doubt, be an important text in the study of and debate on male antisocial behavior and its implications on society.

Finally, my heart, soul, and undying gratitude go out to my longtime devoted assistant and wife, H. Loraine Flowers. Without her patience, understanding, professionalism, talent, and love, this book would never have been written.

R.B.F.

INTRODUCTION

The study of crime and criminals has traditionally been of either a general (or presumed male) nature or focused on females or juvenile offenders. Male criminality has been implicitly or explicitly examined in terms of overall or total criminal behavior. While this approach allows us some perspective on the male criminal offender, it often tends to make all crime synonymous with male deviance. Although males are responsible for the vast majority of serious, violent, and chronic criminality, their motives, means, precursors, and biological, psychological and/or sociological-cultural correlates of deviant behavior do not necessarily reflect the same conditions that may account for female deviance. Furthermore, adult male offenders are typically unlike juvenile offenders in many respects in terms of criminality and motivating factors, though in other ways they are similar in patterns of offenses and precursors to committing crimes. Differences and similarities also exist within racial and ethnic groups of male offenders, as well as between male and female criminals and delinquents.

In *Male Crime and Deviance*, male antisocial behavior is comprehensively examined through various aspects and dimensions, including in comparison with female deviance. It recognizes the distinct dynamics, nature, and characteristics of male aggression, crime, violence, and delinquency, while exploring theories and correlates of male deviance; racial, ethnic, and age disparities; and different subpatterns and subgroups of male crime, violence, and offenders. Legislative efforts at curbing serious and violent offending and increasing penalties against those convicted of such crimes are also discussed.

Particular attention is given to exploring the relationship between male aggression and masculinity, as well as the role testosterone and other biological factors play in male crime and violence. The book also focuses on the correlations between male violence and aggressive behavior and firearms, violence involving intimates, male sexual violence, bias crimes, workplace violence, terrorism, male perpetrated sexual offenses, youth gang crimes, and school violence. These areas of male criminality and deviance are examined within the context of all male offending, arrest, self-report, and inmate data, along with criminological theoretical approaches to understanding the causes and related factors of male deviant behavior.

The book is divided into seven parts in studying the problem of male crime and deviance in American society. Part I discusses biological, psychological, sociological, and cultural and masculinity theories on aggression, crime, and violence, as well as correlates of male deviance.

Part II explores the dynamics of male crime and violent behavior, including racial and ethnic differences, arrest patterns, and characteristics of male inmates in adult and juvenile correctional facilities. Gender differences in criminal behavior are also examined. Part III focuses on male crimes of violence, including homicide, forcible rape, domestic violence, stalking, hate crimes, workplace violence, and terrorism.

Part IV examines property offenses, including robbery, motor vehicle theft, and carjacking. Part V addresses male sex offenses, including incest, child sexual abuse, the relationship between pornography and male violence, and prostitution-related crimes.

Part VI looks at the crime and violence of youth gangs, and school crime and violence. Part VII explores current federal legislation aimed at combating criminal and violent behavior in the United States. An extensive reference section can be found at the end of the book.

CONTENTS

PART I–EXPLAINING MALE CRIME AND DEVIANCE

PART II–THE DYNAMICS OF MALE CRIME

PART III–MALE CRIMES OF VIOLENCE

PART IV–MALE PROPERTY CRIMES

PART V—MALE SEX OFFENSES

PART VI—JUVENILE MALE CRIME AND DELINQUENCY

PART VII—RESPONDING TO MALE CRIME AND DEVIANCE

LIST OF FIGURES AND TABLES

Figures

Tables

MALE CRIME AND DEVIANCE

Part I

EXPLAINING MALE CRIME AND DEVIANCE

Chapter 1

BIOLOGICAL AND PSYCHOLOGICAL
THEORIES

Explanations into male crime and violence have their roots in biological and psychological theories. Biological perspectives have sought to explain male criminality in terms of genetic predisposition to commit crimes and delinquent acts. Much of the biological approaches to crime have been rejected for their biases and unscientific propositions. Recent biological research, such as that associating male aggression and violence with testosterone, has shown more promise in relating criminal behavior with some biological deficiencies, characteristics, or influences, often taking a multidisciplinary perspective in addressing crime.

Psychological theories on male criminality have explored the causes in terms of mental, emotional, and personality disorders. Like biological theories, the psychological school of thought has been problematic in its principles and reliability. Overall, psychological theories appear to be more accepted in criminology in explaining certain aspects of criminal behavior. Most experts agree that such theories tend to have more substance when used in conjunction with cultural and sociological theories (see Chapter 2).

BIOLOGICAL THEORIES ON CRIMINALITY

Early Biogenic Theories

Scientific criminology is believed to have originated with the work of Italian physician Cesare Lombroso. In his 1876 book, *L 'Uomo Delinquente*, Lombroso proposed that some people are biologically predisposed to criminal behavior or born to commit crimes.[1] He believed criminals were a product of atavism or biological throwbacks to earlier genetic forms.

Influenced by the work of Charles Darwin and his theory of evolution, Lombroso derived his proposition from scientific examinations of Italian prisoners and army personnel. He advanced that criminals and noncriminals could be differentiated by physical stigmata—such as large lips, flat nose, and certain shapes of the skull—as well as such preferences as tattoos or involvement in orgies. Various combinations of anomalies distinguished one type of criminal from another.

In spite of later modifying some of his works' shortcomings, Lombroso's theory of atavism was discredited for, among other things, the small size of his prisoner samples, absence of control groups from the general population, and an inability to account for biological determinants of criminality other than through heredity, such as malnutrition.[2]

Body type theories were another early attempt to explain male criminality. In the 1939 book, *Crime and the Man*, Ernest Hooten concluded after comparing the measurements of physical characteristics of prisoners and nonprisoners that most criminals were physically and mentally inferior to noncriminals.[3] He posited that criminals could be distinguished by such traits as mixed eye color or reddish hair, differentiating criminals according to their particular physical characteristics. For example, Hooten believed that tall, heavy men were more likely than others to be murderers.

It was William Sheldon, in the 1940s, who first sought to systematically show a correlation between body type and juvenile delinquency.[4] He described three body types or somatotypes: (1) endomorphics, (2) ectomorphics, and (3) mesomorphics, relating each to certain personality or temperamental traits. Mesomorphics were characterized as muscular, hard, assertive, aggressive, and active. These types were believed to be the most likely to participate in delinquent conduct. Other researchers such as Sheldon and Eleanor Glueck[5] and J. B. Cortes and F. M. Gatti[6] found that mesomorphics were disproportionately represented among delinquent youth.

Body type theories have since been rejected by and large in the understanding of delinquent and criminal behavior due primarily to an inconclusive physiological relationship between body type and delinquency and other methodological weaknesses.

Heredity-Genetic Theories

Heredity theories on criminal behavior have been around for a while. Some biological theorists have sought to explain male crime and abnormal behavior as due to the genetic transmission of certain mental or physical characteristics from generation to generation. Early researchers such as Richard Dugdale[7] and Henry Goddard[8] sought to document intergenerational histories of deviance such as criminality, prostitution, fornication, feeblemindedness, and idiocy.

While genetic transmission theories of criminal behavior have generally been ridiculed as defective and methodologically weak, some recent studies suggest that there may be some basis to the transmitting of violent tendencies intergenerationally.[9]

For instance, studies by Wendy Slutske and associates,[10] and Peter McGuffin and Anita Thapar,[11] found a significant relationship between genetics and conduct disorder, with a strong "estimate of heritability."

Other researchers have found that certain biological characteristics such as low birth weight and other prenatal and perinatal problems may predispose some children to delinquency and criminality.[12]

Twin Studies

The relationship between heredity and antisocial behavior has received more support in the study of twins. Such research has "compared the criminal patterns and incidence of crime among twins developed from a single egg—monozygotic (MZ) twins—or identical twins, to that of twins who came from separately fertilized eggs—dizygotic (DZ) twins—known as fraternal twins."[13] The theory is that if criminal tendencies are in fact inherited, then identical twins should be more alike in their patterns of criminal behavior than fraternal twins.

An important concept in twin studies is concordance, a genetic term in reference to "the degree in which twins or related subject pairings both show a specific condition or behavior."[14] Some early studies, such as Johannes Lange's examination of Bavarian prisoners, found a concordance rate of criminal behavior among identical twins to be six times greater than that of fraternal twins.[15]

More recent research has also found a higher rate of criminal concordance among identical twins, though not as great as found in previous studies. For example, in a study of 444 pairs of Denmark twins who reached the age of 15, Karl Christiansen found the concordance rate for identical twins to be more than three times the rate of fraternal twins for criminal behavior.[16] Similar findings have been reported by James Hudziak and colleagues in their study of 492 pairs of monozygotic and dizygotic twins;[17] and a study of male twins by Jeanette Taylor and associates, who found that the risk of early-onset delinquency was "substantially greater for co-twins in monozygotic pairs (55 percent concordant) than for co-twins in dizygotic pairs (29 percent concordant) in which one boy was an early-starter."[18] The researchers also found that early starting boys in antisocial behavior were much more likely to have first-degree relatives who displayed adult deviant behavior than late starting boys or the control group.

After reviewing twin studies, Hans Eysench concluded that the consistent difference in concordance rates between identical and fraternal twins suggests that heredity is "beyond any doubt . . . an extremely important part in the genesis of criminal behavior."[19] Other researchers have supported this contention.[20]

This notwithstanding, some researchers are not convinced of the positive correlation between genetic influences and deviance. In a study by Odd Dalgaard and Einar Kringlen, there was no significant difference found in concordance rates between identical and fraternal twins.[21] Nevertheless, a number of recent studies have found genetic factors to be highly associated with delinquency and adult criminality.[22] However, most criminologists today who support the link between twins, genetics, and delinquency or criminality, tend to recognize the importance of environment in antisocial behavior, thus diminishing somewhat the role of hereditary influences.

Adoption and Fosterling Studies

The role of genetics in relation to environment has been examined through adoption and fosterling studies. In exploring the correlation between delinquent and criminal behavior of adopted or foster children to that of their biological and adopted or foster parents, such research assumes that "if these children exhibit criminal behavior more like that of their biological parents, then this offers stronger support that behavior is genetically transmitted; [whereas] should adopted children more closely resemble the behavioral characteristics of their adoptive or foster parents, then a more solid case can be made for the environment as the greater influence in deviant behavior."[23]

In one of the first adoption studies conducted by F. Schulsinger in Denmark, in comparing the incidence of psychopathy in the biological families of adoptees, it was found that more than twice the percentage of biological relatives of psychopathic adoptees were classified as psychopathic as the biological families of the control groups.[24] However, the findings were hampered by methodological and definitional weaknesses.

A more advanced examination of genetics and environment in relation to criminal behavior was undertaken by Bernard Hutchings and Sarnoff Mednick. After examining 1,145 male adoptees' and the same number of non-adoptees' criminality compared to that of their biological and adoptive fathers, they found that nearly twice the number of adoptees had criminal records as nonadoptees, with a strong correlation between the criminality of adoptees and criminal involvement of their biological fathers.[25] More than three times as many biological fathers of adoptees had criminal records as did adoptive fathers or fathers of the nonadoptees. The likelihood that an adoptee would become an offender was that much greater when both the biological and adoptive parents had criminal records. In spite of this strong relationship between biological correlates and criminality, the researchers still noted the important role environment plays in criminal behavior.

In an even more comprehensives study of adoptees, Mednick, W. Gabrielli, and Hutchings compared the conviction records of 14,427 adoptees to the conviction records of their biological and adoptive parents.[26] They concluded that the biological predisposition to commit crimes increased the probability of children to become delinquent or criminal offenders.

Recent research has supported these findings. In one such study, Edwin J. G. van den Oord and associates compared 221 pairs of adoptees with 111 pairs of siblings biologically related but living with adoptive parents. The researchers found that genetics were related to 70 percent of the variance in aggression among the subjects, with a 39 percent estimate of heritability reported for delinquent behavior.[27] Weaker genetic correlations were found for such things as depression, anxiety, and withdrawal.

The XYY Chromosome Theory

The theory relating criminality to an XYY chromosomal pattern in males first emerged in the early 1960s when researchers discovered a genetic abnormality in some males.[28] The normal chromosome count is 46, with the configuration for males XY and females XX. The finding that some males had an extra Y sex chromosome or a complement of XYY, caused some to associate this unusual chromosomal configuration with aggressive and violent behavior. Most XYY studies have involved tall prisoners and mentally retarded persons. The XYY males have been found to be in disproportion to the population at large.[29]

In a cohort study of tall men in Denmark, Herman Witkin and colleagues found that XYY men tended to participate in more criminal behavior than XY males of comparable height, age, and social standing.[30] However, the researchers found no evidence that the XYY males were any more prone to violence than the XY group.

Recent research has failed to support a relationship between the XYY chromosomal complement and criminal behavior; some studies even suggesting that XYY males are less likely to exhibit aggressive behavior than those with an XY chromosomal pattern.[31]

Testosterone and Male Offending

There has been considerable study on the relationship between testosterone and male aggression and deviant behavior. Testosterone is defined as a "steroid hormone responsible for the development of male secondary sex characteristics."[32] It is the most essential androgen, which controls and maintains masculine characteristics. Much of the research has found a positive correlation between high levels of testosterone and male violence and aggressive behavior. Early studies focused on testosterone in prisoners. L. E. Kreuz and R. M. Rose found that levels of testosterone were significantly higher in offenders with a history of violent behavior than offenders whose histories were nonviolent.[33] Other researchers found even higher testosterone levels among violent criminals.[34] Similarly, elevated levels of testosterone have been found in studies of violent and aggressive females.[35]

One of the more comprehensive studies of testosterone and aggression was undertaken by J. M. Dabbs and associates, who measured saliva testosterone in young adult inmates. The researchers found that the prisoners with the highest testosterone levels were most likely to have violent criminal histories, while inmates with the lowest levels of testosterone were most likely to have nonviolent criminal histories.[36]

A number of studies on non-offenders have also found a strong correlation between testosterone levels and aggression. R. Lindman and colleagues found a significantly higher level of testosterone among young males who were aggressive while intoxicated, compared to those who were not aggressive.[37] In J. Harris and associates' study of salivary testosterone levels in males and females whose behavior was aggressive or antisocial, males were found to have five times the salivary testosterone as their female counterparts.[38]

Not all studies have supported the strong relationship between testosterone and aggressive behavior. Warwick Peters noted the failure of such studies "to find a concrete correlation between testosterone and criminality,"[39] while some researchers have found little, if any, relationship between testosterone and antisocial behavior.[40] Most experts on male criminality appear to find merit in the role of testosterone in aggressive and violent behavior among males.

Hyperactivity and Antisocial Behavior

Hyperactivity has been shown to be a significant risk factor for delinquent and criminal behavior. Beginning in early childhood, hyperactivity–or being highly or excessively active–is often related to aggressive tendencies, and increases the risk of antisocial personality, conduct disorder, adult criminality, and substance abuse.[41] Rachel Gittleman found that boys with hyperactivity that continued into adolescence were four times as likely as boys not hyperactive to develop deviant behavior and were significantly more likely to have criminal arrests, as well as problems with fighting, larceny, truancy, and expulsion from school.[42] Similarly, half the boys with hyperactivity in James Satterfield's study went on to be arrested for a felony offense, while 25 percent were institutionalized because of antisocial behavior.[43]

A number of studies have been done on attention deficit hyperactivity disorder (ADHD) that demonstrated a strong genetic link. In Joseph Biederman and colleagues' study of children of 31 adults diagnosed with ADHD, 57 percent also fit the diagnostic criteria for having ADHD.[44] The researchers related behavior problems in children as likely more genetic than environmentally based. Heredity was also found to be a significant factor in ADHD in a study of adoptees by Susan Sprich and associates.[45] Eighteen percent of the biological parents of children with ADHD showed symptoms of the disorder, compared to only 6 percent of the adoptive parents. The researchers noted finding high rates of anxiety and mood disorders among the biological parents of children with ADHD, but not among the adoptive parents.

Persons diagnosed with ADHD have been found to be at risk for a number of deviances and abnormal conditions including delinquency, criminality, feelings of worthlessness, psychiatric morbidity, unemployment, family dysfunction, and suicide.[46]

Current Biological Research

The link between biology and criminality has focused more in recent years on various brain and neurological dysfunctions and their effect on behavior.[47] Some research has found abnormal electroencephalogram (EEG) recordings of brain activity in criminals and delinquents, associating it with violent and aggressive behavior, destructiveness, limited impulse control, and weak social adaptations.[48] A higher rate of epilepsy has been found in juvenile delinquents in which seizures may result in a loss of self-control.[49]

Other studies have linked brain dysfunction to such learning disabilities as aphasia, hyperactivity, and dyslexia, which some researchers believe predisposes each such individual to deviant behavior.[50] A correlation between brain tumors and violent criminal behavior has also been noted in the literature,[51] as well as criminality and vitamin deficiencies.[52]

Many behavioral scientists today favor a multidisciplinary perspective in the study of criminal behavior, combining genetics research with environmental studies and other disciplines such as neuroscience, endocrinology, and psychology in exploring delinquency and criminality.

PSYCHOLOGICAL THEORIES ON CRIMINALITY

Psychoanalytic Theories

It was the psychoanalytic theories of Sigmund Freud that is credited with bringing a psychological approach to the study of criminal behavior.[53] Freud, an Austrian physician, founded psychoanalysis through which he advanced that the personality is composed of three integral parts: the id, ego, and super-ego. The id is seen as the source of instinctive energy and biological drives; the ego, the component of the psyche experiencing and reacting to the surrounding worlds; and the superego represents the conscience of the psyche, interceding between the drives of the id and moral values. Fundamentally, psychoanalytic theories see criminal behavior as the conflict between these basic drives and unresolved instincts.

While Freud's proposals established a relationship between "deviant behavior and personality formation, particularly an unconscious sense of guilt the person develops during childhood," psychoanalyst August Aichorn is regarded as most responsible for applying psychoanalytic principles to delinquency and criminality.[54] In his study of juveniles, Aichorn postulated that they were psychologically predisposed toward antisocial behavior, describing this as latent delinquency, which he believed was present in juveniles whose personality made them act instinctively, impulsively, and for self-satisfaction while feeling no guilt.

More recently, C. G. Schoenfeld argued that delinquent conduct was not caused by criminal tendencies, but rather a weak, incomplete, or defective superego that fails to adequately control the primitive and strong urges of early childhood, resulting in deviant behavior.[55]

The major criticism against psychoanalytic theories is their inability to be tested empirically. Since the different parts of the personality are neither observable nor measurable, the conclusions drawn from psychoanalysis are essentially the "analyst's interpretation of a patient's interpretation of what is occurring in the subconscious."[56]

Personality Theories

Personality theories tend to focus on personality disorders in explaining delinquent and criminal behavior, while not necessarily attributing this to unconscious conflicts. Many psychologists and psychiatrists have explored the relationship between emotional problems and criminality, independent of the psychoanalytic approach. In the 1930s, Cyril Burt found that 85 percent of the criminals examined were emotionally impaired.[57] Similarly, in William Healy and Augusta Bronner's comparison study of delinquents and non-delinquent siblings, 90 percent of the delinquents were described as unhappy, discontented, or "extremely emotionally disturbed because of emotion-provoking situations or experiences," compared to 13 percent of the nondelinquents.[58]

Recent studies have failed to support this correlation. In a review of studies of personality variables and delinquency, Gordon Waldo and Simon Dinitz found no significant association between the two components.[59] The same was true for Michael Hakeem, who examined research on emotional disturbances among juvenile delinquents, concluding that the results were more likely due to psychiatric biases than delinquent characteristics.[60]

Psychopathic Personality Theory

Among personality theories, much attention has been placed on the relationship between psychopathy and criminal behavior. The psychopath is defined in the dictionary as "a person with an antisocial personality disorder–[especially] one manifested in aggressive, perverted, or criminal behavior."[61] Psychopathic personalities are commonly regarded as individuals who lack normal feelings of conforming to social norms and are without moral constraints.

According to William McCord and Joan McCord, who have studied psychopathy extensively, there are two traits in particular that sets psychopaths apart from other people: guiltlessness and lovelessness. The researchers advanced that psychopathic personalities originate in brain damage, physical trauma and, most typically, severe childhood emotional deprivation.[62]

In a 30-year follow-up study of patients at a child guidance clinic, Lee Robins sought to explore the link between psychopathic personalities, delinquency, and adult criminalty.[63] More than 70 percent of the clinic juveniles had been referred by the juvenile court for antisocial behavior. Robins found that the majority of the patients in the antisocial category had adult lives characterized by frequent arrests for crimes and drunkenness, psychiatric problems, divorce, and unstable employment. Forty-four percent of the antisocial male patients had been arrested for a serious crime. This compared to only 3 percent of a control group.

The major shortcoming of psychopathic personality theories is the lack of empirical evidence to relate psychopathy to criminal or delinquent behavior.

Furthermore, most evidence indicates that psychopaths represent only a small percentage of the antisocial population. In his study of patterns of criminal behavior, Herbert Quay found that adult psychopathic offenders made up less than one-fourth of all criminals, with juvenile psychopathic offenders constituting a much smaller proportion.[64]

Criminal Personality Theory

The criminal personality theory in explaining crime and delinquency causation was established through the work of Samuel Yochelson and Stanton Samenow.[65] Following years of studying violent criminal patients, the researchers held that in all of their subjects certain patterns of deviant thinking existed. The violent offenders found normal interaction with family and others dull and sought excitement with crime seen as the ultimate form of excitement. Yochelson and Samenow contended that this abnormal pattern of thinking manifests itself in early childhood, rejecting explanations of crime and delinquency outside the individual; though acknowledging that most offenders claim they were victims of family or other violence.

Supporters of the criminal personality theory suggest that it explains the criminality and delinquency of individuals with no apparent intrafamilial or other negative dynamics in their backgrounds who still engage in antisocial behavior. However, critics argue that the theory fails to sufficiently explain how criminality originates. They also point out the lack of a control group and the disregard for explanations of criminal behavior outside the individual such as environmental and social causes.[66]

Intelligence Quotient Theories

The relationship between intelligence and criminal behavior has been explored in crime theories. A number of early theorists found that an intrinsic below average intelligence quotient (IQ) among delinquents and criminals was the major cause for their deviant behavior.[67] Many critics attacked such a view as culturally biased and methodologically weak.

More recent studies appear to support the link between intelligence, delinquency, and criminality. Most notably are the results of a review of IQ research examined by Travis Hirschi and Michael Hindelang.[68] They concluded that a strong correlation exists between delinquency and IQ, independent of race and social class, suggesting that a low IQ affects school performance which in turn leads to antisocial behavior. A review or the literature by R. Loeber and T. Dishion supported these findings.[69]

Other studies have also shown a link between intelligence and deviant behavior. D. J. West and D. P. Farrington found that low intelligence nonverbally was strongly related to low intelligence verbally and low school attainment as predictors of delinquency.[70] Some studies have suggested that a high IQ can act as a protective mechanism against criminal behavior for high-risk children.[71] Longitudinal surveys have consistently shown a correlation between failure in school and delinquent and criminal behavior.[72]

Some researchers have begun to study delinquency in terms of relation to cognitive and neuropsychological disorders along with intelligence, finding evidence of a correlation.[73]

NOTES

1. Cesare Lombroso and William Ferrero, *Criminal Man* (Montclair: Patterson Smith, 1972). Originally titled *L 'Uomo Delinquente* in its 1876 publication.

2. R. Barri Flowers, *The Adolescent Criminal: An Examination of Today's Juvenile Offender* (Jefferson: McFarland, 1990), p. 112.

3. Ernest A. Hooten, *Crime and the Man* (Cambridge: Harvard University Press, 1939).

4. William H. Sheldon, *Varieties of Temperament* (New York: Harper and Row, 1942).

5. Sheldon Glueck and Eleanor T. Glueck, *Physique and Delinquency* (New York: Harper and Row, 1956).

6. J. B. Cortes and F. M. Gatti, *Delinquency and Crime: A Biopsychosocial Approach* (New York: Seminar Press, 1972).

7. Richard L. Dugdale, *The Jukes: A Study in Crime, Pauperism, and Heredity* (New York: Putnam, 1877).

8. Henry H. Goddard, *Feeblemindedness, Its Causes and Consequences* (New York: Macmillan, 1914).

9. See, for example, D. W. Denno, *Biology and Violence* (Cambridge: Cambridge University Press, 1990); L. F. DiLalla and I. I. Gottesman, "Biological and Genetic Contributors to Violence–Widom's Untold Tale," *Psychological Bulletin 109* (1991): 125–29.

10. Wendy Slutske, Andrew Heath, Stephen Dinwiddie, Pamela Madden, Kathleen Bucholz, Michael Dunne, Dixie Statham, and Nicholas Martin, "Modeling Genetic and Environmental Influences in the Etiology of Conduct Disorder: A Study of 2,682 Adult Twin Pairs," *Journal of Abnormal Psychology 106*, 2 (1977): 266–79; "Gene Research Highlights," http://www.crime-times.org/01d/w01dp11.htm.

11. Peter McGuffin and Anita Thapar, "Genetic Basis of Bad Behavior in Adolescents," *The Lancet 350* (1997): 411–412.

12. N. Breslau, N. Klein, and L. Allen, "Very Low Birthweight: Behavioral Sequelae at Nine Years of Age," *Journal of the American Academy of Child and Adolescent Psy-*

chiatry 27 (1988): 605–12; David P. Farrington, "The Explanation and Prevention of Youthful Offending," in J. David Hawkins, ed., *Delinquency and Crime: Current Theories* (Cambridge: Cambridge University Press, 1996), pp. 83–85.

13. Flowers, *The Adolescent Criminal*, pp. 113–14.

14. *Ibid.*, p. 114.

15. Johannes Lange, *Crime as Destiny* (London: George Allen and Unwin, 1931).

16. Karl O. Christiansen, "Seriousness of Criminality and Concordance Among Danish Twins," in R. Hood, ed., *Crime, Criminology and Public Policy* (London: Heinemann, 1977).

17. James J. Hudziak, Lawrence P. Rudiger, Michael C. Neale, Andrew C. Heath, and Richard D. Todd, "A Twin Study of Inattentive, Aggressive, and Anxious/Depressed Behaviors," *Journal of the American Academy of Child and Adolescent Psychiatry 39* (2000): 469–76.

18. Jeanette Taylor, William G. Iacono, and Matt McGue, "Evidence for a Genetic Etiology of Early-Onset Delinquency," *Journal of Abnormal Psychology 109*, 4 (2000): 634–43.

19. Hans J. Eysench, *The Inequality of Man* (San Diego: Edits Publishers, 1973).

20. See, for example, Thalia C. Eley, Paul Lichtenstein, and Jim Stevenson, "Sex Differences in the Etiology of Aggressive and Nonaggressive Antisocial Behavior: Results From Two Twin Studies," *Child Development 70*, 1 (1999): 155–68; Carol A. Prescott and Kenneth S. Kendler, "Genetic and Environmental Contributions to Alcohol Abuse and Dependence in a Population Based Sample of Male Twins," *American Journal of Psychiatry 156*, 1 (1999): 34–40.

21. Odd S. Dalgaard and Einar Kringlen, "A Norwegian Twin Study of Criminality," *British Journal of Criminology 16* (1976): 213–33.

22. See, for example, "Gene Research Highlights;" Kathryn DeMott, "Personality Disorders May Be Genetic," *Clinical Psychiatry News 27*, 12 (1999): 27.

23. Flowers, *The Adolescent Criminal*, pp. 114–15.

24. F. Schulsinger, "Psychopathy: Heredity and Environment," *International Journal of Mental Health 1* (1972): 190–206.

25. Bernard Hutchings and Sarnoff A. Mednick, "Registered Criminality in the Adoptive and Biological Parents of Registered Male Criminal Adoptees," in R. R. Fiene, D. Rosenthal, and H. Brill, eds., *Genetic Research in Psychiatry* (Baltimore: John Hopkins University Press, 1975).

26. S. A. Mednick, W. F. Gabrielli, and B. Hutchings, "Genetic Influences in Criminal Convictions: Evidence from an Adoption Cohort," *Science 234* (1984): 891–94.

27. Edwin J. G. van den Oord, Dorret I. Boomsma, and Frank C. Verhulst, "A Study of Problem Behaviors in 10- to 15-Year Old Biologically Related and Unrelated International Adoptees," *Behavior Genetics 24*, 3 (1994).

28. Flowers, *The Adolescent Criminal*, p. 116.

29. See, for example, A. A. Sandberg, G. F. Koepf, T. Ishiara, and T. S. Hanschka, "An XYY Human Male," *Lancet 262* (1961): 488–89.

30. H. Witkin, S. Mednick, F. Schulsinger, E. Bakkestrom, K. Christiansen, D. Goodenough, K. Hirschorn, C. Lundsteen, D. Owen, J. Philip, D. Rubin, and M. Stocking, "Criminality, Aggression, and Intelligence Among XYY and XXY Men,"

in S. Mednick and K. O. Christiansen, eds., *Biosocial Bases of Criminal Behavior* (New York: Gardner, 1977), pp. 165–87.

31. Flowers, *The Adolescent Criminal*, p. 116; R. Barri Flowers, *Minorities and Criminality* (Westport: Greenwood, 1990).

32. *The American Heritage Dictionary* (New York: Dell, 1994), p. 835.

33. L. E. Kreuz and R. M. Rose, "Assessment of Aggressive Behavior and Plasma Testosterone in a Young Criminal Population," *Journal of Psychosomatic Medicine 34* (1972): 321–32.

34. See, for example, J. H. Brooks and J. R. Reddon, "Serum Testosterone in Violent and Nonviolent Young Offenders," *Journal of Clinical Psychology 52* (1996): 475–83; R. T. Rada, D. R. Laws, and R. Kellner, "Plasma Testosterone Levels in the Rapist," *Psychosomatic Medicine 38* (1976): 257–68.

35. See, for example, J. M. Dabbs, R. B. Ruback, R. Frady, C. H. Hopper, and D. S. Sgoutas, "Saliva Testosterone and Criminal Violence Among Women," *Personality and Individual Differences 9* (1988): 269–75; E. Cashdan, "Hormones, Sex, and Status in Women," *Hormones and Behavior 29* (1995): 354–66.

36. J. M. Dabbs, R. L. Frady, T. S. Carr, and N. F. Besch, "Saliva Testosterone and Criminal Violence in Young Adult Prison Inmates," *Psychosomatic Medicine 49* (1987): 74–182; J. M. Dabbs, T. S. Carr, R. L. Frady, and J. K. Riad, "Testosterone, Crime, and Misbehavior Among 692 Prison Inmates," *Personality and Individual Differences 18* (1995): 627–33.

37. R. Lindman, P. Jarvinen, and J. Vidjeskog, "Verbal Interactions of Aggressively and Nonaggressively Predisposed Males in a Drinking Situation," *Aggressive Behavior 13* (1987): 187–96.

38. J. Harris, J. Rushton, E. Hampson, and D. Jackson, "Salivary Testosterone and Self-Report Aggressive and Pro-Social Personality Characteristics in Men and Women," *Aggressive Behavior 22* (1996): 321–31.

39. Warwick T. Peters, "Phrenology Biological Theories of Crime Criminology," http://members.ozemail.com.au/~wtmp/misc/phrenology.html.

40. See, for example, E. J. Susman, G. Inhoff-Germain, E. D. Nottleman, D. L. Loriaux, G. B. Cutler, and G. P. Chrousos, "Hormones, Emotional Dispositions, and Aggressive Attributes in Young Adolescents," *Child Development 58* (1987): 114–34.

41. "Attention Deficit Hyperactivity Disorder," Commonwealth of Australia, 1997, http://www.health.gov.au/nhmrc/publications/adhd/contents.htm.

42. Cited in Crime Times, 1995, http://www.crime-times.org195c/w95cp9.htm.

43. *Ibid.*

44. *Ibid.*

45. Susan Sprich, Joseph Biederman, Margaret H. Crawford, Elizabeth Mundy, and Stephen V. Fardone, "Adoptive and Biological Families of Children and Adolescents with ADHD," *Journal of the American Academy of Child and Adolescent Psychiatry 39*, 11 (2000): 1432–37.

46. P. Szatmari, D. R. Offord, and M. H. Boyle, "Correlates, Associated Impairments and Patterns of Service Utilization of Children with Attention Deficit Disorder: Findings from the Ontario Child Health Study," *Journal of Child Psychology and Psychiatry 30* (1989): 205–17.

47. Flowers, *The Adolescent Criminal*, pp. 116–17.

48. Vicki Pollock, Sarnoff A. Mednick, and William F. Gabrielli, Jr., "Crime Causation: Biological Theories," in Sanford H. Kadish, ed., *Encyclopedia of Crime and Justice*, Vol. 1 (New York: Free Press, 1983).

49. *Ibid.*

50. Charles A. Murray, *The Link Between Learning Disabilities and Juvenile Delinquency* (Washington: Government Printing Office, 1976); Harold R. Holzman, "Learning Disabilities and Juvenile Delinquency: Biological and Sociological Theories," in C. R. Jeffrey, ed., *Biology and Crime* (Thousand Oaks: Sage, 1979), pp. 77–86.

51. H. D. Kletschka, "Violent Behavior Associated with Brain Tumors," *Minnesota Medicine 49* (1966): 1835–55.

52. "Psychology and Crime," http://faculty.ncwc.edu/toconnor/301/301lect05 .htm.

53. Sigmund Freud, *New Introductory Lectures on Psychoanalysis* (New York: W. W. Norton, 1933).

54. Flowers, *The Adolescent Criminal*, p. 118; August Aichorn, *Wayward Youth* (New York: Viking Press, 1935).

55. C. G. Schoenfeld, "A Psychoanalytic Theory of Juvenile Delinquency," in Edward E. Peoples, ed., *Readings in Correctional Casework and Counseling* (Pacific Palisades: Goodyear, 1975), pp. 23–26.

56. Joseph F. Sheley, *America's "Crime Problem": An Introduction to Criminology* (Belmont: Wadsworth, 1985), p. 202.

57. Cyril Burt, *The Young Delinquent* (London: University of London Press, 1938).

58. Flowers, *The Adolescent Criminal*, p. 119; William Healy and Augusta F. Bronner, *New Light on Delinquency and Its Treatment* (New Haven: Yale University Press, 1936).

59. Gordon Waldo and Simon Dinitz, "Personality Attributes of the Criminal: An Analysis of Research Studies, 1950–1965," *Journal of Research in Crime and Delinquency 4* (1967): 185–202.

60. Michael Hakeem, "A Critique of the Psychiatric Approach," in Joseph S. Roucek, ed., *Juvenile Delinquency* (New York: Philosophical Library, 1958), pp. 89–95.

61. *The American Heritage Dictionary*, 3rd ed. (New York: Dell, 1994), p. 667.

62. William McCord and Joan McCord, *The Psychopath* (Princeton: Van Nostrand, 1964).

63. Lee N. Robins, *Deviant Children Grown Up* (Baltimore: Williams and Wilkins, 1966).

64. Herbert C. Quay, "Crime Causation: Psychological Theories," in S. H. Kadish, ed., *Encyclopedia of Crime and Justice*, Vol. 1 (New York: Free Press, 1983), p. 340.

65. Samuel Yochelson and Stanton E. Samenow, *The Criminal Personality*, Vol. 1 (New York: Jason Arsonson, 1976); Stanton E. Samenow, *Inside the Criminal Mind* (New York: Time Books, 1984).

66. Flowers, *The Adolescent Criminal*, p. 122.

67. *Ibid.*, p. 122; William Healy and Augusta F. Bronner, *Delinquency and Criminals: Their Making and Unmaking* (New York: Macmillan, 1926).

68. Travis Hirschi and Michael J. Hindelang, "Intelligence and Delinquency: A Revisionist Review," *American Sociological Review 42* (1977): 571–86.

69. R. Loeber and T. Dishion, "Early Predictors of Male Delinquency: A Review," *Psychological Bulletin 94* (1983): 68–99.

70. D. J. West and D. P. Farrington, *Who Becomes Delinquent?* (London: Heinemann, 1973).

71. J. L. White, T. E. Moffit, and P. A. Silva, "A Prospective Replication of the Protective Effects of IQ in Subjects at High Risk for Juvenile Delinquency," *Journal of Consulting and Clinical Psychology 57* (1989): 719–24; E. Kandel, S. A. Mednick, L. Kirkegaard-Sorenson, B. Hutchings, J. Knop, R. Rosenberg, and F. Schulsinger, "IQ as a Protective Factor for Subjects at High Risk for Antisocial Behavior," *Journal of Consulting and Clinical Psychology 56* (1988): 224–26.

72. See, for example, K. Polk, C. Alder, G. Bazemore, G. Blake, S. Cordray, G. Coventry, J. Galvin, and M. Temple, *Becoming Adult* (Washington: National Institute of Mental Health, 1981).

73. T. E. Moffit and P. A. Silva, "Neuropsychological Deficit and Self-reported Delinquency in an Unselected Birth Cohort," *Journal of the American Academy of Child and Adolescent Psychiatry 27* (1988): 233–40.

Chapter 2

SOCIOLOGICAL AND CULTURAL THEORIES

Unlike biological and psychological theories that tend to explain criminal behavior in terms of genetic influences and personality disorders, sociological and cultural theories of criminality focus on the relationship between delinquent and criminal behavior and the social structure, culture, environment, and other variables associated with crime causation beyond the individual. The sociological school of thought on antisocial behavior often regards it as normal behavior within the context of the social and cultural influences of the deviant. Sociogenic, criminological, and delinquency theories typically fall under four primary perspectives: social control, strain, cultural transmission, and radical theories.

SOCIAL CONTROL THEORIES

Social control theories posit that all individuals have the potential and opportunity to perpetrate criminality but are restrained through fear and social constraints. Social control theorists explain criminal and delinquent behavior as a reflection of inadequate external social controls and internalized social values for some persons, creating a freedom in which criminality may manifest itself. Control theories are less focused on what motivates one to deviate from the norm than the social institution that produces conditions favorable to either law violating or refraining from such.

While social control theories have shown success in explaining some aspects of criminal and delinquent behavior, they do not adequately explain the role of internalized norms and values, or sufficiently account for the social-structural causes of criminal behavior. This notwithstanding, the basic premise of social control theories has been supported through empirical studies.[1]

Social Disorganization Theory

The notion of social disorganization was established in the early 1960s by sociologists in the University of Chicago's sociology department, referred to as the Chicago School. Social disorganization was used to describe a breakdown in "social conventional structures within a community characterized by largely transitory, heterogeneous, and economically underprivileged people; and the incapability of organizations, groups, and individuals as part of that community to effectively solve its problems."[2]

This social disorganization or lack of social controls in certain areas was found by researchers to correlate with high rates of delinquency. In studying the ecological patterns of crime and delinquency in Chicago, Ernest Burgess and Robert Park found that delinquency rates were highest in central cities and decreased the further the distance from the center.[3] The high rate of inner city crime and delinquency was attributed to their having the highest concentration of physical and social conditions commonly related to criminality and delinquency.

Clifford Shaw and Henry McKay were the first to apply a zonal model of urban ecology and crime systematically. Their research supported the concept of social disorganization in the inner cities and the inverse relationship between rates of delinquency and distance from the city's center.[4]

Social disorganization theory of crime and delinquency was also explained in research on juvenile gangs. In a study of 1,313 Chicago gangs, Frederic Thrasher postulated that youth gangs in socially disorganized neighborhoods reflect the inability of social institutions to control patterns of delinquent behavior.[5] Without social control, he held that juveniles needed no motivation to commit acts of delinquency since unconventional behavior represented a more exciting mode of conduct than conventional behavior. Thrasher further advanced that structured juvenile gangs only emerged due to a perceived threat from an outside source, such as other juvenile gangs.

In spite of the sound propositions of social disorganization theory in explaining the high rate of delinquency in certain areas, it was not until the work of the Chicago School was modified through later social control theories that greater attention was given to the relationship between social disorganization in communities and criminal and delinquent behavior.

Social Bonding Theory

Social bonding theory as a social control theory was established by Travis Hirschi. In the book, *Causes of Delinquency,* he described the social bond that ties juveniles to the social order.[6] It consists of four key components:

(1) attachment (ties to others such as family and peers), (2) commitment (devotion to social conformity), (3) involvement (in legitimate activities), and (4) belief (attitudes toward conformity). The degree and power of these components or an individual's conformity to societal norms and values vary from person to person.

According to Hirschi, the less individuals believe they should follow social convention, the more likely they are to not conform or violate the law. He advanced that delinquents do not possess the intimate attachments, goals, and moral standards that bond most people to the values and norms of society; as such, they are free to perpetrate acts of criminality and delinquency.

Though social bonding theory does have support among many criminologists, some have criticized the theory's proposition that attachment to others helps prevent delinquency, even if these attachments are themselves delinquents. Another shortcoming of social bonding theory is its failure to adequately explain the variance in the frequency of delinquent behavior.

Containment Theory

Another social control theory forwarded by Walter Reckless is containment theory.[7] It posits that youths are restrained from perpetrating antisocial acts by a combination of *inner containment* (positive self-concept, self-components, well-developed superego, high level of tolerance, and positive goal orientation) and *outer containment* (positive social ties, consistent parental supervision, institutional support of the youth's positive self-concept).

According to Reckless, these containments act as buffers against the influences of deviant behavior (such as a delinquent subculture, temptations, and environmental factors). He postulated that while a combination of inner and outer containments were the most effective measure to counter delinquency, strong inner containment could compensate for weak or defective outer containment, or vice versa.

Amongst the criticisms of containment theory are its methodological weaknesses and problems with the validity of the self-concept measure. Overall, it appears that outer containment factors may be more significant in involvement in crime and delinquency than inner containments.[8]

STRAIN THEORIES

Like social control theories, strain theories evolved from the research of the Chicago School. These theories explain deviant behavior as a response to the lack of socially approved opportunities. The concept of strain is viewed as a shared problem of adjustment originating from the social position shared by a group of people.

General strain theory asserts that "actors do not enter interactions with specific outcomes in mind, only that certain distributive justice rules will be followed in establishing equitable relationships. Distress occurs when individuals feel unrewarded for their efforts compared to the efforts and rewards of similar others for similar outcomes. The negative emotions associated with negative relationships may be more successfully handled by engaging in delinquent behavior than nondelinquent behavior."[9]

According to Robert Agnew, general strain theory relates more to the types of strain as opposed to its sources. He postulated that three different types of strain exist: (1) strain as a result of the failure in achieving positive goals such as educational and professional success and wealth, (2) strain due to the removal of positive stimuli as opposed to blocked access to goals, and (3) strain resulting from negative stimuli, such as child abuse and neglect, victimization, and negative associations with family and good friends. Each of these types can apply to the individual or group.[10]

Critics argued that Agnew's strain theory failed to explain why some persons were more likely than others to turn to delinquent behavior in response to strain.

Agnew and colleagues later concluded that delinquency "is higher among those who experience family, school, and neighborhood strain [and] . . . higher among certain categories of juveniles experiencing peer abuse;"[11] and, further, that the likelihood of strain resulting in delinquent conduct was greater among adolescents who were older.[12]

Anomie Theory

The theory of anomie was first introduced in the early 20th century by Emile Durkheim, a preeminent French sociologist.[13] Anomie referred to a "condition of relative normlessness within a group or society."[14] According to Durkheim, this anomie condition occurred when the existing social structure was not able to control man's desires. Anomie was generally seen as a result of social disruption, caused by natural or human disasters such as economic depression and war.

It was Robert Merton who adapted the concept of anomie to societal conditions and cultural values in the United States.[15] He attempted to associate particular types of behavior to the social position of those individuals participating in such behavior. Merton proposed "high rates of deviance are generated in anomie social systems where there is a strong cultural emphasis on economic success coupled with inequality in opportunity to realize such success legitimately."[16] Given that some people have unequal access to approved means, they must deviate from the norm in order to achieve the goals of success in society.

Merton identified five modes of adaptation to the societal goals and means:

- *Conformity* to cultural goals and means.
- *Innovation* refers to the acceptance of culturally prescribed goals of success without also following the moral and institutional means for their attainment.
- *Ritualism* refers to the person who conforms to the mores defining the means, while rejecting the cultural goals.
- *Retreatism* relates to the individual who rejects both the culturally prescribed goals and the institutional means.
- *Rebellion* refers to the rejection of cultural goals and the societal means of attaining them.[17]

A sixth mode of adaptation was forwarded by Martin Haskell and Lewis Yablonsky:

- *Dropping out* refers to rejecting both culturally defined goals and the institutionalized means to achieve by doing nothing to effectuate change.[18]

Merton's anomie propositions have faced strong criticisms. One is its failure to explain why some innovators choose theft and others robbery or why some retreatists use drugs and others alcohol in their rejection of societal goals and conventional means. Another criticism of the theory is that some question whether or not all persons in the United States share the same goals and expectations of success. Furthermore, while anomie theory explains the criminality of those disadvantaged in society, it fails to account for the deviant behavior of upper class individuals or the patterns of crime and delinquency.

In spite of the shortcomings of Merton's strain theory, the sophistication of his work is believed to be most influential in subsequent theoretical perspectives on the relationship between criminality and delinquency and differential economic opportunity.

Recently, an institutional anomie theory was developed by S. Messner and R. Rosenfeld.[19] Referred to as the "American Dream" theory, it holds that attaining material success is shared by all, and that economic interests resulting in material gain have become the dominant theme in our society at the expense of noneconomic interests, such as being a parent and volunteerism.

The theorists regard crime as being caused by anomie, which is fostered by the American dream. Because the most efficient means is desired for achieving economic success, crime is often viewed as such a means for immediate financial gain. The causal variables of beliefs, values, and commitments in relation to the economic forces of competition, individuals, and materialism drives one to pursue monetary gain in any manner required, legal or not.

Subculture Theories

Strain theorists developed subculture theories beginning in the 1950s ad 1960s in the study of juvenile gangs and criminal behavior. Influenced by the research of Durkheim and Merton, a number of criminologists have contributed to the subculture perspective of deviant behavior such as Albert Cohen,[20] Gresham Sykes and David Matza,[21] Walter Miller,[22] and James Short,[23] among others (see also Chapter 18).

A subculture is defined as a "cultural subgroup within a larger cultural group."[24] Such subcultures originate "when individuals in similar circumstances find themselves virtually isolated or neglected by mainstream society. Thus they group together for mutual support. . . . The members of the subculture are different from the dominant culture."[25]

Marvin Wolfgang and Franco Ferracuti proposed a subculture of violence theory in asserting that some subculture's value system effectively promotes violence under certain social circumstances.[26] The criminologists held that subcultures were ruled by a set of "conduct norms" governing the behavior of its members. The transmission of subcultural values consists of a learning process in which an interrelationship between the values and the members is established. But persons can also be born into the subculture.

Wolfgang and Ferracuti first applied the theory to explaining the disproportionate rate of violent crimes among African Americans but described other subcultures as well, such as delinquents and inmates. Critics have attacked subculture of violence theory as biased, not sufficiently tested, and for failure to explain the origins of a subculture of violence[27] (see also Chapter 7).

It was the delinquent subculture theory brought forth by Richard Cloward and Lloyd Ohlin that is most credited with the emergence of this school of thought in explaining delinquency.[28] They argued that there is both a delinquent opportunity structure as well as a legitimate opportunity structure. Subculture theory focuses mainly on the structural conditions that lead to lower class delinquency but also seeks to explain the development of other delinquent subcultures.

According to Cloward and Ohlin, a delinquent subculture is a group fostering beliefs that legitimize delinquent activities. Within this context, subculture theory asserts that the culture, goals, and strategies of the lower class or subgroups within are substantially different from those of the middle class. Lower-class youths are believed to have their own lifestyles, traditions, and focal concerns, which attach importance to such things as "toughness," "living by one's wits," and "hustle." Hence, conforming to this lifestyle suggests a deviation from middle-class standards.

Subculture theory has been attacked for a number of shortcomings. Foremost is the belief by many that the majority of the lower class adopt the middle-class norms of material, educational, and occupational success and opposition to manual labor.[29] There is also evidence to support the contention that most lower-class gang members ultimately abandon criminal activities and turn to more conventional middle-class norms as adults.[30] Further, the theory has been criticized for being inapplicable to the majority of juvenile delinquents.

CULTURAL TRANSMISSION THEORIES

Cultural transmission theories explain delinquency as learned behavior and, as such, a reflection of the norms, values, beliefs, and patterns in behavior people learn from those they interact with. Cultural transmission theorists posit that crime and delinquency are caused primarily by individuals "conforming to the behavioral norms of a culture or subculture that are contrary to conventional norms and values with respect to the behavior and the law."[31] Delinquent norms are also regarded as intergenerational in cultural transmission theories in both the socialization process and the techniques used in perpetrating criminal or delinquent acts.

Differential Association Theory

The cultural transmission theory that has received the most attention among criminologists and sociologists is differential association theory. Developed by Edwin Sutherland and outlined in his 1939 text, *Principles of Criminology,* differential association theory seeks to explain the reasons for the crime or delinquency rate distribution across different groups and why a particular individual participates in or refrains from deviant behavior.[32]

The theory assumes that the probability of criminal behavior varies directly with the priority, frequency, duration, and intensity of an individual's contacts with criminal and delinquent elements, and inversely with their nondeviant contacts. Contact with antisocial elements tends to occur most often when a person's perception of their circumstances are supportive of violations of the norm. As a result, many types of nonconformity such as criminality, delinquency, or mental illness are thought to be concentrated in inner city areas that are characterized by cultural traits that often alienate individuals from one another and middle-class norms.

Differential association theory holds that crime, like other kinds of behavior, is learned. The theory points out the general conditions under which there is likely to be more than less criminal behavior learned and thus a greater likelihood that the person will acquire a set of definitions that are more favorable to criminal activities than noncriminal ones. Furthermore, the theory states that criminality is a social rather than antisocial activity. As such, if the majority of an individual's associations are with persons who frequently violate the law and seek to justify their actions, the individual is more likely to become criminal or delinquent than one who associates with persons who abide by the law and disapprove of such violations.

Differential association theory is supported as a sociological and cultural explanation of criminality and delinquency. However, there are some notable shortcomings. The most glaring is its inability to be validated through empirical testing because of a lack of clarity in its definitions and terminology. The theory also fails to explain the origin of crime and delinquency or outline the nature of the learning process. One final criticism of differential association theory is that it does not establish the basis for differential susceptibility toward criminal behavior for different persons.[33]

Social Learning Theory

As a result of the drawbacks of differential association theory, sociologists sought to revise the theory as a general explanation of deviance. The most prominent theoretical perspective in this regard was formulated by Robert Burgess and Ronald Akers as social learning theory, also referred to as differential association-reinforcement theory.[34]

The basic tenet of social learning theory is that people learn to commit criminal or juvenile acts through social interaction with individuals who represent their primary source of reinforcement. These social reinforcements are seen as mostly symbolic and verbal rewards for supporting group expectations and norms. The lesser role of nonsocial reinforcements that relates mostly to physiological variables that may be relevant for some crimes is also noted.

According to Akers and associates, in social learning theory, social behavior is acquired both through direct conditioning and through *imitation* or modeling of others' behavior. Behavior is strengthened through reward (positive reinforcement) and avoidance of punishment (negative reinforcement) or weakened by aversive stimuli (positive punishment) and loss of reward (negative punishment). Whether deviant or conforming behavior is acquired and persists depends on past and present rewards or punishments for the behavior and the rewards and punishments attached to alternate behavior–*differential reinforcement*.[35]

Critics of social learning theory contend that nonsocial reinforcers are, in fact, stronger than social reinforcers. There is also some question as to whether it can be adequately tested. However, the main principles of social learning theory have been supported through empirical testing.[36] Furthermore, many see the theory as a reflection of incorporating contemporary behavior into sociological approaches to deviance and criminality,[37] as well as being influential in the development of such criminological theories as social control and deterrence theories.[38]

RADICAL CRIMINOLOGICAL THEORIES

Radical or critical theorists tend to concentrate more on the association between capitalism and criminal and juvenile justice than explaining criminality and delinquency. According to radical theory, criminal laws primarily serve the greater interests of the ruling class (owners of the means of production), who use these laws to exploit, dominate, and victimize the lower and working classes in order to perpetuate the political and economic system of capitalism.[39] The theory holds that because the laws are a product of capitalists and the wealthy, their socially harmful "crimes," such as exploitation and demoralization, generally are not considered crimes by the criminal justice system.

Radical criminologists attribute the high rate of lower-class or street crime to the economic functioning of the capitalist system, producing unemployment and underemployment. This is seen as resulting in conditions that lead to criminal and delinquent behavior. David Greenberg applied a radical perspective to the criminality of juveniles, postulating that it explains the high delinquency rates. He identified three pressures faced by juveniles in particular in capitalist societies: (1) deprivation of opportunities for employment necessary to finance the social activities that peer norms stress; (2) stigmatizing, degrading experiences in school by individuals who have a lesser stake in conformity, such as lower-class and unemployed youths, which result in rebellious and often hostile responses; and (3) fear of failure in successfully reaching adult male status positions, resulting in violent, status-defining conduct.[40]

The primary weaknesses of radical criminology theory lie in its predictability, dismissal of objective reality, and an overstatement of its principles. This notwithstanding, a radical or critical approach to criminality is considered by many to be sound in its overall explanation of the capitalist system as it relates to criminal laws, crime definitions, and the criminal justice system.

NOTES

1. R. Barri Flowers, *The Adolescent Criminal: An Examination of Today's Juvenile Offender* (Jefferson: McFarland, 1990), p. 127; Charles E. Frazier, Theoretical Approaches to Deviance: An Evaluation (Columbus: Charles E. Merrill, 1976), pp. 49–71. See also James F. Anderson and Laronistine Dyson, Criminological Theories: Understanding Crime in America (Lanham: University Press of America, 2002).

2. Flowers, *The Adolescent Criminal,* p. 125.

3. Robert E. Park and Ernest W. Burgess, *The City* (Chicago: University of Chicago Press, 1925).

4. Clifford R. Shaw and Henry D. McKay, *Juvenile Delinquency and Urban Areas* (Chicago: University of Chicago Press, 1969).

5. Frederic M. Thrasher, *The Gang* (Chicago: University of Chicago Press, 1927).

6. Travis Hirschi, *Causes of Delinquency* (Berkeley: University of California, 1969).

7. Walter C. Reckless, Simon Dinitz, and Ellen Murray, "Self-Concept as an Insulator Against Delinquency," in James E. Teele, ed., *Juvenile Delinquency: A Reader* (Itasca: Peacock, 1970); Walter C. Reckless, *The Crime Problem,* 5th ed. (Santa Monica: Goodyear, 1973).

8. Gary F. Jenson, "Inner Containment and Delinquency," *Journal of Criminal Law and Criminology 64* (1973): 464–70.

9. "The Varieties of Strain Theory," http://faculty.ncwc.edu/toconnor/301/301lect09.htm.

10. Robert Agnew, "Foundation for a General Strain Theory," *Criminology 30,* 1 (1992): 47–87.

11. Robert Agnew, Timothy Brezina, John P. Wright, and Francis T. Cullen, "Strain, Personality Traits, and Delinquency: Extending General Strain Theory," *Criminology 40,* 1 (2002): 43–70.

12. *Ibid.;* Lisa Broidy, "A Test of General Strain Theory," *Criminology 39* (2001): 9–36; Nicole L. Piquero and Miriam D. Sealock, "Generalizing General Strain Theory: An Examination of an Offending Population," *Justice Quarterly 17* (2000): 449–84.

13. Emile Durkheim, *The Division of Labor in Society* (New York: Free Press, 1933).

14. Flowers, *The Adolescent Criminal,* p. 127.

15. Robert K. Merton, *Social Theory and Social Structure* (Glencoe: Free Press, 1957); Robert K. Merton, "Social Structure and Anomie," *American Sociological Review 3* (1938): 672–82.

16. Dean G. Rojek and Gary F. Jensen, *Exploring Delinquency: Causes and Control* (Los Angeles: Roxbury, 1996), p. 138.

17. Merton, *Social Theory and Social Structure,* pp. 131–60.

18. Martin R. Haskell and Lewis Yablonsky, *Juvenile Delinquency,* 2nd ed. (Chicago: Rand McNally, 1978), p. 397.

19. S. Messner and R. Rosenfeld, *Crime and the American Dream* (Belmont: Wadsworth, 1994); S. Messner, "Merton's Anomie: The Road Not Taken," *Deviant Behavior 9* (1988): 33–53.

20. Albert K. Cohen, *Delinquent Boys* (New York: Free Press, 1955). See also Philip Bean, *Critical Concepts in Sociology* (London: Routledge, 2002).

21. Gresham Sykes and David Matza, "Techniques of Neutralization: A Theory of Delinquency," *American Sociological Review 22* (1957): 664–70.

22. Walter B. Miller, "Lower Class Culture as a Generating Milieu of Gang Delinquency," *Journal of Social Issues 14* (1958): 5–19; Walter B. Miller, "Violent Crimes in City Gangs," *Annals of the American Academy of Political and Social Science 364* (1966): 96–112.

23. James F. Short, Jr., "Gang Delinquency and Anomie," in Marshall B. Clinard, ed., *Anomie and Deviant Behavior* (New York: Free Press, 1964), pp. 98–127.

24. *The American Heritage Dictionary* (New York: Dell, 1994), p. 807.

25. "Overview of Subculture Theories," http://home.attbi.com/~ddemelo/crime/subculture.html.

26. Marvin E. Wolfgang and Franco Ferracuti, *The Subculture of Violence: Towards an Integrated Theory in Criminology* (London: Tavistock, 1967); Marvin E. Wolfgang, *Patterns in Criminal Homicide* (Philadelphia: University of Pennsylvania Press, 1958).

27. See, for example, Barbara Costello, "On the Logical Adequacy of Cultural Deviance Theories," *Theoretical Criminology 1* (1997): 403–28; Ross Matsueda, "Cultural Deviance Theory: The Remarkable Persistence of Flawed Term," *Theoretical Criminology 1* (1997): 429–52; H. S. Erlander, "The Empirical Status of the Sub-Cultures of Violence Thesis," *Social Problems 22* (1974): 280–92.

28. Richard A. Cloward and Lloyd E. Ohlin, *Delinquency and Opportunity* (New York: Free Press, 1960). See also Imogene L. Moyer, *Criminological Theories: Traditional and Nontraditional Voices and Themes* (Thousand Oaks: Sage, 2001).

29. Flowers, *The Adolescent Criminal*, p. 128.

30. *Ibid.*

31. *Ibid.*, p. 129.

32. Edwin H. Sutherland, *Principles of Criminology* (Philadelphia: Lippincott, 1939). See also W. Einstadter and S. Henry, *Criminological Theory* (Fort Worth: Harcourt Brace, 1995).

33. Flowers, *The Adolescent Criminal*, p. 130.

34. Robert L. Burgess and Ronald L. Akers, "A Differential Association-Reinforcement Theory of Criminal Behavior," *Social Problems 14* (1966): 128–47; Ronald L. Akers, Marvin D. Krohn, Lonn Lanza-Kaduce, and Marcia Radosevich, "Social Learning and Deviant Behavior: A Specific Test of a General Theory," in Dean G. Rojek and Gary F. Jensen, eds. *Exploring Delinquency: Causes and Control* (Los Angeles: Roxbury, 1996), pp. 120–27.

35. Ronald L. Akers, Marvin D. Krohn, Lonn Lanza-Kaduce, and Marcia Radosevich, "Social Learning and Deviant Behavior: A Specific Test of a General Theory," *American Sociological Review 44* (1979): 636–55.

36. Albert Bandura, *Social Learning Theory* (Englewood Cliffs: Prentice-Hall, 1977); Barry Mc Laughlin, *Learning and Social Behavior* (New York: Free Press, 1971).

37. George C. Homans, *Social Behavior: Its Elementary Forms* (New York: Harcourt Brace Jovanovich, 1961); J. K. Chadwick-Jones, *Social Exchange Theory: Its Structure and Influence in Social Psychology* (New York: Academic Press, 1976).

38. Rand D. Conger, "Social Control and Social Learning Models of Delinquent Behavior—A Synthesis," *Criminology 14* (1976): 17–40; M. P. Feldman, *Criminal Behavior: A Psychological Analysis* (London: Wiley, 1977).

39. Flowers, *The Adolescent Criminal,* p. 132; R. Barri Flowers, *Minorities and Criminality* (Westport: Greenwood, 1988), pp. 71–72; Thomas Bernard, "The Distinction Between Conflict and Radical Criminology," *Journal of Criminal Law and Criminology* 72 (1981): 366–70; Gresham M. Sykes, "The Rise and Fall of Critical Criminology," Journal of Criminal Law and Criminology 65 (1974): 206–13.

40. David F. Greenberg, "Delinquency and the Age Structure of Society," *Contemporary Crises 1* (1977): 189–224. See also R. Barri Flowers, *Murder, At the End of the Day and Night: A Study of Criminal Homicide Offenders, Victims, and Circumstances* (Springfield: Charles C Thomas, 2002), pp. 210–14.

Chapter 3

MASCULINITY THEORIES

Masculinity theories of male deviance have been put forth by a number of criminologists and sociologists in explaining the relationship between masculinity, crime, and violence. This school of thought presumes that since men are responsible for the majority of serious criminality, it stands to reason that crime is strongly associated with masculinity.[1] The masculinity hypothesis is also used by some to explain the serious criminality of women as a reflection of emancipation, moving away from traditional female social roles, and adopting more traditional male social roles–resulting in more male-like behavior.[2]

However, critics argue that expressing masculinity in and of itself does not make one a criminal, nor does it necessarily lead to aggressive or violent behavior. Others see masculinity as a factor in male crime in conjunction with a complex set of other interrelated biological, psychological, sociological, and cultural variables.

EXPLORING MASCULINITY

What is masculinity and how does it relate to criminality? The term *masculine* is defined as "(1) of or relating to men or boys; (2) marked by qualities generally attributed to a man; (3) of or being the gender of words referring to things classified as male; (4) the masculine gender."[3] Masculinity was defined by David Gilmore as an "approved way of being an adult male in any given society."[4] According to Kenneth Reinicke, masculinity

> has to do with superiority. The competition with other men, and the superiority and dominance over women are central components in the habitus of a macho man. The demonstration of physical strength in front of other men is crucial like the connection between sexuality, power, and conquest. The self-esteem of a macho-man is related to the dominance and exploitation of women.[5]

The terms masculinity and femininity are seen as "relatively recent constructs of Western culture."[6] Robert Connell asserted that in fact there are many masculinities, rather than a single fixed type of masculinity, in Western society.[7] However, criminologists note that there is much homogeneity amongst masculinities, which "as patterns of gender practice, are sustained not only by individuals but also by groups and institutions."[8]

Within the masculinities, the most dominant theme is *hegemonic masculinity*, defined as "the configuration of gender practices, which embodies the currently accepted answer to the problem of legitimacy of patriarchy, which guarantees the dominant position of men and the subordination of women."[9]

Hegemonic masculinity is seen as acting "more as a cultural standard than as an achievable status for the majority of men."[10] While hegemonic masculinity has flexible characteristics that "change depending upon the labor needs of the state in a particular era—it generally connotes dominance, competitiveness, occupational achievement, and heterosexuality."[11]

The term *marginalized masculinity* is used by Connell to describe men, socially and economically disempowered, who engage in violence in a *masculine protest* to overcompensate for their perceived lack of power.[12] According to this view, males who embrace hegemonic masculinity and its gender and normative expectations, but are unable to achieve such expectations because of racial or socioeconomic status, may resort to extreme measures, such as perpetrating violence against homosexuals.[13]

Marginalized masculinity and violence are most likely to occur through socialization in childhood, consisting of social oppression, impoverishment, exposure to violence, and child abuse and neglect. Researchers contend that "one of the hallmarks of the marginalized masculinity that may develop out of childhood poverty and violence is a preoccupation with a masculine front, or the protection of reputation and pride."[14]

Studies have found that in particular sets of males, norms and expectations exist within such violent subcultures that can result in socially aggressive behavior that is predictable and at times ritualistic.[15] In a study of a group of socially and economically disenfranchised young white males, it was found that perceived victimization and powerlessness among the group propelled their social and ritualized aggression against both African Americans and homosexuals.[16]

MACHISMO AND MALES

Machismo is an important concept in masculinity and its relationship to male violent and aggressive behavior. Defined as "a strong or exaggerated sense of masculinity," machismo is "based upon values which has to do with the dimensions of power, envy, self-glorification, and sexuality. . . . [It] also has to do with bodily postures and the way a man looks, speaks, walks and sits. It is embedded in the body in the form of mental dispositions and schemes of perception and thought. Driving may often promote machismo, because the vehicle easily becomes a symbol of the body."[17]

Machismo has been particularly associated with the criminality of Latino men. Many experts attribute their victimization and sexual abuse or exploitation of women in large part to machismo or the macho male, suggesting that violence against women is "more likely to be a product of machismo-oriented cultures than cultures that favor more equality of the sexes."[18] Brazil is an example of a culture that has traditionally condoned male violent aggression against women believed to have insulted their "masculine honor."[19]

Machismo appears to be rooted in Hispanic communities' sense of family and cultural isolation. A number of studies have supported this perspective. In a study of the Latin prison gang, La Familia, anthropologist Theodore Davidson asserted that its emergence was a result of racism, isolation, and the culture of the barrio through which machismo is an intricate part.[20] In Robert Johnson's clinical examination of Hispanic prisoners, 70 percent of the inmate sample's concerns had to do with separation or abandonment by family or their being unable to serve a constructive role within the family.[21]

According to *Minorities and Criminality*, Latino machismo is tied closely to extended family kinships. Through a

> complex interrelationship of duty and dependency, the macho is obligated to his family. He provides for them and is greatly dependent upon them, most notably his wife, for emotional support and nurturance, perpetrating his machismo. Because of this dependency on their separated family, many Latin prisoners suffer from a loss of identity and self-esteem, which has been related to Latin prisoner self-injury and violence.[22]

There is indication that machismo and its intrafamilial and cultural dynamics has been adopted by men of other racial and ethnic groups, as well as other marginalized males.

MASCULINITIES, MALE CRIME, AND VIOLENCE

Masculinity theories on crime primarily seek to demonstrate the relationship between the dynamics of masculinities and male criminality.[23] It was in the early 1990s that criminal justice professionals began to concern themselves with the fact that the overwhelming number of prison inmates were men and how this might relate to such offenses as family violence, sexual abuse, other violence, and juvenile delinquency.[24] The correlation between masculinity and criminality took on greater interest among criminologists and scholars in explaining the interrelated variables in male aggression and anti-social behavior.[25]

A plethora of literature currently exists on the association between masculinity, male violence, and aggressive behavior.[26] Researchers have found that a higher incidence of violent and self-destructive behavior exists among socially marginalized or disadvantaged male youths, suggesting it may be due to a *reactive masculinity* created through the shared rejection from society's mainstream.[27] Violence is seen by these youths as a means of proving one's masculinity, thus achieving social status and power. According to studies on disadvantage and masculinity, violence prevention programs can only work if they are "culturally relevant in all senses of the word 'culture'."[28]

Other masculinity theorists have related various aspects of masculinity to male criminality and other behavior. Jack Katz correlated male deviant behavior to the masculinity traits of being tough and mean, while displaying a willingness to turn it into violence if necessary,[29] while some criminologists have suggested that lower-class criminal and delinquent subcultures are primarily a group response to male role issues.[30]

In detailing the ways that masculinity is expressed, from pimps to white-collar executives, James Messerschmidt advanced: "Men construct masculinity in accordance with their position in social structures and therefore their access to power and resources."[31] He further discussed such male sex offenses as rape, attributing it to men exerting dominance over women as a means to promote their own masculinity when other opportunities to do so are lacking.

Some feminist theorists have characterized masculinity as "intrinsically pathological."[32] In pointing out the wide disparity in male and female violent crimes, Liz Kelly speaks of a "continuum of violence," extending from every-day behavior by males to the more violent acts of criminality such as murder and forcible rape.[33] According to Lynne Segal, masculinity is seen as a burden to men, suggesting that "masculine values are a trap that leads men to self-destruction as it does to the destruction of others."[34]

Critics of masculinity theories on male crime and violence contend that not all men offend or commit acts of violence. Indeed, most men are law abiding and, as such, criminality is uncharacteristic for the majority of men, even if they embody their masculinity in other pursuits and circumstances in life.[35] This notwithstanding, a masculinity approach to male antisocial behavior, aggression, and violence does appear to succeed in tying the male socialization process and biological, cultural, and socioeconomic variables to male crime and aggression. This is particularly true for such male acts of violence as homicide, forcible rape, and terrorism (see Chapter 11).

FEMINIST CRIMINOLOGY AND MASCULINITY CRIME THEORIES

Feminist criminologists are largely critical of traditional criminological theory and its biases and decidedly masculine approach to explaining all crime, victimization, and criminal justice, arguing that "women offenders have been ignored, distorted, or stereotyped within traditional criminology."[36] According to some: "Masculine theorizing tends to be linear, rational, quick, certain, and objective. Feminine theory tends to be slower, intuitive, more circular, iterative, and tentative."[37]

> The construction of masculinity is viewed by Carol Smart as occurring under specific historical and cultural conditions . . . for example, patriarchy [and] neo-colonialism. . . . Masculinity is prioritized and the deployment of power in its multiple forms is gendered. It is, therefore, important for feminist theory to go beyond analyses of law which stop at the point of "recognition" that men...make and implement laws while women . . . are oppressed by them. We need instead to consider the ways in which law constructs and reconstructs masculinity and femininity, and maleness and femaleness, and contributes routinely to a common-sense perception of differences which sustains the social and sexual practices which feminism is attempting to challenge.[38]

Feminist theorists contend that most mainstream theories are "androcentric and sexist," evolving

> out of the experiences of male delinquents/criminals, experiences that subsequently were interpreted through the eyes of predominantly male scholars. Such forms of inquiry either neglected to consider females at all, or if considered, female motivations and behaviors did not deviate from broader societal conceptions of the female nature and role.[39]

In observing that men are studied in non-gendered terms, Ngaire Naffine writes: "In criminology, as in other disciplines, it is men, not women, who supply the essential (and therefore unexamined) 'standard case.' Men, themselves, are not compared with others to see what makes them specific and different."[40]

According to standpoint feminism, which reflects a feminist standpoint of "not just the experience of women, but of women *reflexively* engaged in struggle (intellectual and political),"[41] men and women have different ways of experiencing and perceiving the world. As such, "it is important for women to have a voice in interpreting their behavior, as opposed to having it decided by beliefs and sanctions that do not include women's experiences."[42]

Furthermore, standpoint feminists contend that if crime is regarded as an aggressive act and men are "biologically characterized for their aggressive nature, then not only is criminal theory male centered, so is the criminal practice. If society accepts that men are predisposed to aggression, which leads to crime, then women are socialized as passive actors and consequently many more times victimized. The implications for women are their sense of powerlessness and far reaching dependency upon men."[43]

Feminist criminology holds that crime must be examined from all points of view as the only means to get an accurate picture of criminality, its "actors and reactors."[44] "In order to rewrite criminology with the inclusion of women's identities and perspectives, the masculine view of crime that crime is the activity of men needs to be thrown out."[45] In addition to wanting a greater focus on the seriousness of crimes that victimize women, feminists maintain that with respect to women victims and offenders, "gender be the basis for an analysis of criminology and criminological endeavor rather than simply an additional variable among others."[46]

NOTES

1. See, for example, J. Hood-Williams, "Gender, Masculinities and Crime: From Structures to Psyches," *Theoretical Criminology 5*, 1 (2001): 37–60; Richard Collier, *Masculinities, Crime, and Criminology: Men, Corporeality, and the Criminal(ized) Body* (Thousand Oaks: Sage, 1997); S. Payne, "Masculinity and the Redundant Male: Explaining the Increasing Incarceration of Young Men," *Social & Legal Studies 5*, 2 (1996): 5–14.

2. R. J. Simon and J. Landis, *The Crimes Women Commit, The Punishments They Receive* (Lexington: Lexington Books, 1991); James W. Messerschmidt, *Capitalism, Patriarchy, and Crime: Towards a Socialist Feminist Criminology* (Totowa: Rowman and Littlefield, 1986); J. M. Pollock-Byrne, *Women, Prison, and Crime* (Pacific Grove: Brooks/Cole, 1990).

3. *American Heritage Dictionary* (New York: Dell, 1994), p. 511.

4. David D. Gilmore, *Manhood in the Making: Cultural Concepts of Masculinity* (New Haven: Yale University Press, 1991).

5. Kenneth Reinicke, "Men Facing the 3rd Millennium: A European Comparison," http://www.vidlige.dk/artikler/Men%20in%20the%20face.htm. See also M. D. Schwartz, "Study of Masculinities and Crime," *Criminologist 21*, 1 (1996): 1–5; Emma Ogilvie, "Masculine Obsessions: An Examination of Criminology, Criminality and Gender," *Australian and New Zealand Journal of Criminology 29*, 3 (1996): 62–70.

6. Karen Franklin, "Inside the Mind of Men Who Hate Gays," http://www.pbs.org/wgbh/pages/frontline/shows/assault/roots/franklin.html. See also Ian Harris, *Messages Men Hear: Constructing Masculinities* (Bristol: Taylor and Francis, 1995).

7. Robert Connell, *Masculinities* (Berkeley: University of California Press, 1995); Ingrid Eide, Ingeborg Breines, and Robert Connell, eds., *Male Roles, Masculinities and Violence: A Culture of Peace Perspective* (Paris: UNESCO, 2000). See also David Rose, "Masculinity, Offending and Prison-Based Work," in Bob Pease and Peter Camilleri,

eds., *Working With Men in the Human Services* (Sydney: Allen & Unwin, 2001); S. Robertson, "Separating the Men from the Boys: Masculinity, Psychosexual Development, and Sex Crime in the United States, 1930s–1960s," *Journal of the History of Medicine & Allied Sciences 56*, 1 (2001): 3–35.

8. Reinicke, "Men Facing the 3rd Millennium."

9. *Ibid*; Connell, *Masculinities.*

10. Franklin, "Inside the Mind of Men Who Hate Gays." See also Joachim Kersten, "Culture, Masculinities and Violence Against Women," *British Journal of Criminology 36*, 3 (1996): 381–95; James W. Messerschmidt, *Masculinities and Crime: Critique and Reconceptualization of Theory* (Lanham: Rowman and Littlefield, 1993).

11. Franklin, "Inside the Mind of Men Who Hate Gays." See also P. Bourgis, "In Search of Masculinity: Violence, Respect and Sexuality Among Puerto Rican Crack Dealers in East Harlem," *British Journal of Criminology 36*, 3 (1996): 412–27; James W. Messerschmidt, "From Patriarchy to Gender: Feminist Theory, Criminology and the Challenge of Diversity," in N. Rafter and F. Heidensohn, eds., *International Feminist Perspectives in Criminology* (Milton Keyes: Open University Press, 1995).

12. Connell, *Masculinities*; Hood-Williams, "Gender, Masculinities and Crime;" Sally Holland and Jonathan B. Scourfield, "Managing Marginalized Masculinities: Men and Probation," *Journal of Gender Studies 9*, 2 (2000): 7.

13. Franklin, "Inside the Mind of Men Who Hate Gays;" R. Barri Flowers, *Murder, At the End of the Day and Night: A Study of Criminal Homicide Offenders, Victims, and Circumstances* (Springfield: Charles C Thomas, 2002), pp. 105–14; R. Barri Flowers and H. Loraine Flowers, *Murders in the United States: Crimes, Killers and Victims of the Twentieth Century* (Jefferson: McFarland, 2001), pp. 178–82.

14. Franklin, "Inside the Mind of Men Who Hate Gays;" Holland and Scourfield, "Managing Marginalized Masculinities;" Messerschmidt, *Masculinities and Crime.*

15. Franklin, "Inside the Mind of Men Who Hate Gays;" M. Collinson, "In Search of the High Life: Drugs, Crime, Masculinities and Consumption," *British Journal of Criminology 36*, 3 (1996): 428–33; Gregory M. Herek, ed., *Stigma and Sexual Orientation: Understanding Prejudice Against Lesbians, Gay Men, and Bisexuals* (Thousand Oaks: Sage, 1998).

16. Cited in Franklin, "Inside the Mind of Men Who Hate Gays."

17. *American Heritage Dictionary*, p. 497; Reinicke, "Men Facing the 3rd Millennium." See also Bourgois, "In Search of Masculinity."

18. R. Barri Flowers, *Minorities and Criminality* (Westport: Greenwood, 1990), p. 96. See also J. B. Torres, "Masculinity and Gender Roles Among Puerto Rican Men: Machismo on the U.S. Mainland," *American Journal of Orthopsychiatry 68*, 1 (1998): 16–26; R. Martinez, "Latinos and Lethal Violence: The Impact of Poverty and Inequality," *Social Problems 43* (1996): 131–46.

19. See, for example, Jim Brooke, "Feminism in Foreign Lands: Two Perspectives: Macho Killing in Brazil Spurs Protesters," *Boston Globe* (January 2, 1982): A23; G. Quintero and A. L. Estrada, "Machismo, Drugs and Street Survival in a US-Mexican Border Community," *Free Inquiry in Creative Sociology 26*, 1 (1998): 3–10.

20. Theodore Davidson, *Chicano Prisoners: The Key to San Quentin* (New York: Holt, Rinehart & Winston, 1974). See also Quintero and Estrada, "Machismo, Drugs and

Street Survival in a US-Mexican Border Community;" Keith Carter, "Masculinity in Prison," in Jane Pilcher and Amada Coffey, eds., *Gender and Qualitative Research* (Aldershot: Avebury, 1996).

21. Robert Johnson, *Culture and Crisis in Confinement* (Lexington: D. C. Heath, 1976), pp. 71–75. See also Carter, "Masculinity in Prison;" Bourgois, "In Search of Masculinity;" Torres, "Masculinity and Gender Roles Among Puerto Rican Men."

22. Flowers, *Minorities and Criminality,* p. 97. See also Johnson, *Culture and Crime,* pp. 81–93; J. Moore and R. Pinderhughes, eds., *In the Barrios: Latinos and the Underclass Debate* (New York: Russell Sage, 1993); J. W. Moore, *Homeboys: Gangs, Drugs and Prison in the Barrios of Los Angeles* (Philadelphia: Temple University Press, 1978), pp. 100–106.

23. Messerschmidt, *Masculinities and Crime;* Connell, *Masculinities;* Harris; *Messages Men Hear;* Eide, Breines, and Connell, *Male Roles, Masculinities and Violence;* Michael S. Kimmel, *The Gendered Society* (Oxford: Oxford University Press, 2001).

24. R. Barri Flowers, *Domestic Crimes, Family Violence and Child Abuse: A Study of Contemporary American Society* (Jefferson: McFarland, 2000), pp. 189–218; Tim Newburn and Elizabeth A. Stanko, *Just Boys Doing Business? Men, Masculinities and Crime* (London: Routledge, 1994); Rose, "Masculinity, Offending and Prison-Based Work."

25. Eide, Breines, and Connell, *Male Roles, Masculinities and Violence;* Schwartz, "Study of Masculinities and Crime;" Messerschmidt, "From Patriarchy to Gender;" Connell, *Masculinities.*

26. See, for example, Messerschmidt, *Masculinities and Crime;* Rose, "Masculinity, Offending and Prison-Based Work;" Robertson, "Separating the Men From the Boys;" Carter, "Masculinity in Prison;" Roger Horrocks, *Masculinity in Crisis* (London: Macmillan, 1996).

27. National Crime Prevention, *Working With Adolescents to Prevent Domestic Violence-Rural Town Model,* http://www.ncavac.gov.au/ncp/publications/no3/no3_6sec.2.htm.

28. *Ibid.*

29. Jack Katz, *Seductions of Crime: Moral and Sensual Attractions in Doing Evil* (New York: Basic Books, 1990).

30. Kirstan G. Erikson, Robert Crosnoe, and Sanford M. Dornbusch, "A Social Process Model of Adolescent Deviance: Combining Social Control and Differential Association Perspectives," *Journal of Youth and Adolescence 29* (2000): 395–99; Sui K. Wong, "Acculturation, Peer Relations, and Delinquent Behavior of Chinese-Canadian Youth," *Adolescence 34,* 1 (1999): 107; S. Walklate, *Understanding Criminology: Current Theoretical Debates* (Philadelphia: Open University Press, 1998); L. W. Kennedy and S. W. Baron, "Routine Activities and a Subculture of Violence: A Study of Violence on the Street," *Journal of Research in Crime and Delinquency 30,* 1 (1993): 88–112.

31. Messerschmidt, *Masculinities and Crime,* p. 119. See also Harris, *Messages Men Hear.*

32. See, for example, Horrocks, *Masculinity in Crisis;* Beatrix Campbell, *Goliath: Britain's Dangerous Places* (London: Metheun, 1993).

33. Liz Kelly, "Continuum of Sexual Violence," in Jalna Hanmer and Mary Maynard, eds., *Women, Violence and Social Control* (London: Macmillan, 1987). See also

Kersten, "Culture, Masculinities and Violence Against Women," pp. 316–80; Newburn and Stanko, *Just Boys Doing Business?*

34. Lynn Segal, a review in *Marxism Today* (September 1991). See also Anthony Clare, *On Men: Masculinity and Crises* (London: Chatto and Windus, 2000).

35. H. Croall, *Crime and Society in Britain* (New York: Longman, 1998); Eide, Breines, and Connell, *Male Roles, Masculinities and Violence*; Kimmel, *The Gendered Society*.

36. "Feminist Criminology," http://faculty.newc.edu/toconnor/301/301lect14.htm.

37. *Ibid.*

38. Carol Smart, *Law, Crime and Sexuality: Essays in Feminism* (Thousand Oaks: Sage, 1995), pp. 78–79. See also D. Smith, *The Everyday World as Problematic* (Milton Keyes: Open University Press, 1988); Nancy Levit, "Feminism for Men: Legal Ideology and the Construction of Maleness," *UCLA Law Review 43*, 4 (1996): 1037–1116.

39. Sally Simpson, "Gendered Theory and Single Sex Research," http://www.ou.edu/soc/dwc/simpson2.htm.

40. Ngaire Naffine, *Feminism and Criminology* (Philadelphia: Temple University Press, 1996), pp. 2–3.

41. Smart, *Law, Crime and Sexuality*, p. 43. See also Messerschmidt, "From Patriarchy to Gender;" Sandra Harding, ed., *Feminism and Methodology* (Milton Keyes: Open University Press, 1987).

42. "Feminist Criminology," http://www.Tulane.edu/~femtheory/journals/paper8.html.

43. *Ibid.*

44. *Ibid.*

45. Naffine, *Feminism and Criminology*, pp. 62–64.

46. See, http://library.nothingness.org/articles/SA/en/display/262; Brian D. MacLeun and Dragon Milovanovic, *Thinking Critically About Crime* (Richmond: Collective Press, 1997).

Chapter 4

CORRELATES OF MALE ANTISOCIAL BEHAVIOR

Aside from general crime theories in addressing the causes of male crime and violence, much research has gone into showing a correlation between male criminality and a number of influential factors and circumstances. Of particular importance is the effect of intrafamilial elements on current and future antisocial behavior. These include child abuse and neglect, broken homes, criminality of parents and other family members, parental discipline, and other family dysfunction. Researchers have also looked at the relationship between crime and factors outside the home such as the school, environment, and peer correlates. While such factors are not seen as causative of criminality, per se, they are regarded as significant indicators in crime predictability and preventability for at-risk individuals.

CHILD ABUSE AND NEGLECT

The relationship between child abuse and neglect and delinquent and serious or violent criminal behavior has been strongly documented in the literature. In an examination of the impact of child maltreatment on later antisocial behavior by juveniles, including drug use, Timothy Ireland, Carolyn Smith, and Terrence Thornberry found that persistent maltreatment in childhood and adolescence was strongly and consistently associated with delinquency.[1]

Brandt Steele cited research in which more than 80 percent of the juvenile offenders had a history of being abused, with 43 percent recalling being knocked unconscious by a parent; while D. Lewis and J. H. Pincus reported that violent adolescents had both witnessed and been the victims of severe physical abuse.[2] In a study of 653 young offenders, D. E. Adams, H. A. Ishizula, and K. S. Ishizula found that 43 percent had been abused, neglected, or abandoned at some stage in their lives.[3]

Martin Haskell and Lewis Yablonsky held that juvenile detention facilities are filled with offenders who were victims of child abuse.[4] Similarly, self-report data on prisoners indicate a high percentage had been physically or sexually abused during childhood.[5] After studying chronically violent youthful offenders, Jeanne Cyriaque posited that "violence-dominated lifestyles [of] . . . sexually and physically abusing families, particularly characterize juvenile murderers and sex offenders."[6]

In explaining the relationship between child maltreatment and antisocial behavior, James Garbarino explained: "Many abused children and youth attempt to avoid or escape their parents. In doing so, they are likely to become involved in a variety of [antisocial] behaviors related to their status (unsupervised, uncared for minors) as well as their personal history (inadequate learning of social skills)."[7]

In spite of this persuasive association between child abuse and deviant behavior, not all researchers agree that the two are necessarily interrelated. According to R. W. Weinback and colleagues: "We would be both naïve and grandiose if we were to assert that we can document a relationship of cause and effect when we attempt to associate delinquency and child abuse."[8] However, the overwhelming evidence suggests that child abuse may be one of the strongest factors in aggressive and violent behavior.

FAMILY CYCLE OF VIOLENCE

A number of studies have linked violent behavior to a pattern of antisocial behavior running in the family and transferring itself to outside the family. Vincent Fontana described the family history of some violent adults and abusive parents as being cruel and brutal.[9] Sheldon Glueck and Eleanor Glueck held that the parents of juvenile delinquents were consistently characterized as emotionally disturbed and themselves exhibiting deviant behavior.[10] H. Simmons advanced that "a brutal parent tends to produce a brutal child," and that this brutality then manifests itself beyond the domestic setting.[11]

Other researchers on intergenerational violence have reached similar conclusions. Christopher Ounsted and colleagues advanced that battering parents typically come from families where violence has passed from generation to generation.[12] William McCord described a violence breeds violence hypothesis;[13] and Norman Polansky and associates spoke of an intergenerational cycle of family misfortunes and deviance.[14] In Cathy Widom's retrospective study on the cycle of violence, she found that children who were victims of physical abuse up to the age of 11 were considerably more likely to become violent offenders during the next 15 years of life.[15] While some criminologists have explained generation to generation violent tendencies in terms of genetics, most regard it as learned behavior through the family or socialization process (see Chapters 1 & 2).

BROKEN HOME

The broken home has often been examined in relation to delinquent and criminal behavior. The term "broken home" is generally defined as a home "in which one or both parents are absent due to desertion, divorce, separation, or death—thus depriving the child of a complete, stable family life."[16] Researchers have reached different conclusions in assessing the relationship between broken homes and deviant behavior. J. Bowlby's research in the early 1950s indicated that delinquent youth were much more likely than nondelinquents to have experienced long-term separation from their mothers, causing them to become affectionless and negative in character.[17]

Other early studies reached similar conclusions. Cyril Burt held that delinquents were twice as likely to come from broken homes as nondelinquents.[18] H. Ashley Weeks and Margaret Smith found that 41 percent of the delinquents come from broken homes, compared to 26.7 percent of the control group.[19] The Gluecks found that 60.4 percent of the delinquents as opposed to 34.2 percent of the nondelinquents were from broken homes.[20]

Some researchers have found that broken homes had little effect on the criminality or delinquency of youths. Clifford Shaw and Henry McKay's study of Chicago boys and juvenile court cases concluded that there was only a small correlation between areas with high rates of delinquency and those with high rates of broken homes.[21] Charles Browning found that broken homes were "ineffective . . . as an indicator of family disorganization and other characteristics of family life known to be associated with deviant behavior."[22] F. Ivan Nye also posited that "the structure of the family itself does not cause delinquency."[23]

In a recent comprehensive meta-analysis of the relationship between broken homes and delinquent behavior, L. E. Wells and J. H. Rankin contended that persons from broken homes were 10 to 15 percent more likely to become delinquents than persons from two-parent homes.[24] However, a study of the impact of broken homes on delinquent behavior by Cesar Rebellion suggested a much higher percentage of youths from broken homes were likely to engage in delinquency, with a strong correlation between broken homes and various types of delinquencies, including status offenses, violent crimes, and property crimes.[25]

Some researchers on broken homes and antisocial behavior have focused on the more common loss of the father and its effect on criminality. One study found that divorce or separation in the first five years of a boy's life was predictive of his later being convicted up to the age of 32.[26] Other findings have related not only to broken homes, but the cause of the deviant behavior. In J. McCord's longitudinal study, she found a high prevalence rate of antisocial behavior among boys raised in broken homes absent of an affectionate mother, as well as those raised in homes with both parents beset by conflict.[27] The prevalence rate of criminality was significantly lower for boys from broken homes where an affectionate mother was present. In a longitudinal survey of boys from broken homes due to divorce or separation, an increased probability of delinquent behavior up to the age of 21 was found, compared to boys living in broken homes as a result of death or with both parents present.[28]

PARENTAL DISCIPLINE

Disciplinary practices by parents have been found to be strong factors and predictors of deviant behavior among juveniles. Lax, inconsistent, and harsh discipline have been shown to be more likely to result in antisocial behavior than more consistent, responsible discipline.[29] Extreme parental discipline, in particular, has been related to aggressive and violent juvenile behavior in studies by E. Y. Deykin,[30] A. Buttons,[31] and M. F. Shore.[32] D. J. West and D. P. Farrington found that severe, erratic, and passive parental discipline of youth at the age of eight were predictive of their future convictions.[33]

Some researchers have examined parental discipline in relation to consistency, fairness, and strictness in predicting criminal or delinquent behavior. "Fairness of discipline" was found by Walter Slocum and Carol Stone to be strongly related to conforming behavior by adolescents.[34] Glueck and Glueck reported that lax or erratic parental discipline resulted in a higher percentage of deviant youths than overly strict disciplinary measures.[35] William McCord and colleagues advanced that consistent discipline by parents significantly reduced the incidence of juvenile delinquency.[36]

Parental discipline and supervision in relation to delinquency and criminality has been explored in some studies. Poor supervision by parents was found in one study of adult males to be the most significant predictor of violent crimes and property offenses.[37] Farrington found that weak parental disciplinary measures and poor supervision were strong predictors of juvenile and adult offending and convictions.[38]

PARENTAL AFFECTION

Some researchers have found the lack of parental affection to play an important role in the onset of delinquent behavior. The Gluecks found every pattern of affection in the home–including mother-child, father-child, child-parent, and child-child–to be significantly related to delinquency, with a father's level of affection for his son the most crucial.[39] Similar findings were made by Robert Andry[40] and Slocum and Stone.[41] Leo Davids noted the importance of the father's affection and solid, meaningful relations with his children.[42]

A number of studies have looked at parental rejection in predicting delinquent behavior. In Nye's study of acceptance-rejection, he found a positive correlation between parents rejecting their child and the child's delinquency.[43] McCord and associates found that parental rejection and an absence of maternal warmth were significant factors in antisocial behavior.[44] A study by Albert Bandura and Richard Walters found that the parents of boys described as aggressive delinquents typically denied them an opportunity to express their feelings of dependency.[45]

In examining both affection and discipline in relation to delinquency, S. Kirson Weinberg pointed towards the importance of both variables in affecting the personalities of youths and predisposing to delinquent peers and participation in antisocial behavior.[46]

FAMILY DYSFUNCTION

Dysfunction within the family has been linked in studies with delinquency and criminality. Families that are characterized by discord, tension, conflict, and stress have been found to increase the likelihood of antisocial behavior.[47] Charles Browning found that marital adjustment and family solidarity were significantly related to auto theft and truancy–the two areas of delinquency examined.[48] Glueck and Glueck found that considerably more delinquents than nondelinquents had parents with poor conjugal relations and came from families lacking cohesion.[49] In Lester Jaffee's study of delinquency and anomie, it was observed that "family 'anomie', as measured by the amount of family disagreement on selected value questions, was related with a high score on a 'delinquency proneness' scale."[50]

Family discord has been shown to be closely associated with delinquency in some studies. After studying middle-class, delinquent males, Beatrice Freeman and colleagues found that though none of the subjects' parents had been in contact with social service or law enforcement agencies, their family lives were characterized by inconsistent child-rearing practices, psychological problems, and alcoholism—all seen as disruptive forces within the family.[51] Research has also related emotional disturbances in parents with emotionally disturbed delinquent youth.[52]

Intrafamilial discord and conflict are seen by many as "disrupting the practices of responsible discipline and positive parenting, which in turn increases the likelihood of delinquent behavior."[53] Some studies show that intact families characterized by turmoil and conflict are more closely associated with the formation of delinquency and criminality than broken home families.[54]

CRIMINALITY WITHIN THE FAMILY

A high percentage of juvenile and adult offenders come from families with a history of criminality and incarceration. In L. N. Robins, P. J. West, and B. L. Herjanic's study of two generations of arrests, they found that parents arrested were likely to have children arrested, with similar rates of arrest and types of crimes committed.[55] Robins found that criminal, antisocial, and alcohol-abusing parents tended to have sons who were delinquent.[56] Conversely, in a 30-year study following some 250 delinquent boys, J. McCord found that sons who were convicted were likely to have fathers convicted of crimes.[57]

Most research on intergenerational criminality tends to show a positive correlation between parent offending and child offending. Nearly three in ten fathers convicted of violent offenses in one study had sons convicted of violent crimes.[58] H. Wilson found that parents' convictions were predictive of sons' convictions.[59] More than two times as many sons of parents convicted of crimes were also convicted. According to West and Farrington, a father, mother, or brother convicted by the time a boy turned ten was a strong predictor of his own future convictions.[60]

Studies of incarcerated offenders support the intrafamilial relationship of criminal behavior. In a Justice Department report, 40 percent of prison inmates had at least one member of their immediate family who had spent time behind bars.[61] In a survey of prisoners, nearly 37 percent of male inmates and almost 47 percent of female inmates reported having one or more family members who had been incarcerated.[62]

FAMILY SIZE

Family size has been shown to be a factor in predicting delinquent and criminal behavior. Nye found that male delinquents were more likely to come from large families.[63] J. Newson, E. Newson, and M. Adams[64] reported a large family size to be one of the most significant predictors of criminality, as did J. Ouston.[65] Farrington found large family size as "the most important independent predictor of convictions up to age thirty-two in a logistic regression analysis; 58 percent of boys from large families were convicted up to this age."[66]

Dora Damrin cited a study that related birth order, sex, and family size to the delinquent ratios of juvenile offenders.[67] Albert Reiss used psychiatric terminology such as weak ego and weak superego in differentiating delinquents according to family size.[68] He contended that weak superego delinquents were more likely to come from large families.

CORRELATES OUTSIDE THE FAMILY

A correlation between male crime, delinquency, and violence has been shown in various factors outside the family such as socioeconomic conditions, peer group, and the school. Many of these are addressed in Chapter 18. A number of studies have found male criminality to be associated with the lower class and poverty.[69] Early research such as by Albert Cohen[70] and Richard Cloward and Lloyd Ohlin,[71] found delinquency rates to be highest among youth from a disadvantaged, lower socioeconomic class. More recent research has generally supported the contention that low income and poor living conditions were predictive of juvenile and adult criminality, as reported through official and self-report data.[72]

Some findings have shown peer group pressure to be a strong correlate of male antisocial behavior. F. E. Zimring advanced that most acts of delinquency tend to be perpetrated by a group of youths.[73] According to the National Youth Survey, "having delinquent peers was the best independent predictor of self-reported offending in a multivariate analysis."[74] Despite the relationship between crime and peer group involvement, most such group delinquency tends to decline as juveniles reach the teenage years, though some offenders continue or begin to be influenced by and involved with peers and associates in adulthood criminal behavior.[75]

School-related factors are seen as significant in the onset and continuation of male delinquency and criminality. Some theorists have proposed that the "educational system contributes to delinquent behavior in its fostering of conditions (such as inadequate education, [and] language barriers) that socialize juveniles whose subculture beliefs placed value on delinquent acts."[76]

It has been found that schools with a high rate of delinquency tend to have a high rate of truancy, with under achieving students from the lower classes.[77] Other research has linked learning difficulties, school failure, bullying, and alienation to dropping out of school and delinquency, crime, and violence in childhood and in adulthood.[78]

NOTES

1. Timothy O. Ireland, Carolyn A. Smith, and Terrence P. Thornberry, "Developmental Issues in the Impact of Child Maltreatment on Later Delinquency and Drug Use," *Criminology 40,* 2 (2002): 359–95. See also John H. Lemmon, "How Child Maltreatment Affects Dimensions of Juvenile Delinquency in a Cohort of Low-Income Urban Youths," *Justice Quarterly 16* (1999): 357–76; Suman Kakar, *Child Abuse and Delinquency* (New York: University Press of America, 1996).

2. Brandt F. Steele, "Violence Without the Family," in Ray E. Helfer and C. Henry Kempe, eds., *Child Abuse and Neglect: The Family and the Community* (Cambridge: Ballinger, 1976); R. Barri Flowers, *Children and Criminality: The Child as Victim and Perpetrator* (Westport: Greenwood, 1986), p. 101. See also R. Barri Flowers, *Domestic Crimes, Family Violence and Child Abuse: A Study of Contemporary American Society* (Jefferson: McFarland, 2000), pp. 111–23.

3. D. E. Adams, H. A. Ishizula, and K. S. Ishizula, The Child Abuse Delinquents: An Exploratory/Descriptive Study, unpublished MSW thesis, University of South Carolina, 1977. See also Cindy L. Miller-Perrin and Robin D. Perrin, *Child Maltreatment: An Introduction* (Thousand Oaks: Sage, 2001).

4. Martin R. Haskell and Lewis Yablonsky, *Crime and Delinquency,* 2nd ed. (Chicago: Rand McNally, 1974). See also Peter Stratton, Helga Hanks, and Kevin D. Browne, eds., *Early Prediction and Prevention of Child Abuse: A Handbook* (Hoboken: John Wiley & Sons, 2002).

5. U.S. Department of Justice, Bureau of Justice Statistics, *Sex Offenses and Offenders: An Analysis of Data on Rape and Sexual Assault* (Washington: Office of Justice Programs, 1997), p. 23.

6. Jeanne Cyriaque, "The Chronic Serious Offender: How Illinois Juveniles 'Match Up,'" *Illinois* (February 1982): 4–5. See also Helene Henderson, *Domestic Violence and Child Abuse Sourcebook* (Detroit: Omnigraphics, Inc., 1999).

7. James Garbarino, "Child Abuse and Delinquency: The Developmental Impact of Social Isolation," in Robert J. Hunner and Yvonne E. Walker, eds., *Exploring the Relationship Between Child Abuse and Delinquency* (Montclair: Allanheld, Osmun and Co., 1981), p. 117.

8. Quoted in Flowers, *Children and Criminality: The Child as Victim and Perpetrator,* p. 102.

9. Vincent J. Fontana, *The Maltreated Child: The Maltreatment Syndrome in Children* (Springfield: Charles C Thomas, 1964). See also Ann Buchanan, *Cycles of Child Maltreatment: Facts, Fallacies, and Interventions* (Hoboken: John Wiley & Sons, 1996).

10. Sheldon Glueck and Eleanor T. Glueck, *Delinquents and Non-Delinquents in Perspective* (Cambridge: Harvard University Press, 1968).

11. H. E. Simmons, *Protective Services for Children,* 2nd ed. (Sacramento: Citadel Press, 1970).

12. Christopher Ounsted, Rhoda Oppenheimer, and Janet Lindsay, "The Psychopathology and Psychotherapy of the Families, Aspects Bounding Failure," in A. Franklin, ed., *Concerning Child Abuse* (London: Churchill Livingston, 1975).

13. William McCord, "The Biological Bases of Juvenile Delinquency," in J. S. Roucek, ed., *Juvenile Delinquency* (Freeport: Philosophical Library, 1958). See also Jane Waldfogel, *The Future of Child Protection: How to Break the Cycle of Abuse and Neglect* (Cambridge: Harvard University Press, 2001).

14. Norman A. Polansky, Christine De Souix, and Shlomo A. Sharlin, *Child Neglect: Understanding and Reaching the Parents* (New York: Child Welfare League of America, 1972).

15. Cathy S. Widom, "The Cycle of Violence," *Science 244* (1989): 160–66. See also R. Barri Flowers, *Kids Who Commit Adult Crimes: A Study of Serious Juvenile Criminality and Delinquency* (Binghamton: Haworth, 2002), pp. 130–32.

16. R. Barri Flowers, *The Adolescent Criminal: An Examination of Today's Juvenile Offender* (Jefferson: McFarland, 1990), p. 137.

17. J. Bowlby, *Maternal Care and Mental Health* (Geneva: World Health Organization, 1951).

18. Cyril Burt, *The Young Delinquent* (London: University of London Press, 1925).

19. H. Ashley Weeks and Margaret G. Smith, "Juvenile Delinquency and Broken Homes in Spokane, Washington," *Social Forces 18* (1939): 48–49.

20. Sheldon Glueck and Eleanor T. Glueck, *Family Environment and Delinquency* (Boston: Houghton Mifflin, 1962).

21. Clifford R. Shaw and Henry D. McKay, "Are Broken Homes a Causative Factor in Juvenile Delinquency?" *Social Forces 10* (1932): 514–24.

22. Charles J. Browning, "Differential Impact of Family Disorganization on Male Adolescents," *Social Forces 8* (1960): 37–44.

23. F. Ivan Nye, *Family Relationships and Delinquent Behavior* (New York: John Wiley & Sons, 1958). See also Jan Sokil-Katz, Roger Dunham, and Rick Zimmerman, "Family Structure Versus Parental Attachment in Controlling Adolescent Deviant Behavior: A Social Control Model," *Adolescence 32* (1997): 199–215.

24. L. Edward Wells and Joseph H. Rankin, "Families and Delinquency: A Meta-Analysis of the Impact of Broken Homes," *Social Problems 38* (1991): 73–93; L. Edward Wells and Joseph H. Rankin, "The Broken Homes Model of Delinquency: Analytic Issues," *Journal of Research in Crime and Delinquency 23* (1986): 68–93.

25. Cesar J. Rebellion, "Reconsidering the Broken Homes/Delinquency Relationship and Exploring Its Mediating Mechanism(s)," *Criminology 40,* 1 (2002): 103–33.

26. I. Kolvin, F. W. Miller, M. Fleeting, and P. A. Kolvin, "Social and Parenting Factors Affecting Criminal-Offense Rates: Findings from the Newcastle Thousand Family Study (1947–1980), *British Journal of Psychiatry 152* (1988): 80–90.

27. J. McCord, "A Longitudinal View of the Relationship between Paternal Absence and Crime," in J. Gunn and D. P. Farrington, eds., *Abnormal Offenders, Delinquency, and the Criminal Justice System* (New York: John Wiley & Sons, 1982), pp. 113–28.

28. M. Wadsworth, *Roots of Delinquency* (London: Martin Robertson, 1979).

29. Flowers, *The Adolescent Criminal*, pp. 135–36.

30. E. Y. Deykin, "Life Functioning in Families of Delinquent Boys: An Assessment Model," *Social Services Review 46*, 1 (1971): 90–91.

31. A. Buttons, "Some Antecedents of Felonious and Delinquent Behavior," *Journal of Child Clinical Psychology 2* (1973): 35–37.

32. M. F. Shore, "Psychological Theories of the Causes of Antisocial Behavior," *Crime and Delinquency 17*, 4 (1971): 456–58.

33. D. J. West and D. P. Farrington, *Who Becomes Delinquent?* (London: Heinemann, 1973).

34. Walter Slocum and Carol L. Stone, "Family Culture Patterns and Delinquent-Type Behavior," *Marriage and Family Living 25* (1963): 202–8.

35. Sheldon Glueck and Eleanor T. Glueck, *Unraveling Juvenile Delinquency* (New York: Commonwealth Press, 1950).

36. William McCord, Joan McCord, and Irving K. Zola, *Origins of Crime* (New York: Columbia University Press, 1959).

37. J. McCord, "Some Child-Rearing Antecedents of Criminal Behavior in Adult Men," *Journal of Personality and Social Psychology 37* (1979): 1477–86.

38. David P. Farrington, "The Explanation and Prevention of Youthful Offending," in J. David Hawkins, ed., *Delinquency and Crime: Current Theories* (New York: Cambridge University Press, 1996), pp. 88–90.

39. Glueck and Glueck, *Unraveling Juvenile Delinquency*.

40. Robert G. Andry, "Paternal Affection and Delinquency," in Marvin F. Wolfgang, Leonard Savitz, and Norman Johnson, eds., *The Sociology of Crime and Delinquency* (New York: John Wiley & Sons, 1962), pp. 342–52.

41. Slocum and Stone, "Family Culture Patterns and Delinquent-Type Behavior."

42. Leo Davids, "Delinquency Prevention through Father Training: Some Observations and Proposals," in Paul C. Friday and V. Lorne Stewart, eds., *Youth, Crime and Juvenile Justice: International Perspectives* (New York: Holt, Rinehart & Winston, 1977).

43. Nye, *Family Relationships and Delinquent Behavior*.

44. McCord, McCord, and Zola, *Origins of Crime*. See also Sung J. Jang and Carolyn A. Smith, "A Test of Reciprocal Causal Relationships Among Parental Supervision, Affective Ties, and Delinquency," *Journal of Research in Crime and Delinquency 344* (1997): 307–36.

45. Albert Bandura and Richard H. Walters, "Dependency Conflicts in Aggressive Delinquents," *Journal of Social Issues 4* (1958): 52–65.

46. S. Kirson Weinberg, "Sociological Processes and Factors in Juvenile Delinquency," in Joseph S. Roucek, ed., *Juvenile Delinquency* (New York: Philosophical Library, 1958), pp. 113–32.

47. Flowers, *Children and Criminality*, pp. 144–48.

48. Browning, "Differential Impact of Family Disorganization on Male Adolescents."

49. Glueck and Glueck, *Unraveling Juvenile Delinquency.*

50. Flowers, *Children and Criminality,* p. 145. See also Lester D. Jaffe, "Delinquency Proneness and Family Anomie," *Journal of Criminal Law, Criminology and Police Science 54* (1963): 146–54.

51. Beatrice Freeman, George Savastano, and J. J. Tobias, "The Affluent Suburban Male Delinquent," *Crime and Delinquency 16* (1970): 274–72.

52. See, for example, S. Liverant, "MMPI Differences Between Parents of Disturbed and Non-Disturbed Children," *Journal of Consulting Psychology 23* (1959): 256–60.

53. Flowers, *The Adolescent Criminal,* p. 139.

54. *Ibid.;* M. Rutter, "Parent-Child Separation: Psychological Effects on the Children," *Journal of Child Psychology and Psychiatry 12* (1971): 233–60.

55. L. N. Robins, P. J. West, and B. L. Herjanic, "Arrests and Delinquency in Two Generations: A Study of Black Urban Families and Their Children," *Journal of Child Psychology and Psychiatry 16* (1975): 125–40.

56. L. N. Robins, "Study Childhood Predictors of Adult Outcomes: Replications from Longitudinal Studies," in J. E. Barrett, R. M. Rose, and G. L. Klerman, eds., *Stress and Mental Disorder* (New York: Raven Press, 1979), pp. 219–35.

57. J. McCord, "A Comparative Study of Two Generations of Native Americans," in R. F. Meier, ed., *Theory in Criminology* (Thousand Oaks: Sage, 1977), pp. 83–92.

58. *Ibid.*

59. H. Wilson, "Parental Supervision Re-examined," *British Journal of Criminology 27* (1987): 275–301.

60. West and Farrington, *Who Becomes Delinquent?*

61. U.S. Department of Justice, Bureau of Justice Statistics, *Report to the Nation on Crime and Justice: The Data* (Washington: Government Printing Office, 1983), pp. 30–40.

62. Cited in R. Barri Flowers, *Drugs, Alcohol and Criminality in American Society* (Jefferson: McFarland, 1999), pp. 163–64.

63. Nye, *Family Relationships and Delinquent Behavior.*

64. J. Newson, E. Newson, and M. Adams, "The Social Origins of Delinquency," *Criminal Behavior and Mental Health 3* (1993): 19–29.

65. J. Ouston, "Delinquency, Family Background, and Educational Attainment," *British Journal of Criminology 24* (1984): 2–26.

66. Farrington, "The Explanation and Prevention of Youthful Offending," pp. 94–95.

67. Dora E. Damrin, "Family Size and Sibling Age, Sex, and Position as Related to Certain Aspects of Adjustment," *Journal of Social Psychology 29* (1949): 93–102.

68. Albert J. Reiss, Jr., "Social Correlates of Psychological Types of Delinquency," *American Sociological Review 17* (1961): 710–18.

69. Flowers, *Children and Criminality,* pp. 147–48; Albert J. Reiss and Albert J. Rhodes, "The Distribution of Juvenile Delinquency in the Social Class Structure," *American Sociological Review 26* (1961): 720–32; D. R. Offord, M. H. Boyle, and Y.

Racine, "Ontario Child Health Study: Correlates of Disorder," *Journal of the American Academy of Child and Adolescent Psychiatry 28* (1989): 856–60.

70. Albert K. Cohen, *Delinquent Boys* (New York: Free Press, 1955).

71. Richard A. Cloward and Lloyd E. Ohlin, *Delinquency and Opportunity* (New York: Free Press, 1960).

72. Flowers, *The Adolescent Criminal;* D. P. Farrington, "Juvenile Delinquency," in J. C. Coleman, ed., *The School Years,* 2nd ed. (London: Routledge, 1992), pp. 123–63.

73. F. E. Zimring, "Kids, Groups and Crime: Some Implications of a Well-Known Secret," *Journal of Criminal Law and Criminology 72* (1981): 867–85.

74. Farrington, "The Explanation and Prevention of Youthful Offending," p. 98. See also D. S. Elliott, D. Huizinga, and S. S. Ageton, *Explaining Delinquency and Drug Use* (Thousand Oaks: Sage, 1985).

75. Flowers, *Drugs, Alcohol and Criminality in American Society;* D. P. Farrington and D. J. West, "The Cambridge Study in Delinquent Development: A Long-Term Follow-Up of 411 London Males," in H. J. Kerner and G. Kauser, eds., *Criminality: Personality, Behavior, Life History* (Berlin: Springer-Verlag, 1990), pp. 115–38.

76. Flowers, *Children and Criminality,* p. 151.

77. M. Rutter, B. Maughan, P. Mortimore, and J. Ouston, *Fifteen Thousand Hours* (London: Open Books, 1979).

78. Flowers, *The Adolescent Criminal,* p. 129; Flowers, *Kids Who Commit Adult Crimes,* pp. 59–61.

Part II

THE DYNAMICS OF MALE CRIME

Chapter 5

THE NATURE OF MALE CRIME AND VIOLENCE

Serious crime has seen an increase recently in the United States after a number of years of declining rates in violent crimes; this, in spite of more effective intervention strategies, anticrime statutes, law enforcement powers, and community awareness. This is attributed to a faltering economy, the release into society of hundreds of thousands of prisoners, an increase in the teen population, easy access to and use of firearms, and drug use and abuse. Millions of people continue to be the victims of crime in this country every year, with a rippling effect on the nation itself in terms of costs, crime prevention, and incarceration of offenders.

Males are predominantly responsible for the vast majority of serious and violent criminality including murder, forcible rape, aggravated assault, domestic and workplace violence, terrorist acts, gang crime and violence, and school violence. Related offenses such as alcohol and drug crimes are also significantly male-oriented. Minority males are disproportionately represented as both offenders and victims of crimes, while males in general are more likely to be victims of crime than females.

Inmate data indicates that a high percentage of male offenders were under the influence of alcohol or drugs and used weapons during the commission of their crime. Many such criminals had long histories of antisocial behavior and/or were the victims of child physical or sexual abuse or otherwise came from dysfunctional families or violent backgrounds.

MALE VIOLENCE

Few would argue that criminal violence has shaped our society through its incidence, attempt to prevent, punishment for law violators, laws against violent crime, the threat of such violence perpetrated against citizens, and the high cost of violence in human and economic terms.

The significant relationship between males and violence has been examined in numerous studies with respect to homicides, firearms, domestic violence, child abuse, drug abuse, street crime, workplace violence, youth violence, hate crimes, terrorism, and incarceration. Most experts on violence regard it as largely a male phenomenon in society as a reflection of masculinity, power, aggressive tendencies, position of authority, testosterone, poverty, culture and subcultures, opportunity, learned behavior, cycles of violence, personality disorders, substance abuse, and interrelated societal and individual variables.

Higher levels of testosterone have been found in violent males compared to their nonviolent counterparts,[1] while a subculture of violence theory has related male violence to a set of "conduct norms" that fosters such behavior among those within the subculture.[2] In studies, males have been found to have a tendency to be more aggressive than women where it results in pain or physical injury, attributing this to the "perceived consequences of aggression that are learned as aspects of gender roles and other social roles."[3]

Violence itself can generally be broken into two types: (1) *behavioral violence* and (2) *structural violence.* According to Mark Thomas:

> Acute behavioral violence is usually sudden in onset and short in duration, and the effects are usually immediately realized. Violent crime is typically acute, [such as] assaults, murder, and rape. It is typically committed by individuals or groups on intended or recognized victims. Structural violence is the result of systemic, institutional, and social factors; it is typically chronic and great in duration; its causes and effects are not always recognized or perceived.[4]

Behavioral violence can be subcategorized into two broad types: (1) *intrafamilial violence* and (2) *extrafamilial violence.* Extrafamilial violence, or violence outside the family such as violent street crime, tends to get much of the attention from law enforcement, the media, and our collective psyches. But intrafamilial violence and structural violence occur most often, "which can be determined either by quantifying the number of incidents or by quantifying the amount of injuries and deaths that result from them."[5]

Structural violence and criminality are seen as being highly influenced by racism, classism, sexism, and patriarchy, as stated by James Messerschmidt.[6] "Cultural crime and violence" is defined as "a culture in which structural crime and violence are considered normative by most people in that culture."[7] Poverty is a type of structural violence that is considered the norm in society, and amongst the most deadly kind of violence.[8]

According to James Gilligan, the root cause of intrafamilial and extrafamilial violence, as well as social oppression, in American society and culture are the ways in which masculinity and femininity are defined.[9] Hegemonic masculinity is seen as leading to the abuse, degradation, and violent oppression of women,[10] whereas racism and classism are seen as resulting in the abuse, degradation, and oppression of racial minorities and the poor.[11] The criminal justice system as such is viewed as a "violent means of controlling males of the 'oppressed' groups."[12]

The high rate of street and domestic violence and other serious offenses attributed primarily to males continues to influence our perception of criminality and aggression in society and how it is responded to.[13]

VICTIMIZATION AND MALE OFFENDERS

According to the Department of Justice's annual, report, National Crime Victimization Survey (NCVS)—which collects information on crime, victims, and offender characteristics—there were an estimated 25.9 million crimes in the United States in 2000.[14] Nearly three-quarters of these were property crimes, around one-quarter violent crimes, and about 1 percent were personal thefts (see Fig. 5.1).

In corresponding NCVS data from 1995, males were perceived by victims to be the perpetrator in more than eight out of ten victimizations of the single-offender victimizations and around seven in ten multiple-offender victimizations (see Table 5.1). More than nine in ten rapes or sexual assaults and robberies were believed to have been committed by males in single-offender victimizations, while multiple-offender victimizations involving all male offenders were identified as being responsible for over nine out of ten sexual assaults and nearly nine in ten robbery offenses.

The NCVS reported the following characteristics on crime victims in 2000:

- Persons 12 to 24 years of age had the highest rates of violent victimization.
- Persons 16 to 19 years of age were much more likely to be sexually assaulted than persons 50 to 64 years of age.
- Persons 16 to 19 years old were around ten times more likely to be robbery victims as persons 65 years of age or older.
- Males had higher overall rates of violent crime victimization than females.
- Females had significantly higher rates of rape or sexual assault victimizations than males.
- Blacks had the highest rates of violent crime victimization.
- Hispanics and non-Hispanics experienced similar rates of violent crime victimization.

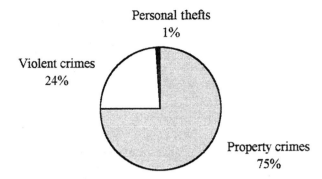

Figure 5.1. Criminal Victimization in the United States, by Type, 2000. *Source:* National Crime Victimization Survey, 2000, http://www.ojp.usdoj.gov/bjs/cvictgen.htm

- Hispanics were more likely than non-Hispanics to be robbery victims.
- Persons 65 years of age and older were disproportionately likely to be victims of property crimes.
- More than nine in ten crimes against elderly victims were property offenses.
- Less than four in ten crimes against persons 12 to 24 years of age were property offenses.[15]

HOMICIDE VICTIMS AND OFFENDERS

The homicide rate rose more than 3 percent in 2001, after a decade on the decline.[16] In 2000, an estimated 15,517 persons were murdered in the United States, down some 21 percent from 1996 and 37.2 percent since 1991 (see Fig. 5.2). Males are most likely to be both the perpetrators and victims of homicide. They are nine times as likely as females to murder males and females, as well as be murdered by males in single-offender homicides.[17] Males are also most likely to be killed by female murderers.[18]

According to data from the Federal Bureau of Investigation's annual crime report, *Crime in the United States: Uniform Crime Reports* (UCR), in 2000:

- Males constituted 90 percent of known murder perpetrators.
- More than three-quarters of murder victims were male.
- More than nine in ten murder offenders were persons 18 years of age and older.
- Nearly nine out of ten murder victims were age 18 or older.
- More than half the homicide offenders were black.
- Over 46 percent of homicide offenders were white.

Table 5.1

PERCENT DISTRIBUTION OF SINGLE- AND MULTIPLE-OFFENDER VICTIMIZATIONS, BY TYPE OF CRIME AND
PERCEIVED SEX OF OFFENDER, 1995

Type of crime	Number of single-offender victimizations	Perceived sex of offender	Number of multiple-offender victimizations	Perceived sex of offenders	
		Male		All male	Male and female
Crimes of violence	7,287,430	84.4%	2,147,890	71.6%	16.9%
Completed violence	2,023,180	85.8	720,030	77.8	11.5
Attempted/threatened violence	5,264,250	83.9	1,427,860	68.5	19.7
Rape/sexual assault[a]	303,240	97.5	32,480	94.0	0.0
Robbery	623,710	92.9	496,710	87.9	8.7
Completed/property taken	381,850	91.2	346,500	87.7	8.8
With injury	90,660	94.0	127,110	85.5	10.0
Without injury	291,190	90.3	219,380	89.0	8.1
Attempted to take property	241,850	95.7	150,200	88.6	8.3
With injury	51,130	95.0	43,420	89.5	5.4
Without injury	190,720	95.9	106,770	88.2	9.5
Assault	6,360,470	83.0	1618,700	66.2	19.8
Aggravated	1,346,930	88.1	497,580	76.3	14.8
Simple	5,013,530	81.6	1,121,110	61.7	22.0

[a] Includes verbal threats of rape and threats of sexual assault.

Source: Adapted from U.S. Department of Justice, Bureau of Justice Statistics, *Criminal Victimization in the United States, 1995: A National Crime Victimization Survey Report* (Washington: Office of Justice Programs, 2000), pp. 47, 51.

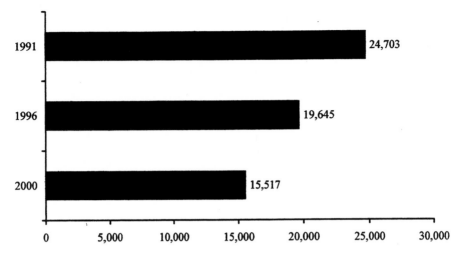

Figure 5.2. Homicides in the United States, 1991–2000. *Source:* Derived from U.S. Department of Justice, Federal Bureau of Investigation, *Crime in the United States: Uniform Crime Reports 2000* (Washington: Government Printing Office, 2001), pp. 15, 66.

- Around half the victims of homicide were white, more than 48 percent black, while less than 3 percent were of other races.
- More than nine in ten black victims of murder were killed by black offenders.
- Nearly nine in ten white murder victims were killed by white offenders.[19]

Male murderers tend to kill strangers or acquaintances most often. However, males are also most likely to be the perpetrators of intimate homicides. Nearly three in four murders involving an intimate partner are committed by males.[20] Studies show that an estimated three out of ten women slain in the United States are victims of a male intimate.[21] (See further discussion on homicide in Chapters 7 and 11.)

FIREARMS AND MALE OFFENDERS

The number of crimes perpetrated with firearms in the United States has dropped since the early 1990s. However, use of firearms in crimes remains a serious problem, and one distinctly of a male nature.[22] In 2000, there were 533,470 victims of violent crimes such as rape, sexual assault, robbery, and aggravated assault, who reported that the offender possessed a firearm, according to the NCVS.[23] Victimizations in which a firearm was used constituted an estimated 8 percent of the 6.3 million crimes of violence. A weapon was present in more than one-fourth of all violent crimes, while the perpetrator possessed or used a weapon in more than half of all robberies.

Homicides are most often perpetrated with firearms, particularly handguns. In 2000, firearms constituted nearly two-thirds of the murder weapons in the United States. Of these, more than half the murders involved the use of a handgun; with shotguns used in almost 4 percent of the murders, rifles just over 3 percent, and more than 7 percent perpetrated with other guns.[24] Around one-third of homicides are committed with other lethal weapons including knives and blunt objects.

Male offenders commit the vast majority of firearms-related crimes. In 2000, there were 96,831 arrests of males for weapons-related offenses, representing nearly 92 percent of all weapons charges.[25] In a survey of prison inmates, of those possessing a handgun during their crime, 28 percent had obtained through an illicit means such as a drug dealer, 9 percent from a theft; while 10 percent had stolen one or more guns and 11 percent had traded or sold stolen firearms.[26]

According to the U.S. Justice Department's report on firearm injury and death, from 1993 to 1997:

- Nearly three in ten nonfatal violent crimes were perpetrated with a firearm.
- More than six in ten nonfatal firearm-related injuries treated in hospital emergency departments were the result of an assault.
- Of firearm-related deaths, more than four in ten were homicides.
- Four in five victims of fatal and nonfatal gunshot wounds as a result of a crime were male.
- More than eight out of ten victims of firearm homicide were male.
- Nearly half of all victims of fatal and nonfatal injuries from firearms resulting from a crime were black males.
- Almost 20 percent of nonfatal gunshot wound victims of a crime were Hispanic.
- More than half of victims of nonfatal gunshot wounds as a result of a crime were under the age of 25.
- Victims of fatal gunshot wounds due to criminality tended to be older.[27]

ARRESTS AND MALE OFFENDERS

According to the UCR, there were nearly 7.1 million arrests of males for all offenses in the United States in 2000 (see Table 5.2). This accounted for around 80 percent of all arrests. More than 84 percent of the male arrestees were age eighteen and over. Over 343,000 arrests were for crimes of violence, while nearly 758,000 were for property crimes. In all, of some 1.1 million Crime Index arrests–representing violent and property crimes–about 73 percent of the arrestees were males 18 years of age and older.

Table 5.2
ARRESTS OF MALES, BY AGE, 2000

Offense charged	Total all ages	Ages under 18	Ages 18 and over
TOTAL	7,096,187	1,128,529	5,967,658
Percent distribution[a]	100.0	15.9	84.1
Murder and nonnegligent manslaughter	7,783	715	7,068
Forcible rape	17,712	2,903	14,809
Robbery	65,026	16,592	48,434
Aggravated assault	252,921	33,633	219,288
Burglary	164,165	55,278	108,887
Larceny-theft	501,106	153,381	347,725
Motor vehicle theft	83,149	28,196	54,953
Arson	9,065	4,965	4,100
Violent crime[b]	343,442	53,843	289,599
Percent distribution[a]	100.0	15.7	84.3
Property crime[c]	757,485	241,820	515,665
Percent distribution[a]	100.0	31.9	68.1
Crime Index total[d]	1,100,927	295,663	805,264
Percent distribution[a]	100.0	26.9	73.1

[a] Due to rounding, the percentages may not add to total.
[b] Includes murder, forcible rape, robbery, and aggravated assault.
[c] Includes burglary, larceny-theft, motor vehicle theft, and arson.
[d] Includes arson.
Source: Adapted from U.S. Department of Justice, Federal Bureau of Investigation, *Crime in the United States: Uniform Crime Reports 2000* (Washington: Government Printing Office, 2001), p. 227.

Race and Arrests

Blacks are disproportionately likely to be arrested for crimes relative to their population figures, while whites are most often arrested. As shown in Figure 5.3, for Crime Index offenses in 2000, more than 64 percent of the arrestees were white, with blacks comprising almost 33 percent of the total, followed by Asians at 1.5 percent, and Native Americans at just over 1 percent of those arrested. Blacks represented more than half the arrestees for robbery and nearly half the persons arrested for murder and nonnegligent manslaughter.[28]

Drug- and Alcohol-Related Arrests

Alcohol and drug abuse and other drug offenses have been commonly related to more serious and violent male crimes including homicide, forcible rape, domestic violence, and robbery.[29] In 2000, there were more than 2.3

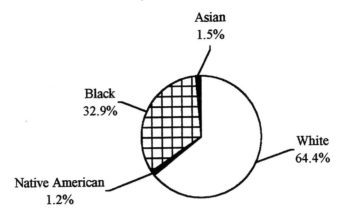

Figure 5.3. Arrests for Crime Index Offenses, by Race,[a] 2000. *Source:* Derived from U.S. Department of Justice, Federal Bureau of Investigation, *Crime in the United States: Uniform Crime Reports 2000* (Washington: Government Printing Office, 2001), p. 234.
[a] Native Americans include American Indians or Alaskan Natives; Asians include Pacific Islanders.

million male arrests for alcohol- and drug-related crimes (see Table 5.3). Nearly 860,000 of these were arrests for drug abuse violations. Among alcohol-related arrests, 765,680 were for driving under the influence. This constituted more than twice the number of arrests for drunkenness or liquor law violations, at 367,825 and 335,618 arrests, respectively. More than 91 percent of the males arrested in 2000 for drug- or alcohol-related offenses were persons age 18 or over.

Trends in Male Arrests

Overall and for serious crimes, male arrests have been on the decline in the United States. As seen in Table 5.4, between 1991 and 2000, arrests of males for total crimes dropped nearly 4 percent. For Crime Index offenses, arrests fell by almost 30 percent. Male arrests for violent crimes decreased around 17 percent, while male property crime arrests dropped about 34 percent.

For individual Crime Index offenses, the greatest drop in arrests occurred for murder and nonnegligent manslaughter, which fell more than 42 percent; motor vehicle theft, declining over 39 percent; and robbery, which dropped nearly 33 percent. The smallest declines in male arrests for serious offenses were for aggravated assault at just over 9 percent and arson at nearly 18 percent.

Other significant declines in male arrests in 2000 occurred for gambling at almost 44 percent, vagrancy at 36 percent, and stolen property and weapons-related charges, both of which dropped more than 31 percent.[30]

Table 5.3
MALE ARRESTS FOR DRUG- AND ALCOHOL-RELATED OFFENSES, 2000

Offense charged	Total all ages	Ages under 18	Ages 18 and over
Total	2,327,756	207,182	2,120,574
Drug abuse violations	858,633	115,013	743,620
Driving under the influence	765,680	10,839	754,841
Liquor laws	335,618	69,738	265,880
Drunkenness	367,825	11,592	356,233

Source: Adapted from U.S. Department of Justice, Federal Bureau of Investigation, *Crime in the United States: Uniform Crime Reports 2000* (Washington: Government Printing Office, 2001), p. 228.

Male arrests rose over the ten-year span for curfew and loitering law violations at more than 70 percent, drug abuse violations at over 47 percent, offenses against family and children increased more than 24 percent, and other assaults climbed nearly 13 percent. Arrests of males also rose for white-collar offenses such as embezzlement and forgery and counterfeiting.[31]

MALE INMATES

The overall number of persons being held in correctional facilities has risen as the criminal justice system cracks down on serious and violent offenders and habitual criminals through tougher laws, law enforcement, and sentences. According to the Department of Justice, in 2000 there were 2,071,686 inmates in jails, state and federal prisons, military facilities, and juvenile facilities in the United States (see Fig. 5.4).

The vast majority of inmates under correctional authority are male, constituting more than 93 percent of state and federal prisoners, nearly 89 percent of jail inmates, and around 86 percent of persons held in juvenile residential facilities.[32]

Race and Ethnicity of Male Inmates

Minority male offenders are disproportionately likely to be in jail, prison, or juvenile corrections (see Table 5.5). Black males constitute more than 46 percent of inmates in prison, and around 41 percent of inmates in jail or juvenile facilities. Hispanic males account for more than 16 percent of prison inmates, more than 15 percent of those in jail, and 19 percent of the juveniles

Table 5.4
TEN-YEAR TOTAL AND CRIME INDEX MALE ARREST TRENDS, 1991–2000

Offense charged	1991	2000	Percent change
TOTAL[a]	6,000,210	5,771,866	−3.8
Murder and nonnegligent manslaughter	10,772	6,237	−42.1
Forcible rape	20,475	14,382	−29.8
Robbery	81,000	54,624	−32.6
Aggravated assault	234,479	212,297	−9.5
Burglary	224,420	135,735	−39.5
Larceny-theft	596,714	409,577	−31.4
Motor vehicle theft	106,545	64,825	−39.2
Arson	9,161	7,539	−17.7
Violent crime[b]	346,726	287,540	−17.1
Property crime[c]	936,840	617,676	−34.1
Crime Index total[d]	1,283,566	905,216	−29.5

[a] Does not include suspicion.
[b] Violent crimes are offenses of murder, forcible rape, robbery, and aggravated assault.
[c] Property crimes are offenses of burglary, larceny-theft, motor vehicle theft, and arson.
[d] Includes arson.
Source: Adapted from U.S. Department of Justice, Federal Bureau of Investigation, *Crime in the United States: Uniform Crime Reports 2000* (Washington: Government Printing Office, 2001), p. 221.

in residential placement. White males represent nearly 36 percent of prison inmates, almost 42 percent of those in jail, and 36 percent of males in juvenile detention. Other racial minorities account for just under 2 percent of the male prison and jail inmates, and 3 percent of those confined in juvenile correctional facilities.

According to the Justice Department, as of midyear 2000, approximately 12 percent of the nation's black males, 4 percent of Hispanic males, and 1.7 percent of white males in their twenties to early thirties were either in jail or prison.[33]

Trends in the Inmate Population

The inmate population continues to rise in the United States, though the growth has slowed down in recent years. From 1990 to 2000, the number of males in state or federal penitentiaries grew by 77 percent.[34] As shown in Table 5.6, from midyear 1999 to midyear 2000, the total number of inmates under correctional supervision rose 3 percent. The federal prison inmate population increased by more than 11 percent. By comparison, between 1990 and midyear 2000, the number of inmates nationwide rose an average of

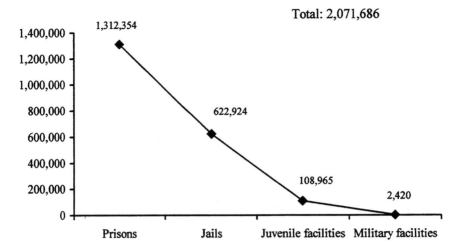

Figure 5.4. Inmates in Correctional Facilities in the United States,[a] 2000. *Source:* Derived from U.S. Department of Justice, Bureau of Justice Statistics Bulletin, *Prisoners in 2000* (Washington: Office of Justice Programs, 2001), p. 1.
[a] Totals include inmates held in territorial prisons, U.S. Immigration and Naturalization Service facilities, and jails under Indian jurisdiction.

Table 5.5
RACIAL DISTRIBUTION OF MALES IN CORRECTIONAL FACILITIES

Race	Percent of Inmates		
	Prisons	Jails	Juvenile facilities[b]
White	35.7%	41.9%	36.0%
Black	46.2%	41.3%	41.0%
Hispanic	16.4%	15.1%	19.0%
Other[a]	1.7%	1.6%	3.0%

a Includes Asians and Native Americans.
b Includes juveniles being held in residential placement.
Source: Derived from U.S. Department of Justice, Bureau of Justice Statistics Bulletin, *Prisoners in 2000*, (Washington: Office of Justice Programs, 2001), p. 11; U.S. Department of Justice, Bureau of Justice Statistics Bulletin, *Prison and Jail Inmates at Midyear 2000* (Washington: Office of Justice Programs, 2001), p. 7; U.S. Department of Justice, *Juvenile Offenders and Victims: 1999 National Report* (Washington: Office of Juvenile Justice and Delinquency Prevention, 1999), p. 195.

almost 6 percent annually, with the annual rate of growth among state, federal, and jail inmate populations at 5.9 percent, 8.8 percent, and 4.6 percent, respectively. The average rate of increase for prisoners in state custody in

2000, was the lowest since 1972.[35] This notwithstanding, in 2000 there were still 1.2 million state prison inmates in this country, the vast majority male.[36]

Drug and Alcohol Use by Inmates

A high percentage of inmates used alcohol and/or drugs prior to or during the commission of their offense. Nearly four in ten convicted offenders were drinking at the time the crimes was perpetrated.[37] According to research, an estimated 38 percent of violent offenders in state prisons, 41 percent in local jails, 20 percent in federal prisons, and 41 percent on probation had been drinking when committing the offense.[38]

Similarly, studies show that many inmates used drugs when committing crimes. A 1997 survey of inmates in state and federal prisons found that one-third of state prisoners and more than two in ten federal prisoners committed their crimes while using drugs.[39] More than half of all prison inmates reported using alcohol or drugs during the commission of the crime. Around four in ten drug offenders and property offenders incarcerated were under the influence of drugs when perpetrating their offense.

In 1998, more than one-third of convicted jail inmates were estimated to have used drugs at the time they committed their crime.[40] According to the Bureau of Justice Statistics (BJS), 65 percent of mentally ill persons in jail and 57 percent of others in jail were under the influence of alcohol and drugs during the commission of the crime.[41]

A strong relationship has been shown between inmates convicted of intimate crimes and drug or alcohol use at the time of the offense.[42] Among parents incarcerated, more than half reported using drugs in the month prior to the crimes, while more than eight in ten had ever used drugs.[43]

Physical and Sexual Abuse of Inmates

Many inmates in correctional facilities have been the victims of physical or sexual abuse prior to their incarceration, often believed by criminologists to be a precursor to serious violent or sexual offending. According to BJS surveys, from 1995 to 1997, nearly 19 percent of state prison inmates, around 10 percent of those in federal penitentiaries, and almost 16 percent of local jail inmates reported being the victims of physical or sexual abuse prior to their present sentence (see Table 5.7).

Just over 16 percent of total male inmates had ever been physically or sexually abused, with state prisoners and jail inmates the most likely to experience physical or sexual abuse. Male inmates were more likely to have been

Table 5.6
PERSONS HELD IN STATE OR FEDERAL PRISONS OR IN LOCAL JAILS, 1990–2000

Year	Total inmates in custody	Prisoners in custody — Federal	Prisoners in custody — State	Inmates held in local jails	Incarceration rate[a]
1990	1,148,702	58,838	684,544	405,320	458
1991	1,219,014	63,930	728,605	426,479	481
1992	1,295,150	72,071	778,495	444,584	505
1993	1,369,185	80,815	828,566	459,804	528
1994	1,476,621	85,500	904,647	486,474	564
1995	1,585,586	89,538	989,004	507,044	601
1996	1,646,020	95,088	1,032,440	518,492	618
1997	1,743,643	101,755	1,074,809	567,079	648
1998	1,816,931	110,793	1,113,676	592,462	669
1999[b]					
June 30	1,875,199	117,995	1,151,261	605,943	687
December 31	–	125,682	1,158,220	–	
2000					
June 30	1,931,859	131,496	1,179,214	621,149	702
Percent change, 6/30/99–6/30/00	3.0%	11.4%	2.4%	2.5%	
Annual average increase, 12/31/90–6/30/00	5.6%	8.8%	5.9%	4.6%	

Note: Jail counts are for midyear (June 30). Counts for 1994–2000 exclude persons who were supervised outside of a jail facility. State and federal prisoner counts for 1990–98 are for December 31.

[a] Total number of persons in custody per 100,000 residents in each reference year.

[b] In 1999, 15 states expanded their reporting criteria to include inmates held in privately operated correctional facilities. For comparisons with previous years, the state count 1,136,582 and the total count 1,860,520 should be used for June 30, 1999.

Source: U.S. Department of Justice, Bureau of Justice Statistics Bulletin, *Prison and Jail Inmates at Midyear 2000* (Washington: Office of Justice Programs, 2001), p. 2.

Table 5.7
PRIOR ABUSE OF MALE CORRECTIONAL POPULATIONS

	Percent experiencing abuse before sentence		
	Total	*Ever*	*Before 18*
Ever abused before admission			
State prison inmates	18.7%	16.1%	14.4%
Federal prison inmates	9.5	7.2	5.8
Jail inmates	16.4	12.9	11.9
Probationers	15.7	9.3	8.8
Physically abused			
State prison inmates	15.4	13.4	11.9
Federal prison inmates	7.9	6.0	5.0
Jail inmates	13.3	10.7	–
Probationers	12.8	7.4	–
Sexually abused			
State prison inmates	7.9	5.8	5.0
Federal prison inmates	3.7	2.2	1.9
Jail inmates	8.8	5.6	–
Probationers	8.4	4.1	–

– Not available.

Source: Adapted from U.S. Department of Justice, *Prior Abuse Reported by Inmates and Probationers* (Washington: Bureau of Justice Statistics, 1999), p. 1.

physically than sexually abused. The vast majority of abused male inmates had been sexually or physically abused before the age of 18.

GANGS IN CORRECTIONAL INSTITUTIONS

Gangs are a major concern in adult and juvenile correctional facilities, much like in society as a whole. In a survey of administrators of juvenile detention and correctional institutions, it was estimated that around 40 percent of institutionalized youths were in gangs.[44] In another survey, more than three-quarters of the correctional facilities that responded reported a problem with gangs.[45]

In surveying over 800 serious and violent male inmates in six juvenile correctional institutions close to urban areas with gang problems, J. F. Sheley and J. D. Wright reported that more than two-thirds of the inmates said they were involved with a gang or quasi-gang.[46] More than eight in ten of the gang-related members owned a firearm and over half said they carried the gun almost always prior to their incarceration.

A high percentage of imprisoned gang members were drug-involved before becoming inmates. In a survey of gang-related inmates in state prisons, over 80 percent had ever used drugs, while nearly 70 percent reported selling, manufacturing, or importing drugs.[47]

Some evidence suggests that along with the gangs' relationship to violence in correctional facilities, gangs can also develop as well as recruit members in the institutional setting.[48] Furthermore, being confined in a juvenile detention or correctional institution has been found to be significantly predictive of membership in an adult prison gang.[49]

HIV AMONG MALE INMATES

At the end of 1999, there were an estimated 22,175 male inmates in state prison who tested positive for the Human Immunodeficiency Virus (HIV), according to the Justice Department.[50] This represented around 2.2 percent of the inmate population that were infected with HIV, the precursor to AIDS (Acquired Immunodeficiency Syndrome). New York had the most HIV-positive male inmates by state with 6,240, followed by Florida at 2,439, and Texas at 2,238.

The number of male prisoners with the HIV virus is rising. Between 1998 and 1999, HIV-positive male inmates increased by 130, with an average annual increase of HIV infection at 1.2 percent from 1995 to 1999. However, the percentage of male inmates testing positive for the virus has remained fairly stable over the five-year span at just over 2 percent of the inmate population (see Table 5.8)

CAPITAL PUNISHMENT AND MALE PRISONERS

There were 3,593 state and federal prisoners under a death sentence in the United States at yearend 2000, as reported by the BJS bulletin, *Capital Punishment 2000*.[51] Characteristics of death row inmates can be seen in Table 5.9. Inmates under a death sentence are overwhelmingly male, constituting 98 percent of those on death row in 2000.

Although more than 55 percent of the inmates under sentence of death were white, racial and ethnic minorities were overrepresented among death row inmates. Blacks comprised nearly 43 percent of the inmates on death row and Hispanics made up almost 11 percent of the total.

Table 5.8
MALE STATE PRISON INMATES WITH HIV

Year	Estimated number of HIV-positive inmates	Percent HIV/AIDS in custody year population
1995	21,144	2.3%
1996	21,299	2.2%
1997	20,608	2.1%
1998	22,045	2.2%
1999	22,175	2.2%
Annual average change, 1995–99: 1.2%		

Source: U.S. Department of Justice, Bureau of Justice Statistics Bulletin, *HIV in Prisons and Jails, 1999* (Washington: Office of Justice Programs, 2001).

Death row inmates most often tended to have a ninth grade to high school graduation or GED education. More than half the inmates under a sentence of death were never married.

There were 214 prisoners sentenced to death and 161 removed from death row in 2000. Relative to their population figures, black and Hispanic prisoners were disproportionately likely to be both admitted to and removed from death row.

The youngest inmate under sentence of death was 18 years old, while the oldest was 85 years of age. The average age of death row inmates when arrested for current offense was twenty-eight, while 2 percent of inmates on death row were under the age of eighteen.[52]

In 2000, 83 male death row inmates were executed, 11 less than in 1999. Forty-nine of those executed were white, 35 were black, and one was Native American. Six of the inmates executed were whites of Hispanic ethnicity. Nine out of ten executions in 2000 were by lethal injection, in comparison to five out of ten people put to death in 1990.[53]

Between 1977 and 2000, of 6,588 persons on death row, only one in ten were executed with more than one in three receiving a disposition other than execution.[54]

NOTES

1. See, for example, J. M. Dabbs, R. L. Frady, T. S. Carr, and N. F. Besch, "Saliva Testosterone and Criminal Violence in Young Adult Prison Inmates," *Psychosomatic Medicine 49* (1987): 74–182; A. Campbell, S. Muncer, and J. Odber, "Aggression

Table 5.9
DEMOGRAPHIC CHARACTERISTICS OF PRISONERS UNDER SENTENCE
OF DEATH, 2000

| Characteristic | Prisoners under sentence of death, 2000 | | |
	Yearend	Admission	Removals
Total number under sentence of death[a]	3,593	214	161
Gender			
Male	98.5%	96.3%	96.9%
Female	1.5	3.7	3.1
Race			
White	55.4%	57.0%	57.1%
Black	42.7	40.2	41.0
All other races[b]	1.9	2.8	1.9
Hispanic origin			
Hispanic	10.6%	17.0%	8.6%
Non-Hispanic	89.4	83.0	91.4
Education			
8th grade or less	14.4%	17.6%	12.7%
9th–11th grade	37.3	34.1	39.6
High school graduate/GED	38.2	39.8	40.3
Any college	10.1	8.5	7.5
Median	11th	11th	11th
Marital status			
Married	22.6%	23.5%	27.5%
Divorced/separated	21.0	18.7	25.4
Widowed	2.8	3.2	4.2
Never married	53.6	54.5	43.0

[a] Calculations are based on those cases for which data were reported.
[b] At yearend 1999, "other" consisted of 28 American Indians, 24 Asians, and 13 self-identified Hispanics. During 2000, 2 American Indians and 4 Asians were admitted; 1 American Indian, 1 Asian, and 1 self-identified Hispanic were removed.
Source: U.S. Department of Justice, Bureau of Justice Statistics Bulletin, *Capital Punishment 2000* (Washington: Office of Justice Programs, 2001), p .8.

and Testosterone: Testing a Bio-Social Model," *Aggressive Behavior 23* (1997): 229–38; J. H. Brooks and J. R. Reddon, "Serum Testosterone in Violent and Nonviolent Young Offenders," *Journal of Clinical Psychology 52* (1996): 475–83.

2. Marvin E. Wolfgang and Franco Ferracuti, *The Subculture of Violence: Towards an Integrated Theory in Criminology* (London: Tavistock, 1967); C. G. Ellison, "An Eye For An Eye? A Note on the Southern Subculture of Violence Thesis," *Social Forces 69* (1991): 1223–39; J. Dixon and A. J. Lizotte, "Gun Ownership and the Southern Subculture of Violence," *American Journal of Sociology 93* (1987): 383–405.

3. "Sex and Violence," http://www.dic.gov.au/research/cvp/ncv/vda-secD8. html; A. H. Eagly and V. J. Steffen, "Gender and Aggressive Behavior: A Meta-Analytic Review of the Social Psychological Literature," *Psychological Bulletin 100* (1986): 309–30.

4. Mark Thomas, "A Study on the Psychospiritual Rehabilitation of the American Nation: The Patterns and Processes in Transforming a Culture of Crime and Violence," http://www.neteze.com/mkthomas/proposal.htm.

5. *Ibid.*

6. James W. Messerschmidt, *Masculinities and Crime: Critique and Reconceptualization of Theory* (Lanham: Rowman and Littlefield, 1993).

7. Thomas, "A Study on the Psychospiritual Rehabilitation of the American Nation."

8. James Gilligan, *Violence: Reflections on a National Epidemic* (New York: Vintage, 1997), p. 91.

9. *Ibid.*

10. Messerschmidt, *Masculinities and Crime.*

11. *Ibid.*; Gilligan, *Violence: Reflections of a National Epidemic.*

12. Thomas, "A Study on the Psychospiritual Rehabilitation of the American Nation;" A. Davis, "Masked Racism: Reflections on the Prison Industrial Complex," *ColorLines 1*, 2 (1998): 11–17.

13. Benjamin B. Wolman, *Antisocial Behavior* (Amherst: Prometheus Books, 1999); S. Donziger, ed., *The Real War on War: The Report of the National Criminal Justice Commission* (New York: Harper Collins, 1996).

14. National Crime Victimization Survey, 2000, http://www.ojp.usdoj.gov/bjs/cvictgen.htm.

15. *Ibid.*

16. Dan Eggen, "FBI: U.S. Crime Rate is on Rise–Increase in Incidents of Major Violence Ends 10-Year Decline," http://www.detnews.com/2002/nation/0206/24/nation-522429.htm.

17. U.S. Department of Justice, Federal Bureau of Investigation, *Crime in the United States: Uniform Crime Reports 2000* (Washington: Government Printing Office, 2001), p. 15.

18. U.S. Department of Justice, Bureau of Justice Statistics Crime Data Brief, *Homicide Trends in the United States: 1998 Update* (Washington: Office of Justice Programs, 2000), p. 2; R. Barri Flowers and H. Loraine Flowers, *Murders in the United States: Crimes, Killers and Victims of the Twentieth Century* (Jefferson: McFarland, 2001), pp. 109–46.

19. *Crime in the United States*, p. 15.

20. R. Barri Flowers, *Domestic Crimes, Family Violence and Child Abuse: A Study of Contemporary American Society* (Jefferson: McFarland, 2000), pp. 62–63; Angela Browne, Kirk R. Williams, and Donald G. Dutton, "Homicide Between Intimate Partners," in M. Dwayne Smith and Margaret A. Zahn, eds., *Studying and Preventing Homicide: Issues and Challenges* (Thousand Oaks: Sage, 1999), pp. 55–58.

21. Flowers, *Domestic Crimes, Family Violence and Child Abuse*, p. 62; R. Barri Flowers, *Murder, At the End of the Day and Night: A Study of Criminal Homicide Offenders, Victims, and Circumstances* (Springfield: Charles C Thomas, 2002), pp. 51–63.

22. *Crime in the United States*, pp. 216, 225.

23. National Crime Victimization Survey, http://www.ojp.usdoj.gov/bjs/.

24. *Crime in the United States*, p. 18.

25. *Ibid.*, p. 233.

26. Firearms and Crime Statistics, http://www.ojp.usdoj.gov/bjs/.

27. U.S. Department of Justice, *Firearm Injury and Death From Crime, 1993–97* (Washington: Office of Justice Programs, 2000), pp. 1–5.

28. *Crime in the United States*, p. 234.

29. R. Barri Flowers, *Drugs, Alcohol and Criminality in American Society* (Jefferson: McFarland, 1999), pp. 32–44; Marvin E. Wolfgang and R. B. Strohm, "The Relationship Between Alcohol and Criminal Homicide," *Quarterly Journal of Studies on Alcoholism 17* (1956): 411–26; U.S. Department of Justice, Bureau of Justice Statistics, *Drugs, Crime, and the Justice System* (Washington: Government Printing Office, 1992).

30. *Crime in the United States*, p. 221.

31. *Ibid.*

32. U.S. Department of Justice, Bureau of Justice Statistics Bulletin, *Prisoners in 2000* (Washington: Office of Justice Programs, 2001), p. 1; U.S. Department of Justice, Bureau of Justice Statistics Bulletin, *Prison and Jail Inmates at Midyear 2000* (Washington: Office of Justice Programs, 2001), p. 7; U.S. Department of Justice, *Juvenile Offenders and Victims: 1999 National Report* (Washington: Office of Juvenile Justice and Delinquency Prevention, 1999), p. 195.

33. *Prison and Jail Inmates at Midyear 2000*, p. 1.

34. *Prisoners in 2000*, p. 1

35. *Ibid.*, p. 3.

36. *Ibid.*, pp. 10–11.

37. Bureau of Justice Statistics, http://www.ojp.usdog.gov/bjs/.

38. *Ibid.*

39. U.S. Department of Justice, Bureau of Justice Statistics, *Substance Abuse and Treatment, State and Federal Prisoners, 1997* (Washington: Office of Justice Programs, 1999).

40. U.S. Department of Justice, Bureau of Justice Statistics, *Drug Use, Testing, and Treatment in Jails* (Washington: Office of Justice Programs, 2000).

41. U.S. Department of Justice, Bureau of Justice Statistics, *Mental Health and Treatment of Inmates and Probationers* (Washington: Office of Justice Programs, 1999).

42. Cited in Flowers, *Domestic Crimes, Family Violence and Child Abuse*, pp. 198–99; Flowers, *Drugs, Alcohol and Criminality in American Society*, pp. 168–73.

43. U.S. Department of Justice, Bureau of Justice Statistics, *Incarcerated Parents and Their Children* (Washington: Office of Justice Programs, 2000).

44. U.S. Department of Justice, *Youth Gangs: An Overview* (Washington: Office of Juvenile Justice and Delinquency Prevention, 1998).

45. G. W. Knox, *An Introduction to Gangs* (Barrien Springs: Vande Vere Publishing, 1991).

46. J. F. Sheley and J. D. Wright, *In the Line of Fire: Youth, Guns and Violence in Urban America* (Hawthorne: Aldine De Gruyter, 1995).

47. U.S. Department of Justice, Bureau of Justice Statistics, *Drugs and Crime Facts, 1994* (Washington: Government Printing Office, 1995), p. 29.

48. J. W. Moore, D. Vigil, and R. Garcia, "Residence and Territoriality in Chicano Gangs," *Social Problems 31* (1983): 182–94.

49. P. Ralph, R. J. Hunter, J. W. Marquart, S. J. Cuvelier, and D. Merianos, "Exploring the Differences Between Gang and Non-Gang Prisoners," in C. R. Huff, ed., *Gangs in America*, 2nd ed. (Thousand Oaks: Sage, 1996), pp. 241–56.

50. U.S. Department of Justice, Bureau of Justice Statistics Bulletin, *HIV in Prisons and Jails, 1999* (Washington: Office of Justice Programs, 2001).

51. U.S. Department of Justice, Bureau of Justice Statistics Bulletin, *Capital Punishment 2000* (Washington: Office of Justice Programs, 2001), p. 1.

52. *Ibid.*

53. *Ibid.*

54. *Ibid.*

Chapter 6

COMPARING MALE-FEMALE CRIME

Traditionally males have far exceeded females where it concerns serious criminality and delinquency. For years there has been debate on whether or not females are beginning to close the gap with males in terms of crimes committed, types of crimes, arrests, and imprisonment. There is some indication that the antisocial behavior of males and females is becoming more alike, especially among juveniles. Further, certain serious forms of deviance, such as child abuse and neglect and domestic violence, are believed by some experts to involve at least as many female offenders as male. Females are also well represented in some sexual offenses, such as prostitution, along with involvement in substance abuse-related offenses and the status offense of running away from home. This notwithstanding, overall serious and violent criminal behavior continues to be mostly a male phenomenon and preoccupation.

GENDER AND CRIMINALITY

The relationship between gender and antisocial behavior has been explored in various studies.[1] Much of the research has focused on explaining the disparity between male crime and female crime. Crime rates are typically higher—often considerably higher for males—particularly for crimes of violence and aggression,[2] but also sex offenses,[3] property crimes, and drug and alcohol offenses.[4] Nearly eight in ten persons arrested in the United States are male,[5] while also representing more than nine in ten persons behind bars.[6] Over 98 percent of persons on death row in this country are male.[7]

So why do males commit more crimes or are generally recognized as perpetrating more offenses? Some have contended that females benefit from more lenient treatment in the criminal justice system—from discretionary practices in arrest, to differential sentencing decisions, and time in confinement—than their male counterparts.[8] This has been attributed to chivalry, paternalism, and patriarchy.[9] However, others have disputed this contention, finding that women–particularly minority women–are not more likely than men to receive a favorable outcome from their involvement with law enforcement, the courts, or corrections.[10] Indeed, the evidence indicates that for prostitution, women are more likely to face arrest and detention than men,[11] though studies show that at least as many males as females are selling their bodies or otherwise involved in the sex-for-sale industry.[12]

Traditional gender role expectations for males and females are seen as strong indicators of their criminality and propensity to commit certain types of crimes.[13] Sex role theorists posit that male-female differences in deviant behavior are not intrinsic, but learned behavior through the socialization process. This is especially true for violent crimes. A. H. Eagly and V. J. Steffen found a greater tendency for men to be more aggressive than women where such aggression resulted in pain and injury, suggesting that sex differences in aggressive behavior reflect the perception of the consequences of such that comes through learning as part of gender and social roles.[14] According to Mark Warr, differential socialization between males and females makes the latter tend to be less willing to become involved in harmful behavior, such as violent criminality.[15]

Masculinity and femininity have also been used to explain gender differences in criminal behavior. Masculinity theories basically hold that men commit more crimes and acts of aggression because it is a reflection of their masculine values, gender, nature, socialization and physical superiority to be more powerful, violent, aggressive, controlling, and a reflection of a culture and society that is largely male dominated.[16] Conversely, feminine values and socialization tend to make women less violent and aggressive, thus they commit fewer acts of serious criminality. Women who follow more traditional male sex roles in their deviant behavior are seen as becoming "masculinized."[17]

The significantly higher rate of aggressive behavior by men compared to women has been further linked to testosterone. Elevated levels of testosterone has been found to correlate with aggression in males and females in studies by J. M. Dabbs and colleagues,[18] among others,[19] but has primarily been associated with male aggression and crimes of violence.[20] Other researchers believe that the relationship between testosterone and aggression is weak at best, and not as strong a factor in explaining criminality as environmental and sociological variables.[21]

The lower overall incidence of criminality among women is seen as a reflection of greater intrafamilial and societal social controls. Studies have shown that females tend to have more close supervision than males, a stronger attachment to parents and offspring, and exhibit a greater willingness to conform to conventional values, while being less likely to participate in antisocial behavior.[22] Warr argued that while moral inhibitions blocked both males and females from offending, the effect was much greater for females.[23]

Other researchers have attributed gender differences in deviant behavior to females being more empathetic, nurturing, and altruistic than males, relating this to "brain systems and hormones that mediate bonding and maternal care."[24] Anthony Walsh asserted that "sex differences in aggression, dominance seeking, and promiscuity are related to parental investment rather than sex per se. It is the level of parental investment that exerts pressure for the selection of the neurohormonal mechanisms that underlie these behaviors."[25]

Many criminologists believe that when females do commit crimes, they do so as a reflection of their marginal status in society. One study found that women inmates shared backgrounds characterized by domestic violence and childhood abuse, substance abuse, low educational achievement, impoverishment, self-abuse, and psychological problems.[26] Other research has linked female criminality, in particular, to intrafamilial sexual and physical abuse; a dysfunctional family; poor parent-child communication; and low paying, unsatisfying work.[27]

OFFICIAL DATA ON GENDER AND CRIME

Male and Female Arrests

According to official arrest figures, an estimated 14 million arrests for criminal infractions were made in the United States in 2000.[28] The vast majority of persons arrested were males. There were nearly 7.1 million arrests of males for criminal offenses, compared to just over two million arrests of females. Males constituted nearly eight of every ten persons arrested (see Fig. 6.1). Around 3.5 males were arrested for every female. A greater proportion of adult males are arrested for criminal acts than adult females. About 84 percent of all male arrests involve persons age eighteen and over, while just over 78 percent of female arrests are of persons 18 years of age and over.[29]

For Crime Index offenses—representing what are considered the most serious violations of the law—there were an estimated 1.5 million arrests in 2000, as shown in Table 6.1. Of these, some 1.1 million arrests were of males, with less than 400,000 arrests of females. Almost three out of every four Crime Index arrests involved male arrestees, while just over one in four arrests were of females.

The differential by gender was greater for violent crime arrests than property crime arrests. About 83 percent of those arrested for violent crimes were male, compared to just over 17 percent female. Nearly 90 percent of persons

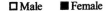

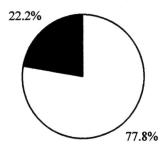

Figure 6.1. Total Arrests, by Sex, 2000. Source: Derived from U.S. Department of Justice, Federal Bureau of Investigation, *Crime in the United States: Uniform Crime Reports 2000* (Washington: Government Printing Office, 2001), p. 233.

arrested for robbery and about 90 percent of those arrested for forcible rape in 2000 were male. Males constituted around 70 percent of persons arrested for property crimes, while nearly 30 percent of persons arrested for property offenses were female. More than 84 percent of the arrestees for motor vehicle theft and arson were male. Female property crime arrestees were most likely to be arrested for larceny-theft, representing nearly 36 percent of those arrested.

Arrest Trends

Arrest trends indicate that arrests have been on the decline overall. However, arrests of females have shown an increase in total arrests and a smaller decrease than males in arrests for Crime Index offenses. Between 1991 and 2000, while total male arrests fell almost 4 percent, total female arrests grew nearly 18 percent (see Fig. 6.2). For Crime Index offenses, arrests of males declined by about 30 percent. By comparison, arrests of females decreased just over 10 percent during the ten-year span (see Fig. 6.3). In spite of this, the overall gap between male and female arrestees remains considerable.

Male and Female Inmates

Data on jail and prison inmates reveal that males are far more likely to be incarcerated than females. In 2000, there were around 12 times as many men in jail or prison as women.[30] As seen in Figure 6.4, in 2000 males constituted nearly 89 percent of the nation's local jail inmates at midyear, while females

Table 6.1
ARRESTS FOR CRIME INDEX OFFENSES, BY SEX, 2000

Offense charged	Number of persons arrested			Percent male	Percent female
	Total	Male	Female		
TOTAL	**9,116,967**	**7,096,187**	**2,020,780**	**77.8**	**22.2**
Murder and nonnegligent manslaughter	8,709	7,783	926	89.4	10.6
Forcible rape	17,914	17,712	202	98.9	1.1
Robbery	72,320	65,026	7,294	89.9	10.1
Aggravated assault	316,630	252,921	63,709	79.9	20.1
Burglary	189,343	164,165	25,178	86.7	13.3
Larceny-theft	782,082	501,106	280,976	64.1	35.9
Motor vehicle theft	98,697	83,149	15,548	84.2	15.8
Arson	10,675	9,065	1,610	84.9	15.1
Violent crime[a]	415,573	343,442	72,131	82.6	17.4
Property crime[b]	1,080,797	757,485	323,312	70.1	29.9
Crime Index total[c]	1,496,370	1,100,927	395,443	73.6	26.4

[a] Violent crimes are offenses of murder, forcible rape, robbery, and aggravated assault.
[b] Property crimes are offenses of burglary, larceny-theft, motor vehicle theft, and arson.
[c] Includes arson.

Source: Adapted from U.S. Department of Justice, Federal Bureau of Investigation, *Crime in the United States: Uniform Crime Reports 2000* (Washington: Government Printing Office, 2001), p. 233.

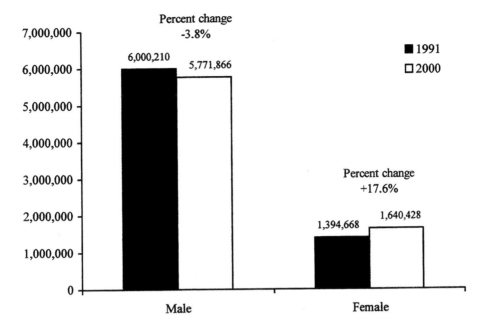

Figure 6.2. Ten-Year Total Arrest Trends, by Sex, 1991–2000. *Source:* Derived from U.S. Department of Justice, Federal Bureau of Investigation, *Crime in the United States: Uniform Crime Reports 2000* (Washington: Government Printing Office, 2001), p. 221.

made up just over 11 percent of the jail inmate population. There were an estimated 543,120 adult males in jail at midyear in 2000, compared to 70,414 adult females.[31]

Among prison inmates, an even higher proportion are male. There were around 1.2 million male prisoners in 2000, compared to some 91,612 female prisoners. As shown in Figure 6.5, males constituted 93.4 percent of all state and federal prison inmates in the United States, while females made up 6.6 percent of the total. Relative to their population numbers, men were fifteen times more likely than women to be imprisoned in a state or federal penitentiary.[32]

Trends in the Inmate Population

Long-term inmate trends show a growth in the jail inmate population among females and an increase in the male and female prison population. From 1990 to 2000, the percentage of female jail inmates rose by more than 2 percent, while the percentage of male inmates decreased over 2 percent (see Table 6.2). The adult female jail inmate population grew 6.6 percent each

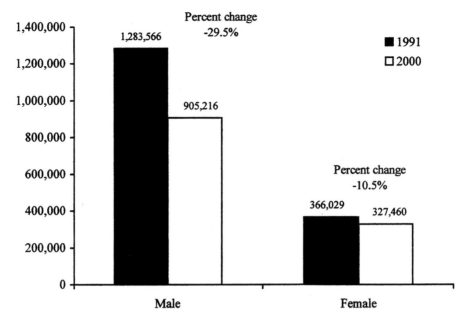

Figure 6.3. Ten-Year Crime Index[a] Arrest Trends, by Sex, 1991–2000. *Source:* Derived from U.S. Department of Justice, Federal Bureau of Investigation, *Crime in the United States: Uniform Crime Reports 2000* (Washington: Government Printing Office, 2001), p. 221.

[a] Includes arrests for violent crimes and property crimes.

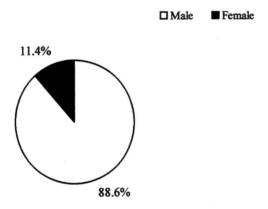

Figure 6.4. Jail Inmate Population, by Sex, Midyear 2000. *Source:* Derived from U.S. Department of Justice, Bureau of Justice Statistics Bulletin, *Prison and Jail Inmates at Midyear 2000* (Washington: Government Printing Office, 2001), p. 7.

year on average over the span, compared to an almost 4 percent average growth in the adult male jail inmate population.[33]

□ Male ■ Female

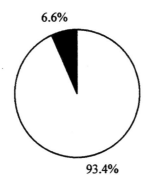

6.6%

93.4%

Figure 6.5. State and Federal Prison Inmate Population, by Sex, 2000. *Source:* Derived from U.S. Department of Justice, Bureau of Justice Statistics Bulletin, *Prisoners in 2000* (Washington: Office of Justice Programs, 2001), p. 1.

Table 6.2
LOCAL JAIL INMATES, BY SEX, MIDYEAR 1990–2000

	Percent of jail inmates						
	1990	*1995*	*1996*[b]	*1997*	*1998*	*1999*	*2000*
Total[a]	100%	100%	100%	100%	100%	100%	100%
Male	90.8	89.8	89.2	89.4	89.2	88.8	88.6
Female	9.2	10.2	10.8	10.6	10.8	11.2	11.4

[a] Detail may not add to total because of rounding.
[b] Data for 1996 were based on all persons under jail supervision
Source: Adapted from U.S. Department of Justice, Bureau of Justice Statistics Bulletin, *Prison and Jail Inmates at Midyear 2000* (Washington: Office of Justice Programs 2001), p. 7.

Although males comprise more than nine in ten inmates in prison, the female prison population has risen at a greater pace than the male prison population (see Table 6.3). Between 1990 and 2000, the number of females in prison has more than doubled, rising an average of 7.6 percent per year, compared to an annual growth rate of 5.9 percent among male prisoners. From 1999 to 2000, the number of female inmates increased 1.3 percent, with the number of female inmates rising by 1.2 percent.

In spite of the greater growth in the female prison population, at the end of 2000, there were 915 sentenced male prisoners per 100,000 men, in comparison to 59 sentenced female prisoners per 100,000 women in the United States.

Table 6.3
PRISONERS UNDER THE JURISDICTION OF STATE OR FEDERAL
CORRECTIONAL AUTHORITIES, BY GENDER, YEAREND 1990, 1999, AND 2000

	Men	*Women*
All inmates		
Advance 2000	1,290,280	91,612
Final 1999	1,273,171	90,530
Final 1990	729,840	44,065
Percent change, 1999–2000	1.3%	1.2%
Average annual 1990–2000	5.9%	7.6%
Incarceration rate[a]		
2000	915	59
1990	572	32

[a] The number of prisoners with sentences of more than one year per 100,000 residents on December 31.
Source: Adapted from U.S. Department of Justice, Bureau of Justice Statistics Bulletin, *Prisoners in 2000* (Washington: Office of Justice Programs, 2001), p. 5.

VIOLENT CRIME

The rate, range, and rise in violent female crime in relation to violent male crime have been debated sine the 1970s when some suggested the presence of a new female criminal. In the book, *Sisters in Crime: The Rise of the New Female Criminal,* Freda Adler associated the women's movement, assertiveness by women, and the entry of females into nontraditional occupations with an increase in crimes of violence. She asserted that "although males continue to commit the greater number of offenses, it is [females] who are committing those same crimes at yearly rates of increase now running as high as six or seven times faster than males."[34]

Critics have challenged Adler's findings. In his examination of gender differences in adult criminality, Darrell Steffensmeier found little change in female patterns of arrest over the 12-year period studied.[35] After comparing official data from the United States and England, Carol Smart argued against the "tendency to fixate on monocausal explanations of female criminality such as the women's movement, when studies of male deviance indicate several possible etiological perspectives."[36]

As shown in Figure 6.6, between 1991 and 2000, female arrests for violent crimes nationwide increased by nearly 33 percent, while male arrests decreased by around 17 percent. Despite this apparent narrowing of the gap in male-female arrests for violent crimes, males are still far more likely to commit violent acts than females as is documented consistently through official, victimization, and self-report data.

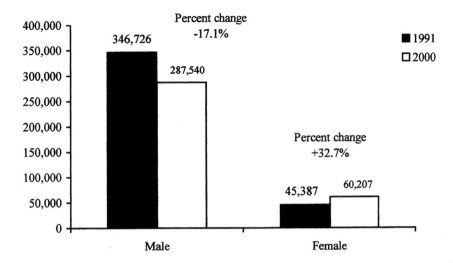

Figure 6.6. Ten-Year Violent Crime Arrest Trends, by Sex, 1991–2000. *Source:* Derived from U.S. Department of Justice, Federal Bureau of Investigation, *Crime in the United States: Uniform Crime Reports 2000* (Washington: Government Printing Office, 2001), p. 221.

PROPERTY CRIME

The growth in the property crime rate among females in recent decades has led some researchers to believe that the male-female disparity in property crimes may be steadily narrowing. After examining arrest data from 1953 to 1972, Rita Simon posited that if the current trends in female arrest rates for property crimes were to continue, "approximately equal numbers of men and women will be arrested for larceny and for fraud and embezzlement by the 1990s; and for forgery and counterfeiting the proportions should be equal by the 2010s."[37]

These conclusions have been rejected for the most part as inaccurate and methodologically weak. For instance, George Noblit and Janie Burcart argued that Simon failed to examine age groups in arrest rates, was inconsistent in the use of official data, and did not allow for changes in the population.[38]

Recent arrest trends of male and female arrestees for property crime do not indicate a significant shrinking in arrests relative to gender. As seen in Figure 6.7, between 1991 and 2000, the decrease in male arrests for property crimes in the United States of around 34 percent was more than twice that of female arrests for property crimes, which dropped nearly 17 percent. Although males and females appear closer in their participation in property offenses than violent offenses, the ratio of male-female arrests for property crimes is still is 2.3 to 1. Moreover, the differential is much greater for certain high incidence seri-

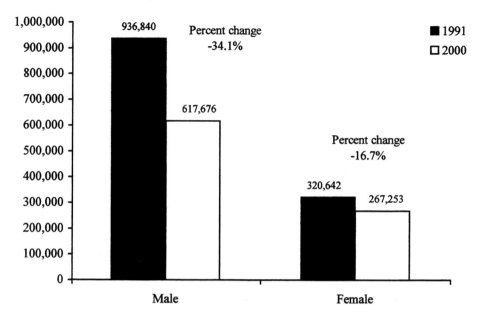

Figure 6.7. Ten-Year Property Crime Arrest Trends, by Sex, 1991–2000. *Source:* Derived from U.S. Department of Justice, Federal Bureau of Investigation, *Crime in the United States: Uniform Crime Reports 2000* (Washington: Government Printing Office, 2001), p. 221.

ous property offenses such as burglary, with a male-female ratio of arrests at 6.2 to 1, and motor vehicle theft with a ratio of 5.2 to 1.[39]

DRUG AND ALCOHOL VIOLATIONS

Males are much more likely to use and abuse alcohol and drugs than females, according to most findings. In 2000, more than 82 percent of the more than a million persons arrested for drug abuse violations in the United States were male (see Table 6.4). Similarly, males constituted around 84 percent of the more than 915,000 arrestees for driving under the influence, 77 percent of the over 435,000 arrestees for liquor law violations, and nearly 87 percent of the more than 423,000 arrested for drunkenness. Thus, females represented less than two in ten persons arrested for drug abuse violations, driving under the influence, and drunkenness; and just over two in ten arrestees for violations of liquor laws.

Other national data generally support arrest figures. A National Institute of Mental Health survey found that the highest rate of serious alcohol abuse occurred among adult males, single, separated, and divorced persons.[40]

Table 6.4
ARRESTS FOR DRUG/ALCOHOL-RELATED VIOLATIONS, BY SEX, 2000

Offense charged	Number of persons arrested			Percent male	Percent female
	Total	*Male*	*Female*		
Drug abuse violations	1,042,334	858,633	183,701	82.4	17.6
Driving under the influence	915,931	765,680	150,251	83.6	16.4
Liquor laws	435,672	335,618	100,054	77.0	23.0
Drunkenness	423,310	367,825	55,485	86.9	13.1

Source: Adapted from U.S. Department of Justice, Federal Bureau of Investigation, *Crime in the United States: Uniform Crime Reports 2000* (Washington: Government Printing Office, 2001), p. 233.

According to the National Household Survey on Drug Abuse, nearly four in ten males had ever used marijuana compared to around one in four females; while males were twice as likely as females to have used crack, inhalants, or stimulants at some time in their life.[41]

For males and females, substance abuse is linked to other crimes such as violent crimes, property crimes, and drug dealing. The National Institute of Justice recently found that more than half the men and women arrested for crimes of violence in New York and Washington had been using one or more illicit drugs.[42] Similarly, the Drug Use Forecasting Program reported that 60 percent or more of male arrestees and 50 percent of female arrestees for property crimes and robberies tested positive for drug use.[43]

INTIMATE VIOLENCE

Where it concerns lethal violence between intimates, men are far more likely to kill an intimate partner than be killed by one (see Chapter 7). Women are more than two times as likely to be the victims than perpetrators of domestic homicide.[44] According to the Bureau of Justice Statistics, between 1976 and 1996, there were 31,260 women killed by a husband, ex-husband, boyfriend, or other intimate, compared to 20,311 males slain by a female intimate (see Fig. 6.8). Most male intimate killers tend to kill as a reflection of intimate battering, sexual jealousy, or separation;[45] whereas most female intimate murderers tend to kill due to being physically abused, threatened, or in self-defense from a violent mate.[46]

Most studies indicate that women are far more likely to be on the receiving end of nonfatal intimate violence as well. A woman is beaten by a spouse every nine seconds in the United States, with some estimates going as high as

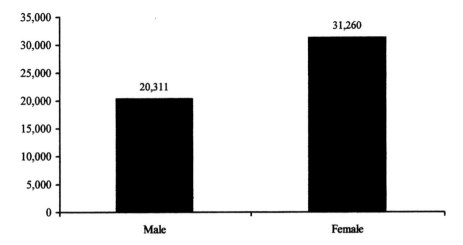

Figure 6.8. Murdered Intimates,[a] by Sex of Victim, 1976–1996. *Source:* Derived from U.S. Department of Justice, Bureau of Justice Statistics Factbook, *Violence by Intimates: Analysis of Data on Crimes by Current or Former Spouses, Boyfriends, and Girlfriends* (Washington: Government Printing Office, 1998), p. 6.

[a] Perpetrators include husbands, ex-husbands, wives, ex-wives, boyfriends, girlfriends, and other intimates.

one victim out of every two women.[47] Diana Russell found that more than two in ten females who had ever been married reported being battered by a husband at some time in their life.[48] Dating violence against females has been found in some studies to be just as prevalent as marital violence.[49]

Some studies have found that males may be the victims of intimate violence just as often as females. Suzanne Steinmetz estimated that around 300,000 men are victims of domestic violence annually in the United States.[50] Robert Langley and Richard Levy estimated that 12 million men in this country have ever been the victims of intimate violence by a spouse.[51]

According to Murray Straus, approximately two-thirds of all married couples engage in some type of physical violence during their relationship, with one-fourth considered of a serious nature.[52] Richard Gelles found that nearly one-third of the wives in his sample had been violent at some time in the relationship, compared to nearly half the husbands.[53] Most experts agree that female intimates are much more likely than male intimates to be the victims of severe intimate violence with the most serious implications.

CHILD ABUSE

There are more than a million victims of child abuse in the United States each year. While males are far more likely to be the perpetrators of child sexual abuse, studies show that women or mothers are as likely, if not more, as men or fathers to perpetrate physical child abuse. According to data from the National Child Abuse and Neglect Data System, females were the perpetrator in more than 55 percent of reported child physical abuse, almost 72 percent of neglect cases, 78 percent of medical neglect cases, and 57 percent of the cases of emotional maltreatment.[54] Overall, nearly 61 percent of child abuse cases involved female perpetrators.

Other studies have supported these findings. David Gil found that child abusers were more likely to be female than male.[55] B. F. Steele and C. Pollock found the mother to be the child abuser in 50 out of 57 cases,[56] while Richard Gelles reported that 68 percent of the mothers and 58 percent of the fathers reported at least one act of violent child abuse during the survey years.[57]

Such researchers as S. Zalba[58] and Blair Justice and Rita Justice[59] found child abuse to be roughly equal between male and female abusers.

PROSTITUTION

Of the crimes recorded by the Uniform Crime Reporting Program, prostitution and the often interrelated runaways, are the only offenses for which there are more arrests of females than males. In 2000, there were 38,146 female arrests for prostitution and commercialized vice in the United States, compared to 23,237 male arrests.[60] Females constituted more than 62 percent of the arrestees, while males made up just under 38 percent of the total. In spite of this apparent discrepancy in female-male arrests, there is some evidence that females are the victims of a double standard in law enforcement with respect to arrests and incarceration for prostitution-involved offenses.[61] Moreover, some prostitution experts believe that there are at least as many males selling sexual favors in this country as females.[62] There are also studies that suggest males involved in prostitution are more likely than their female counterparts to participate in other types of more serious criminal behavior, including violent and property crimes and drug-related offenses.[63]

GENDER AND JUVENILE CRIME

Boys commit most of the serious juvenile crimes, much like men perpetrate the majority of serious adult crimes when considering gender. However, the gap between boys and girls in overall crime appears to be narrowing and, in some respects, girls seem to be becoming more like boys in the types of crimes and delinquencies they commit. Arrest figures show that while the ratio of male-female arrests for persons age eighteen and over is around 3.8 to 1, the ratio of arrests for males and females under the age of 18 is roughly 2.6 to 1.[64] For Crime Index offenses, or the more serious violent and property crimes, the ratio of arrest for male and female juveniles is slightly closer at about 2.5 to 1.[65]

Recent self-report surveys on gender differentials in juvenile offending generally support official data. R. Mawby found that boys were much more likely to commit serious offenses than girls.[66] A similar self-report survey on juvenile aggression found that about half the boys had been in a fight within the past year, compared to around one-third of the girls.[67] Boys were two to three times as likely to report having carried a weapon in the previous month.

S. W. Henggeler reported that young boys were more likely to engage in antisocial behavior than young girls.[68] This conclusion was also reached by R. E. Tremblay and associates in a longitudinal study of children and youth in Canada.[69] In the National Longitudinal Survey of Youth in the United States, 18 percent of the 12-year-old boys admitted participating in at least one assault compared to 10 percent of the 12-year-old girls.[70] Thirteen percent of the boys reported carrying a firearm, compared to just 2 percent of the girls. However, in most of the other types of delinquent acts, the rates were similar for boys and girls.

Studies show that males are much more likely than females to commit aggressive acts in school such as fighting, bullying, and carrying weapons; and that most such acts of aggression are perpetrated against other males.[71] However, the rate of girl involvement in school aggression is not insignificant. For instance, in D. W. Webster, P. S. Gainer, and H. R. Champion's study of weapons possession among inner city junior high schoolers, 67 percent of the girls were found to carry knives, compared to 40 percent of the boys.[72]

Official data indicates that girls are more likely to engage in such status or underage behaviors as truancy and running away than boys.[73] However, some researchers have found that a gender bias may be at work here. According to M. Chesney-Lind and R. G. Shelden, female juveniles are disproportionately more likely to be arrested for status offenses than male juveniles in order to sexualize and seek to control their antisocial behavior.[74] A double standard has also been shown in a higher rate of girls' involvement than boys' with the juvenile and criminal justice system for minor offenses in a number of studies.[75]

This suggests that, in addition to committing the majority of juvenile violent and other serious offenses, boys may be at least as likely to perpetrate minor and status offenses as girls, while being less likely to face punishment.[76]

Gender disparities in juvenile involvement in deviant behavior have largely been attributed to differential opportunities among juvenile males and females for committing antisocial acts, as well as differences in methods of socialization practiced by parents with respect to boys and girls.[77]

NOTES

1. See, for example, D. Steffensmeier and E. Allan, "Gender and Crime: Toward a Gendered Theory of Female Offending," *Annual Review of Sociology 22* (1996): 459–87; R. J. Simon & J. Landis, *The Crimes Women Commit, The Punishments They Receive* (Lexington: Lexington Books, 1991); A. Worrall, "Gender, Criminal Justice and Probation," in G. McIvor, ed., *Working With Offenders: Research Highlights in Social Work 26* (London: Jessica Kingsley, 1995).

2. See, for example, K. Kempf-Leonard and L. L. Sample, "Disparity Based on Sex: Is Gender-Specific Treatment Warranted?" *Justice Quarterly 17*, 1 (2000): 89–128; D. Barash and J. Lipton, "Making Sense of Sex," in D. Barash, ed., *Understanding Violence* (Boston: Allyn & Bacon, 2001), pp. 20–30; Darrell Steffensmeier and Dana Haynie, "Gender, Structural Disadvantages and Urban Crime: Do Macrosocial Variables also Explain Female Offending Rates," *Criminology 38*, 2 (2000): 403–38.

3. R. Barri Flowers, *Sex Crimes, Predators, Perpetrators, Prostitutes, and Victims: An Examination of Sexual Criminality and Victimization* (Springfield: Charles C Thomas, 2001); Diana E. Russell, *Rape in Marriage* (New York: Macmillan, 1990); Brenda J. Vander Mey & Ronald L. Neff, *Incest as Child Abuse: Research and Applications* (New York: Praeger, 1986).

4. R. Barri Flowers, *Kids Who Commit Adult Crimes: Serious Criminality by Juvenile Offenders* (Binghamton: Haworth, 2002); R. Barri Flowers, *Drugs, Alcohol and Criminality in American Society* (Jefferson: McFarland, 1999); H. J. Kerner, E. G. Weitekamp, and J. Thomas, "Patterns of Criminality and Alcohol Abuse: Results of the Tuebinger Criminal Behavior Development Study," *Criminal Behavior & Mental Health 7*, 4 (1997): 401–20.

5. U.S. Department of Justice, Federal Bureau of Investigation, *Crime in the United States: Uniform Crime Reports 2000* (Washington: Government Printing Office, 2001), pp. 228, 230.

6. U.S. Department of Justice, Bureau of Justice Statistics Bulletin, *Prisoners in 2000* (Washington: Office of Justice Programs, 2001), pp. 5, 11.

7. U.S. Department of Justice, Bureau of Justice Statistics Bulletin, *Capital Punishment 2000* (Washington: Office of Justice Programs, 2001), p. 1.

8. See, for example, Worrall, "Gender, Criminal Justice and Probation;" Lizanne Dowds and Carol Hedderman, "The Sentencing of Men and Women," in C. Hedderman and L. Gelsthorpe, eds., *Understanding the Sentencing of Women* (London: Home Office, 1997); R. G. Shelden, "Gender Bias in the Juvenile Justice System," *Juvenile and Family Court Journal 49*, 1 (1998): 11–26.

9. Barbara A. Koons-Witt, "The Effect of Gender on the Decision to Incarcerate Before and After the Introduction of Sentencing Guidelines," *Criminology 40*, 2 (2002): 297–327; Joanne Belknap, *The Invisible Woman: Gender, Crime, and Justice* (Belmont: Wadsworth, 2001); Keith A. Crew, "Sex Differences in Criminal Sentencing: Chivalry or Patriarchy?" *Justice Quarterly 8* (1991): 59–83.

10. See, for example, Belknap, *The Invisible Woman*; Nicole Rafter, *Pretrial Justice: Women, Prisons, and Social Control* (New Brunswick: Transaction Publishers, 1990); Evelyn Gilbert, "Crime, Sex, and Justice; African-American Women," in Sandy Cook

and Susanne Davies, eds., *Harsh Punishment: International Experience of Women's Impris-onment* (Boston: Northeastern University Press, 1999).

11. R. Barri Flowers, *Runaway Kids and Teenage Prostitution: America's Lost, Aban-doned, and Sexually Exploited Children* (Westport: Greenwood, 2001); pp. 95–105; R. Barri Flowers, *The Prostitution of Women and Girls* (Jefferson: McFarland, 1998), pp. 20–21, 145–52.

12. Flowers, *The Prostitution of Women and Girls*, pp. 134–47; Flowers, *Runaway Kids and Teenage Prostitution*, pp. 119–39; Kathleen Barry, *The Prostitution of Sexuality* (New York: New York University Press, 1995); D. Kelly Weisberg, *Children of the Night: A Study of Adolescent Prostitution* (Lexington: Lexington Books, 1985).

13. Mark Warr, *Companions in Crime: The Social Aspects of Criminal Conduct* (New York: Cambridge University Press, 2002); H. Lytton and D. Romney, "Parents' Dif-ferential Socialization of Boys and Girls: A Metaanalysis," *Psychological Bulletin 109* (1991): 267–96; A. H. Eagly and V. J. Steffen, "Gender and Aggressive Behavior: A Meta-Analytic Review of the Social Psychological Literature," *Psychological Bulletin 100* (1986): 309–30; J. L. Bernard, S. L. Bernard, and M. L. Bernard, "Courtship Vio-lence and Sex-Typing," *Family Relations 34* (1985): 573–76.

14. Eagly and Steffen, "Gender and Aggressive Behavior."

15. Warr, *Companions in Crime*, p. 117.

16. David Rose, "Masculinity, Offending and Prison-Based Work," in Bob Pease and Peter Camilleri, eds., *Working With Men in the Human Services* (Sydney: Allen & Unwin, 2001); Kenneth Polk, *Why Men Kill: Scenarios of Masculine Violence* (Cambridge: Cambridge University Press, 1994); Tim Newburn and Elizabeth A. Stanko, *Just Boys Doing Business? Men, Masculinities and Crime* (London: Routledge, 1994); Roger Hor-rocks, *Masculinity in Crisis* (London: Macmillan, 1996); Joachim Kersten, "Culture, Masculinities and Violence Against Women," *British Journal of Criminology 36*, 3 (1996): 381–95.

17. Simon and Landis, *The Crimes Women Commit, the Punishments They Receive*; J. Hood-Williams, "Gender, Masculinities and Crime: From Structures to Psyches," *The-oretical Criminology 5*, 1 (2001): 37–60; Nancy C. Jurik and Susan E. Martin, "Femi-ninities, Masculinities, and Organizational Conflict: Women in Criminal Justice Occupations," in Claire M. Renzetti and Lynne Goodstein, eds., *Women, Crime and Criminal Justice* (Los Angeles: Roxbury, 2001), pp. 264–81.

18. J. M. Dabbs, R. L. Frady, T. S. Carr, and N. F. Besch, "Saliva Testosterone and Criminal Violence in Young Adult Prison Inmates," *Psychosomatic Medicine 49* (1987): 74–182; J. M. Dabbs, R. B. Ruback, R. Frady, C. H. Hopper, and D. S. Sgoutas, "Sali-va Testosterone and Criminal Violence Among Women," *Personality and Individual Differences 9* (1988): 269–75.

19. See, for example, J. H. Brooks and J. R. Reddon, "Serum Testosterone in Vio-lent and Nonviolent Young Offenders," *Journal of Clinical Psychology 52* (1996): 475–83; C. L. Ehlers, K. C. Rickler, and J. E. Hovey, "A Possible Relationship Between Plas-ma Testosterone and Aggressive Behavior in a Female Outpatient Population," in M. Girgis and L. G. Kiloh, eds., *Limbic Epilepsy and Dyscontrol Syndrome* (Amsterdam: Elsevier/North Holland Biomedical Press, 1980), pp. 183–94; J. A. Harris, J. P. Rush-ton, E. Hampson, and D. Jackson, "Salivary Testosterone and Self-Report Aggressive

and Prosocial Personality Characteristics in Men and Women," *Aggressive Behavior 22* (1996): 321–31.

20. See, for example, J. M. Dabbs, T. S. Carr, R. L. Frady, and J. K. Riad, "Testosterone, Crime, and Misbehavior Among 692 Prison Inmates," *Personality and Individual Differences 18* (1995): 627–33; H. G. Pope and D. L. Katz, "Homicide and Near-Homicide by Anabolic Steroid Users," *Journal of Clinical Psychiatry 51* (1989): 28–31; J. Archer, "The Influence of Testosterone on Human Aggression," *British Journal of Psychology 82* (1991): 1–28.

21. A. Lloyd, *Doubly Deviant, Doubly Damned* (Sydney: Penguin, 1995); M. Miedzian, *Boys Will Be Boys: Breaking the Link Between Masculinity and Violence* (London: Virago Press, 1992); J. D. Constantino, D. Grosz, P. Saenger, D. Chandler, R. Nandi, and F. Earls, "Testosterone and Aggression in Children," *Journal of the American Academy of Child & Adolescent Psychiatry 32* (1993): 1217–22.

22. Anne Campbell, "Staying Alive: Evolution, Culture, and Women's Intrasexual Aggression," *Behavioral and Brain Sciences 22* (1999): 203–15; Lytton and Romney, "Parents Differential Socialization of Boys and Girls;" American Psychological Association, Commission on Violence and Youth, *Violence and Youth: Psychology's Response* (Washington: American Psychological Association, 1993); John Hagan, John Simpson, and A. R. Gillis, "Class in the Household: A Power-Control Theory of Gender and Delinquency," *American Journal of Sociology 92* (1987): 788–816.

23. Warr, *Companions in Crime.*

24. Anthony Walsh, "Companions in Crime: A Biosocial Perspective," http://human-nature.com/nibbs/02/walsh.html; D. Geary, "Evolution and Proximate Expression of Human Paternal Investment," *Psychological Bulletin 126* (2000): 55–77; J. Panksepp, "The Psychobiology of Prosocial Behaviors: Separation Distress, Play, and Altruism," in C. Zahn-Wazler, E. Cummings, and R. Ianotti, eds., *Altruism and Aggression: Biological and Social Origins* (Cambridge: Cambridge University Press, 1986), pp. 19–57.

25. Walsh, "Companions in Crime: A Biosocial Perspective."

26. L. Acoca, "Defusing the Time Bomb: Understanding and Meeting the Growing Health Care Needs of Incarcerated Women in America," *Crime & Delinquency 44*, 1 (1998): 44–69; Mary E. Gilfus, "From Victims to Survivors to Offenders: Women's Routes of Entry and Immersion into Street Crime," *Women & Criminal Justice 4*, 1 (1992): 63–89; B. Rivera and C. S. Widom, "Childhood Victimization and Violent Offending," *Violence & Victims 5*, 1 (1990): 19–35.

27. See, for example, Scottish Office, *Women Offenders–A Safer Way: A Review of Community Disposals and the Use of Custody for Women Offenders in Scotland* (Edinburgh: The Stationery Office, 1998), p. 13; A. Leibling, "Suicide Among Women Prisoners," *Howard Journal 33*, 1 (1994): 1–9; B. Owen and B. Bloom, "Profiling Women Prisoners: Findings from National Surveys and a California Sample," *Prison Journal 75*, 2 (1995): 165–85.

28. *Crime in the United States*, p. 215.

29. *Ibid.*, pp. 228, 231.

30. U.S. Department of Justice, Bureau of Justice Statistics Bulletin, *Prison and Jail Inmates at Midyear 2000* (Washington: Office of Justice Programs, 2001).

31. *Ibid.*, p. 7.

32. *Prisoners in 2000*, p. 5.

33. *Prison and Jail Inmates at Midyear 2000*, p. 7.

34. Freda Adler, *Sisters in Crime: The Rise of the New Female Criminal* (New York: McGraw-Hill, 1975), p. 15. See also K. Daly, "Women's Pathways to Felony Court: Feminist Theories of Lawbreaking and Problems of Representation," *Review of Law and Women's Studies 2* (1992): 11–52; P. Pearson, *When She Was Bad: Violent Women and the Myth of Innocence* (Toronto: Random House, 1997).

35. Darrell J. Steffensmeier, "Sex Differences in Patterns of Adult Crime, 1965–77: A Review and Assessment," *Social Forces 58* (1980): 1098–99. See also Steffensmeier and Haynie, "Gender, Structural Disadvantages and Urban Crime."

36. Carol Smart, "The New Female Criminal: Reality or Myth," *British Journal of Criminology 19* (1979): 50–59. See also Carol Smart, *Law, Crime and Sexuality: Essays in Feminism* (Thousand Oaks: Sage, 1995); R. Barri Flowers, *Female Crime, Criminals and Cellmates: An Exploration of Female Criminality and Delinquency* (Jefferson: McFarland, 1995), pp. 44–58.

37. Rita J. Simon, *Women and Crime* (Lexington: D.C. Heath, 1975), p. 42. See also Owen and Bloom, "Profiling Women Prisoners;" Ralph C. Allen, "Socioeconomic Conditions and Property Crime: A Comprehensive Review and Test of the Professional Literature," *American Journal of Economics and Sociology 55* (1996): 293–308.

38. George W. Noblit and Janie M. Burcart, "Women and Crime: 1960–1970," *Social Science Quarterly 56* (1976): 656–57. See also Walter R. Gove, Michael Hughes, and Michael Geerken, "Are Uniform Crime Reports a Valid Indicator of the Index Crimes? An Affirmative Answer with Minor Qualifications," *Criminology 23* (1985): 451–500.

39. *Crime in the United States*, p. 221.

40. Cited in R. Barri Flowers, *Demographics and Criminality: The Characteristics of Crime in America* (Westport: Greenwood, 1989), p. 129.

41. U.S. Department of Health and Human Services, Substance Abuse and Mental Health Services Administration, *National Household Survey on Drug Abuse: Population Estimates 1995* (Rockville: U.S. Department of Health and Human Services, 1996), pp. 23–27, 29–39, 41–51, 83–87. See also Erich Labouvie, "Maturing Out of Substance Use: Selection and Self-Correction," *Journal of Drug Issues 26*, 2 (1996): 457–76.

42. Cited in Flowers, *Drugs, Alcohol and Criminality in American Society*, p. 42.

43. U.S. Department of Justice, Bureau of Justice Statistics, *Drugs, Crime and the Justice System* (Washington: Government Printing Office, 1992), p. 7.

44. R. Barri Flowers, *Murder, At the End of the Day and Night: A Study of Criminal Homicide Offenders, Victims, and Circumstances* (Springfield: Charles C Thomas, 2002), pp. 51–63; Angela Browne, Kirk R. Williams, and Donald G. Dutton, "Homicide Between Intimate Partners," in M. Dwayne Smith and Margaret A. Zahn, eds., *Studying and Preventing Homicide: Issues and Challenges* (Thousand Oaks: Sage, 1999), p. 57.

45. R. Barri Flowers, *Domestic Crimes, Family Violence and Child Abuse: A Study of Contemporary American Society* (Jefferson: McFarland, 2000), pp. 62, 90; U.S. Department of Justice, Bureau of Justice Statistics Factbook, *Violence by Intimates: Analysis of Data on Crimes by Current or Former Spouses, Boyfriends, and Girlfriends* (Washington:

Government Printing Office, 1998), pp. 5–6; Ximena B. Arriaga and Stuart Oskamp, eds., *Violence in Intimate Relationships* (Thousand Oaks: Sage, 1999).

46. P. D. Chimbos, *Marital Violence: A Study of Interspousal Homicide* (San Francisco: R & E Research Associates, 1978); A. Goetting, "Homicidal Wives: A Profile," *Journal of Family Issues 8* (1987): 332–41; M. Daly and M. Wilson, *Homicide* (New York: Aldine de Gruyter, 1988); S. Rutherford McDill and Linda McDill, *Dangerous Marriage: Breaking the Cycle of Domestic Violence* (Grand Rapids: Baker Books, 1998); Angela Browne, *When Battered Women Kill* (New York: Free Press, 1987).

47. Cited in Flowers, *Domestic Crimes, Family Violence and Child Abuse*, pp. 72–73. See also Nancy Crowell and Ann W. Burgess, eds., *Understanding Violence Against Women* (Washington: National Academy Press, 1996); Richard B. Felson, "Arrest for Domestic and Other Assaults," *Criminology 39* (2001): 501–21.

48. Russell, *Rape in Marriage*. See also Richard B. Felson, Steven F. Mesner, Anthony W. Hoskin, and Glenn Deane, "Reasons for Reporting and Not Reporting Domestic Violence to the Police," *Criminology 40*, 3 (2002): 617–46.

49. See, for example, Flowers, *Domestic Crimes, Family Violence and Child Abuse*, pp. 72–80; Barrie Levy, ed., *Dating Violence: Young Women in Danger* (Seattle: Seal Press, 1998); W. S. De Keseredy, "Women Abuse in Dating Relationships: The Relevance of Social Support Theory," *Journal of Family Violence 3*, 1 (1988): 1–14.

50. Suzanne K. Steinmetz, "The Battered Husband Syndrome," *Victimology 2* (1978): 507.

51. Robert Langley and Richard C. Levy, *Wife Beating: The Silent Crisis* (New York: Dutton, 1977). See also Murray Straus, "Physical Assaults by Wives: A Major Social Problem," in Richard J. Gelles and Denise R. Loseke, eds., *Current Controversies on Family Violence* (Thousand Oaks: Sage, 1993).

52. Cited in Flowers, *Female Crime, Criminals and Cellmates*, p. 93. See also Murray Straus, Richard J. Gelles, and Suzanne K. Steinmetz, *Behind Closed Doors: Violence in the American Family* (New York: Anchor Books, 1980); Sharon D. Herzberger, *Violence Within the Family: Social Psychological Perspectives* (Boulder: Westview Press, 1996); A. Ferrante, F. Morgan, D. Indermaur, and R. Harding, *Measuring the Extent of Domestic Violence* (Sydney: Hawkins Press, 1996).

53. Richard J. Gelles, *The Violent Home* (Thousand Oaks: Sage, 1985), pp. 50–52; Richard J. Gelles and Murray A. Straus, *Intimate Violence* (New York: Simon & Schuster, 1988); Richard J. Gelles and Claire P. Cornell, *Intimate Violence in Families* (Thousand Oaks: Sage, 1990).

54. U.S. Department of Health and Human Services, Children's Bureau, *Child Maltreatment 1996: Reports From The States to the National Child Abuse and Neglect Data System* (Washington: Government Printing Office, 1998), p. 2–15; Cindy L. Miller-Perrin and Robin D. Perrin, *Child Maltreatment: An Introduction* (Thousand Oaks: Sage, 2001).

55. David G. Gil, *Violence Against Children: Physical Child Abuse in the United States* (Cambridge: Harvard University Press, 1970), p. 117. See also Peter Stratton, Helga Hanks, and Kevin D. Browne, eds., *Early Prediction and Prevention of Child Abuse: A Handbook* (Hoboken: John Wiley & Sons, 2002); David Finkelhor, "The Victimization

of Children: A Developmental Perspective," *American Journal of Orthopsychiatry 65* (1995): 177–93.

56. B. F. Steele and C. Pollock, "A Psychiatric Study of Parents Who Abuse Infants and Small Children," in R. E. Helfer and C. H. Kempe, eds., *The Battered Child* (Chicago: University of Chicago Press, 1968), pp. 89–133; Flowers, *Domestic Crimes, Family Violence and Child Abuse*, pp. 22–25, 111–29; Vincent J. Fontana and Douglas J. Besharov, *The Maltreated Child* (Springfield: Charles C Thomas, 1995); Jennifer A. Hurley, *Child Abuse* (San Diego: Greenhaven Press, 1999).

57. Richard J. Gelles, "Violence Toward Children in the United States," *American Journal of Orthopsychiatry 48*, 4 (1978): 580–92. See also Murray A. Straus and Richard J. Gelles, eds., *Physical Violence in American Families: Risk Factors and Adaptations to Violence in 8,145 Families* (New Brunswick: Transaction, 1990); D. Finkelhor and J. Dziuba-Leatherman, "Victimization of Children," *American Psychologist 49*, 3 (1994): 173–83.

58. S. Zalba, "Battered Children," *Trans-Action 8* (1971): 58–61. See also U.S. Department of Health and Human Services, *Child Maltreatment 1999* (Washington: Government Printing Office, 2001); Sandra Azar and David Wolfe, "Child Physical Abuse and Neglect," in Eric J. Mash and Russell A. Barkley, eds., *Treatment of Childhood Disorders*, 2nd ed. (New York: Guilford Press, 1998).

59. Blair Justice and Rita Justice, *The Abusing Family* (New York: Human Sciences Press, 1976), p. 90. See also Flowers, *Domestic Crimes, Family Violence and Child Abuse*; Cynthia C. Tower, *Understanding Child Abuse and Neglect* (Needham Heights: Allyn & Bacon, 1998).

60. *Crime in the United States*, p. 233.

61. *Women Offenders—A Safer Way*; Flowers, *The Prostitution of Women and Girls*, pp. 145–48; M. Reitsma-Street, "Justice for Canadian Girls: A 1990s Update," *Canadian Journal of Criminology 41*, 3 (1999): 335–63.

62. Flowers, *The Prostitution of Women and Girls*, p. 1; Joan J. Johnson, *Teen Prostitution* (Danbury: Franklin Watts, 1992).

63. Flowers, *The Prostitution of Women and Girls*, pp. 142–43; Weisberg, *Children of the Night*, p. 75; Flowers, *Runaway Kids and Teenage Prostitution*.

64. *Crime in the United States*, pp. 221, 233.

65. *Ibid.*, pp. 221, 223, 233.

66. R. Mawby, "Sex and Crime: The Results of a Self-Report Study," *British Criminology of Sociology 31*, 4 (1980): 537–43. See also L. Yiaoru and H. B. Kaplan, "Explaining the Gender Differences in Adolescent Delinquent Behavior: A Longitudinal Test of Mediating Mechanisms," *Criminology 37*, 1 (1999): 195–215.

67. Girls Incorporated, *Prevention and Parity: Girls in Juvenile Justice* (Indianapolis: Girls Incorporated National Resource Center, 1996).

68. S. W. Henggeler, *Delinquency in Adolescence* (Thousand Oaks: Sage, 1989).

69. R. E. Tremblay, B. Boulerice, P. W. Harden, P. McDuff, D. Perusse, R. O. Pihl, and M. Zoccolillo, *Do Children in Canada Become More Aggressive As They Approach Adolescence? Growing Up in Canada: National Longitudinal Survey of Children and Youth* (Ottawa: Human Resources Development Canada and Statistics Canada, 1996), pp. 127–36.

70. C. M. Puzzanchera, *Self-Reported Delinquency by 12-Year-Olds, 1997*, OJJDP Fact Sheet (Washington: Office of Juvenile Justice and Delinquency Prevention, 2000).

71. See, for example, Jennifer Watson, Michele Cascardi, and Daniel O'Leary, "High School Students' Responses to Dating Aggression," *Violence and Victims 16*, 3 (2001): 339–43; Delbert S. Elliott, Beatrix A. Hamburg, and Kirk R. Williams, eds., *Violence in American Schools* (New York: Cambridge University Press, 1998); D. J. Flannery, *School Violence: Risk, Preventive Intervention, and Policy* (New York: Teachers College, ERIC Clearinghouse on Urban Education, 1997).

72. D. W. Webster, P. S. Gainer, and H. R. Champion, "Weapon Carrying Among Inner-City Junior High School Students: Defensive Behavior versus Aggressive Delinquency," *American Journal of Public Health 83* (1993): 1604–08.

73. *Crime in the United States*, pp. 221, 233; M. Chesney-Lind and R. G. Shelden, *Girls, Delinquency, and Juvenile Justice* (Belmont: West/Wadsworth, 1998).

74. Chesney-Lind and Shelden, *Girls, Delinquency, and Juvenile Justice*. See also Reitsma-Street, *Justice for Canadian Girls*.

75. See, for example, Emily Gaarder and Joanne Belknap, "Tenuous Borders: Girls Transferred to Adult Court," *Criminology 40*, 3 (2002): 481–517; R. Corrado, C. Odgers, and I. M. Cohen, "The Incarceration of Female Young Offenders: Protection for Whom?" *Canadian Journal of Criminology 42*, 2 (2000): 189–207; Kempf-Leonard and Sample, "Disparity Based on Sex," pp. 89–128.

76. R. Barri Flowers, *The Adolescent Criminal: An Examination of Today's Juvenile Offender* (Jefferson: McFarland, 1990); David P. Farrington, "The Explanation and Prevention of Youthful Offending," in J. David Hawkins, ed., *Delinquency and Crime: Current Theories* (New York: Cambridge University Press, 1996), pp. 68–82.

77. Kempf-Leonard and Sample, "Disparity Based on Sex;" David P. Farrington, "Epidemiology," in H. C. Quay, ed., *Handbook of Juvenile Delinquency* (New York: Wiley, 1987), pp. 33–61; D. J. Flannery and C. R. Huff, eds., *Youth Violence: Prevention, Intervention, and Social Policy* (Washington: American Psychiatric Press, 1999); Yiaoru and Kaplan, "Explaining the Gender Differences in Adolescent Delinquent Behavior," pp. 195–215.

Part III

MALE CRIMES OF VIOLENCE

Chapter 7

HOMICIDE

The murder rate in the United States rose in 2001 after a decline in murders over the past decade. This excluded the mass murder as a result of a terrorist attack on September 11. Firearms-related homicides by young adults and juveniles have risen sharply since the mid 1980s, indicative of the easy access to illegal guns and related youth violence. Males are much more likely to be perpetrators and victims of homicide than females. Around nine in ten of all murders in this country are committed by males.[1] The majority of such crimes are perpetrated against strangers or acquaintances. However, males are considerably more likely to be the perpetrators in intimate homicides; women are killed by male intimates more than any other type of killer.[2] Males are almost solely responsible for serial killings and mass murder; as well as most likely to be homicide offenders and victims among racial minorities.[3] Substance abuse and other drug-related offending often play a strong role in homicidal behavior. Murder itself is commonly seen as an accurate measure of all violent criminality in society. Evidence suggests that three strikes laws are generally ineffective as a deterrent in the commission of homicides.[4]

OFFICIAL DATA AND MURDER

Official information on the scope of murder in this country comes mainly from the Federal Bureau of Investigation's (FBI) Uniform Crime Reports (UCR). The UCR defines murder and nonnegligent manslaughter as "the willful (nonnegligent) killing of one human being by another . . . not [including] deaths caused by negligence, suicide, or accident; justifiable homicides; and attempts to murder or assaults to murder."[5]

According to UCR data, there were an estimated 15,517 persons murdered in the United States in 2000, a total virtually unchanged from the estimate for

Table 7.1
MURDER OFFENDERS, BY AGE AND SEX, 2000

		Sex		
Age	Total	Male	Female	Unknown
Total	12,943	9,840	3,076	27
Percent distribution[a]	100.0	76.0	23.8	0.2
Under 18[b]	1,300	879	420	1
Under 22[b]	3,247	2,523	723	1
18 and over[b]	11,380	8,791	2,587	2

[a] Because of rounding, the percentages may not add to total.
[b] Does not include unknown ages.
Source: Adapted from U.S. Department of Justice, Federal Bureau of Investigation, Crime in the United States: Uniform Crime Reports 2000 (Washington: Government Printing Office, 2001), p. 17.

1999 but down more than 37 percent since 1991.[6] More than three out of four murder victims were male, while nearly nine in ten were age 18 and over. Forty-nine percent of homicide victims in 2000 were white, 48.5 percent black, and 2.5 percent were victims of other races.

Figures on murder perpetrators nationwide, by sex and age, in 2000 can be seen in Table 7.1. Based on data for 14,697 murder offenders, males constituted over 90 percent of the offenders reported by gender, and nearly 76 percent of murder offenders when including those for which the gender was unknown. Male murder offenders were predominantly age 18 and over, accounting for more than 89 percent of all male murderers. However, more than one-fourth of the total male murder offenders were males under the age of 22.

Table 7.2 reveals the relationship between murder victims and offenders, by sex and race, for single victim/offender homicides in 2000. In nearly 89 percent of the homicides, both the offender and victim were male, while nearly 91 percent of female homicide victims were killed by males.

Most murders are intraracial in nature. Almost 94 percent of black victims in single victim/offender murders in 2000 were slain by black offenders; similarly, some 86 percent of white murder victims were killed by white perpetrators.

More than four in ten victims of murder knew their killer in 2000, while more than three in ten were acquainted with the perpetrator. Husbands or boyfriends were responsible for one-third of the murders of females. Three out of ten murders for the year occurred because of arguments, representing the most likely circumstance leading to murder.[7]

Preliminary FBI figures show that the number of murders committed in the United States rose 3.1 percent in 2001 from 2000.[8] Had the murders resulting from the terrorist attack on September 11 been included in figures, the number of murders would have risen by 26 percent over the period.

Table 7.2
VICTIM/OFFENDER RELATIONSHIP, BY RACE AND SEX, 2000

Single Victim/Single Offender

Victim	Total	Sex of offender			Race of Offender			
		Male	Female	Un-known	White	Black	Other	Un-known
Race of victim								
White victims	3,352	2,985	332	35	2,860	417	40	35
Black victims	2,927	2,565	341	21	178	2,723	5	21
Other race victims	169	150	18	1	43	22	103	1
Unknown race	66	48	2	16	30	19	1	16
Sex of victim								
Male victims	4,542	3,983	518	41	2,004	2,397	100	41
Female victims	1,906	1,717	173	16	1,077	765	48	16
Unknown sex	66	48	2	16	30	19	1	16

Source: Adapted from U.S. Department of Justice, Federal Bureau of Investigation, *Crime in the United States: Uniform Crime Reports 2000* (Washington: Government Printing Office, 2001), p. 18.

Homicides climbed significantly in a number of cities across the country, including a 67 percent increase in Boston and double-digit gains in Atlanta, Houston, Phoenix, and St. Louis, among other cities.[9]

Criminologists attribute the growth in the murder rate to the weak economy, property crimes, and a rise in the number of men being released from prison.

Male Arrests and Murder

There were an estimated 13,227 total arrests for murder and nonnegligent manslaughter in the United States in 2000. Nearly nine in ten of those arrested for murder were males, and more than 90 percent of them were age 18 and over.[10] Males were most likely to be arrested for murder and nonnegligent manslaughter in cities, followed by the suburbs, and rural areas.[11]

Ten-year arrest trends for 1991–2000 indicate a sharp decline in males being arrested for murder. As seen in Figure 7.1, total male arrests for murder and nonnegligent manslaughter dropped by more than 42 percent over the span. For males under the age of 18, arrests declined over 67 percent during the period.

Overall, the murder rate of 5.7 murders per 100,000 inhabitants in 2000 in the United States represented a 3.1 percent drop from 1999.[12]

MALE PRISONERS AND HOMICIDE

Although arrests for murder and other violent offenses have been on the decline, the number of violent offenders incarcerated in this country has risen. From 1990 to 2000, the average annual increase in persons held in jails and state and federal prisons was 5.3 percent.[13] The number of violent male offenders rose by 53 percent between 1990 and 1999.[14] As shown in Figure 7.2, in 1999, of an estimated 141,500 total persons held in state prison for murder and nonnegligent manslaughter, 134,900 were male. Sentenced male inmates made up more than 95 percent of those in prison for murder (see also Chapter 5).

FIREARMS AND HOMICIDE

There is a significant correlation between homicides and use of guns. According to the UCR, in 2000 firearms were the weapons most often used

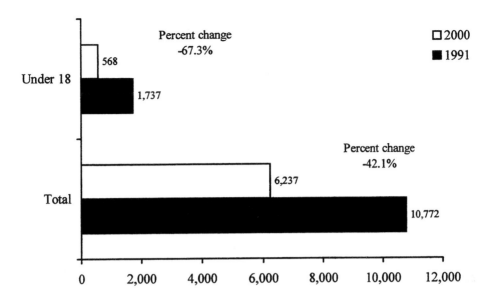

Figure 7.1. Ten-Year Male Arrest Trends for Murder,[a] 1991–2000. *Source:* Derived from U.S. Department of Justice, Federal Bureau of Investigation, *Crime in the United States: Uniform Crime Reports 2000* (Washington: Government Printing Office, 2001), p. 221.
[a] Includes nonnegligent manslaughter.

in committing murder (see Table 7.3). A firearm was involved in an estimated 66 percent of homicides in the United States. More than half of the murders in which the weapon was established involved the use of a handgun, while shotguns represented nearly 4 percent of the weapons, and rifles around 3 percent. Other types of firearms were involved in over 7 percent of the homicides. Nonfirearm lethal weapons used in perpetrating murders included knives or other cutting instruments, making up more than 13 percent of weapons, and blunt objects—such as hammers or clubs—accounted for nearly 5 percent of the total.

Some perspective on the interrelationship between firearms, homicides, offenders, and victims can be seen in Table 7.4, which compares homicide data from different sources between 1993 and 1997. Findings from the Vital Statistics and FBI's Supplementary Homicide Reports and on nonfatal firearm injury resulting from criminality indicate that black males are the most frequently victimized from firearms, representing nearly half the victims. Around one-third of victims of firearm-related homicides or nonfatal injury are white males. Homicide victims and nonfatally injured firearm victims are primarily younger persons, with most between 20 and 34 years of age. When firearms are involved in the commission of a crime, older victims

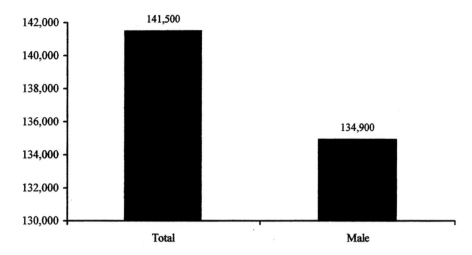

Figure 7.2. Sentenced Prisoners Under State Jurisdiction for Murder,[a] 1999. *Source:* Derived from U.S. Department of Justice, Bureau of Justice Statistics Bulletin, *Prisoners in 2000* (Washington: Office of Justice Programs, 2001), p. 11.

[a] Includes nonnegligent manslaughter.

Table 7.3
MURDER VICTIMS, TYPES OF WEAPONS USED, 2000

Weapons	1999
Total	12,943
Total firearms	8,493
Handguns	6,686
Rifles	396
Shotguns	468
Other guns	51
Firearms, not stated	892
Knives or cutting instruments	1,743
Blunt objects (clubs, hammers, etc.)	604
Personal weapons (hands, fists, feet, etc.)[a]	900
Poison	8
Explosives	9
Fire	128
Narcotics	20
Drowning	15
Strangulation	166
Asphyxiation	89
Other weapons or weapons not stated	768

[a] Pushed is included in personal weapons.

Source: Derived from U.S. Department of Justice, Federal Bureau of Investigation, *Crime in the United States: Uniform Crime Reports 2000* (Washington: Government Printing Office, 2001), p. 19.

Table 7.4
VARIOUS SOURCES OF DATA ON FIREARM HOMICIDES AND NONFATAL
FIREARM INJURY, 1993–1997

Firearm homicides, 1993–1997

	Vital statistics[a]	*FBI's Supplementary Homicide Reports*	*Nonfatal firearm injury from assault*
Race and Gender			
White male	36%	34%	33% (b)
White female	9	9	5 (b)
Black male	46	47	49
Black female	6	7	6
Other	3	2	4
Age			
0–14	3%	2%	3%
15–19	17	17	26
20–24	22	22	25
25–34	29	29	26
35–44	17	16	12
45 and older	13	13	7
Unknown	0	1	0

[a] Includes legal intervention homicides.

[b] For comparison, Hispanics who were included in the other racial category in the original data were included in the white racial category. Hispanic origin is not sufficiently reported in the Supplementary Homicide Reports to allow comparison.

Sources: U.S. Department of Justice, *Firearm Injury and Death from Crime, 1993–97* (Washington: Office of Justice Programs, 2000), p. 3; Vital Statistics of the United States, Centers for Disease Control and Prevention National Center for Health Statistics, 1993–97; Federal Bureau of Investigation, *Uniform Crime Reports,* Supplementary Homicide Reports, 1993–97; Centers for Disease Control and Prevention, National Center for Injury Prevention, Firearms Injury Surveillance Study, 1993–97.

appear more likely to suffer a fatality than not, possibly because of being less able to recover from their injuries.

Prisoner data corresponds with these findings on the correlation between male offenders, firearms, and murder. According to the Bureau of Justice Statistics (BJS), nearly one in five males in state prisons and more than one in six in federal prisons possessed a firearm during the commission of the crime they were convicted of.[15] In 1997, nearly 43 percent of state prison inmates and more than 39 percent of federal prisoners were in possession of a firearm in committing a homicide.[16]

Young prison inmates and minority prisoners were more likely to have possessed a gun during the commission of a homicide than older or white prisoners. The BJS reported that in 1997, nearly 30 percent of state inmates under 25 years of age carried a firearm when perpetrating the crime, in comparison to 15 percent of prisoners age 35 and older. Around 21 percent of black inmates and nearly 18 percent of Hispanic inmates in state institutions were in possession of a gun during the commission of the offense, while less than 15 percent of the white prisoners carried a firearm when committing the crime they were incarcerated for.[17]

DRUGS, ALCOHOL AND MURDER

Studies have shown that a high percentage of murders involve drug or alcohol use by the offender and/or victim.[18] FBI data indicates that in 2000 there were 278 murders committed in the United States from brawls that were due to the influence of alcohol or drugs. Another 572 murders were attributed to circumstances related to narcotic drug laws.[19]

Inmate data supports the relationship between alcohol, drugs, and violent crime. Around four in ten violent offenders in jail or prison were under the influence of alcohol during the commission of their offense.[20] Nearly four in ten state prisoners convicted of a violent crime had used cocaine in the month before committing the crime, while nearly half had used another drug.[21]

Other findings further relate violence with alcohol or drugs. An analysis of national data on alcohol and crime found that 40 percent of violent victimizations involved alcohol use.[22] The FBI's National Incident-Based Reporting System (NIBRS) indicated that around half of the intimate violence recorded was alcohol-related. An estimated one in five NIBRS alcohol-related violent offenses involved a weapon aside from the offender's fists, hands, or feet.[23]

Some studies have focused on alcohol with respect to its effect of patterns of behavior, including homicide, aggression, and cognitive functioning.[24] Other researchers have found a relationship between persons who kill, cocaine, and polydrug use.[25] In some research, drug-related homicide has been found to be more common among racial and ethnic minority offenders.[26] Other studies have shown a lower rate of drug or alcohol use by some minority homicide perpetrators.[27] Overall, the indication is that killers and their victims may be more involved with substance abuse and drug-related criminality than the population at large.[28]

Male perpetrated homicide has been shown to be related to drug dealing and related drug offending. In a study of street gangs by M. W. Klein, C. L. Maxson, and L. C. Cunningham, it was found that almost 70 percent of gang-related murders involved drugs.[29] P. Goldstein and associates' study on drugs and homicide found that almost half of crack-associated homicides were directly related to drug trafficking and distribution, with almost two in ten homicides involving robbing a drug dealer.[30]

TYPES OF MALE MURDERERS

Sex-Related Killers

Many male perpetrated homicides can be classified as sex-related murders, or murders that are by their very nature sexually related. These include murders involving an intimate, rape or sexual assault, prostitute, or other sexual motivation or circumstance. Most of these are intimate murders. In 2000, there were 1,015 females murdered by husbands and boyfriends in the United States.[31] Between 1976 and 1996, nearly 75 percent of the victims of an intimate murder were wives and girlfriends.[32] Around 30 percent of women murdered in this country are killed by male intimates.

Studies show that men who murder intimates often do so in relation to real or perceived infidelity by the female intimate, sexual jealousy, the killer's unfaithfulness, or fears that a partner will leave[33] (see also Chapter 9).

Serial Killers

Serial killers are almost entirely male. Serial murders (defined as multiple murders occurring at different times by one or more killers) represent perhaps less than 1 percent of the nation's homicides. However, serial killers command attention because of the multiple numbers of homicides and often their brutal nature and media interest. Most serial killers are sexual murderers, with targets including children, women, young men, and prostitutes.

Recent examples of serial killers in the United States include:

- In the early 1990s, cannibal serial killer Jeffrey Dahmer lured boys to his Wisconsin apartment where he drugged, strangled, and fed on them. He confessed to 17 such murders. In 1994, he was beaten to death in prison while serving a life sentence.
- Between 1974 and 1978, Ted Bundy sexually assaulted and murdered as many as 40 females across the United States. After a number of escapes from custody, he was convicted of murder. He was executed in Florida's electric chair in 1989.
- Between 1972 and 1978, John Gacy raped, tortured, and murdered 33 boys and young men, burying them beneath his house in Chicago, Illi-

nois. He was convicted and sentenced to death, dying by lethal injection in 1994.

- In the early 1980s, Robert Hansen confessed to raping and murdering 17 women in Anchorage, Alaska. He was convicted of four murders and given a life sentence in prison.
- Between 1979 and 1981, Wayne Williams is believed to have murdered 27 African American children in Atlanta, Georgia. He was convicted on two counts and sentenced to life in prison.
- Between 1990 and 1998, Robert Yates murdered as many as 17 women, mostly prostitutes and homeless, in Washington. After pleading guilty to 13 slayings, he received a sentence of 408 years behind bars.
- In the early 1990s, Keith Jesperson raped, beat, and strangled to death at least eight women in five states. He confessed to several of the killings to avoid the death penalty and received a sentence of life imprisonment in Oregon State Prison.[34]

In studying serial killers, a number of criminologists have developed profiles. D. T. Lunde characterized a high percentage of serial killers as sexual sadists who related sexuality to violence beginning at an early age.[35] Almost 20 percent of serial killers studied by J. Levin and J. A. Fox were identified as sexual sadists.[36]

In R. R. Hazelwood and colleagues' examination of sexually sadistic serial killers, 43 percent had participated in homosexual acts in adulthood, while 20 percent had perpetrated such acts as voyeurism and exhibitionism.[37] P. E. Dietz characterized one type of serial murderer as a psychopathic sexual sadist, contending that every serial killer with ten or more victims was a male possessing sexually sadistic tendencies and characterized with an antisocial personality disorder.[38]

Mass Murderers

Mass murder refers to the killing of usually three or more people at the same time and location. Mass murderers in the United States have been predominantly male. Like serial killers, there are relatively few in comparison to other types of killers. However, as the term mass murder implies, mass killers draw attention to themselves more than most killers on the basis of a single, often extremely violent, incident of multiple murders.[39]

Recently, mass murder in this country has taken on a new and frightening dimension with the September 2001 hijacking of four airliners and murder-suicide terrorist attack on the World Trade Center and Pentagon, taking the lives of almost 3,000 people. The 19 reported hijacker-mass murderers were all identified as males. Other notable mass murderers on American soil include:

- On April 19, 1995, Timothy McVeigh and Terry Nichols perpetrated what at the time was the United States' worst terrorist attack when a bomb blew up the Alfred P. Murrah Building in Oklahoma City, Oklahoma, killing 168 people and injuring hundreds of others. Both men were convicted of the crime. McVeigh was executed in 2001, while Nichols was sentenced to life in prison.
- In 1955, Jack Graham planted a bomb in an airplane taking off from Denver, Colorado, killing his mother and 43 others. He was convicted of the mass murder and executed in the gas chamber in 1957.
- On July 18, 1984, James Huberty, heavily armed, entered a McDonald's restaurant in San Ysidro, California. He opened fire, killing 20 people before he was shot to death by police.
- On March 25, 1990, Julio Gonzalez, a Cuban émigré, set fire to a social club in the Bronx in New York, killing 87 people. He was convicted on 174 counts and sentenced to 20 years to life behind bars.[40]

See other recent examples of school mass murders in Chapter 19.

R. M. Holmes and J. T. Holmes identified five types of mass murderers:

- *Disciple mass murderers* kill because they were given orders to do so, such as by a Charles Manson-type charismatic figure.
- *Family annihilator mass murderers* kill the entire family at once, usually a male head of household with a history of psychological problems and substance abuse.
- *Pseudocommando mass murderers* stockpile weapons and go on a one-man shooting spree at a targeted location.
- *Disgruntled employee mass murderers* go to a former or current workplace and murder the supervisor or boss, colleagues, and randomly anyone else in sight.
- *Set-and-run mass murderers,* such as McVeigh, plant a bomb or other killing device, including poison, at the desired place and leave the scene, waiting for the mass murder to occur, while distancing themselves from the crime scene.[41]

WHAT CAUSES ONE TO MURDER?

There have been a number of theories seeking to offer explanations on murder and those committing this act. Much of these tend to focus on mental disorders and physiological abnormalities or sociological factors. More general theories on male crime and violence can be found in Part I.

Psychological Hypotheses

Most experts believe that only a small number of killer's actions can be blamed on insanity or other mental illness. Some studies suggest that severe childhood and adolescent frustration may lead to a build up in anger and hostility that can manifest itself in murder or other acts of violence. In a comparison of killers and nonkillers, S. Palmer found that killers had suffered twice as many traumas in their childhood and adolescence as nonkillers—including difficult births, major illnesses, serious accidents, violence, and excessive discipline.[42] The killers were also more likely than nonkillers to wet the bed, stutter, and have problems in school, indicating a high level of stress and frustration, leading to further stresses and strains.

Two types of murderers were put forth by E. I. Megargee, based on an ability to keep aggressive impulses under control: ***undercontrolled*** and ***overcontrolled*** murders.

- ***Undercontrolled murderers*** have little to no control over aggressive impulses. Thus, even upon the slightest pretext or some form of frustration, irritation, or vexation, they may explode in aggressive behavior such as fights or other violence, including murder.
- ***Overcontrolled murderers*** are able to inhibit any outward expression of anger, often unaware of it. The unexpressed anger can build over the years before erupting, possibly without warning, resulting in a violent and deadly attack, often against family members.[43]

Biological Hypotheses

Studies have found that abnormal electrical brain activity, indicating brain damage, can be found in around 24 percent of killers.[44] This compares to about 12 percent of the general population. Around 65 percent of people who are serious repeat assaultive offenders possess abnormal electrical brain activity, or more than 2.5 times that of killers. As such, the relationship between brain damage and homicide in and of itself is weakened. Such abnormalities of the brain may be genetically linked or due to previous head trauma.

Some researchers have related the abnormal XYY chromosomal pattern in men to less intelligence, larger bones, and a greater probability of brain damage—resulting in violent behavior.[45] Since most XYY males are not law violators, few give any credence to this notion (see also Chapter 1).

Testosterone has also been studied in its relationship to male aggression and violence, the implication being that men with higher levels of testosterone or a hormonal imbalance are more likely to commit violent crimes. A number of studies on prisoners have found significantly higher testosterone levels among those with violent histories than those without violence in their histories.[46] Among the most comprehensive was a study done by J. M. Dabbs and colleagues, who found that the subjects with the highest levels of testosterone were most likely to have a history of violent crime, compared to the subjects with the lowest testosterone levels.[47]

These findings notwithstanding, some researchers have found only a limited or weak causal relationship between violent criminality and testosterone,[48] whereas others have found no correlation between the two variables.[49]

The relationship between murderers and lack of socially acceptable means for channeling aggressive instincts, such as sports, has been studied by some. For instance, Palmer found that killers had fewer socially acceptable ways for releasing anger than nonkillers.[50]

Sociological Hypotheses

Sociologists tend to explain murder in terms of learned behavior, subcultural norms, inadequate social controls, and other factors related to the social structure, culture, and environment. Some criminologists posit that violent subcultures exist in this country that include high murder rates and use of illegal firearms. Marvin Wolfgang and Franco Ferracuti have argued that some youths—particularly young, black, lower-class males and gang members—resort to murder and other violent acts as a reflection of the pressures and frustrations of the lower class, suggesting that more than 90 percent were "normatively prescribed" violent offenders belonging to a subculture of violence.[51]

According to the researchers, this subculture contained a series of "conduct norms" that governed the actions of its members under particular circumstances and, further, that values of the subculture came through both learning and being born into a subculture of violence. Wolfgang and Ferracuti originally used this hypothesis to explain why the black rate of murder and other violent crimes was disproportionately high. A subculture of violence model has since been applied to the high violent crime and homicide rate among males in general, youths and street crime, criminality in the south, and the relationship between murder and gun ownership.[52]

Critics have attacked the subculture of violence theory as racist, unsound, and a poor explanation of subcultural violence.[53] However, some continue to support the theory,[54] while others find it reliable in conjunction with other approaches on violent behavior.[55]

R. M. Holmes and J. DeBurger postulated that society itself cultivates a subculture of violent behavior, including homicide, through such things as:

* A high degree and condoning of interpersonal violence as a means of solving interpersonal struggles.
* A strong focus on desired societal goods and comforts.
* The anonymous, impersonal nature of urban America.
* A high rate of mobility and migration.
* The many role models for violent behavior in sports, entertainment, and neighborhoods.
* An emphasis on instant satisfaction.
* A high rate of resentment and blame on other people for one's frustrations, troubles, and misfortunes.[56]

Further discussion on social and cultural perspectives on violent behavior can be found in Chapters 2 and 3.

NOTES

1. U.S. Department of Justice, Federal Bureau of Investigation, *Crime in the United States: Uniform Crime Reports 2000* (Washington: Government Printing Office, 2001), p. 15; U.S. Department of Justice, Bureau of Justice Statistics Crime Data Brief, *Homicide Trends in the United States: 1998 Update* (Washington: Office of Justice Programs, 2000).

2. Angela Browne, Kirk R. Williams, and Donald G. Dutton, "Homicide Between Intimate Partners," in M. Dwayne Smith and Margaret A. Zahn, eds., *Studying and Preventing Homicide: Issues and Challenges* (Thousand Oaks: Sage, 1999), p. 57; A. L. Kellerman and J. A. Mercy, "Men, Women, and Murder: Gender-Specific Differences in Rates of Fatal Violence and Victimization," *Journal of Trauma 33* (1992): 1–5.

3. R. Barri Flowers and H. Loraine Flowers, *Murders in the United States: Crimes, Killers and Victims of the Twentieth Century* (Jefferson: McFarland, 2001), pp. 78–83, 86–105; David Lester, *Serial Killers: The Insatiable Passion* (Philadelphia: The Charles Press, 1995); *Crime in the United States*, pp., 15, 18.

4. See, for example, Tomislav V. Kovandzic, John J. Sloan III, and Lynne M. Vieraitis, "Unintended Consequences of Politically Popular Sentencing Policy: The Homicide Promoting Effects of 'Three Strikes' in U.S. Cities (1980–1999)," *Criminology 1,* 3 (2002): 399–424; Thomas B. Marvell and Carlisle E. Moody, "The Lethal Effects of Three Strikes Laws," *Journal of Legal Studies 30* (2001): 89–106.

5. *Crime in the United States,* p. 14.

6. *Ibid.,* p. 15.

7. *Ibid.,* pp. 18, 20.

8. Dan Eggen, "FBI: U.S. Crime Rate is on Rise–Increase in Incidents of Major Violence Ends 10-Year Decline," http://www.detnews.com/2002/nation/0206/24/nation-522429.htm.

9. *Ibid.*

10. *Crime in the United States,* pp., 224, 228.

11. *Ibid.,* pp. 238, 251, 256.

12. *Ibid.,* p. 14.

13. U.S. Department of Justice, Bureau of Justice Statistics Bulletin, *Prisoners in 2000* (Washington: Office of Justice Programs, 2001), p. 2

14. *Ibid.,* p. 12

15. U.S. Department of Justice, Bureau of Justice Statistics Special Report, *Firearm Use by Offenders* (Washington: Office of Justice Programs, 2001), p. 1.

16. *Ibid.,* p. 3.

17. *Ibid.,* p. 4.

18. R. Barri Flowers, *Drugs, Alcohol and Criminality in American Society* (Jefferson: McFarland, 1999), pp. 146–50; R. Lindquist, "Homicides Committed by Abusers of Alcohol and Illicit Drugs," *British Journal of Addiction 86* (1991): 321–26.

19. *Crime in the United States,* p. 21.

20. Flowers, *Drugs, Alcohol and Criminality in American Society,* pp. 171–72; U.S. Department of Justice, *An Analysis of National Data on the Prevalence of Alcohol Involvement in Crime,* http://www.ojp.usdoj.gov/bjs/.

21. U.S. Department of Justice, Bureau of Justice Statistics, *Drugs and Crime Facts,* http://www.ojp.usdoj.gov/bjs/.

22. *An Analysis of National Data on the Prevalence of Alcohol Involvement in Crime.*

23. *Ibid.*

24. See, for example, S. A. Brown, "Drug Effect Expectancies and Addictive Behavior Change," *Experimental and Clinical Psychopharmacology 1* (1993): 55–67; K. E. Leonard and S. P. Taylor, "Exposure to Pornography, Permissive and Nonpermissive Cues, and Male Aggression Toward Females," *Motivation and Emotion 7* (1983): 291–99.

25. Kathleen Auerhahn and Robert N. Parker, "Drugs, Alcohol, and Homicide," in M. Dwayne Smith and Margaret A. Zahn, eds., *Studying and Preventing Homicide: Issues and Challenges* (Thousand Oaks: Sage, 1999), pp. 99–106; M. C. Ray and R. L. Simons, "Convicted Murderers' Accounts of Their Crimes: A Study of Homicide in Small Communities," *Symbolic Interaction 10* (1987): 57–70.

26. R. Bachman, "The Social Causes of American Indian Homicide as Revealed by the Life Experiences of Thirty Offenders," *American Indian Quarterly 15* (1991): 468–92; E. L. Abel, "Drugs and Homicide in Erie County, New York," *International Journal of the Addictions 22* (1987): 195–200.

27. W. Wieczorek, J. Welte, and E. Abel, "Alcohol, Drugs, and Murder: A Study of Convicted Homicide Offenders," *Journal of Criminal Justice 18* (1990): 217–27.

28. Flowers, *Drugs, Alcohol and Criminality in American Society;* B. Spunt, H. H. Brownstein, P. Goldstein, M. Fendrich, and H. J. Liberty, "Drug Use by Homicide Offenders," *Journal of Psychoactive Drugs 27* (1995): 125–34.

29. M. W. Klein, C. L. Maxson, and L. C. Cunningham, "Crack, Street Gangs, and Violence," *Criminology 29* (1991): 623–50.

30. P. Goldstein, H. H. Brownstein, P. J. Ryan, and P. A. Bellucci, "Crack and Homicide in New York City, 1988: A Conceptually Based Event Analysis," *Contemporary Drug Problems 16* (1989): 651–87.

31. *Crime in the United States,* p. 19.

32. Cited in R. Barri Flowers, *Sex Crime, Predators, Perpetrators, Prostitutes, and Victims: An Examination of Sexual Criminality and Victimization* (Springfield: Charles C Thomas, 2001), p. 9.

33. Jacquelyn C. Campbell, "If I Can't Have You, No One Can: Issues of Power and Control in Homicide of Female Partners," in J. Radford and D. E. Russell, eds., *Femicide: The Politics of Women Killing* (Boston: Twayne, 1992); R. E. Dobash and R. P. Dobash, *Violence Against Wives* (New York: Free Press, 1979).

34. Flowers and Flowers, *Murders in the United States,* pp. 86–106. See also R. Barri Flowers, *Murder, At the End of the Day and Night: A Study of Criminal Homicide Offenders, Victims, and Circumstances* (Springfield: Charles C Thomas, 2002), pp. 159–178.

35. D. T. Lunde, *Murder and Madness* (New York: Norton, 1979).

36. J. Levin and J. A. Fox, *Mass Murder* (New York: Plenum, 1985).

37. R. R. Hazelwood, P. E. Dietz, and J. Warren, "The Criminal Sexual Sadist," *FBI Law Enforcement Bulletin 61* (1992): 477–91.

38. P. E. Dietz, "Mass, Serial, and Sensational Homicides," *Bulletin of the New York Academy of Medicine 62* (1986): 477–91.

39. Flowers, *Murder, At the End of the Day and Night,* pp. 180–86.

40. Flowers and Flowers, *Murders in the United States,* pp. 78–83.

41. R. M. Holmes and S. T. Holmes, "Understanding Mass Murder," *Federal Probation 56,* 1 (1992): 53–61.

42. S. Palmer, *A Study of Murder* (New York: Thomas Y. Crowell, 1960).

43. E. I. Megargee, "Uncontrolled and Overcontrolled Personality Types in Extreme Antisocial Aggression," *Psychological Monographs 80,* 3 (1966): 611.

44. Lester, *Serial Killers,* p. 6.

45. *Ibid.;* A. A. Sandberg, G. F. Koepf, T. Ishiara, and T. S. Hanschka, "An XYY Human Male," *Lancet 262* (1961): 488–89.

46. See, for example, "Hormone Responses and Male Aggression," http://www.aic.gov.au/research/cvp/ncv/vda-sec08.html; J. Bain, R. Langevin, R. Dickey, and M. Ben-Aron, "Sex Hormones in Murderers and Assaulters," *Behavioral Science and the Law 5* (1987): 95–101; J. Archer, "The Influence of Testosterone on Human Aggression," *British Journal of Psychology 82* (1991): 1–28.

47. J. M. Dabbs, R. L. Frady, T. S. Carr, and N. F. Besch, "Saliva Testosterone and Criminal Violence in Young Adult Prison Inmates," *Psychosomatic Medicine 49* (1987): 74–182; J. M. Dabbs, T. S. Carr, R. L. Frady, and J. K. Riad, "Testosterone, Crime, and Misbehavior Among 692 Prison Inmates," *Personality and Individual Differences 18* (1995): 627–33.

48. See, for example, "Hormone Responses and Male Aggression;" Warwick T. Peters, "Phrenology Biological Theories of crime Criminology," http://members.ozemail.com/au/~wtmp/misc/phrenology.html; A. Mazur and A. Booth, "Testosterone and Dominance in Men," http://www.thehormoneshop.com/testosteroneanddominanceinmen.htm.

49. See, for example, Peters, "Phrenology Biological Theories of Crime Criminology;" Mazur and Booth, "Testosterone and Dominance in Men;" A. Mattsson, D. Schalling, D. Olweus, H. Low, and J. Stevenson, "Plasma Testosterone, Aggressive

Behavior, and Personality Dimensions in Young Male Delinquents," *Journal of the American Academy of Child Psychiatry 19* (1980): 476–90.

50. Palmer, *A Study of Murder*. See also E. Gonzalez-Bono, A. Salvador, J. Ricarte, M. A. Serrano, and M. Arnedo, "Testosterone and Attribution of Successful Competition," *Aggressive Behavior 26* (2000): 235–40.

51. Marvin E. Wolfgang and Franco Ferracuti, *The Subculture of Violence; Toward an Integrated Theory in Criminology* (London: Tavistock, 1967); "Marvin Wolfgang's Subculture of Violence Theory," http://www.criminology.fsu.edu/criminology/wolfgang.htm; R. N. Parker, "Poverty, Subculture of Violence, and Type of Homicide," *Social Forces 67* (1989): 983–1007.

52. See, for example, L. W. Kennedy and S. W. Baron, "Routine Activities and a Subculture of Violence: A Study of Violence on the Street," *Journal of Research in Crime and Delinquency 30,* 1 (1993): 88–112; R. B. Felson, A. E. Liska, S. J. South, and T. L. McNulty, "The Subculture of Violence and Delinquency: Individual vs. School Context Effects," *Social Forces 73,* 1 (1994): 155–73; J. Dixon and A. J. Lizotte, "Gun Ownership and the Southern Subculture of Violence," *American Journal of Sociology 93* (1987): 383–405.

53. See, for example, Parker, "Poverty, Subculture of Violence, and Type of Homicide;" E. Shihadeh and D. J. Steffensmeir, "Economic Inequality, Family Disruption, and Urban Black Violence: Cities as Units of Stratification and Social Control," *Social Forces 73,* 1 (1994): 729–51.

54. Dixon and Lizotte, "Gun Ownership and the Southern Subculture of Violence;" C. G. Ellison, "An Eye for an Eye? A Note on the Southern Subculture of Violence Thesis," *Social Forces 69* (1991): 1223–39.

55. See, for example, Kennedy and Baron, "Routine Activities and a Subculture of Violence;" J. R. Benedict, *Athletes and Acquaintance Rape* (Thousand Oaks: Sage, 1998).

56. R. M. Holmes and J. DeBurger, *Serial Murder* (Thousand Oaks: Sage, 1988).

Chapter 8

FORCIBLE RAPE

Violent sex offenses are primarily perpetrated by males and directed at females. This is particularly true for rape, though some females have been known to rape other females or children. Forcible rape by males is a common occurrence in our society, victimizing millions of women, children, and men. There is one forcible rape every six minutes in the United States. Although stranger rape is most often viewed as the more likely kind of forcible rape, most rapists are not strangers to their victims. Acquaintance rapists include marital and date rapists and other offenders familiar to those victimized. Many rapists are serial rapists and are often involved in other types of violent behavior. Studies reveal that most men who rape tend to be under the influence of alcohol or drugs and commit rape as a reflection of masculinity, sexual aggression, power, and opportunity. Rape is seen as learned behavior that is often rooted in child sexual abuse and family violence.

DEFINING FORCIBLE RAPE

The word *rape* itself derives from the Latin term *rapere*, which means to "steal, seize, or carry away."[1] According to the American Heritage Dictionary, rape is "(1) the crime of forcing a person to submit to sexual intercourse, (2) seizing and carrying off by force; abduction; and (3) violation: a rape of justice."[2] Traditionally, the act of rape has been defined in terms of a male aggressor and a female victim. Typically, definitions of rape have been broken down into two categories: legal and nonlegal definitions.

Legal Definitions of Forcible Rape

Legal definitions of forcible rape are rooted in traditional common law and statute law. According to common law, rape is defined as "the unlawful carnal knowledge of a woman by force and against her will."[3] Any kind of sexual penetration, no matter how slight, was sufficient to make it a criminal offense, assuming the presence of the other elements as defined. A standard of resistance was applied for the victim "in order to distinguish forcible carnal knowledge (rape) from consensual carnal knowledge (fornication and adultery).[4]

In common law, both forms of carnal knowledge were considered criminal acts, but if the act was forcible, the victim received no punishment for adultery or fornication.

Forcible rape is considered a crime in every state today. Most states have adopted a statutory definition of forcible rape "as the act of sexual intercourse with a woman other than the perpetrator's wife committed without her lawful consent."[5] As with common law, only the slightest penetration is necessary for it to be the crime of rape. Excluded from this definition are forced sexual assaults such as oral and anal copulation and homosexual sex offenses.

The FBI's Uniform Crime Reporting Program defines forcible rape as "the carnal knowledge of a female forcibly and against her will. Assaults or attempts to commit rape by force or threat of force are also included."[6] Statutory rape and other sexual offenses are excluded from this definition.

A number of state statutes use the terms "sexual battery" and "criminal sexual assault" in addressing sex offenses beyond forced intercourse,[7] while every state now considers marital rape a crime.[8] Some states have defined rape in sex-neutral terms, allowing for the act to be considered a criminal offense beyond the traditional female victim-male offender dynamics.[9]

Nonlegal Definitions of Forcible Rape

Nonlegal definitions of forcible rape tend to be broader in their interpretation than legal definitions, while generally examining the issue of rape within a social context. According to many social scientists, rape and rapists are seen as an "extension of normative sexual attitudes and relations in a society that demands and objectifies women."[10] Largely influenced by the feminist movement, some rape scholars have pointed towards the social and cultural factors in creating sexual aggression, contending that rather than being an individual pathology, rape is a "product of the patriarchal society in which it is imbedded."[11]

Nontraditional views on forcible rape typically include forced sexual or exploitative contact such as incest, molestation, and sodomy as rape in its definition. Some researchers have studied rape in terms of victim perception, traditional sex role expectations, and normative influences.[12]

THE EXTENT OF FORCIBLE RAPE

What is the prevalence and incidence of forcible rape in the United States? Rape experts such as Diana Russell and Rebecca Bolen see rape and sexual assault as an epidemic.[13] A number of studies and surveys illustrate the magnitude of the problem. According to a National Violence Against Women (NVAW) Survey, nearly one in five women have been victimized by a completed or attempted rape in their life, affectingly nearly 18 million women in this country (see Table 8.1). Almost 15 percent of the women surveyed had been victims of a completed rape, while fewer than 3 percent had been victims of an attempted rape. In their study of rape in America, D. G. Kilpatrick, C. N. Edmunds, and A. K. Seymour estimated that one in eight women had ever been the victim of forcible rape.[14]

Other prevalence studies of sexual assault have yielded similar findings. For example, 13 percent of women in a National Women's Study have been the victims of completed forcible rape at some point in their life,[15] whereas the National Health and Social Life Survey found that 22 percent of the women surveyed had ever been forced to participate in some form of sexual act.[16]

Incidence studies of rape also reveal its high numbers in our society. The NVAW Survey estimated that 876,064 rapes are perpetrated against women in the United States annually, affecting 302,091 victims (see Table 8.2). This results in a victimization rate of 8.7 rapes per 1,000 females 18 years of age or older. The average number of rape victimizations per victim was found to be nearly three. In Russell's survey of rape victims, the researcher estimated that 1.5 million rapes and attempted rapes took place in this country every year.[17] According to the U.S. Justice Department, approximately one in every six rapes are perpetrated against victims under the age of twelve.[18]

Although forcible rape is predominantly a male perpetrator-female or -child victim violent crime, men are also rape victims. The NVAW estimated that nearly three million American men have been the victims of attempted or completed rape during their lifetime.[19] Approximately one in every ten victims of rape are male.[20]

In spite of these staggering numbers, the vast majority of rapes go unreported, according to official data and experts on rape. In a study of rape in America, Nancy Gager and Cathleen Schurr estimated that as many as nine out of ten forcible rapes go unreported.[21] Susan Brownmiller estimated that anywhere from one in five rapes to as little as one in 20 rapes are ever reported.[22] Kilpatrick and colleagues found that only 16 percent of the rape victims in their nationally representative sample reported being raped to law enforcement.[23]

Table 8.1
WOMEN RAPE VICTIMS IN LIFETIME, BY TYPE OF VICTIMIZATION

Type of victimization	*Percentage*	*Number*[a]
Total Rape	17.6	17,722,672
Completed	14.8	14,903,156
Attempted only	2.8	2,819,516

[a] Based on estimates of females age 18 and older.
Source: Adapted from U.S. Department of Justice, *Full Report of the Prevalence, Incidence, and Consequences of Violence Against Women: Findings From the National Violence Against Women Survey* (Washington: National Institute of Justice, 2000), p. 14.

Table 8.2
ESTIMATED NUMBER OF ADULT FEMALE RAPE VICTIMS ANNUALLY

Estimated number of victims	*Average number of victimizations per victim*	*Estimated total number of victimizations*	*Annual rate of victimizations*
302,091	2.9[a]	876,064[a]	8.7

[a] Relative standard error exceeds 30 percent.
Source: Adapted from U.S. Department of Justice, *Full Report of the Prevalence, Incidence, and Consequences of Violence Against Women: Findings From the National Violence Against Women Survey* (Washington: National Institute of Justice, 2000), p. 15.

The National Crime Victimization Survey found that the most common reason victims report rape is to prevent the rapists from repeating the offense, whereas victims are least likely to report being raped because they consider it a personal matter.[24]

Arrests and Forcible Rape

Only a small percentage of rapists ever enter the criminal justice system. According to official figures, there were 90,186 reported rapes in the nation in 2000, nearly nine in ten of which were classified as forcible rapes.[25] Less than half of these were cleared by law enforcement agencies. Across the country, there were an estimated 27,469 persons arrested for forcible rape in 2000.[26] Just over 45 percent of the arrestees were under the age of 25, and nearly two-thirds were white.

Arrest trends reveal that fewer persons are being arrested for forcible rape, though the number of recorded forcible rapes of females in 2000 increased for the first time in eight years (see Fig. 8.1). Between 1991 and 2000, arrests for forcible rape in the United States dropped by nearly 30 percent. During

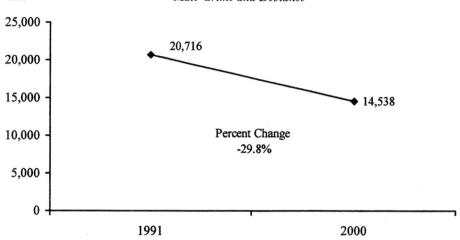

Figure 8.1. Ten-Year Arrest Trends for Forcible Rape, 1991–2000. *Source:* Derived from U.S. Department of Justice, Federal Bureau of Investigation, *Crime in the United States: Uniform Crime Reports 2000* (Washington: Government Printing Office, 2001), p. 216.

this span, the decrease was smaller for arrestees under the age of 18, falling 26.4 percent; whereas a slightly higher percentage drop occurred for arrestees age 18 or older, decreasing 30.5 percent.[27]

According to the Department of Justice, almost 60 percent of convicted rapists and other sex offenders are under correctional supervision other than incarceration.[28] A 1993 Congressional report found that:

- Ninety-eight percent of rape victims fail to see their rapists arrested, tried, and imprisoned.
- Over half of all rape prosecutions result in dismissal prior to trial or acquittal.
- Almost one-quarter of convicted rapists never go to prison.
- One in four convicted rapists receive only a jail sentence.
- A convicted rapist is 50 percent more likely to receive probation than a convicted robber.[29]

CHARACTERIZING FORCIBLE RAPE VICTIMS AND PERPETRATORS

The majority of forcible rapists are neither reported nor apprehended by law enforcement authorities.[30] Studies show that rapists tend to most often target juvenile and single female victims. More than half the victims in the Kilpatrick and associates study and the NVAW Survey were under the age of

18 when the rape occurred.[31] Russell found that 85 percent of the rape victims surveyed were single at the time the rape or attempted rape took place.[32]

Using detailed data from three states, the National Incident-Based Reporting System characterized the dynamics of forcible rape as follows:

- Nine out of ten forcible rapes conformed to the traditional male offender-female victim definition of rape.
- In nearly nine in ten forcible rapes, the offender and victim were the same race.
- Around eight in ten rape victims were younger than age 30.
- Half of rape victims were under the age of 18.
- Four in ten rapists were age 30 and older.
- One in eight rapists were younger than 18.
- Rape victims older than 30 were around 12 times more likely as rape victims under 12 to have been raped by a stranger.
- Two-thirds of rape victims between the ages of 18 and 29 were intimately involved with their rapist.
- Eighty percent of rapes involved physical force only.
- In around 12 percent of rapes, the rapist used a gun or knife.
- Around six in ten rapes occurred in a residence.[33]

Profiling the Rapist

According to the 2000 National Crime Victimization Survey and other government sources, the following profile has emerged about rapists:

- The average rapist's age at time of arrest is 31.
- More than half of rapists are white.
- More than six in ten rapists know their victim.
- Around four in ten rape a friend or acquaintance.
- About one-third of rapists are strangers to their victims.
- More than half the rapists on probation will be rearrested within three years for committing another crime.
- Of those, more than one in four will be arrested for another violent crime.[34]

Probability data on a rapist's involvement with the criminal justice system was estimated by the National Center For Policy Analysis, which found that:

- For reported rapes, there is nearly a 51 percent chance it will result in an arrest.
- If arrested, there is an 80 percent probability that the rape suspect will be prosecuted.

- With a prosecution, there is a 58 percent chance that it will result in a felony conviction.
- With a felony conviction, there is a 69 percent probability that the rapist will be incarcerated.
- Less than 17 percent of reported rapists will serve time behind bars.
- Only one in 20, or 5 five percent, of rapists will ever spend any time incarcerated.[35]

TYPES OF FORCIBLE RAPISTS

Researchers have identified over 50 types of rapists.[36] Many of these types fit into multiple classifications. Paul Gebhard and associates found that there were six types of rapists whom they classified collectively as "heterosexual aggressors":

- *Assaultive rapists:* the most common type of rapist, characterized by sadistic, hostile feelings toward women.
- *Amoral delinquents:* the second most common type of rapist; nonsadistic, with a desire to have sexual relations whether the victim agrees to it or not.
- *Drunken variety:* rapists as common as amoral delinquents.
- *Explosive variety:* rapists whose history gives no indication of their potential to rape; the behavior often contains psychotic elements.
- *Double-standard variety:* rapists who divide females into good ones to respect, and bad ones to disrespect.
- *Other types:* a combination of the prior five types of rapists, along with rapists who are mentally defective or psychotic.[37]

Psychiatrist Richard Rada also identified five categories of rapists:

- *Psychotic rapists:* acutely psychotic and violent rapists; neither victim nor offender are in control of the episode.
- *Situational rapists:* rarely very violent or dangerous rapists with no history of violent or sexual deviations; rape is typically the result of situational stress.
- *Masculine identity conflict rapists:* a broad range of rapists characterized by an actual or perceived deficiency in their masculinity; rape is often planned, dangerous, and violent.
- *Sadistic rapists:* comprising only a small percentage of rapists; usually plans the rape, has a history of sexual perversion, and gains pleasure in the ritualistic degrading of women.

- *Sociopathic rapists:* the most common type of rapist; generally impulsive and motivated primarily by sex, with the rape a manifestation of antisocial behavior.[38]

Researchers have found that rapists typically fall into two categories: power rapists and anger rapists. Power rapists constitute around 55 percent of all rapists.[39] Their crimes are often premeditated, repeat offenses, and borne out of fantasies and exposure to pornography. Two subtypes of power rapists are power-assertive rapists and power-reassurance rapists.

- *Power-assertive rapists* tend to feel powerless with the rape an expression of masculinity, dominance, command, and often feelings of entitlement.
- *Power-reassurance rapists* commit rapes largely for reassurance of their masculinity and sexual adequacy; these rapists try to make their victims feel helpless and powerless.[40]

Anger rapists account for about 40 percent of all rapists.[41] They tend to be more impulsive, spontaneous, and dangerous than power rapists–often using foul language in intimidating and degrading their victims. The two subtypes of anger rapists identified are anger-retaliation rapists and anger-excitation rapists.

- *Anger-retaliation rapists:* often rape to show their hostility towards women; the rape is meant to degrade, hurt, and act as revenge against women they believe have wronged them in some way.
- *Anger-excitation rapists:* ties anger to sexual arousal; such rapists derive excitement and pleasure in their victims' pain and suffering and their own violence and aggression.[42]

Marital Rapists

Another type of forcible rapist is the marital rapist. Marital rape is defined as "any unwanted sexual intercourse or penetration (vaginal, anal, or oral) obtained by force, threat of force, or when the wife is unable to consent."[43] Within this definition, researchers have identified three subtypes of marital rape:

- *Force only rape*–where the spouse rapist uses only the required force to get the wife to submit.
- *Battering rape*–where the husband rapes and beats his wife; the abuse may occur before, after, or simultaneous with the rape.
- *Sadistic/obsessive rape*–where the spouse rapist uses torture or sexual perversions during the rape.[44]

Many rape experts contend that the dynamics of rape in marriage also apply to rape and sexual assaults involving a live-in partner or other intimates who are unmarried, including rape in dating relationships.[45]

Studies on marital rape reveal its impact on society. The Crime Victims Research and Treatment Center (CVC) reported that more than a million women have ever been the victims of marital rape.[46] The CVC and National Victim Center estimates that more than 61,000 women are raped by spouses and ex-spouses in the United States every year.[47] Marital rape researchers estimate that between 10 and 14 percent of all married women have been victimized by rape in marriage.[48]

Husband rapists have been characterized as domineering men, condoning wife battering, and viewing their spouses as personal and sexual property.[49] Kersti Yllo and David Finkelhor describe three types of marital rapists:

- Men motivated mainly by uncontrolled anger.
- Men who use rape as a way to gain power over their wives.
- Men obsessed with sex who receive satisfaction out of perverse and sadistic acts.[50]

Almost half the marital rapists studied were identified as uncontrolled anger types. These men often raped their wives during or after battering them. Men who raped their wives to gain power over them tended to use only the force necessary to have sexual intercourse.

Although marital rape is now recognized as a sex crime in every state, in more than half the states there continues to be some marital rape exemptions in statutes in prosecuting men who rape their wives.[51]

Acquaintance Rapists

Acquaintance or date rapists represent a growing threat in society. Especially vulnerable to this type of forcible rapist are teenage females and young women in college. Acquaintance rape is defined as forced sex against a person's will by someone she or he is familiar with such as a date, friend, coworker, or neighbor. Rape is now defined in many statutes as "nonconsensual sexual penetration by physical force, by threat of bodily harm, or when the victim is incapable of giving consent by virtue of mental illness, mental retardation, or intoxication."[52]

A number of recent studies have documented the seriousness of acquaintance or date rape in the United States.[53] According to the National Resource Center on Domestic Violence, more than one in three women victims of reported rape or battering since the age of 18 identified their offender as a current spouse or live-in intimate, ex-intimate, or date.[54] It is estimated that more than 50 percent of rapes are perpetrated against adolescent teenage victims, with the vast majority of perpetrators acquaintances or dates.[55]

Much of the research on acquaintance or date rape has focused on college students. According to the Bureau of Justice Statistics, approximately 3 percent of women in college are the victims of an attempted or completed rape during a given college year.[56] In a *Ms.* magazine study, one in four females interviewed reported being the victims of a rape or attempted rape.[57] Eighty-four percent of the perpetrators were described as acquaintances, while 57 percent were identified as dates. Similar findings have been made by other researchers.[58] Some researchers have found a correlation between stalking and date rape,[59] as well as substance abuse.[60]

"Date rape drugs" such as Rohypnol or "Roofies" and GHB (Gamma hydroxy butyrate) have recently been linked to forced sexual relations often by defenseless victims.[61] The tasteless and odorless drugs are powerful enough to cause one to lose consciousness, become physically incapacitated, or impair memory. Potential victims who consume alcohol at bars or parties are particularly susceptible to rape victimization.

Acquaintance or date rapists are seen by rape experts as reflecting masculinity and sex role expectations of power and domination in their actions, along with gender stereotyping.[62] Many such rapists are also often characterized by anger, a fixation on the victim of aggression, and a history of violence or exposure to it.

THEORIES ON FORCIBLE RAPE

A number of theories have been applied to forcible rape in understanding its dynamics and causes. Most tend to fall under four general theoretical approaches: (1) interactionist theories, (2) psychoanalytic theories, (3) opportunity structure theories, and (4) biological predisposition theories.

Interactionist Theories

Interactionist theories posit that "social interaction is mediated by signs and symbols, by eye contact, gestures, and words."[63] Thus, a person views and interprets another person's actions, responding accordingly. Rape is often seen as the consequence of such a response. Interactionist theories hold that rape is the product of the way males and females communicate their feelings and attitudes towards one another.[64]

Victim-precipitation theories fall under the interactionist theoretical base. In concentrating on the rapist's reaction to the rape victim, supporters of this approach refer to rape cases "in which the victim–actually or so it was interpreted by the offender–agreed to sexual relations but retracted before the actual act or did not resist strongly enough."[65]

Rape experts have criticized interactionist theories for their inapplicability to all types of rape, as well as the failure to "question the oppressive sexist norms that regulate women's lives."[66] Researchers Julia Schwendinger and Herman Schwendinger argue that interactionist theories "tacitly minimize the structural realities of the situation and the power differentials that characterize the overwhelming number of forcible rapes."[67]

Psychoanalytic Theories

Only a small percentage of men who rape are believed to be psychotic. However, psychoanalytic theorists postulate that most rapists are mentally disturbed, developed strong childhood hatred for women, and many have harbored experiences "that triggered their latent homosexual tendencies."[68] As such, rape is regarded as an act perpetrated by men who are "obsessively motivated by hatred of women and an overpowering need to assure themselves of their own masculinity."[69] Psychoanalytic research is also a critical component in some sociological theories on criminality–such as the subculture of violence theory–applied to forcible rapists by such criminologists as Menachem Amir and Brownmiller.[70]

Psychoanalytic theories fall short in explaining rape, primarily because of the systematic failure to be tested scientifically. Psychoanalysis tends to put too much emphasis on the number of rapes associated with personality disorders without the empirical validity to back up its propositions.

Opportunity Structure Theories

An opportunity structure theory has been advanced by Lorenne Clark and Debra Lewis to explain rape.[71] They contend that men view women as possessing saleable sexual properties that can be bought and sold. The theory assumes that men of lesser means or physically unappealing may use force to achieve their sexual desires if unable to bargain successfully for sexual favors.

Lower-class men are seen as often choosing to rape middle-class women because they lack the necessary means to attract such women and desire what is normally unattainable to them. According to the researchers, the act of forcible rape "will always be an inevitable consequence of the fact that some men do not have the means to achieve sexual relations with women, except through physical violence."[72]

Opportunity structure theory has been attacked by critics in its concept of sex as a commodity, as well as ignoring the fact that many rapists are also wealthy, handsome, and charming. Further, there is little evidence that lower class rapists are more likely to rape middle class women. On the contrary, most studies suggest that the majority of rape victims are also from the lower class.[73]

Biological Theories of Rape

Some theorists have argued that rape and other violence is a reflection of biological predisposition or other inherent factors and tendendicies.[74] Brownmiller, in particular, has advanced a biological theory of rape in her book, *Against Our Will: Men, Women and Rape.* She holds that "had it not been for this accident of biology, an accommodation requiring the locking together of two separate parts, penis and vagina, there would be neither copulation nor rape as we know it. . . . In terms of human anatomy, the possibility of forcible intercourse incontrovertibly exists."[75]

Biological rape theories are generally rejected by most criminologists as being unscientific and too simplistic. Brownmiller's approach further places too little emphasis on man's biological superiority physically over women in using the biological imbalance to their advantage, while perpetuating traditional male stereotypes (see also Chapter 1).

NOTES

1. R. Barri Flowers, *Women and Criminality: The Woman as Victim, Offender, and Practitioner* (Westport: Greenwood, 1987), p. 28.

2. *American Heritage Dictionary* (New York: Dell, 1994), p. 683.

3. Flowers, *Women and Criminality*, p. 28.

4. *Ibid.* See also Merril D. Smith, *Sex Without Consent: Rape and Sexual Coercion in America* (New York: New York University Press, 2002).

5. R. Barri Flowers, *Sex Crimes, Predators, Perpetrators, Prostitutes, and Victims: An Examination of Sexual Criminality and Victimization* (Springfield: Charles C Thomas, 2001), p. 21.

6. U.S. Department of Justice, Federal Bureau of Investigation, *Crime in the United States: Uniform Crime Reports 2000* (Washington: Government Printing Office, 2001), p. 25.

7. Flowers, *Sex Crimes, Predators, Perpetrators, Prostitutes, and Victims*, pp. 21–22.

8. Patricia Mahoney and Linda M. Williams, "Sexual Assault in Marriage: Prevalence, Consequences, and Treatment of Wife Rape," in Jana L. Jasinski and Linda M.

Williams, eds., *Partner Violence: A Comprehensive Review of 20 Years of Research* (Thousand Oaks: Sage, 1998), p. 119.

9. Richard A. Posner and Katharine B. Silbaugh, *A Guide to America's Sex Laws* (Chicago: University of Chicago Press, 1996), pp. 5–43; Battelle Law and Justice Study Center Report, *Forcible Rape: An Analysis of Legal Issues* (Washington: Government Printing Office, 1977), p. 34.

10. Mary E. Odem and Jody Clay-Warner, *Confronting Rape and Sexual Assault* (Wilmington: Scholarly Resources, Inc., 1998), p. xiv.

11. *Ibid.* See also Carole J. Sheffield, "Sexual Terrorism," in Jo Freeman, ed., *Women: A Feminist Perspective*, 4th ed. (Mountain View: Mayfield, 1984), pp. 3–19.

12. Smith, *Sex Without Consent*; T. W. Herbert, *Sexual Violence and American Manhood* (Cambridge: Harvard University Press, 2002); Susan H. Klemmack and David L. Klemmack, "The Social Definition of Rape," in Marcy J. Walker and Stanley L. Brodsky, eds., *Sexual Assault* (Lexington: Lexington Books, 1976), pp. 144–45.

13. Diana E. Russell and Rebecca M. Bolen, *The Epidemic of Rape and Child Sexual Abuse in the United States* (Thousand Oaks: Sage, 2000).

14. D. G. Kilpatrick, C. N. Edmunds, and A. K. Seymour, *Rape in America: A Report to the Nation* (Charleston: Medical University of South Carolina, Crime Victims Research and Treatment Center, 1992).

15. Cited in U.S. Department of Justice, *Full Report of the Prevalence, Incidence, and Consequences of Violence Against Women: Findings From the National Violence Against Women Survey* (Washington: National Institute of Justice, 2000), p. 13.

16. R. T. Michael, J. H. Gagnon, E. O. Lauman, and G. Kolata, *Sex in America: A Definitive Survey* (New York: Warner, 1994).

17. Diana E. Russell, *Sexual Exploitation: Rape, Child Abuse, and Workplace Harassment* (Thousand Oaks: Sage, 1984), p. 47.

18. U.S. Department of Justice, Bureau of Justice Statistics, *Child Rape Victims, 1992* (Washington: Office of Justice Programs, 1994), pp. 1–2.

19. Cited in Rape, Abuse & Incest National Network (RAINN) Statistics, http://www.rain.org/statistics.html.

20. *Ibid.*

21. Nancy Gager and Cathleen Schurr, *Sexual Assault: Confronting Rape in America* (New York: Grosset and Dunlap, 1976), p. 91. See also Russell and Bolen, *The Epidemic of Rape and Child Sexual Abuse.*

22. Susan Brownmiller, *Against Our Will: Men, Women and Rape* (New York: Simon & Schuster, 1975), p. 190. See also Mary P. Koss, "The Undetection of Rape: Methodological Choices Influence Incidence Estimates," *Journal of Social Issues 48* (1992): 61–75.

23. Kilpatrick, Edmunds, and Seymour, *Rape in America.*

24. Cited in Flowers, *Sex Crimes, Predators, Perpetrators, Prostitutes, and Victims*, p. 24.

25. *Crime in the United States*, pp. 25–27.

26. *Ibid.*, p. 27.

27. *Ibid.*, p. 216.

28. U.S. Department of Justice, Bureau of Justice Statistics, *Sex Offenses and Offenders: An Analysis of Data on Rape and Sexual Assault* (Washington: Office of Justice Programs, 1997), p. 15.

29. Cited in Lorraine Dusky, *Still Unequal: The Shameful Truth About Women and Justice in America* (New York: Crown, 1996), p. 381.

30. Flowers, *Sex Crimes, Predators, Perpetrators, Prostitutes, and Victims*, p. 25.

31. Kilpatrick, Edmunds, and Seymour, *Rape in America; National Violence Against Women Survey*, p. 35.

32. Russell, *Sexual Exploitation*, p. 88.

33. *Sex Offenses and Offenders*, pp. 11–12.

34. 2000 National Crime Victimization Survey, Bureau of Justice Statistics, http://www.ojp.usdoj.gov/bjs. See also Menachem Amir, *Patterns in Forcible Rape* (Chicago: University of Chicago Press, 1971).

35. National Center for Policy Analysis, *Crime and Punishment in America: 1999*, U.S. Department of Justice, http://www.ncpd.org/studies/s229/s229.html.

36. A. Nicholas Groth and H. Jean Birnbaum, *Men Who Rape: The Psychology of the Offender* (Cambridge: Perseus, 2001); Stanley L. Brodsky and Susan C. Hobart, "Blame Models and Assailant Research," *Criminal Justice and Behavior 5* (1978): 379–88.

37. Paul H. Gebhard, John H. Gagnon, Wardell B. Pomeroy, and Cornelia V. Christenson, *Sex Offenders: An Analysis of Types* (New York: Harper & Row, 1965), pp. 198–204; Herbert, *Sexual Violence and American Manhood*.

38. Richard T. Rada, *Clinical Aspects of the Rapist* (New York: Grune and Stratton, 1978), pp. 122–30.

39. Groth and Birnbaum, *Men Who Rape*; Robert E. Freeman-Longo and Geral T. Blanchard, *Sexual Abuse in America: Epidemic of the 21st Century* (Brandon: Safer Society Press, 1988), p. 48.

40. Freeman-Longo and Blanchard, *Sexual Abuse in America*, pp. 48–49; Dawn J. Graney and Bruce A. Arrigo, *Power Serial Rapist: A Criminology-Victimology Typology of Female Victim Selection* (Springfield: Charles C Thomas, 2002).

41. *Ibid.*, p. 49.

42. *Ibid.*

43. VAWnet Applied Research Forum, National Electronic Network on Violence Against Women, "Marital Rape," National Resource Center on Domestic Violence, San Francisco, 1999.

44. See http://www.sccadvasa.org/marital_rape.htm; Diana E. Russell, *Rape in Marriage* (New York: Macmillan, 1990).

45. Flowers, *Sex Crimes, Predators, Perpetrators, Prostitutes, and Victims*, pp. 51–57; Barrie Levy, ed., *Dating Violence: Young Women in Danger* (Seattle: Seal Press, 1998).

46. Cited in Andrea Gross, "A Question of Rape," *Ladies Home Journal 110*, 11 (November 1993), p. 170.

47. *Ibid.*

48. Russell, *Rape in Marriage*; David Finkelhor and Kersti Yllo, *License to Rape: Sexual Abuse of Wives* (New York: Holt, Rinehart & Winston, 1985).

49. J. C. Campbell and P. Alford, "The Dark Consequences of Marital Rape," *American Journal of Nursing 1* (1989): 946–49.

50. Cited in Gross, "A Question of Rape." See also Finkelhor and Yllo, *License to Rape.*

51. Mahoney and Williams, "Sexual Assault in Marriage," p. 119; R. K. Bergen, *Wife Rape: Understanding Responses of Survivors and Service Providers* (Thousand Oaks: Sage, 1996).

52. See http://www.sccadvasa.org/saacquaince.html.

53. See, for example, Heather M. Karjane, Bonnie S. Fisher, and Francis T. Cullen, *Campus Sexual Assault: How America's Institutions of Higher Education Respond. Final Report* (Washington: National Institute of Justice, 2001); Sally K. Ward, Kathy Chapman, Ellen Cohn, Susan White, and Kirk Williams, "Acquaintance Rape and the College Social Scene," *Family Relations 40* (1991): 65–71; Charlene L. Muehlenhard and Melaney A. Linton, "Date Rape and Sexual Aggression in Dating Situations: Incidence and Risk Factors," *Journal of Consulting Psychology 34* (1987): 186–96; Walter De Keseredy and Katharine Kelly, "The Incidence and Prevalence of Women Abuse in Canadian University and College Dating Relationships," *Canadian Journal of Sociology 18* (1993): 137–59.

54. National Institute of Justice and Centers for Disease Control and Prevention, *Prevalence, Incidence, and Consequences of Violence Against Women: Findings from the National Violence Against Women Survey,* November 1998.

55. Cited in R. Barri Flowers, *Domestic Crimes, Family Violence and Child Abuse: A Study of Contemporary American Society* (Jefferson: McFarland, 2000), p. 88.

56. Bureau of Justice Statistics, National Institute of Justice, 2001.

57. Mary P. Koss, "Hidden Rape: Sexual Aggression and Victimization in a National Sample of Students in Higher Education," in Ann W. Burgess, ed., *Rape and Sexual Assault II* (New York: Garland, 1988), pp. 3–25.

58. Flowers, *Sex Crimes, Predators, Perpetrators, Prostitutes, and Victims,* pp. 51–57; Joanne Belknap and Edna Erez, "The Victimization of Women on College Campuses: Courtship Violence, Date Rape, and Sexual Harassment," in Bonnie S. Fisher and John J. Sloan III, eds., *Campus Crime: Legal, Social, and Policy Perspectives* (Springfield: Charles C Thomas, 1995); E. J. Kanin and S. R. Parcell, "Sexual Aggression: A Second Look at the Offended Female," *Archives of Sexual Behavior 6* (1977): 67–76.

59. T. K. Logan, Carl Leukefeld, and Bob Walker, "Stalking as a Variant of Intimate Violence: Implications From a Young Adult Sample," *Violence and Victims 15* (2000): 91–111; Bonnie S. Fisher, Francis T. Cullen, and Michael G. Turner, "Being Pursued: Stalking Victimization in a National Study of College Women," *Criminology & Public Policy 1,* 2 (2002): 257–308.

60. Flowers, *Sex Crimes, Predators, Perpetrators, Prostitutes, and Victims,* pp. 55–56; Koss, "Hidden Rape;" Timothy M. Rivinus and Mary E. Larimer, "Violence, Alcohol, Other Drugs, and the College Student," in Leighton C. Whitaker and Jeffrey W. Pollard, eds., *Campus Violence: Kinds, Causes, and Cures* (Binghamton: Haworth, 1993).

61. Flowers, *Sex Crimes, Predators, Perpetrators, Prostitutes, and Victims,* pp. 55–56. See also "Dating Violence," http://www.sccadvasa.org/saacqvaince.html.

62. Martha R. Burt, "Cultural Myths and Support for Rape," *Journal of Personality and Social Psychology 38* (1980): 217–30; Patricia L. Donat and John D'Emilio, "A Feminist Redefinition of Rape and Sexual Assault: Historical Foundations and Change," in Mary E. Odem and Jody Clay-Warner, eds., *Confronting Rape and Sexual Assault* (Wilmington: Scholarly Resources Inc., 1998), pp. 43–44; James W. Messerschmidt, *Masculinities and Crime: Critique and Reconceptualization Theory* (Lanham: Rowman and Littlefield, 1993).

63. Julia R. Schwendinger and Herman Schwendinger, *Rape and Inequality* (Thousand Oaks: Sage, 1983), p. 65.

64. Flowers, *Sex Crimes, Predators, Perpetrators, Prostitutes, and Victims*, p. 29–30.

65. Amir, *Patterns in Forcible Rape*, p. 346.

66. Flowers, *Women and Criminality*, p. 39.

67. Schwendinger and Schwendinger, *Rape and Inequality*, p. 68.

68. *Ibid.*, p. 71.

69. Flowers, *Women and Criminality*, p. 40.

70. Amir, *Patterns in Forcible Rape*; Brownmiller, *Against Our Will.*

71. Lorenne M. Clark and Debra J. Lewis, *Rape: The Price of Coercive Sexuality* (Toronto: Canadian Women's Educational Press, 1977), pp. 28–31.

72. *Ibid.*, p. 131.

73. Flowers, *Women and Criminality*, p. 41.

74. See, for example, Jeanette Taylor, William G. Iacono, and Matt McGue, "Evidence for a Genetic Etiology of Early-Onset Delinquency," *Journal of Abnormal Psychology 109*, 4 (2000): 634–43; D. Fishbein, "Biological Perspectives in Criminology," *Criminology 28*, 1 (1990): 27–72; P. Brain, "Hormonal Aspects of Aggression and Violence," in A. Reiss and J. Roth, eds., *Understanding and Preventing Violence* (Washington: National Academy Press, 1993), pp. 173–244; Cesare Lombroso, *Crime, Its Causes and Remedies* (Boston: Little, Brown, 1918); E. A. Hooten, *The American Criminal: An Anthropological Study* (Cambridge: Harvard University Press, 1939).

75. Brownmiller, *Against Our Will*, pp. 13–14.

Chapter 9

DOMESTIC VIOLENCE

Domestic violence has proven to be a persistent and disturbing problem in our society and, indeed, worldwide. In a 2000 UNICEF study, it was reported that 20 to 50 percent of the world's female population will be victimized through domestic violence.[1] Experts estimate that millions of women and men were involved in domestic violence of a serious nature in the United States. Women are far more likely than men to be the victims of severe battering in an intimate relationship and, as such, most often experience injuries from domestic violence requiring medical attention or are fatal in nature. Male batterers come from all sociodeomographic groups and are often repeat offenders. Their violence toward intimates is typically a reflection of power, dominance, sexual aggression, sexual jealousy, pregnancy, stress, and related dynamics. Most abusive men are also likely to perpetrate other acts of intrafamilial violence or violent behavior outside the family.

WHAT IS DOMESTIC VIOLENCE?

Domestic violence generally refers to violence occurring within the family, usually between spouses or involving intimates or ex-intimates. According to the Family Violence Prevention Fund, domestic violence is defined as: "the actual or threatened physical, sexual, psychological or economic abuse of an individual by someone with whom they have or had an intimate relationship."[2] An expert on domestic violence defined it as "a pattern of assaultive and coercive behaviors, including physical, sexual, and psychological attacks, as well as economic coercion, that adults or adolescents use against their intimate partners."[3]

Various terms are used interchangeably to describe domestic violence including marital violence, relationship violence, spousal violence, and intimate violence–defined in the Bureau of Justice Statistics Factbook, *Violence by*

Intimates, as "violence between people who have had an intimate relationship–spouses, ex-spouses, boyfriends, girlfriends, and former boyfriends and girlfriends."[4]

Domestic violence is most often associated with violence toward female intimates, who are five to eight times more likely than male intimates to be the victims of domestic battering.[5] Battered woman or wife abuse is typically defined in broad terms as "physical beatings with fists or other objects, choking, stabbing, burning, whipping–any form of [intimate] inflicted physical violence–as well as psychological mistreatment in the form of threats, intimidation, isolation, degradation [and] mind games."[6] Some have included sexual violence such as marital rape in the definition of battered women[7] (see also Chapter 8).

According to studies on domestic violence:

- Intimate violence accounts for one in five violent crimes against females.[8]
- Ninety-five percent of domestic violence assaults on spouses or ex-spouses are committed by men against women.[9]
- The rate of female intimate violence victimization is about five times that of male intimate violence victimization.[10]
- Male intimate violence against women is much more likely to cause serious injury than female intimate violence against men.[11]
- Women are the victims in almost three out of four murders involving intimates.[12]

THE EXTENT OF INTIMATE VIOLENCE

Most research indicates that the prevalence and incidence of violence between intimates is significant and widespread. The National Crime Victimization Survey (NCVS) estimates that there are 840,000 nonlethal violent crimes involving an intimate each year in the United States.[13] According to the Department of Justice, an estimated 960,000 violent victimizations against a spouse, ex-spouse, boyfriend, girlfriend, or former boyfriend or girlfriend occur annually.[14] Murray Straus estimated that 65 percent of all married couples were involved in domestic violence, with 25 percent considered serious.[15]

Researchers have found that much of the violence between intimate partners involves being pushed, shoved, hit, slapped, and grabbed.[16] These can often lead to more serious forms of domestic violence such as choking, punching, hitting with an object, stabbing, or shooting the victim. Even less serious domestic physical assaults can have dire consequences. For instance, "a woman or man who is pushed down the stairs could suffer a concussion or even death, while a woman or man who is slapped or hit could suffer a perforated eardrum or eye injury."[v]

Data on female victims of domestic violence has yielded even higher numbers of victimization and incidents of severity. In some studies, females have been found to constitute as many as 90 percent of the victims of intimate violence.[18] A woman is physically assaulted by her husband every nine seconds in this country.[19] One in four women have ever been the victims of intimate violence.[20] About 20 percent of battered women have reported being the victims of at least three violent incidents within the past six months.[21] Nearly one-third of women admitted to hospital emergency rooms had injuries sustained through domestic violence;[22] while around one-third of all female murder victims were killed by husbands, boyfriends, or other intimates.[23]

The Commonwealth Fund estimated that 3.9 million women were beaten by husbands or live-in lovers in the United States in the last year.[24] The National Violence Against Women (NVAW) Survey estimated that 1.3 million women are the victims of nearly 4.5 million physical assaults committed by intimates every year (see Table 9.1). This amounts to an average of more than three incidents per victim, with a victimization rate of 44.2 per 1,000 persons annually.

The NVAW Survey reported that 22 percent of the women in this country have been the victims of an assault by an intimate at some point during their lifetime. An estimated 22.2 million women were ever the victims of domestic violence.[25] As shown in Table 9.2, most of the victimizations consisted of pushing, grabbing, shoving, slapping, and hitting. Nearly 8 percent of women reported ever being victimized by an intimate through the threat or actual use of a gun or knife.

The Bureau of Justice further reported that:

- Females age 16 to 24 are the most likely to be victims of domestic violence.
- While African American and white women experience similar levels of intimate violence overall, African American women experience higher levels of victimization than white women for those age 20 to 24.
- Hispanic women tend to be less victimized by domestic violence than non-Hispanic women.[26]
- Only around half the cases of domestic violence are ever reported to the police.[27]

Dating Violence

As a reflection of intimate violence, recent research has focused on the scope of dating violence. An Iowa study found that 60 percent of young

Table 9.1
ESTIMATED NUMBER OF PHYSICAL ASSAULTS PERPETRATED AGAINST
WOMEN BY INTIMATES ANNUALLY

Estimated number of victims	*Average number of victimizations per victim*	*Estimated total number of victimizations*	*Annual rate of victimizations per 1,000 persons*
1,309,062	3.4	4,450,807	44.2

Source: Adapted from U.S. Department of Justice, *Full Report of the Prevalence, Incidence, and Consequences of Violence Against Women: Findings From the National Violence Against Women Survey* (Washington: National Institute of Justice, 2000), p. 27.

Table 9.2
WOMEN PHYSICALLY ASSAULTED BY AN INTIMATE PARTNER[a] IN LIFETIME,
BY TYPE OF ASSAULT

Type of assault	*Percentage*
Total Reporting Physical Assault by Intimate Partner	**22.1**
Threw something that could hurt	8.1
Pushed, grabbed, shoved	18.1
Pulled hair	9.1
Slapped, hit	16.0
Kicked, bit	5.5
Choked, tried to drown	6.1
Hit with object	5.0
Beat up	8.5
Threatened with gun	3.5
Threatened with knife	2.8
Used gun	0.7
Used knife	0.9

[a] Intimate partners include current and former spouses, opposite-sex and same-sex cohabitating partners, boyfriends/girlfriends, and dates.
Source: Adapted from U.S. Department of Justice, *Full Report of the Prevalence, Incidence, and Consequences of Violence Against Women: Findings From the National Violence Against Women Survey* (Washington: National Institute of Justice, 2000), p. 28.

women during a six-month period were currently involved in an abusive relationship.[28] Studies show that one out of three dating females will be beaten by a boyfriend prior to reaching the age of 18.[29]

Dating violence has been found to be similar to marital violence in its dynamics. "Victims dating their batterers experience the same patterns of power and control as their counterparts in abusive marriages or cohabitation and clearly dating violence can be just as lethal."[30]

Male violence in dating relationships appears to differ from that in marital relationships insofar as the rationale given by the batterer for violent behavior. In dating situations, "young men admit to abusing their young partners in order to intimidate them into giving in to their demands, while violent husbands more commonly blame their aggression on reasons out of their control such as drinking, drugs, anger, and stress"[31] (see also Chapter 8).

Unreported Intimate Violence

In spite of the magnitude of intimate violence, much of it goes unreported. Around half of the incidents of domestic violence are never reported to law enforcement, according to the NCVS.[32] Some experts on intimate violence believe the actual number of victims who report being battered may be much lower. One estimate of reported domestic violence put it at only one in 270 cases.[33] Lenore Walker found that less than 10 percent of battered women ever reported serious intimate violence to police.[34] Common reasons given for not reporting domestic violence include fear of reprisal, denial, shame, and lack of confidence that the matter could be resolved by authorities

MALES AND FATAL
DOMESTIC VIOLENCE

Women are much more likely to be killed by an intimate partner than men. According to the Uniform Crime Reports, husbands or boyfriends were responsible for 33 percent of the murders of females in the United States in 2000, compared to wives or girlfriends accounting for just over 3 percent of the murders of males.[35] More than twice the number of women are killed by intimate partners as strangers.[36] Studies have found that about seven out of ten murdered women are the victims of a husband, ex-husband, boyfriend, or ex-boyfriend.[37] Two in three such victims of homicide are battered women.[38]

Many male perpetrators of intimate homicides kill their victims after a violent relationship had ended through separation or divorce. One study found that as many as one in two women were slain by abusive intimates after they were separated.[39] Another study reported that one in four women were the victims of murder by an intimate while attempting to separate.[40]

To put the incidence of intimate homicides by males in perspective, between 1976 and 1996, there were 31,260 female victims of domestic homicides in the United States (see Fig. 9.1). Sixty-three percent of the victims were slain by husbands, 32 percent by nonmarital intimates, and 5 percent by an ex-husband. During the same span, there were 20,311 males killed by female intimates.[41] Thirty percent of the total number of females killed over

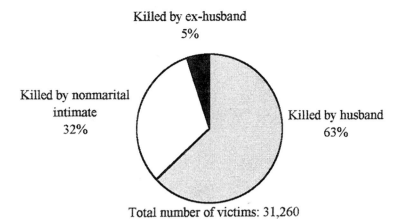

Killed by ex-husband
5%

Killed by nonmarital
intimate
32%

Killed by husband
63%

Total number of victims: 31,260

Figure 9.1. Female Victims of Homicide by Intimate Partners, 1976–1996. *Source:* Constructed from U.S. Department of Justice, Bureau of Justice Statistics Factbook, *Violence by Intimates: Analysis of Data on Crimes by Current or Former Spouses, Boyfriends, and Girlfriends* (Washington: Government Printing Office, 1998), p. 6.

the two decades was attributed to domestic violence, compared to 6 percent of the males killed.[42]

CHARACTERISTICS OF MALE BATTERERS

Abusive men in intimate relationships come from every racial, economic, and educational background. However, there are some particular characteristics that may distinguish male batterers from nonabusive men, as noted in the book, *Domestic Crimes, Family Violence and Child Abuse*:

> The battering man is typically seen as possessing a dual personality. He is regarded as either extremely charming or especially cruel. Selfishness and generosity are parts of his personality and depend upon his mood. Substance abuse, while sometimes present, is not a central feature in the battering pattern itself. On the other hand, jealousy and possessiveness are considered an integral part of mate-inflicted violence. Most batterer's greatest fear is that [the] woman will leave them.[43]

Male batterers have been identified as intractable or treatable, dependent upon their perception of the violence exhibited. "The intractable abuser finds no fault in his abusive action, whereas the treatable husband experiences guilt and remorse after the violence. In the latter instance, it is possible that with counseling the offender can learn nonviolent means of coping."[44]

After a four-year study of violent intimate relationships, Maria Roy profiled male batterers and domestic violence as follows:

- Most abusive men are between 26 and 35 years of age, followed by between the ages of 35 and 50.
- The majority of children living in domestic violence environments fall between the ages of one and 13.
- Most violent couples have joint incomes.
- Most domestic violence occurs during the first 15 years of the relationship.
- In more than two-thirds of the intimate violence cases, the battering of women occurred almost immediately after the relationship started.
- Nine out of ten abusive men do not have a criminal record.
- More than eight in ten male batterers were abused in childhood, or came from violent families.
- Significant changes in life such as unemployment, death, or moving increases the probability or level of domestic violence in long-term relationships.
- Most intimate violence is physical and does not include the use of weapons.
- More than one-third of abusive men abused alcohol, while only one-tenth were enrolled in substance abuse treatment programs.[45]

Researchers have identified three broad types of batterers:

- *Family-only batterer*–is abusive only within the family; violence tends to not be severe, with psychological or sexual maltreatment relatively rare; and little to no indication of psychopathology.
- *Dysphoric/borderline batterer*–violence can vary from moderate to severe; primarily directed toward an intimate or family member; tends to be emotionally unstable or dysphoric.
- *Violent/antisocial batterer*–intimate violent behavior ranges from moderate to severe; most likely to commit violence outside the family, have a long history of criminality and substance abuse; and psychopathology or antisocial personality disorder.[46]

Risk factors that have been associated with abusive men include witnessing intimate violence during childhood or adolescence, being the victim of child physical and/or sexual abuse, physical or sexual violence directed towards other family members, lower-class status, and chronic alcohol or drug abuse.[47]

A high percentage of batterers have been found in clinical studies to have mental disorders such as "schizoidal/borderline, personality, antisocial or narcisstic, passive dependent/compulsive disorders."[48] Violent male intimates have also been shown to possess higher levels of anger and hostility than nonviolent male intimates.[49] Studies show that abusive men may be lacking in such interpersonal skills as communication than men who are not abusive.[50]

FACTORS IN MALE BATTERING

Pregnancy and Battering

Many incidents of male violence against an intimate occur during the woman's pregnancy.[51] Studies have "frequently noted the propensity of battering husbands to punch and kick their pregnant partners in the stomach, with resultant miscarriages and injuries to their reproductive organs."[52] In one study, 42 percent of the women reported being battered during pregnancy.[53] Studies by Lenore Walker[54] and Richard Gelles[55] found a high degree of battering during a woman's first, second, and third pregnancies. Some men become violent merely in learning about the pregnancy; often continuing thereafter, including lashing out against other family members.[56]

Common dynamics shown to be involved in the onset and continuation of male violence against pregnant intimates include:

- The added strain placed on relationship and finances.
- Unplanned pregnancy.
- The number of children already in family.
- Resentment and jealousy toward unborn child.
- Sexual problems.
- Substance abuse.
- Unemployment.
- Control and power.[57]

Sexual Problems

Many abusive men become violent against their significant others because of sexual problems. Studies show that such issues as impotency, frigidity, perceived infidelity, and jealousy can play important roles in domestic violence against women.[58] These problems can lead to arguments and confrontations, escalating into physical violence. The abuser often "doubts his own virility, is insecure, possessive, and questions his wife's fidelity, at times even casting doubt on the paternity of his children."[59] Conversely, some women display sexual jealousy when suspecting a spouse of being unfaithful, which may then trigger a violent response both ways.

THEORIES ON DOMESTIC VIOLENCE

Domestic violence is often seen by experts as a reflection of a number of interrelated forces such as external stresses, a history of intrafamilial or childhood violence, substance abuse, and inadequate means in controlling violent impulses.

General theories on domestic violence typically concentrate on four primary schools of thought: psychological theories, social stress theories, social-structural theories, and social-cultural theories.

Psychological Theories

Psychological theories on domestic violence tend to focus on personality disorders. Early theorists such as W. Goode advanced that "one reason intimates commit violence against one another is that they are in each other's presence a lot, and few others can anger one so much as those who are close;"[60] while G. Levinger cited mental and emotional cruelty between divorcing spouses as significant in intimate violence.[61] However, critics have argued that psychological views on domestic violence fail to account for aggressive and violent behavior learned from violent role models or through childhood abuse.[62]

Many theorists today prefer multifactorial or interactionist approaches to domestic and family violence. For instance, K. Browne and M. Herbert advanced that aggression should be considered a social form of behavior that is controlled through a person's self-esteem, strong relationships, and stress management—which are all dependent upon one's particular personality traits and background factors.[63]

According to researchers on domestic violence: "By specifying mechanisms that connect environmental, cognitive and behavior factors, the more recent psychological models provide testable theories and suggest multiple points of entry for preventive interventions that can be adequately evaluated."[64]

Using a cultural-psychological perspective, psychologists have described battering men as adhering to traditional masculine norms or possessing a weak and immature personality.

> Enactment of compulsive masculinity, often referred to as "machismo," is an effort to maintain complete dominance over his wife. On the other extreme, many batterers' personalities contain elements of helplessness and dependency. The violent husband has been characterized as a "little boy wanting to be grown up and superior," as he's been taught he should be.[65]

Social Stress Theories

Social stress theories hold the position that domestic violence is a reflection of a patriarchal ideology or social construction, in which men are socialized as the head of the household with women being inferior and there to serve them. This perspective contends that intimate violence can occur when wives are resistant to the husband's authority role. Such theorists as Nancy Chodorow[66] and K. Daly[67] have focused on the relationship between masculinity, patriarchal ideology, and male perpetrated domestic violence. Criminality or violence under this thesis is seen as a way of attaining masculinity when other traditional means fail–such as being unemployed–and therefore unable to derive masculinity through supporting one's family.[68]

Social stress theories give prominence to social class factors such as unemployment, low income, and social isolation in explaining intimate violence. A number of studies have found a higher rate of occurrence of domestic violence among families from the lower socioeconomic class.[69] However, other research has suggested that domestic or family violence may be just as high in the middle or upper classes, even if there are more avenues available for avoiding violence.[70]

Social-Structural Theories

Social-structural theories associate domestic violence with the external and environmental influences that affect domestic life, as well as the individual interactions between spouses. R. Whitehurst theorized that increased jealousy among male spouses in response to a trend toward socioeconomic equality for women was a major factor in wife battering.[71] Murray Straus's general systems approach to domestic violence examines it as related to intrafamilial group characteristics such as beliefs, values, organization, and position within the social structure.[72] Some other theorists focus on a socialization of aggression approach in linking domestic violence to the environment.[73]

Social-Cultural Theories

Social-cultural theories tend to focus on influences outside the family in explaining domestic violence, such as socially structured inequality and cultural norms. David Gil looked at societal power struggles and its effect on domestic violence.[74] Cultural values and attitudes were noted by D. Abrahamsen as sanctioning violence as a way of life.[75]

More recently, J. Mugford and S. Mugford argued that domestic violence cannot be prevented, as it is a reflection of our culture of masculinity, gender construction, and socialization.[76]

Such prominent theories as structural-functional theory and subculture of violence theory are seen as influential in the social-cultural school of thought in studying intimate and family violence.[77] See Chapter 2 for further discussion on social and cultural theories on male criminality.

NOTES

1. Sushma Kapoor, *Domestic Violence Against Women and Girls*, UNICEF: Innocenti Research Center, 2000, http://www.sccadvasa.org/Domestic%20Violence.htm. See also Helene Henderson, *Domestic Violence and Child Abuse Sourcebook* (Detroit: Omnigraphics, 1999).

2. Family Violence Prevention Fund, San Francisco, http://www.fvpf.org.

3. Anne L. Ganley, "Understanding Domestic Violence," Family Violence Prevention Fund, http://www.fvpf.org.

4. U.S. Department of Justice, Bureau of Justice Statistics Factbook, *Violence by Intimates: Analysis of Data on Crimes by Current or Former Spouses, Boyfriends, and Girlfriends* (Washington: Government Printing Office, 1998), p. v.

5. R. Barri Flowers, *Domestic Crimes, Family Violence and Child Abuse: A Study of Contemporary American Society* (Jefferson: McFarland, 2000), p. 18.

6. *Ibid.*, p. 71.

7. *Ibid.*, pp. 82–84. See also Kersti Yllo and David Finkelhor, *License to Rape: Sexual Abuse of Wives* (New York: Free Press, 1985).

8. Flowers, *Domestic Crimes, Family Violence and Child Abuse*, p. 18; Christopher Maxwell, Joel Garner, and Jeffrey Fagan, *The Effects of Arrest on Intimate Partner Violence: New Evidence from the Spouse Assault Replication Program* (Washington: National Institute of Justice, 2001).

9. Cited in Flowers, *Domestic Crimes, Family Violence and Child Abuse*, p. 72.

10. *Ibid.*, p. 18.

11. Murray A. Straus and Richard J. Gelles, *Physical Violence in American Families: Risk Factors and Adaptations to Violence in 8,145 Families* (New Brunswick: Transaction Publishers, 1990).

12. *Violence by Intimates*, pp. 3–6.

13. *Ibid.*, p. v. See also A. Ferrante, F. Morgan, D. Indermaur, and R. Harding, *Measuring the Extent of Domestic Violence* (Sydney: Hawkins Press, 1996).

14. *Ibid.*, p. 3.

15. Cited in R. Barri Flowers, *The Victimization and Exploitation of Women and Children: A Study of Physical, Mental and Sexual Maltreatment in the United States* (Jefferson: McFarland, 1994), p. 30.

16. Flowers, *Domestic Crimes, Family Violence and Child Abuse*, pp. 14–16.

17. U.S. Department of Justice, *Full Report of the Prevalence, Incidence, and Consequences of Violence Against Women: Findings From the National Violence Against Women Survey* (Washington: National Institute of Justice, 2000), p. 27.

18. "LawLink NSW: Preventing Violence," http://www.lawlink.nsw.gov.au/cpd.nsf/pages/violrep_chapter 7.

19. Flowers, *Domestic Crimes, Family Violence and Child Abuse*, p. 72.

20. Lieberman Research, Inc., *Domestic Violence Advertising Campaign Tracking Survey*, conducted for the Advertising Council and Family Violence Prevention Fund, July–October 1996.

21. U.S. Department of Justice, Bureau of Justice Statistics, *Highlights from 20 Years of Surveying Crime Victims: The National Crime Victimization Survey, 1973–92* (Washington: Government Printing Office, 1993).

22. Flowers, *Domestic Crimes, Family Violence and Child Abuse*, p. 17.

23. U.S. Department of Justice, Federal Bureau of Investigation, *Crime in the United States: Uniform Crime Reports 2000* (Washington: Government Printing Office, 2001), p. 18.

24. The Commonwealth Fund, *First Comprehensive National Health Survey of American Women*, July 1993. See also S. Rutherford McDill and Linda McDill, *Dangerous Marriage: Breaking the Cycle of Domestic Violence* (Grand Rapids; Baker Books, 1998).

25. *Findings from the National Violence Against Women Survey*, p. 26.

26. Callie M. Rennison, *Intimate Partner Violence and Age of Victim, 1993–1999* (Washington: U.S. Department of Justice, 2001).

27. *Violence by Intimates*, p. 19.

28. Rebecca Bettin, Young Women's Resource Center, testimony at Iowa House of Representatives Public Hearing on Dating Violence, March 31, 1992.

29. S. Kuehe, "Legal Remedies for Teen Dating Violence," in Barrie Levy, ed., *Dating Violence: Young Women in Danger* (Seattle: Seal Press, 1998), p. 73.

30. Quoted in Flowers, *Domestic Crimes, Family Violence and Child Abuse*, p. 78.

31. "Final Report of the Supreme Court Task Force on Courts' and Communities' Response to Domestic Abuse," submitted to the Supreme Court of Iowa, August 1994, p. 13. See also D. Sugarman and G. Hotaling, "Dating Violence: A Review of Contextual and Risk Factors," in Barrie Levy, ed., *Dating Violence: Young Women in Danger* (Seattle: Seal Press, 1998), pp. 116–17.

32. *Violence by Intimates*, p. 19.

33. Suzanne K. Steinmetz, *The Cycle of Violence: Assertive, Aggressive, and Abusive Family Interaction* (New York: Praeger, 1977); McDill and McDill, *Dangerous Marriage*.

34. Lenore E. Walker, "Treatment Alternatives for Battered Women," in Jane R. Chapman and Margaret Gates, eds., *Women into Wives: The Legal and Economic Impact of Marriage* (Thousand Oaks: Sage, 1976), p. 144.

35. *Crime in the United States*, p. 18.

36. A. L. Kellerman and J. A. Mercy, "Men, Women, and Murder: Gender-Specific Differences in Rates of Fatal Violence and Victimization," *Journal of Trauma 33* (1992): 1–5.

37. Jacquelyn Campbell, "Prediction of Homicide of and by Battered Women," in J. Campbell and J. Milner, eds., *Assessing Dangerousness: Potential for Further Violence of Sexual Offenders, Batterers, and Child Abusers* (Thousand Oaks: Sage, 1995).

38. *Ibid.*; *Violence by Intimates*, pp. 5–6.

39. U.S. Department of Justice, Bureau of Justice Statistics, *Female Victims of Violent Crime* (Washington: Government Printing Office, 1991), p. 5.

40. *Ibid.* See also Linda Saltzman and James Mercy, "Assaults Between Intimates: The Range of Relationships Involved," in Anna Wilson, ed., *Homicide: The Victim/Offender Connection* (Cincinnati: Anderson, 1993).

41. *Violence by Intimates,* p. 6.

42. *Ibid.*; Flowers, *Domestic Crimes, Family Violence and Child Abuse,* pp. 62–64.

43. Flowers, *Domestic Crimes, Family Violence and Child Abuse,* p. 76.

44. Terry Davidson, *Conjugal Crime: Understanding and Changing the Wife-Beating Pattern* (New York: Hawthorne, 1979), p. 23.

45. Maria Roy, "Four Thousand Partners in Violence: A Trend Analysis," in Maria Roy, ed., *The Abusive Partner: An Analysis of Domestic Battering* (New York: Van Nostrand Reinhold, 1982), pp. 34–35.

46. A. Holtzworth-Munroe and G. L. Stuart, "Typologies of Male Batterers: Three Subtypes and the Differences Among Them," *Psychological Bulletin 116,* 3 (1994): 476–97; D. G. Saunders, "A Typology of Men Who Batter Women: Three Types Derived From Cluster Analysis," *American Orthopsychiatry 62* (1992): 264–75; E. W. Gondolf, "Who Are Those Guys? Toward A Behavioral Typology of Batterers," *Violence and Victims 3* (1988): 187–203.

47. G. T. Totaling and D. B. Sugarman, "An Analysis of Risk Markers in Husband to Wife Violence: The Current State of Knowledge," *Violence and Victims 1* (1986): 101–24; E. Aldarondo and D. B. Sugarman, "Risk Marker Analysis of the Cessation and Persistence of Wife Assault," *Journal of Consulting and Clinical Psychology 64,* 5 (1996): 1010–19.

48. "Male Batterers," http://www.cdc.gov/ncipc/factsheets/malebat.htm; K. L. Hamberger and J. E. Hastings, "Characteristics of Male Spouse Abusers Consistent with Personality Disorders," *Hospital and Community Psychiatry 39* (1988): 763–70.

49. "Male Batterers;" D. J. Boyle and D. Vivian, "Generalized versus Spouse-Specific Anger/Hostility and Men's Violence Against Intimates," *Violence and Victims 11* (1996): 293–317.

50. A. Holtzworth-Munroe, "Social Skill Deficits in Maritally Violent Men: Interpreting the Data Using a Social Information Processing Model," *Clinical Psychology Review 12* (1992): 605–17.

51. Flowers, *Domestic Crimes, Family Violence and Child Abuse*; A. S. Helton, M. S. McFarlane, and E. T. Anderson, "Battered and Pregnant: A Prevalence Study," *American Journal of Public Health 77* (1987): 10.

52. "Final Report of the Supreme Court Task Force," p. 18.

53. Cited in Cynthia Gillespie, *Justifiable Homicide: Battered Women, Self-Defense, and the Law* (Columbus: Ohio State University Press, 1989), p. 52.

54. Lenore E. Walker, *The Battered Woman Syndrome* (New York: Springer, 1984), p. 51.

55. Richard J. Gelles, "Violence and Pregnancy: A Note on the Extent of the Problem and Needed Services," *Family Coordinator 24* (1975): 81–86.

56. "Final Report of the Supreme Court Task Force," p. 18.

57. *Ibid.*, pp. 17–18.

58. Flowers, *Domestic Crimes, Family Violence and Child Abuse*, p. 90; E. Hilberman and L. Munson, "Sixty Battered Women," *Victimology 2*, 3–4 (1978): 460–71.

59. Flowers, *Domestic Crimes, Family Violence and Child Abuse*, p. 90.

60. W. Goode, "Violence Among Intimates," *Crimes and Violence 13* (1969): 941–77.

61. G. Levinger, "Sources of Marital Dissatisfaction Among Applicants for Divorce," *American Journal of Orthopsychiatry 36*, 5 (1966): 803–7.

62. "LawLink NSW;" K. Browne and M. Herbert, *Preventing Family Violence* (Chichester: Wiley & Sons, 1997).

63. *Ibid.*

64. "LawLink NSW."

65. R. Barri Flowers, *Women and Criminality: The Woman as Victim, Offender, and Practitioner* (Westport: Greenwood, 1987), p. 20. See also Davidson, *Conjugal Crime*, p. 29; Kathleen H. Hofeller, *Social, Psychological and Situational Factors in Wife Abuse* (Palo Alto: R. & E Research Associates, 1982), p. 39.

66. Nancy Chodorow, *Feminism and Psychoanalytic Theory* (New Haven: Yale University Press, 1989).

67. K. Daly, "Different Ways of Conceptualizing Sex/Gender in Feminist Theory and Their Implications for Criminology," *Theoretical Criminology 1*, 1 (1997).

68. H. Nancarrow, "Crime Prevention and Social Justice: Preventing Domestic Violence," unpublished MA paper, Griffith University, Queensland, 1998.

69. See, for example, *Developmental Crime Prevention Consortium, Pathways to Prevention: Developmental and Early Intervention Approaches to Crime in Australia (Full Report)* (Canberra: National Crime Prevention, 1999); Ferrante, Morgan, Indermaur, and Harding, *Measuring the Extent of Domestic Violence.*

70. See, for example, Flowers, *Domestic Crimes, Family Violence and Child Abuse*, pp. 31–35; Lenore E. Walker, *The Battered Woman* (New York: Harper & Row, 1979); Terry Davidson, *Conjugal Crime: Understanding and Changing the Wife-Beating Pattern* (New York: Hawthorne, 1979).

71. R. Whitehurst, "Violently Jealous Husbands," *Sexual Behavior 1*, 4 (1971): 32–38, 40–41.

72. Murray A. Straus, "A General System Theory Approach to a Theory of Violence Between Family Members," *Social Science Information 12*, 3 (1973): 101–25.

73. See, for example, F. Ilfeld, Jr., "Environmental Theories of Violence," in D. Danield, M. Gilula and F. Ochberg, eds., *Violence and the Struggle for Existence* (Boston: Little Brown, 1970).

74. David G. Gil, *Violence Against Children: Physical Child Abuse in the United States* (Cambridge: Harvard University Press, 1970).

75. D. Abrahamsen, *Our Violent Society* (New York: Funk and Wagnalls, 1970).

76. J. Mugford and S. Mugford, "Policing Domestic Violence," in P. Moir and H. Eijkman, eds., *Policing Australia: Old Issues, New Perspectives* (South Melbourne: MacMillan, 1992), pp. 321–51. See also D. Gil, "Societal Violence in Families," in J. M. Eekelaar and S. N. Katz, eds., *Family Violence* (Toronto: Butterworths, 1978).

77. R. Barri Flowers, *Demographics and Criminality: The Characteristics of Crime in America* (Westport: Greenwood, 1989), p. 159.

Chapter 10

STALKING

Stalking is a crime of violence, intimidation, harassment, and control. Its perpetrators often engage in aggressive behavior in fixating on a victim and psychologically, physically, and/or sexually terrorizing them. Stalking has only been recognized as a serious behavioral problem since the late 1980s, resulting in antistalking laws across the country. Although stalkers can be both male and female, the vast majority are male, while stalking victims are overwhelmingly female.

Stalking cases involving celebrity victims have drawn attention to this offense. Such notable examples include ex-Beatle John Lennon, who was shot to death by a man who had stalked him; tennis star Monica Seles, seriously injured when she was stabbed by a stalker; and the stalking of director Steven Spielberg and actor/comedian Jerry Lewis, to name a few. However, the majority of stalking victims are non-celebrities. It is believed that millions of ordinary citizens have been stalked at one time or another in their lives.

Moreover, cyberstalking has become a new and dangerous threat to society, potentially affecting even more people as the laws and criminal justice system try to keep up.

DEFINING STALKING

What is stalking? According to the National Violence Against Women (NVAW) Survey, stalking is defined as "a course of conduct directed at a specific person that involves repeated visual or physical proximity; nonconsensual communication; or verbal, written, or implied threats, or a combination thereof, that would cause a reasonable person fear."[1] In a U.S. Department of Justice Research in Brief, stalking is seen as "harassing or threatening behavior that an individual engages in repeatedly."[2] Stalking has further been defined as "an abnormal or long-term pattern of threat or harassment that (a) is directed repeatedly toward a specific individual; (b) is experienced as unwelcome or intrusive; and (c) is reported to trigger fear or concern."[3] Such behavior can include following someone, showing up at a person's home or business, making unwanted and often persistent phone calls or leaving intimidating answering machine messages, sending tormenting mail, or committing acts of vandalism against the stalking victim's property. More recently, stalking through electronic communication has been included in the definition.[4] Stalking can often escalate beyond psychological harassment and intimidation of the victim into sexual or physical assault and, in some cases, murder.

Legal definitions of stalking behavior tend to vary from one state to another. In general, states define stalking as "the willful, malicious and repeated following or harassing of another person," with a "credible threat of bodily harm."[5]

According to the Ohio stalking law: "No person by engaging in a pattern of conduct shall knowingly cause another to believe that the offender will cause physical harm to the other person or cause mental distress to the other person."[6] A minimum of two stalking incidents that can each be proven beyond a reasonable doubt are required before one can be charged with stalking. Some states include such conduct as surveillance, harassment over the phone or through the mail, lying in wait, and vandalism in their definitions of stalking;[7] or charge stalkers who fall outside the legal definition with related offenses, if applicable, such as criminal trespass and violating a protection order.

A typical example of stalking was given before a Senate Judiciary Committee, illustrating both the problem and, until recently, the frustrations on the part of the victims:

> Members of the 16-man, 2-woman Senate Judiciary Committee listened raptly as Kathleen Tobin Krueger, 34, wife of newly appointed Texas Senator Bob Krueger, delivered her tale of terror. Last summer, she said, she walked to the mailbox to find a note that read, "Look how close I can get to you. See, I could kill you right now if I wanted to."
>
> Krueger knew immediately who had written the note. For the past nine years, she and her husband and, from birth, their two daughters, have been stalked by a former employee who has rung their doorbell repeatedly, screamed obscenities over the telephone, and delivered countless death threats. When the Kruegers complained to the police, they were told that unless the harasser tried to harm them physically, there was nothing that the authorities could do.[8]

ANTISTALKING LAWS

The seriousness of stalking in this country has led to major legislative responses in attacking the problem and its perpetrators. In 1990, following the murder of actress Rebecca Schaeffer by an obsessed fan, California became the first state to enact legislation into law making stalking a crime.[9] Today, all 50 states and the District of Columbia have passed stalking legislation.[10] Stalkers can be charged with committing a felony or misdemeanor, depending on the state. This, along with such issues as violating a restraining order or repeat offenses, can result in up to ten years behind bars for a stalker.

On the federal level, passage of the Violence Against Women Act (VAWA) as part of Title IV of the Violent Crime Control and Law Enforcement Act of 1994 and reauthorized as the Violence Against Women Act of 2000, further addresses violence against women as a gender inequality issue.[11] This includes domestic violence, sexual assault, and stalking offenses. The federal interstate stalking law of 1996 also added another weapon in the fight against stalking and the victimization of women.[12]

In a report to Congress on stalking and domestic violence in 2001, it was noted: "Stalking creates a psychological prison that deprives its victims of basic liberty of movement and security in their homes. We must address these crimes effectively by working together to protect stalking victims and to hold perpetrators responsible for their criminal behavior. To eradicate stalking, we must act with the full force of the law.[13]

THE EXTENT OF STALKING

Just how big is the problem of stalking in the United States? Experts have estimated that between 20,000 and 200,000 Americans are presently being stalked.[14] An estimate by forensic psychiatrist Park Dietz put the number of women who were ever stalked at 5 percent, with approximately 200,000 women stalked annually in this country.[15] Recent indicators suggest stalking is even more prevalent. According to the NVAW Survey, around 8 percent of women and just over 2 percent of men in this country have ever been stalked (see Table 10.1). Using U.S. Census population figures, this means that an estimated 8.2 million women and two million men have been the victims of a stalker at some point in their life. The survey found that more than one million women and nearly 400,000 men are stalking victims each year in the United States.

When applying a broader definition of stalking, the prevalence rate is even higher. The NVAW Survey found that when defining stalking in terms of the victim being only slightly frightened by the stalker's conduct, lifetime prevalence rate for women increased to 12 percent and men to 4 percent.[16] The annual prevalence rates for women being stalked went from 1 percent to 6 percent, compared to men going from 0.4 percent to 1.5 percent. According

Table 10.1
NUMBER OF WOMEN AND MEN STALKED IN THE UNITED STATES, BY LIFE-TIME AND THE PAST TWELVE MONTHS[a]

| | Adult Victims of Stalking Over Lifetime | | Adult Victims of Stalking Annually | |
	Estimated Number	Percent	Estimated Number	Percent
Women	8,156,460	8.1	1,006,970	1.0
Men	2,040,460	2.2	370,990	0.4

[a] Based on estimates of persons 18 years of age and older, U.S. Bureau of the Census, Current Population Survey, 1995.
Source: Constructed from Patricia Tjaden and Nancy Thoennes, *Stalking in America: Findings From the National Violence Against Women Survey*, Research in Brief, National Institute of Justice, Centers for Disease Control and Prevention (Washington: National Institute of Justice, 1998), p. 3.

to these higher rates of prevalence, it is estimated that more than 12 million women and nearly four million men are stalked every year in the United States.[17]

Approximately 80 percent of all incidents of stalking involve females who are being victimized by stalker ex-spouses or ex-boyfriends.[18] Some experts believe that as many as 90 percent of victims of domestic violence-related fatalities had been stalked by their killers.[19]

THE NATURE OF STALKING

Stalking is a crime that affects men, women, and children, young and old, from all races and nationalities, and every walk of life. Stalkers are often ex-spouses, lovers, or others with some romantic involvement or infatuation with the victim. Other stalkers may have no direct relationship or connection to their victims but may have developed a dangerous obsession with the person who could be anything from a co-worker or neighbor to a celebrity or other well-known personality, or even a total stranger.

Females are far more likely to be victims than perpetrators of stalking. Conversely, males are much more likely to be perpetrators than victims of stalking. The NVAW Survey reported women constituted 78 percent of the stalker victims compared to men at 22 percent. Contrarily, men were identified as the stalker by 94 percent of female victims and 60 percent of male victims. Males accounted for nearly 90 percent of the stalkers of all victims.[20]

In their clinical study of stalkers, J. R. Melody and S. Gothard found that approximately 90 percent of the stalkers were males targeting females.[21] Stud-

ies have indicated that the vast majority of stalking incidents involve hetero-
sexuals, with less than 1 percent of the cases pertaining to homosexuals.[22]

Stalkers have been found in studies to be older than other types of offenders, with a high level of education.[23] R. B. Harmon, R. Rosner, and H. Owen
found that 42 percent of their stalker sample in criminal court had some high
school education, with 22 percent high school graduates, and 6 percent college graduates.[24]

While race and ethnicity do not appear to be significant demographic factors among stalkers overall, a clinical study of offenders found most offenders
to be racial or ethnic minorities.[25] R. Lloyd-Goldstein reported that immi-
grants constituted up to 10 percent of stalkers in the United States, suggesting
immigration as a risk factor in certain stalking cases.[26]

Most stalker victims tend to be young. More than half the victims surveyed
by the NVAW were between 18 and 29 years of age, with more than two in
ten between 30 and 39 years of age. The average age of a stalking victim was
28.

The NVAW Survey found that most victims are stalked by nonstrangers.
Nearly three out of every four female victims were stalked by someone they
knew. Female stalking victims are most likely to be stalked by someone with
whom they have been intimately involved, such as a current or ex-spouse, or
current or ex-mate. The survey found that almost six in ten female victims
were stalked by a romantic acquaintance.

Although men are more likely to be stalked by strangers and acquaintances than women, females are prevalently more at risk for victimization from a
stranger or acquaintance stalker.[27]

Other important findings on the nature of stalking include the following:

- Nearly nine in ten stalkers are male.
- Almost eight in ten stalking victims are female.
- More than one in two stalking victims are between age 18 and 29.
- Around half of the stalkers of intimate partners stalk while still involved
  with the victim.
- The majority of stalking cases involve nonstrangers.
- About eight in ten female stalking victims are targeted by someone they
  are familiar with.
- Nearly six in ten victimized females are stalked by an intimate.
- Around eight in ten women stalked by a current or former intimate were
  battered, and three in ten were sexually assaulted by the stalker.
- In general, there are no statistical differences in the prevalence of stalk-
  ing among racial and ethnic groups.
- Native American women have a higher rate of stalking victimization
  than women of other racial or ethnic groups.

- There is a strong correlation between stalking and other types of intimate violence.
- Under half of all stalkers directly threaten their victims.
- Around half of stalking incidents are reported to the police by victims.
- Around one in four female stalking victims obtain restraining orders against the person stalking them.
- Stalking incidents last nearly two years on average.
- Three in ten female victims of stalking undergo psychological counseling as a consequence of the stalking.[28]

STALKING OF COLLEGE STUDENTS

There is some indication that college students are at an even greater risk of stalking victimization than those in the general public. According to a study funded by the National Institute of Justice (NIJ), 13.1 percent of female students in the year surveyed were stalking victims; similarly, a survey of females in college by Elizabeth Mustaine and Richard Tewksbury yielded a six-month prevalence rate of stalking victimization at 10.5 percent.[29] These findings are considerably higher than the annual national rate of women's stalking victimization of 1 percent as reported in the NVAW Survey.

Like stalking incidents outside the college environment, most stalkers of female college students are male intimates or acquaintances of the victim. The NIJ study found that:

- More than four in ten known stalkers were boyfriends.
- Around one in four stalkers were classmates.
- One in ten nonstranger stalkers were acquaintances.
- The common types of stalking incidents were telephone calls, lying in wait, being followed, sent letters, and e-mailed.
- Two-thirds of victims reported being stalked from two to six times per week.
- Most stalking incidents involved psychological abuse.
- Around one in ten stalking situations involved a sexual assault.
- Stalking lasted on average about two months.
- Almost three in four stalking victims took some kind of action against the stalker, including avoidance and confrontation.
- Alcohol, dating relationships, and living alone were risk factors for being the target of a stalker.

Researchers have applied a lifestyle-routine theory of stalking victimization in assessing risk for college students. The theory postulates that four factors related to lifestyle or routines increase the chance of becoming a stalker's target. These include (1) being in close proximity to a motivated offender, (2) being in high-risk or dangerous circumstances that exposes one to criminality, (3) being seen as an attractive target to a perpetrator, and (4) being without adequate guardianship to act as a deterrent to a stalker.[30]

Although media stories on stalking suggest a high incidence of homicidal or serial violence on college campuses across the country, most recent studies seem to indicate that students are more vulnerable to sexual victimization than other types of stalker violence.[31]

STALKER TYPOLOGIES

Experts have established a number of stalker typologies in identifying common and different characteristics and motivating factors. According to V. J. Geberth, stalkers fit into two broad classifications: (1) *psychopathic personality stalkers* and (2) *psychotic personality stalkers.*[32] Psychopathic personality stalkers tend to be male, have no mental disorder, are familiar with the target, and have a stress factor that often precipitates the stalking. Psychotic personality stalkers may be male or female, suffer from delusions, tend to fixate on strangers, make contact with the victim, and usually have no stress element to precipitate the stalking.

In a typology reflecting the victim-offender relationship, M. A. Zona and associates broke down stalking into three categories:

- *Simple obsessional*–usually involves a prior relationship between victim and stalker. Most stalking incidents fit into this classification and it is the most dangerous for the victim. Motivation for the stalker includes desire to reestablish the relationship and revenge through intimidation and fear.
- *Love obsessional*–usually there is no previous relationship. Stalker often knows victim as a celebrity, public figure, or from the Internet. This represents the second most common group of stalkers. Many suffer from such mental disorders as bipolar disorder or schizophrenia.
- *Erotomanic*–stalking cases in which the offender has a delusion that the victim is in love with him or her. The smallest number of stalkers fit into this category. Subcategories include *primary erotomania* where there are no other major disorders suffered by the stalker, and *secondary erotomania* in which the stalking is caused by another major influencing disorder.[33]

The researchers added a fourth category called *false victimization syndrome,* in which the victim falsely accuses another, real or imagined, person of stalking in order to receive support and sympathy from others.[34]

A similar stalker typology was established by J. A. Wright and colleagues, who wrote the FBI's *Crime Classification Manual*.[35] They divided stalkers into two broad categories:

- *Non-domestic stalkers*–have no personal relationship to the person targeted. Subtypes include *organized* and *delusional* stalkers.
- *Domestic stalkers*–have a prior relationship with the targeted person and wish to reestablish to the point of violence. This category represents 60 percent of stalkers.

THE MEN WHO STALK

Stalkers can be categorized into two basic types: (1) those who stalk an intimate or acquaintance, and (2) those who stalk strangers.[36] Most male stalkers fit into the former category and include victims who are current or ex-intimate partners or otherwise acquainted. The NVAW Survey found that 38 percent of stalkers stalked females who were current or ex-wives. Another 10 percent stalked current or ex cohabitating partners, and 14 percent stalked present or former girlfriends.[37] Nearly six out of every ten cases of male stalking of females involved an intimate relationship.

Men who stalk have been further broken down into the following subtypes:[38]

- *Rejected stalkers*–turn to stalking after the relationship has ended, motivated by hopes of renewing romance or revenge. They are often the most persistent and dangerous type of stalker, as well as least likely to stop the stalking in spite of efforts taken by the victim to that effect.
- *Resentful stalkers*–stalks victim for revenge due to the victim having angered them or perceived as oppressive. Intent is to terrorize victim, who may be known or a stranger to the stalker. These men are typically paranoid and the most obsessive type of stalker. Legal remedies for discontinuing the stalking are less effective the longer it persists.
- *Predatory stalkers*–target victims with the intent to attack, often sexually, with the motivation being power over the victim and sexual gratification. These stalkers usually have a poor self-esteem and are sexual deviants. Victims can be strangers or nonstrangers. Offenders typically give no warning of stalking and plan to physically victimize.
- *Intimacy seekers*–attempt to start a romantic relationship with victim. These stalkers delusionally believe that the victim loves them and vice versa. Any type of response from the targeted person may be viewed as encouragement. They typically suffer from such mental disorders as

schizophrenia or narcissistic personality disorder and are potentially violent. They are amongst the most persistent kind of stalkers and tend to disregard legal restraints.

- *Incompetent suitors*—stalk in order to begin a romantic relationship with victim, whom they are usually acquainted with but can be a total stranger. Such men tend to have limited social and dating skills with a lower than average intelligence. These offenders usually stalk for a shorter length of time than other types and, in many instances, have stalked other victims previously. The stalking will often cease when legal steps are taken by the victim.

- *Erotomanic and morbidly infatuated stalkers*—become fixated on victim, whom they believe is in love with them. These stalkers may suffer from acute paranoia or delusions due to such mental disorders as borderline personality disorder and schizophrenia. Unless they undergo psychological and drug therapy, these men will likely not respond to legal efforts to discontinue the stalking.

Most men who stalk intimates tend to have a history of battering or sexually assaulting the victim. The NVAW survey reported that more than eight in ten stalkers had physically assaulted the female stalking victim, while more than three in ten of the stalkers had sexually abused the victim.[39] Many male stalkers were also found to have subjected the intimate targets of their stalking to emotional abuse.[40]

WHY MEN STALK

Why do men stalk? The reasons vary, as seen in the categories and subtypes of stalkers discussed. These include extreme jealousy, obsession, control, manipulation, intimidation, fear of losing the person, and other unnatural urges or responses to perceived loss of control or strong desire to be with or around the stalking victim. Sometimes the victim may be little more than a casual acquaintance and as perplexed as anyone over the stalker's interest. Notes one expert on stalking of targeted women: "They often wonder if there were signs they should have looked for that would have told them that a fascination was deadly."[41]

Nine in ten stalkers are believed to suffer from some type of mental disorder such as manic depression, paranoia, bipolar disorder, and schizophrenia. "Often, they delude themselves into believing that the victim has a romantic interest in them, a condition known as erotomania. Some of the people with these delusions are quite intelligent, but they tend to be socially isolated.

Many are withdrawn and lonely, never able to develop relationships. Most have limited sexual experience."[42]

According to psychologist James Wulach, stalkers are typically unable to deal with rejection and feelings of aggression.

> When some men suffer a blow to their self-esteem, as in unrequited love, they use aggression as a way to restore the equilibrium to their sense of self. . . . Men stalk to boost their self-esteem and restore a sense of power. It's most likely to happen with men in their twenties and thirties who are often immature and need to prove themselves.[43]

Most stalkers are persistent in their targeting of victims and the actions taken to this effect. "They will find out everything they need to know about the object of their desire–from where she lives and works to the most intimate details of her life."[44]

CYBERSTALKING

A new threat to victims from stalkers has emerged recently by way of the Internet and online services. Cyberstalking–in reference to stalking behavior through e-mail, chat rooms, and other online communication–has expanded the range and means for stalkers to operate. As such, it poses a serious issue for both would-be victims and law enforcement.

There are no reliable national figures on the extent of cyberstalking, but many experts believe it to be a widespread and growing problem, potentially affecting hundreds of thousands of computer users.[45] Nearly 40 percent of the cases in the New York Police Department's Computer Investigations and Technology Unit concern electronic harassment and threats.[46] Around 20 percent of cases in the Manhattan District Attorney's Office Sex Crimes Unit are estimated to involve cyberstalking.[47] Likewise, roughly 20 percent of the Los Angeles District Attorney's Office cases referred to its Stalking and Threat Assessment Unit are related to e-mail or other online communication.[48] It is estimated that one in four incidents of stalking women on college campuses involve cyberstalking.[49]

Similar to offline stalking, the vast majority of cyberstalkers are men and the vast majority of stalking victims are women and children. Most cyberstalking involves people intimately acquainted. However, stranger cyberstalking is also a common occurrence on the Internet. Most stalkers on and offline seek to control their victims through fear, intimidation, and harassment.

Cyberstalking differs from offline stalking primarily in the stalker's ability to stalk a victim through electronic communication anywhere in the world and with less means of detection and identification. Because cyberstalkers have various ways of terrorizing a victim (such as identity theft, message boards e-mail, and chat rooms), the effect can be just as damaging and frightening to victims. There have also been cases of cyberstalkers who become offline stalkers to the same victims.

In response to the growing threat of cyberstalking, federal and state laws have been enacted or strengthened to protect victims and go after offenders. Congress passed the Amy Boyer's Law in 2000, prohibiting the unauthorized sale or display of a person's social security number over the Internet.[50] This followed the 1999 murder of a 20-year-old woman by a man who had stalked her online, where he was able to purchase her social security number from an investigation firm.

Many states have added provisions to current stalking and harassment statutes criminalizing electronic stalking or use of computers for the purpose of stalking.[51] In spite of these measures, most experts agree that the laws and means to enforce them are not keeping pace with the cyberstalkers and the means afforded them to prey online often to unsuspecting victims.[52]

NOTES

1. Patricia Tjaden and Nancy Thoennes, *Stalking in America: Findings From The National Violence Against Women Survey*, Research in Brief, National Institute of Justice, Centers for Disease Control and Prevention (Washington: National Institute of Justice, 1998), p. 2.

2. *Ibid.*, p. 1.

3. See http://homepage.psy.utexas.edu/homepage/Group/BussLAB/stalkinghelp.org/whatisstalking.html.

4. U.S. Department of Justice, *Cyberstalking: A New Challenge for Law Enforcement and Industry*, Attorney General's Report to the Vice President (Washington: U.S. Department of Justice, 1999).

5. R. Barri Flowers, *The Victimization and Exploitation of Women and Children: A Study of Physical, Mental and Sexual Maltreatment in the United States* (Jefferson: McFarland, 1994), p. 190. See also Claire Serant, "Stalked: Any Woman Can Become a Victim of This Heinous Crime," *Essence* (October, 1993), p. 73.

6. 2903.211 O.R.C. See also http://crimevictimservices.org/victimtypes/index/stalking/definition/definition.html.

7. Tjaden and Thoennes, *Stalking in America*, p. 1.

8. Quoted in Flowers, *The Victimization and Exploitation of Women and Children*, p. 190.

9. Flowers, *The Victimization and Exploitation of Women and Children*, p. 192.

10. Donna Hunzeker, "Stalking Laws," *State Legislative Report 17*, 19 (1992): 1–6; National Criminal Justice Association, *Project to Develop a Model Anti-Stalking Code for States* (Washington: National Institute of Justice, 1993); Ellen Sohn, "Antistalking

Statutes: Do They Actually Protect Victims?" *Criminal Law Bulletin 30*, 3 (1994): 203–41.

11. Public Law 103–322.

12. 18 U.S.C. §§ 2261A (1996).

13. "Stalking and Domestic Violence Report to Congress," May 2001, Office of Justice Programs, www.ojp.usdoj.gov.

14. Cited in The Crime Library, http://www.crimelibrary.com/criminology/cyber-stalking/3.htm.

15. Park Dietz and Daniell Martell, "Threatening and Otherwise Inappropriate Letters to Members of the United States Congress," *Journal of Forensic Sciences 36*, 5 (1991).

16. Tjaden and Thoennes, *Stalking in America*, p. 4.

17. *Ibid.*

18. Cited in Marie D'Amico, "The Law vs. Online Stalking," http://www.mad-capps.com/writings/faqabout.htm.

19. "Murderous Obsession: Can New Laws Deter Spurned Lovers and Fans From 'Stalking' or Worse?" *Newsweek 120* (July 13, 1992), p. 61.

20. Tjaden and Thoennes, *Stalking in America*, p. 5.

21. J. R. Meloy and S. Gothard, "Demographic and Clinical Comparison of Obsessional Followers and Offenders with Mental Disorders," *American Journal of Psychiatry 152*, 2 (1995): 258–62. See also P. E. Mullen, M. Pathe, R. Purcell, and G. W. Stuart, "A Study of Stalkers," *American Journal of Psychiatry 156* (1999): 1244–49.

22. Meloy and Gothard, "Demographic and Clinical Comparison of Obsessional Followers and Offenders." See also P. Tjaden, N. Thoennes, and C. J. Allison, "Comparing Stalking Victimization From Legal and Victim Perspectives," *Violence and Victims 15* (2000): 7–22.

23. Cited in The Crime Library. See also J. R. Meloy, "Stalking (Obsessional Following): A Review of Some Preliminary Studies," *Aggression and Violent Behavior 1*, 2 (1996): 147–62.

24. R. B. Harmon, R. Rosner, and H. Owen, "Obsessional Harassment and Erotomania in a Criminal Court Population," *Journal of Forensic Sciences 40*, 2 (1995): 188–96.

25. *Ibid.*

26. R. Lloyd-Goldstein, "De Clerembault On-Line: A Survey of Erotomania and Stalking from the Old World to the World Wide Web," in J. R. Meloy, ed., *The Psychology of Stalking: Clinical and Forensic Perspectives* (San Diego: Academic Press, 1998).

27. Tjaden and Thoennes, *Stalking in America*, pp. 5–7.

28. *Ibid.*, pp. 2–5; U.S. Department of Justice, *Domestic Violence, Stalking, and Antistalking Legislation: An Annual Report to Congress Under the Violence Against Women Act* (Washington: National Institute of Justice, 1996).

29. Bonnie S. Fisher, Francis T. Cullen, and Michael G. Turner, *The Sexual Victimization of College Women* (Washington: National Institute of Justice, 2000), pp. 27–29; Elizabeth E. Mustaine and Richard Tewksbury, "A Routine Activity Theory Explanation of Women's Stalking Victimizations," *Violence Against Women 5*, 1 (1999): 43–62.

30. Bonnie S. Fisher, Francis T. Cullen, and Michael G. Turner, "Being Pursued: Stalking Victimization in a National Study of College Women," *Criminology & Public Policy 1*, 2 (2002): 257–308; Terance D. Miethe and Robert F. Meier, *Crime and Its Social Context: Toward an Integrated Theory of Offenders, Victims, and Situations* (Albany: State University of New York Press, 1994).

31. See, for example, Joanne Belknap and Edna Erez, "The Victimization of Women on College Campuses: Courtship Violence, Date Rape, and Sexual Harassment," in Bonnie S. Fisher and John J. Sloan III, eds., *Campus Crime: Legal, Social and Policy Perspectives* (Springfield: Charles C Thomas, 1995); Nancy A. Crowell and Ann W. Burgess, eds., *Understanding Violence Against Women* (Washington: National Academy Press, 1996); Martin D. Schwartz and Victoria L. Pitts, "Exploring a Feminist Routine Activities Approach to Explaining Sexual Assault," *Justice Quarterly 12* (1995): 9–31.

32. Vernon J. Geberth, *Practical Homicide Investigation: Tactics, Procedures and Forensic Techniques* (Boca Raton: CRC Press, 1996).

33. M. A. Zona, R. E. Palarea, and J. C. Lane, "Psychiatric Diagnosis and the Offender-Victim Typology of Stalking," in J. R. Meloy, ed., *The Psychology of Stalking: Clinical and Forensic Perspectives* (San Diego: Academic Press, 1998); M. A. Zona, K. K. Sharma, and M. D. Lane, "A Comparative Study of Erotomanic and Obsessional Subjects in a Forensic Sample," *Journal of Forensic Sciences 38* (1993): 894–903.

34. Zona, Palarea, and Lane, "Psychiatric Diagnosis and the Offender-Victim Typology of Stalking;" P. E. Mullen and M. Pathe, "The Pathological Extensions of Love," *British Journal of Psychiatry 165* (1994): 614–23.

35. J. A. Wright, A. G. Burgess, A. W. Burgess, A. T. Laszlo, G. O. McCrary, and J. E. Douglas, "A Typology of Interpersonal Stalking," *Journal of Interpersonal Violence 11*, 4 (1996): 487–503.

36. Flowers, *The Victimization and Exploitation of Women and Children*, p. 191; Doreen Orion, *I Know You Really Love Me: A Psychiatrist's Journal of Erotomania, Stalking, and Obsessive Love* (New York: Macmillan, 1997).

37. Tjaden and Thoennes, *Stalking in America*, pp. 5–6.

38. StalkingHelp.org; D. Schwartz-Watts and D. W. Morgan, "Violent versus Nonviolent Stalkers," *Journal of the American Academy of Psychiatry Law 26* (1998): 241–45; F. L. Coleman, "Stalking Behaviour and the Cycle of Domestic Violence," *Journal of Interpersonal Violence 12*, 3 (1997): 420–32.

39. Tjaden and Thoennes, *Stalking in America*, p. 8.

40. *Ibid.*; R. Barri Flowers, *Domestic Crimes, Family Violence and Child Abuse: A Study of Contemporary American Society* (Jefferson: McFarland, 2000).

41. Serant, "Stalked," p. 76.

42. Shirley Streshinsky, "The Stalker and Her Prey," *Glamour* (August 1992), p. 238.

43. Quoted in Serant, "Stalked," p. 73.

44. *Ibid.*, p. 76.

45. Trudy M. Gregorie, "Cyberstalking: Dangers on the Information Superhighway," http://www.ncvc.org/src/help/cyberstalking.html; U.S. Department of Justice,

Cyberstalking: A New Challenge for Law Enforcement and Industry—A Report From the Attorney General to the Vice President (Washington: U.S. Department of Justice, 1999).

46. "Stalking and Domestic Violence Report."

47. *Ibid.*

48. *Ibid.*

49. Cited in *Ibid.*

50. 42 U.S.C., Sec. 1320 B-23, P. L. 106–553 (2000).

51. Gregorie, "Cyberstalking: Dangers on the Information Superhighway."

52. "Stalking and Domestic Violence Report;" *Cyberstalking: A New Challenge.*

Chapter 11

OTHER VIOLENT CRIMES

A disturbing trend in recent years has been the rise in hate crimes and workplace violence in the United States. Terrorism has also made a major impact on this country, punctuated with the September 11, 2001 terrorist attack. Offenders are predominantly male in each of these forms of violence—fueled by growing racial, ethnic, religious, and sexual orientation intolerance with respect to bias-related offenses; domestic instability, stresses, strains, frustration, and often revenge where it concerns workplace violence; and usually politically-motivated violence and intimidation in perpetrating terrorist attacks. Although these forms of violent behavior may differ in their dynamics, they are similar in their masculine nature and use of male aggression, fear, and violent criminality in committing offenses. Many involved in hate crimes, workplace violence, and terrorism have precursors in their behavioral patterns and psychological makeup that make them susceptible to such antisocial conduct. Current and new laws are addressing these issues in targeting, identifying, and penalizing offenders while protecting the public from future attackers.

HATE CRIMES

What are hate crimes? According to the Justice Department, a hate crime, also referred to as a bias crime, is "a criminal offense committed against a person, property, or society which is motivated, in whole or in part, by the offender's bias against a race, religion, disability, sexual orientation, or ethnicity/national origin."[1]

Although hate crimes have had a long history in the United States, particularly with respect to acts of violence against racial and ethnic minorities,[2] only recently has the government begun to officially recognize this as a cate-

162

gory of criminality. Due to growing public concern over bias-motivated offenses, the Hate Crimes Statistics Act (HCSA) was signed into law in 1990. It required the Department of Justice to collect data on crimes "that manifest evidence of prejudice based on race, religion, sexual orientation, or ethnicity."[3]

In 1994, the Violent Crime Control and Law Enforcement Act amended the HCSA to include physical and mental disabilities as possible factors in bias crimes to be reported on. The collection of hate crime data became a permanent part of the Federal Bureau of Investigation's Uniform Crime Reporting (UCR) Program by mandate of the Church Arson Prevention Act of 1996.[4] The act was enacted as a response to a series of arson attacks aimed mostly at African American churches.[5]

The threat of hate crime violence has impacted all areas of society. A 1999 Gallup Poll found that 13 percent of people were worried about becoming a victim of a hate crimes; whereas 13 percent of respondents also said they personally knew someone they felt was capable of perpetrating a hate crime.[6] More than eight in ten racial, ethnic, and religious minorities and better than three in four homosexuals feared hate crime victimization.

The Extent of Hate Crimes

According to the UCR, there were 8,152 hate crime incidents reported in the United States in 2000 (see Table 11.1). Of these, there were 9,524 different offenses, with 10,021 victims, and 7,642 known offenders. The vast majority of incidents were single-bias.

Racial bias or prejudice was the greatest motivating factor, constituting 4,368 hate crime incidents and 5,206 offenses with 5,435 victims and 4,498 known offenders. Blacks were far more likely to be the victims of racial bias than any other race, representing more than two-thirds of those targeted.

Religious bias motivations reflected the second greatest number of incidents and offenses with 1,483; followed by sexual orientation bias with 1,330 incidents; ethnicity and nationality bias with 927 incidents; and disability bias with 36 hate crime incidents. In particular, there have been an increased number of incidents and offenses related to religious and sexual orientation biases recently. These are often reflected in circumstances or incidents that might heighten emotions in motivating hate criminality. For example, after the hijacking and crashing of four U.S. airliners in September 2001–resulting in the worst terrorism attack in U.S. history–there was a surge in bias crimes against Muslims and Arab Americans after all the suspects were identified as Muslims from the Middle East.

Table 11.1

NUMBER OF HATE CRIME INCIDENTS, OFFENSES, VICTIMS, AND KNOWN
OFFENDERS, BY BIAS MOTIVATION, 2000

Bias motivation	Incidents	Offenses	Victims[a]	Known offenders[b]
Total	**8,152**	**9,524**	**10,021**	**7,642**
Single-Bias Incidents	**8,144**	**9,507**	**10,003**	**7,632**
Race	**4,368**	**5,206**	**5,435**	**4,498**
Anti-White	886	1,061	1,091	1,182
Anti-Black	2,904	3,433	3,562	2,832
Anti-American Indian/Alaskan Native	57	62	64	58
Anti-Asian/Pacific Islander	281	317	339	273
Anti-Multi-Racial Group	240	333	379	153
Religion	**1,483**	**1,568**	**1,711**	**590**
Anti-Jewish	1,119	1,172	1,280	417
Anti-Catholic	56	61	63	33
Anti-Protestant	59	62	62	23
Anti-Islamic	28	33	36	20
Anti-Other Religious Group	173	188	211	78
Anti-Multi-Religious Group	44	46	52	18
Anti-Atheism/Agnosticism/etc.	4	6	7	1
Sexual Orientation	**1,330**	**1,517**	**1,589**	**1,471**
Anti-Male Homosexual	925	1,052	1,089	1,112
Anti-Female Homosexual	181	213	230	173
Anti-Homosexual	182	210	226	153
Anti-Heterosexual	22	22	24	18
Anti-Bisexual	20	20	20	15
Ethnicity/National Origin	**927**	**1,180**	**1,232**	**1,037**
Anti-Hispanic	567	745	773	711
Anti-Other Ethnicity/National Origin	360	435	459	326
Disability	**36**	**36**	**36**	**36**
Anti-Physical	20	20	20	22
Anti-Mental	16	16	16	14
Multiple-Bias Incidents[c]	**8**	**17**	**18**	**10**

[a] The term *victim* may refer to a person, business, institution, or society as a whole.

[b] The term *known offender* does not imply that the identity of the suspect is known, but only that an attribute of the suspect is identified which distinguishes him/her from an unknown offender.

[c] A *multiple-bias incident* is any hate crime in which two or more offense types were committed as a result of two or more bias motivations.

Source: U.S. Department of Justice, Federal Bureau of Identification, *Crime in the United States: Uniform Crime Reports 2000* (Washington: Government Printing Office, 2001), p. 60.

Multiple bias crimes are relative rare. Only eight such incidents were reported to the FBI in 2000, involving 17 offenses and 18 victims, with ten known offenders.

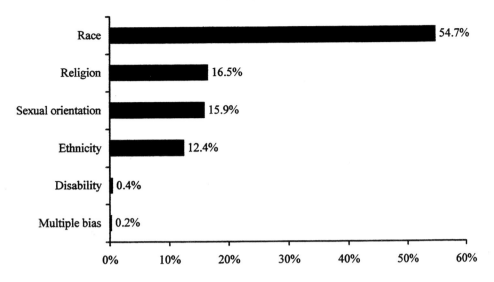

Figure 11.1. Bias-Motivated Offenses, 2000. *Source:* Derived from U.S. Department of Justice, Federal Bureau of Investigation, *Crime in the United States: Uniform Crime Reports 2000* (Washington: Government Printing Office, 2001), p. 62.

Over half of all hate crimes in 2000 were racially motivated (see Fig. 11.1). Nearly 55 percent of offenses were motivated by racial bias, 16.5 percent a religious bias, 15.9 percent a sexual orientation bias, and 12.4 percent were a reflection of an ethnicity/nationality bias. Less than 1 percent of the hate crimes were motivated by disability or multiple biases.

Some notable hate crimes can be seen as follows:

- On June 12, 1963, NAACP activist Medgar Evars was shot to death in Jackson, Mississippi. More than three decades later, white supremacist Byron De La Beckwith was convicted of the crime.
- On January 10, 1966, black civil rights worker Vernon Dahmer was the victim of a firebombing in Mississippi. Following five trials for the murder, former Ku Klux Klan leader Samuel Bowers was found guilty of the murder in August 1998.
- On January 7, 1973, Mark Robert Essex, an African American, sat atop a Howard Johnson Motor Lodge in New Orleans. Armed with a rifle, he shot to death six people, wounding 15 others, before being killed by a Marine sharpshooter. Essex reportedly had developed a hatred for whites.
- On December 19, 1986, a group of white youths used bats and fists to severely beat three African Americans in Howard Beach in New York. One of the victims was struck and killed by a car while trying to escape his attackers.

- On October 12, 1998, gay college student Matthew Shepard was beaten to death by Aaron McKinney and Russell Henderson in Laramie, Wyoming. Both men received life sentences behind bars. The vicious murder increased efforts toward new anti-hate legislation.[7]

Most hate crimes reported to law enforcement are crimes against persons (see Table 11.2). Nearly two-thirds of bias-motivated offenses in 2000 were crimes against persons, representing 6,223 offenses and victims with 6,266 known offenders. Intimidation occurred most often among crimes against persons, constituting almost 53 percent of the total. This was followed by simple assault and aggravated assault, at 26 percent and 20.5 percent of the total, respectively.

Crimes against property accounted for more than one-third of the reported hate crimes, consisting of 3,242 offenses, with 3,739 victims and 1,653 known offenders. The vast majority of these crimes were property destruction, damage, or vandalism, followed by robbery, burglary, and larceny-theft.

Less than 1 percent of all bias-motivated offenses reported to law enforcement were classified as crimes against society.

Most experts believe that the majority of bias-related crimes are either never reported or misclassified by law enforcement authorities. It is estimated that there are anywhere from 10,000 to 40,000 hate crimes in the United States annually.[8] As many of these are directed toward racial and ethnic minorities and homosexuals, their strained relations with police and often within their communities contributes to the low reporting rate and failure by police departments to recognize them as a bias crime.

Who Are the Perpetrators of Hate Crimes?

Most hate crimes are committed by young white males.[9] According to the UCR, 64.2 percent of known offenders of bias crimes in 2000 were white (see Fig. 11.2). Black offenders made up 18.9 percent of the total, with 7.2 percent of other races, and 9.7 percent of unknown races.

Common perception is that the majority of hate crimes are committed by neo-Nazis, skinheads, or other hate groups. However, research suggests otherwise. For example, in a study of 1,459 hate crimes perpetrated in Los Angeles between 1994 and 1995, less than 5 percent of the perpetrators belonged to an organized hate group.[10]

Young people are responsible for committing a high proportion of hate crimes in this country. Fifty-six percent of all bias-motivated homicides are committed by persons under the age of 21.[11] Many of these youths are seen as thrill-seekers, as opposed to persons considered hardcore in their hatred. In

Table 11.2
NUMBER OF OFFENSES, VICTIMS, AND KNOWN OFFENDERS,
BY OFFENSE, 2000

Offense	Offenses	Victims[a]	Known offenders[b]
Total	**9,524**	**10,021**	**7,642** (c)
Crimes against persons	**6,223**	**6,223**	**6,266** (c)
Murder and nonnegligent manslaughter	19	19	26
Forcible rape	4	4	5
Aggravated assault	1,274	1,274	1,734
Simple assault	1,616	1,616	2,062
Intimidation	3,294	3,294	2,421
Other[d]	16	16	18
Crimes against property	**3,242**	**3,739**	**1,653** (c)
Robbery	139	160	327
Burglary	138	158	76
Larceny-theft	114	121	81
Motor vehicle theft	11	12	10
Arson	52	70	48
Destruction/damage/vandalism	2,766	3,193	1,092
Other[d]	22	25	19
Crimes against society[d]	**59**	**59**	**78** (c)

[a] The term *victim* may refer to a person, business, institution, or society as a whole.

[b] The term *known offender* does not imply that the identity of the suspect is known, but only that an attribute of the suspect is identified which distinguishes him/her from an unknown offender.

[c] The actual number of known offenders is 7,642. Some offenders, however, may be responsible for more than one offense and are, therefore, counted more than once in this table.

[d] Includes additional offenses collected in NIBRS.

Source: U.S. Department of Justice, Federal Bureau of Identification, *Crime in the United States: Uniform Crime Reports 2000* (Washington: Government Printing Office, 2001), p. 61.

a Northeastern University study of hate crimes, 60 percent of offenders committed their crimes for the thrill of it.[12]

Drugs or alcohol are often factors in hate crime offenses. However, most such crimes are primarily a reflection of prejudice against those targeted, "a situation that colors people's judgment, blinding the aggressors to the immorality of what they are doing."[13] This prejudice or hatred is typically borne out of "an environment that disdains someone who is 'different' or sees that difference as threatening. One expression of this . . . is the perception that society sanctions attacks on certain groups."[14] For instance, "in some settings, offenders perceive that they have societal permission to engage in violence against homosexuals."[15]

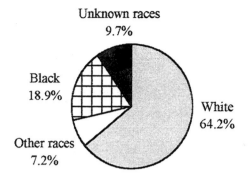

Figure 11.2. Known Offenders of Hate Crimes, by Race, 2000. *Source:* Derived from U.S. Department of Justice, Federal Bureau of Investigation, *Crime in the United States: Uniform Crime Reports 2000* (Washington: Government Printing Office, 2001), p. 61.

Types of Hate Crime Offenders

Researchers have identified different types of persons who commit hate crimes, including thrill seekers, reactive offenders, hardcore fanatics, and self-defense assailants:

- *Thrill seekers* are the most common type of hate crime perpetrator. They are typically adolescent youths who commit assaultive hate crimes out of boredom, for fun, excitement, and a feeling of power.
- *Reactive offenders* are the second most common type of perpetrator of hate crimes. They view their actions as a response to such things as a remark by the victim, interracial dating, community integration, or separation from a battered wife.
- *Hardcore fanatics* are hate crime offenders reflecting a racial, ethnic, religious, or sexual orientation bigotry ideology. They are often members, or potential ones, of an extremist group.
- *Self-defense assailants* perceive their acts of hatred as self-defense. This is particularly true when attacking homosexuals, whom they see as sexual predators seeking to proposition them.[16]

WORKPLACE VIOLENCE

The workplace has been referred to by the Department of Justice as the most dangerous place to be in the United States. According to the National Crime Victimization Survey, workplace violence is defined as "violent acts against a person at work or on duty, including physical assaults (rape and sexual assault and aggravated and simple assault) and robbery. Attempts are included with complete victimizations."[17]

The Centers for Disease Control has classified violence in the workplace as a national epidemic. Workplace homicide has become the fastest growing category of homicide in the United States, and the leading cause of death on the job for women and second leading cause for men.[18] Males are predominantly likely to be the perpetrators of lethal violence in the place of work. The following recent examples of deadly workplace violence attests to its chilling impact on society, victims, and offenders:

- On August 21, 1986, a 44-year-old heavily armed part-time postal worker, Patrick Sherrill, entered the post office in Edmond, Oklahoma and opened fire. He killed 14 employees and wounded six others, before shooting himself to death.

- On December 7, 1987, David Burke, a former employee of Pacific Southwest Airlines' parent company, boarded their Flight 1771. He shot the pilots in flight, causing the jet to crash into a California hillside. All 43 on board were killed.

- On February 16, 1998, 39-year-old Richard Farley, obsessed with a female coworker at a Silicon Valley defense plant, entered the company's Sunnyvale, California offices where he shot to death seven and wounded four. He was convicted and sentenced to death.

- On July 29, 1999, 44-year-old day trader Mark Barton entered two brokerage firms in Atlanta, Georgia. He shot to death nine workers and injured 12 before eventually committing suicide. Earlier he had bludgeoned to death his wife and two young children.

- On November 2, 1999, 40-year-old Byran Uyesugi, a Xerox employee, entered the Xerox Corporation building in Honolulu, Hawaii, where he shot and killed seven people. He was convicted on all counts and sentenced to life in prison.

- On March 20, 2000, 28-year-old Robert Harris, a disgruntled ex-employee, shot to death five people at a car wash in Dallas, Texas. He was convicted and given a death sentence.

- On December 26, 2000, Michael McDermott, a software engineer for the Internet consulting firm Edgewater Technology, entered the workplace in Wakefield, Massachusetts. Heavily armed, he fatally shot seven people. He was convicted on seven murder counts and sentenced to life in prison.

- On February 7, 2001, 66-year-old former employee, William Baker, entered the International Truck and Engine Corporation plant near Chicago, Illinois. He shot to death four employees, before committing suicide.[19]

Although workplace homicide is rare, the threat and reality of such violence has permeated throughout society and the fear it causes. According to a Gallup Poll, more than four in ten persons were worried to some degree about the threat of workplace violence.[20] Four in ten respondents were not confident that there were appropriate security measures at their workplace to prevent violence.

The Scope of Workplace Violence

Most experts on workplace violence concur that it is a growing and costly problem. According to the U.S. Department of Labor's Occupational Safety and Health Administration (OSHA), homicide represents the second leading cause of occupational injury resulting in death in the United States.[21] Almost 1,000 workers are homicide victims and an estimated 1.5 million are victims of assault in the United States annually.[22] Domestic violence on the job accounts for 30,000 to 40,000 incidents of workplace violence each year, according to the Bureau of Justice Statistics;[23] with firearms used in nearly two-thirds of the fatal domestic homicides in this country.[24] The Justice Department supports these findings, reporting that nearly two million people are victims of violence in the workplace in the United States each year.[25] One in four workers is threatened, harassed, or assaulted on the job with medical costs estimated at $13.5 billion annually.

Assaults constitute the most common type of workplace violence. As shown in Table 11.3, from 1993 to 1999, there were nearly 1.3 million simple assaults in the workplace on average annually, representing 75.2 percent of all occupational victimizations nationwide. There were 325,500 reported aggravated assaults each year, comprising nearly 19 percent of the offenses. This was followed by 70,100 robberies and 36,500 rape and sexual assaults, representing 4.0 percent and 2.1 percent, respectively, of all workplace violence annually. There were 900 workplace homicides each year, constituting less than 1 percent of all crimes.

In a national survey of U.S. workers, 42 percent said that verbal abuse occurred at the workplace, with 29 percent saying that they had been verbally abusive.[26] This can often be a precursor to more serious acts of aggression. One in ten respondents reported working in an atmosphere where physical violence had taken place, while 14 percent said that angry or disgruntled workers had damaged equipment or machinery on the job.

Other findings on the nature of workplace violence include:

- Around four in ten victims of nonfatal workplace violence knew their attacker.
- Male victims outnumbered female victims by around two to one.

Table 11.3
VICTIMS OF WORKPLACE VIOLENCE, 1993–1999

Type of violence	Annual average	Percent
Total	1,744,300	100.0
Homicide	900	0.1
Rape/Sexual assault	36,500	2.1
Robbery	70,100	4.0
Aggravated assault	325,000	18.6
Simple assault	1,311,700	75.2

Source: U.S. Department of Justice, Bureau of Justice Statistics Special Report, *Violence in the Workplace, 1993–99* (Washington: Office of Justice Programs, 2001), p. 2.

- Almost nine in ten victims of workplace violence are white.
- Around seven in ten victims are between 25 and 49 years of age.
- More than eight in ten rape or sexual assault victims are female.
- Nearly three in four victims of aggravated assault are male.
- Workplace victimizations are largely intraracial.
- Around 12 percent of nonfatal violence on the job involves injury to the victim.
- More than two-thirds of physical and verbal assaults in the workplace are perpetrated by strangers or customers.
- Intimates are the perpetrators in around 1 percent of all workplace violence.
- More than eight in ten workplace homicides were perpetrated with a gun.
- Nearly four in ten robberies on the job occur against victims in the retail or transportation sector.
- Workplace victimizations occur most often in law enforcement, followed by retail sales, medical work, teaching, and transportation.[27]

Who Are the Perpetrators of Workplace Violence?

Males are overwhelmingly responsible for much of the workplace violence. Between 1993 and 1999, more than 82 percent of the workplace violence committed in the United States was perpetrated by male offenders (see Table 11.4). Another two percent of violence on the job involved male and female perpetrators.

More than five out of ten offenders were white, with around three in ten black, and less than one in ten of another race. Most perpetrators of workplace violence were age 30 and over, constituting more than four of every ten

Table 11.4
CHARACTERISTICS OF OFFENDERS WHO COMMITTED WORKPLACE
VIOLENCE, 1993–1999

Characteristics of offenders	Percent of violent workplace victimizations[a]
Gender	100.0
Male	82.3
Female	13.0
Male and female	2.0
Unknown	2.7
Race	100.0
White	54.7
Black	30.2
Other	9.2
More than one race	1.8
Unknown	4.0
Age	100.0
Under 17	13.5
18 to 20	7.0
21 to 29	26.1
30 or older	43.0
Mixed ages	5.0
Age unknown	5.3
Number of Offenders	100.0
One	85.7
Two	5.9
Three	2.5
Four or more	3.3
Number unknown	2.6

[a] Details may not add to totals because of rounding.
Source: U.S. Department of Justice, Bureau of Justice Statistics Special Report, *Violence in the Workplace, 1993–99* (Washington: Office of Justice Programs, 2001), p. 7.

offenders. Just over one in four offenders were 21 to 29 years of age. The perpetrator of violence in the workplace operated alone in nearly 86 percent of the incidents.

A profile of the typical workplace violence offender has been established as follows:

• White male.
• Thirty-five to 45 years old.
• A loner without close family relations or social network.
• Often disgruntled.
• Relates to violence.

Table 11.5
WHETHER THE OFFENDER IN WORKPLACE VIOLENCE WAS ARMED,
BY VICTIM'S OCCUPATION, 1992–1996

	Percent of violent victimizations in the workplace		
Victim's occupation	*Offender armed*	*Offender unarmed*	*Unknown*
Medical	7.2	89.2	3.5
Mental health	14.9	83.5	1.6 (a)
Teaching	11.9	82.4	5.7
Law enforcement or security	21.5	75.1	3.4
Retail sales	26.6	65.6	7.9
Transportation	34.3	55.3	10.4
Other	20.6	71.9	7.6

ᵃ Fewer than ten sample cases.
Source: U.S. Department of Justice, Bureau of Justice Statistics Special Report, *Workplace Violence 1992–96* (Washington: Government Printing Office, 1998), p. 5.

- Tends to blame others when things go awry.
- Is unable to take criticism well.
- Problem with substance abuse.
- Has a fascination with firearms and other lethal weapons.[28]

An estimated 20 percent of all workplace violent episodes are perpetrated by an armed offender. The relationship between workplace violence and the perpetrator being armed varies depending on the victim's occupation. As shown in Table 11.5, between 1992 and 1996, the offender was most likely to possess a gun, knife, or other weapon for violence against transportation, retail sales, and law enforcement or security workers. They were least likely to carry a weapon in medical, teaching, and mental health workplace violence. More than one-third of transportation violence victimizations involved an armed perpetrator; whereas more than one-fourth of retail sales and over two in ten law enforcement or security workplace victimizations were perpetrated by an offender carrying a gun, knife, or other weapon.

Studies reveal that as many as 85 percent of the persons who commit workplace violence exhibit warning signs. These include:

- Previous history of violence towards women, children, or animals.
- Emotional difficulties such as depression or low self-esteem.
- Bad temper
- Poor hygiene.
- Frequent mood swings.
- Substance abuse, including drug abuse, alcohol abuse, or both.

- Career troubles such as long-term employment on same job, an inconsistent employment history, or recent termination.
- Threatening colleagues and/or supervisors.
- Poor relationships with other people.
- Increase in domestic troubles.
- Suicidal ideation.
- An obsession with weapons, a person, violent acts, the job, extremists, or something else.[29]

Causes of Workplace Violence

Workplace violence can occur for a number of reasons, including relationship or family difficulties, job stresses, financial troubles, mental problems, and road rage. Many experts believe that one of the greatest predictors of violence in the workplace is the conditions on the job that may foster violent behavior. Increased workloads, promotions, demotions, overcrowding, and lack of policies to deal with employee issues can all contribute to or trigger job rage.

Some blame the strong economy of recent years and a shortage of workers as a result for an increase in workloads and stress on the job. According to one expert on workplace violence: "Stress in the workplace, and the pressure to produce, is uncommonly high. More people are being asked to do more than they can handle."[30] This can often manifest itself into "all these different rages–road rage, air rage, whatever rage."[31]

Overcrowding in the workplace is seen by many as a growing problem and symptom of workplace crime and violence. This is particularly true in big cities with a high rate of occupancy. Employers are often forced to spend increasingly more per square foot of space and, as such, seek to squeeze as many employees into cramped areas as possible to maintain or increase profits. Already overstressed, overworked employees can react negatively in some respect, including violently.

Those who are already on the edge from other personal or professional troubles are at particular risk to lash out in workplace violence. Symptoms of such potential rage include insomnia, hypertension, and alcohol and drug abuse. As more employers recognize the signs of workers who may become violent, more can be done to prevent violence from occurring in the workplace.

TERRORISM

Terrorism has become one of the most frightening and examined forms of male violence in the United States in recent years, with the Oklahoma City bombing in 1995 and the September 2001 terrorist attack on America. Although violent street crime is much more common in this country, the devastation that a crime of terrorism can bring makes it an important issue to confront. The recent passage of the U.S.A. Patriot Act and stepped up federal efforts at prosecuting and incarcerating terrorists as part of the war on terrorism illustrates this very point.[32]

What exactly is terrorism? The term *terrorism* originated in the late 1700s during the French Revolution, reflecting what was known as the Reign of Terror, in which violence was used by some revolutionists to seize and maintain power.[33] The dictionary defines terrorism as "(1) the political use of violence or intimidation and (2) the systematic use of terror especially as a means of coercion."[34]

According to Title 22 of the U.S. Code, the definition of terrorism is "premeditated, politically-motivated violence perpetrated against noncombatant targets by subnational groups or clandestine agents, usually intended to influence an audience."[35] *International terrorism* is defined as terrorism "involving the territory or the citizens of more than once country;"[36] while a "terrorist group" is defined as "any group that practices, or has significant subgroups that practice international terrorism."[37]

Terrorist Attacks Against the U.S. and American Interests

There have been a number of deadly terrorist attacks in recent years against America, both in the United States and abroad. Some of the most notable are as follows:

- On February 26, 1993, a truck bomb exploded in the underground parking garage of New York's World Trade Center, killing six and injuring more than 1,000 people. Mastermind Ramzi Yousef, a 29-year-old Kuwati, and five other Islamic extremists were convicted for the crimes and sent to prison.
- On April 19, 1995, a bomb exploded inside a Ryder rental truck parked outside the Alfred P. Murrah Federal Building in Oklahoma City, Oklahoma. The powerful explosion killed 168 people and wounded hundreds of others. A 29-year-old Gulf War veteran, Timothy McVeigh, and 40-year-old Terry Nichols, were tried and convicted of the terrorist attack. McVeigh received a death sentence and was executed in June 2001, while Nichols received a life sentence in prison.
- On June 25, 1996, a fuel truck packed with explosives detonated outside the Al Khubar U.S. military housing complex near Dhahran, Saudi Ara-

bia, killing 19 Americans in the military and wounding 372 others. On June 21, 2001, 14 terrorists were indicted for the attack.

- On August 7, 1998, terrorists exploded bombs at the U.S. Embassies in Nairobi, Kenya and Dar es Salaam, Tanzania, killing 224 people, including 12 Americans, and injuring more than 1,000 others. Terrorist Osama bin Laden and his Al Qaeda network were blamed for the attack. In November 1998, a Federal Grand Jury indicted bin Laden on charges in connection with the attack.
- On September 11, 2001, 19 Muslim extremists and members of Al Qaeda hijacked four American airliners, crashing two into the twin towers of the World Trade Center in New York, causing both to collapse. A third plane crashed into the Pentagon in Washington, D.C., and the fourth airliner crashed in a field in Pennsylvania. Nearly 3,000 people lost their lives in the deadliest terrorist attack in U.S. history.[38]

Although American terrorists such as Timothy McVeigh and the "Unabomer," Theodore Kaczynski, as well as terrorist-related organizations in this country such as the Ku Klux Klan and People for the Ethical Treatment of Animals (PETA), have left their mark on society through their deadly acts of terrorism, the majority of terrorist attacks against America and U.S. interests are perpetrated by international terrorists. As shown in Table 11.6, between 1981 and 2000, there were 2,939 casualties involving American citizens as a result of international terrorism. Of these, 670 Americans were killed and 2,269 wounded. Prior to the September 2001 terrorist attack, most terrorist-related casualties occurred outside the United States.

For terrorist attacks that do occur in this country, bombings are the most likely form of attack. Between 1980 and 1999, more than 70 percent of the terrorist incidents were bombings (see Table 11.7). Kidnappings, assaults, hijackings, and assassinations made up the next most common incidents of terrorism. During this time span, terrorist attacks took place most often in the Northeast, Puerto Rico, and the West.

Characterizing the Terrorist

Terrorists are typically young males, often poor, who are "easily influenced by radial extremists and their message of hatred towards and violence against groups, governments, and individuals."[39] Notes one terrorism expert: "The receptivity of young men to terror's radical message is enormously increased by [the] legacy of conflict, dislocation, and . . . poverty."[40]

However, some point out that even those from wealthy Western nations can be susceptible to the message. "These people can still powerfully identify with communities elsewhere that they believe have been exploited, vic-

Table 11.6
CASUALTIES RESULTING FROM INTERNATIONAL TERRORISM INVOLVING
U.S. CITIZENS, BY TYPE OF CASUALTY, 1981–2000

| | U.S. Citizens | | |
	Total	*Killed*	*Wounded*
Total	2,939	670	2,269
1981	47	7	40
1982	19	8	11
1983	386	271	115
1984	42	11	31
1985	195	38	157
1986	112	12	100
1987	54	7	47
1988	231	192	39
1989	34	16	18
1990	43	9	34
1991	23	7	16
1992	3	2	1
1993	1,011(a)	7	1,004
1994	11	6	5
1995	70	10	60
1996	535(b)	25	510
1997	27	6	21
1998	23	12	11
1999	11	5	6
2000	62	19	43

[a] The bombing of the World Trade center in New York City on February 26, 1993 accounts
for this increase.
[b] The bombing of the Al Khubar U.S. military housing complex near Dhahran, Saudi Arabia
on June 25, 1996 accounts for this increase.
Source: U.S. Department of Justice, Bureau of Justice Statistics Special Report, *Sourcebook of
Criminal Justice Statistics 2000* (Washington: Government Printing Office, 2001), p. 348.

timized, reduced to crushing poverty, or otherwise treated with disrespect."[41]
With respect to radical Islamic extremists, their grievances "are often
expressed as anger over American policy toward Israel and Iraq and American support for 'un-Islamic' Middle Eastern governments."[42]

Suicide terrorists tend to regard their deaths not as suicide, but rather mar-
tyrdom for the cause. Terrorist organization leaders are viewed as "cold and
rational, rather than suicidal. For them, suicide terrorism has inherent tactical
advantages over 'conventional' terrorism."[43] These advantages include keeping operational costs low, while ensuring mass causalities and damage with no
captured terrorists to reveal information about the terrorist group and their
activities.

Table 11.7
TERRORIST INCIDENTS, BY TYPE OF INCIDENT AND REGION,
UNITED STATES, 1980–1999

Terrorist Incident	Number
Total	457
Type of Incident	
Bombing attacks[a]	321
Malicious destruction of property; sabotage	15
Shootings	19
Hostile takeover	10
Arson	19
Kidnapping; assaults; hijackings; assassinations	31
Robbery; attempted robbery	13
Other	29
Region	
Northeast	140
North Central	52
South	68
West	82
Puerto Rico	103
Other/Unknown	12

[a] Includes detonated and undetonated devices, tear gas, pipebombs, letterbombs, and fire-bombs.

Source: U.S. Department of Justice, Federal Bureau of Investigation, *Terrorism in the United States, 1999* (August 28, 2001), pp. 28, 41, http://www.fbi.gov/publications/terror/terror99.pdf.

Terrorists and Masculinity

The relationship between terrorism and masculinity has been studied by some researchers.[44] American terrorists and Middle Eastern terrorists have common masculine traits of young malehood, disenfranchisement, anger against those they oppose, political agenda for their actions, and an exaggerated sense of power in inflicting their terror on innocent victims.

American white terrorists—often seen as white supremacists—typically vent their frustrations on racial, ethnic, religious, and gender minorities. According to Michael Kimmel, these terroristic white supremacists offer men "the restoration of their masculinity—a manhood in which individual white men control the fruits of their own labor and are not subject to emasculation by Jewish-owned finance capital or a black and feminist-controlled welfare state."[45]

Middle Eastern terrorists, such as Al Qaeda, oppose globalization and the influence of the West in the Middle East. Their anger or political agenda is directed largely toward America and those leaders of Arab states who they see as buckling under to American interests. Some experts view Middle Eastern terrorism as "fueled by a fatal brew of antiglobalization politics, convoluted Islamic theology, and virulent misogyny. . . . Central to their political ideology is the recovery of manhood from the emasculating politics of globalization."[46]

Kimmel argued that among terrorists, it is their masculinity, sense of entitlement, and frustrations in achieving goals that drives their anger in committing acts of terrorism.[47]

NOTES

1. U.S. Department of Justice, Federal Bureau of Investigation, *Crime in the United States: Uniform Crime Reports 2000* (Washington: Government Printing Office, 2001), p. 59.

2. R. Barri Flowers, *Minorities and Criminality* (Westport: Greenwood, 1988); Jeannine Bell, *Policing Hatred: Law Enforcement, Civil Rights, and Hate Crime* (New York: New York University Press, 2002).

3. *Crime in the United States*, p. 60; 28 U.SC. 534.

4. *Crime in the United States*; 18 U.S.C. 247; Frederick M. Lawrence, *Punishing Hate: Bias Crimes and American Law* (Cambridge: Harvard University Press, 2002).

5. Cited in http://www.civilrights.org/issues/hate/history/index.html; Bell, *Policing Hatred*.

6. George Gallup, Jr. and Alec Gallup, *The Gallup Poll Monthly*, No. 401 (Princeton: The Gallup Poll, 1999), pp. 28–29.

7. R. Barri Flowers and H. Loraine Flowers, *Murders in the United States: Crimes, Killers and Victims of the Twentieth Century* (Jefferson: McFarland, 2001), pp. 178–82.

8. William Lin, "Perpetrators of Hate," *Yale Political Quarterly 19*, 2 (1997): 12; James Bennett, "Clinton Backs Expanding Definition of a Hate Crime," *New York Times* (November 11, 1997), p. A20.

9. See http://www.civilrights.org/pulications/cause_for_concern/p.10.html; http://www.teemings.com/issue05/hatecrimes.html.

10. American Psychological Association, 1998, http://www.apa.org/pubinfo/hate/#who.

11. Cited in Lin, "Perpetrators of Hate."

12. Cited in http://www.civilrights.org/publications/cause_for_concern/p.10.html.

13. See http://www.apa.org/pubinfo/hate/#who.

14. *Ibid.*

15. *Ibid.*

16. See http://www.civilrights.org/publications/cause_for_concern/plo.html; http://www.education.mcgill.ca/455-410-03/abdou/hate3.htm.

17. U.S. Department of Justice, Bureau of Justice Statistics Special Report, *Workplace Violence, 1992–96* (Washington: Office of Justice Programs, 1998), p. 1.

18. Cited in http://workplace-violence-hq.com/. See also Martin Gill, Bonnie Fisher, and Vaughan Bowie, eds., *Violence at Work* (Devon: Willan Publishing, 2001).

19. Flowers and Flowers, *Murders in the United States*, pp. 78–83; Stephanie Armour, "Employers' New Measures to Fight Workplace Violence," *USA Today* (May 9, 2002), http://www.usatoday.com.

20. George Gallup, Jr. and Alec Gallup, *The Gallup Monthly*, No. 410 (Princeton: The Gallup Poll, 1999), p. 32.

21. Cited in Louisiana Department of Justice, "Violence in the Workplace," http://www.laag.org/violence.shtml.

22. *Ibid.*

23. *Ibid.*

24. *Ibid.*

25. *Workplace Violence, 1992–96*, p. 1; U.S. Department of Justice, Bureau of Justice Statistics Special Report, *Violence in the Workplace, 1993–99* (Washington: Office of Justice Programs, 2001), p. 1.

26. Cited in http://www11.cnn.com/2000/CAREER/trends/11/15/rage/.

27. *Violence in the Workplace, 1993–99*, p. 1; *Workplace Violence, 1992–96*, pp. 1–4.

28. Jurg W. Mattman, "Preventing Violence in the Workplace," http://www.noworkviolence.com/articles/preventing_violence.htm.

29. See http://www.workplace-violence-hq.com/; Mattman, "Preventing Violence in the Workplace."

30. See http://www11.cnn.com/2000/ CAREER/trends/11/15/rage/.

31. *Ibid.* See also Bonnie Fisher and Elaine Gunnison, "Violence in the Workplace Gender Similarities and Differences," *Journal of Criminal Justice 29* (2001): 145–55.

32. P.L. 107-56 (2001); Brent L. Smith, Kelly R. Damphouse, Freedom Jackson, and Amy Sellers, "The Prosecution and Punishment of International Terrorists in Federal Courts: 1980–1988," *Criminology 1*, 3 (2002): 311–37.

33. M. Cherif Bassiouni, "Terrorism," World Book Online Americas Edition, 2001, http://www.cssve.worldbook.compuserve.com/wbol/wbpage/na/ar/co/551940; Harvey W. Kushner, *Encyclopedia of Terrorism* (Thousand Oaks: Sage, 2002).

34. *American Heritage Dictionary* (New York: Dell, 1994), p. 835; http://www.yourdictionary.com.

35. U.S. Code, Title 22, Sec. 2656(f).

36. *Ibid.*

37. *Ibid.*; http://jurist.law.pitt.edu/terrorism1.htm.

38. R. Barri Flowers, *Murder, At the End of the Day and Night: A Study of Criminal Homicide Offenders, Victims, and Circumstances* (Springfield: Charles C Thomas, 2002), pp. 117–18; Victor D. Hanson, *An Autumn of War: What America Learned from September 11 and the War on Terrorism* (New York: Vintage Books, 2002).

39. Flowers, *Murder, At the End of the Day and Night*, p. 122.

40. Thomas H. Dixon, "Why Root Causes are Important," http://www.pugwash.org/September11/letter-homerdixon.htm.

41. *Ibid.*

42. *Ibid.*

43. National Center for Policy Analysis, "Suicide Terrorists," http://www.ncpd.org/pi/congress/pd091201e.html.

44. See, for example, Sally Haslanger, Gender and the Events of 9/11," http://web.mit.edu/cms/reconstructions/interpretations/gender.html; Michael Kimmel, "Gender, Class, and Terrorism," http://www.xyonline.net/terror.shtml.

45. Kimmel, "Gender, Class, and Terrorism."

46. *Ibid.*

47. *Ibid.*

Part IV

MALE PROPERTY CRIMES

Chapter 12

ROBBERY

Robbery is one of the country's most serious crimes, costing victims near-ly half a billion dollars each year. Considered both a violent and proper-ty crime, robbery offenders are decidedly male. The number of robberies committed in the United States has been on the rise recently, attributed to a downturn in the economy and the reentry of hundreds of thousands of state and federal prisoners, among other reasons. More than eight out of ten rob-beries involve the use of firearms or strong-armed tactics. Robberies are responsible for over 1,000 murders annually, representing the most common circumstance for felony homicides. The crime of robbery often correlates with such factors as substance abuse, unemployment, lower socioeconomics, and mental health problems. Most offenders tend to be involved in other forms of violence and with other criminals, and often have backgrounds fraught with abuse, violence, and family discord.

THE DYNAMICS OF ROBBERY

According to the Uniform crime Reports (UCR) of the Federal Bureau of Investigation (FBI), robbery is defined as "the taking or attempting to take anything of value from the care, custody, or control of a person or persons by force or threat of force or violence and/or by putting a victim in fear."[1]

As such, robbery is at once a property offense and a crime against the per-son. In order for a crime to be classified as a robbery, the use of force or threat therein must create a reasonable sense of fear by the victim, therefore differentiating it from larceny-theft. As an example, assuming a perpetrator "grabs a purse, billfold or other piece of property from the victim so quickly that he or she cannot offer any resistance, in some jurisdictions the crime will be classified s larceny, not robbery."[2]

For other jurisdictions, the crime would be categorized as robbery as a result of the possibility of using force. If the offender and victim become involved in a struggle, in all likelihood the crime would be classified as a robbery. Oftentimes robbery is also broken down by the degree of force or threat of used by the robber. Hence, armed robbery would be considered a more serious offense than unarmed robbery.[3]

Robbery is considered by many to be perhaps the most frightening crime, for it "not only entails loss of property, but also the threat—or actual use—of violence. . . . Even when victims do not sustain extensive injury or loss, they are often forced to suffer threats of violence and bodily harm at the hands of their assailant. Both property and personal safety are placed at substantial risk during a robbery."[4]

Total loss of control was reported by Morton Bard and Dawn Sangrey as typical for victims in a face-to-face encounter with a robber.[5] With an armed robbery, the sense of loss can be that much more severe, and result in short- or long-term effects for the victim.

THE EXTENT OF ROBBERY

Robberies occur hundreds of thousands of times each year in the United States. A robbery takes place every 54 seconds, according to the FBI.[6] In 2000, there were an estimated 407,842 robberies nationwide, or a rate of 144.9 robberies per 100,000 inhabitants, according to official data.[7] Robberies outnumbered homicides by more than 26 to one and forcible rapes by nearly five to one.[8] Robbery was the motivating circumstance in 1,048 murders in 2000.[9] Every year, some 49,000 carjackings occur, in which victims are abducted and robbed of their vehicles.[10] Robbery is also often a factor in other acts of criminality such as workplace violence[11] (see also Chapter 11).

Regionally, in 2000, robberies occurred most often in the South, with more than 37 percent of the nation's total. This was followed by the regions in the West, Northeast, and Midwest with 22 percent, 20.5 percent, and 20 percent of the robberies, respectively (see Fig. 12.1).

With respect to community type, metropolitan areas have the highest volume and rate of robberies. As shown in Table 12.1, in 2000 an estimated 388,817 robberies—representing more than 95 percent of all robberies in the United States—occurred in metropolitan statistical areas at a rate of 173.0 per 100,000 inhabitants. This was followed by cities outside of metropolitan areas with 13,622 robberies at a rate of 59.9, and rural counties, which had approximately 5,403 robberies at a rate of 15.9.

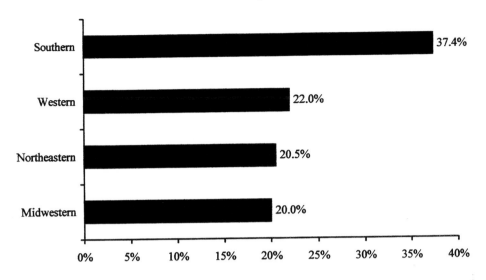

Figure 12.1. Robberies in the United States, by Region, 2000. *Source:* Derived from U.S. Department of Justice, Federal Bureau of Investigation, *Crime in the United States: Uniform Crime Reports 2000* (Washington: Government Printing Office, 2001), p. 30.

Official data indicates that the total number of robberies nationally declined less than 1 percent between 1999 and 2000. Long-term trends show that the volume of robberies dropped nearly 41 percent from 1991 to 2000, and decreased almost 24 percent between 1996 and 2000, with the rate of robberies also declining less during the spans.[12] These figures notwithstanding, preliminary estimates suggest that the number of robberies in 2001 increased significantly in the United States from the previous year.[13]

Arrests of Robbery Suspects

In 2000, law enforcement agencies cleared or solved around one in every four robberies in the United States with an arrest.[14] There were an estimated 106,130 arrests for robbery.[15] Nearly nine out of ten persons arrested for robbery are male.[16] Persons age 18 and over account for nearly three out of four male robbery arrestees.[17]

Black males are disproportionately represented in arrests for robbery. As seen in Figure 12.2, blacks accounted for more than half the persons arrested for robbery nationwide in 2000. Whites constituted over 44 percent of the robbery arrestees, while Native Americans and Asians made up less than 2 percent of the total.

Arrest trends reveal that fewer persons are being arrested for robbery. Between 1991 and 2000, male arrests for robbery dropped by more than 32

Table 12.1
ROBBERIES IN THE UNITED STATES, BY COMMUNITY TYPE, 2000

Area	Population[a]	Robbery
United States Total	281,421,906	407,842
Rate per 100,000 inhabitants		144.9
Metropolitan Statistical Area	224,805,902	
Area actually reporting[b]	92.6%	378,602
Estimated totals	100.0%	388,817
Rate per 100,000 inhabitants		173.0
Cities Outside Metropolitan Area	22,738,278	
Area actually reporting[b]	80.7%	11,430
Estimated totals	100.0%	13,622
Rate per 100,000 inhabitants		59.9
Rural Counties	33,877,726	
Area actually reporting[b]	79.8%	4,662
Estimated totals	100.0%	5,403
Rate per 100,000 inhabitants		15.9

[a] Populations are Bureau of the Census 2000 decennial census counts and are subject to change.

[b] The percentage reported under "Area actually reporting" is based upon the population covered by agencies providing three months or more of crime reports to the FBI.

Source: U.S. Department of Justice, Federal Bureau of Identification, Crime in the United States: Uniform Crime Reports 2000 (Washington: Government Printing Office, 2001), p. 67.

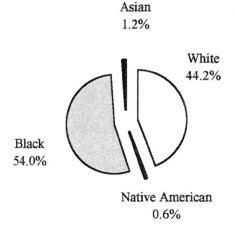

Figure 12.2. Arrests for Robbery, by Race,[a] 2000. *Source:* Adapted from U.S. Department of Justice, Federal Bureau of Investigation, *Crime in the United States: Uniform Crime Reports 2000* (Washington: Government Printing Office), p. 234.

[a] Native Americans include American Indians and Alaskan Natives; Asians include Pacific Islanders.

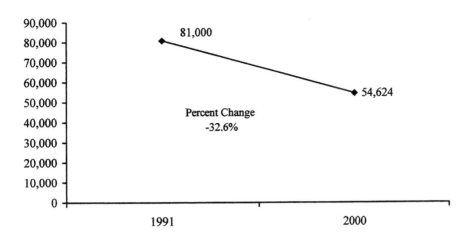

Figure 12.3. Ten-Year Male Arrest Trends for Robbery, 1991–2000. *Source:* Derived from U.S. Department of Justice, Federal Bureau of Investigation, *Crime in the United States: Uniform Crime Reports, 2000* (Washington: Government Printing Office, 2001), p. 221.

percent (see Fig. 12.3). However, for the five-year trend from 1996 to 2000, the decline was less at just over 23 percent; while for the period from 1999 to 2000, arrests for robbery were down, at less than 3 percent.[18]

Convicted robbers make up the largest segment of inmates incarcerated for violent or property offenses, attesting to the seriousness of the crime of robbery, arresting suspected offenders, convicting them, and sentencing them to prison.[19]

THE NATURE OF LOSS FROM ROBBERY

Robberies are most likely to occur on the streets or highways, according to the UCR (see Fig. 12.4). In 2000, 46 percent of robberies in the United States were perpetrated on streets/highways. This was followed by commercial houses and residences, which accounted for 13.9 percent and 12.2 percent of the robberies, respectively. Convenience stores, gas stations, and banks were the targets of robbers in over 11 percent of the robberies; with nearly 17 percent of robberies classified as miscellaneous. Robberies tended to occur most often in October, December, and August, and occurred least often in February, April, and March in 2000.[20]

Robbers are most likely to use firearms or strong-armed tactics to perpetrate their crimes. As seen in Figure 12.5, in 2000, nearly 41 percent of robberies in the United States were committed while using a gun, with more than

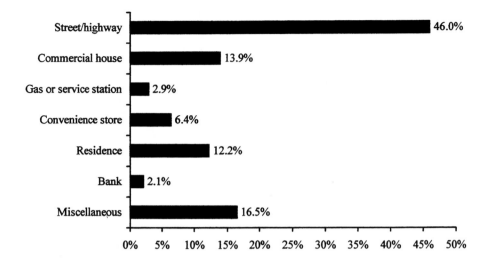

Figure 12.4. Robberies, by Place of Occurrence, 2000. *Source:* Derived from U.S. Department of Justice, Federal Bureau of Investigation, *Crime in the United States: Uniform Crime Reports 2000* (Washington: Government Printing Office, 2001), p. 30.

40 percent involving strong-arm tactics. Other weapons were used by offenders in over 10 percent of the robberies, while more than 8 percent were perpetrated with knives or other cutting instruments.

Studies reveal that robbery offenders carrying firearms are least likely to experience resistance by the victim or injury in successfully perpetrating the robbery, compared to unarmed offenders.[21] Since firearms-related injuries have a greater likelihood of resulting in death to the robbery victim, the rate of fatality for armed robberies using a gun is around three times that of robberies in which the offender uses a knife, and ten times the rate of robberies perpetrated with other weapons.[22]

Some researchers have found that aside from the purpose of killing robbery victims, some robbers use firearms as a means to secure an advantage over victims who are less vulnerable to attack. These can include men, older teenagers, groups of people, and businesses.[23] Conversely, guns tend to be used less often when robbing victims considered more vulnerable, such as children, women, and elderly targets.

The loss from robbery is staggering on society. In 2000, the Justice Department reported that more than $477 million was stolen from victims in the United States. As seen in Table 12.2, the average dollar loss per robbery was $1,170. Losses were highest from banks, with bank robberies resulting in an average loss of $4,437. Commercial houses and residences yielded losses with an average value of $1,705 and 1,358, respectively. Losses from robbery were

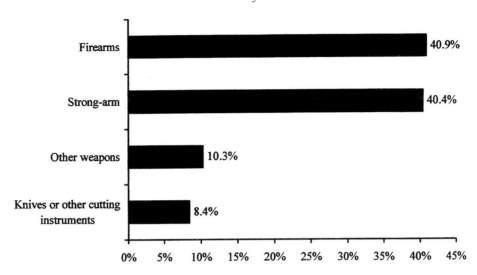

Figure 12.5. Armed Robberies, by Type of Weapons Used, 2000. *Source:* Derived from U.S. Department of Justice, Federal Bureau of Investigation, *Crime in the United States: Uniform Crime Reports 2000* (Washington: Government Printing Office, 2001), p. 31.

lowest for convenience stores, with an average dollar loss of $544; and service stations, which lost on average $693 during a robbery.

Most of the losses sustained from robberies are never recovered. Furthermore, robbery victims often incur losses other than the value of their property—including physical injuries and mental trauma—which can have long-term ramifications and an immeasurable cost to victims.[24]

PROFILING THE ROBBER

Perpetrators of robbery are usually persons in their late teens, twenties, and thirties. Researchers have reported that 90 percent of robbery offenders are black males, and 82 percent are strangers to the victim.[25] Around half of all robberies are perpetrated by more than one offender.[26]

According to experts on property offenders, the classic method of operation of the robber includes:

- Specializes in a type of victim.
- Looks for a particular place or person to target.
- Often relies on same method or ploy to commit crime.
- May work alone or have partners in robbery.
- May leave a calling card at scene of crime.[27]

Table 12.2
MONETARY LOSSES FROM ROBBERIES, BY TYPE OF ROBBERY, 2000

Robbery Location	Percent distribution[a]	Average dollars lost
Total	**100.0**	**1,170**
Street/highway	46.0	879
Commercial house	13.9	1,705
Gas or service station	2.9	693
Convenience store	6.4	544
Residence	12.2	1,358
Bank	2.1	4,437
Miscellaneous	16.5	1,298

[a] Because of rounding, the percentages may not add to total.
Source: U.S. Department of Justice, Federal Bureau of Identification, Crime in the United States: Uniform Crime Reports 2000 (Washington: Government Printing Office, 2001), p. 204.

Furthermore, robbers and burglars who stakeout or case a target for victimization typically use such ploys as:

- Acting like a drunk.
- Faking having a flat tire or being out of gas.
- Feigning being lost.
- Pretending to be a salesman or repairman.
- Having money handy to bribe security or others if caught.
- Reduce suspicion by having family waiting in getaway car.[28]

Robbers have been shown to commonly "possess attitudes, values, and beliefs favorable towards violating the law,"[29] and belong to a subculture that is supportive of criminal activity.[30]

Robbery offenders often have a history of alcohol and/or drug use or abuse. In a survey of robbers, over two-thirds had a high prevalence of drug use and around three-quarters had abused alcohol over their lifetime.[31] This contention has been supported through studies of prisoners convicted of robbery with a history of substance abuse or being under the influence of drugs or alcohol when committing the robbery.[32]

Many robbery offenders have been found to possess Antisocial Personality Disorders, characterized by a history of antisocial behavior, often beginning in early childhood and extending into adulthood, and poor work performance over a number of years. In a study comparing the lifetime rates of prevalence of mental disorders among serious offenders, the likelihood of meeting the criteria for Antisocial Personality Disorder was highest for robbers.[33]

Signs of the disorder typically include such things during childhood as lying, fighting, stealing, truancy, and aversion to authority; and adolescent behaviors such as aggressive sexual conduct and alcohol and drug abuse; as well as being unable to function properly in adulthood as a parent or in employment, while rejecting social convention in abiding the law.[34] Studies show that the most troublesome features of Antisocial Personality Disorder–such as promiscuity, fighting, vagrancy, and criminal behavior–may lessen after the age of thirty.[35] One recent study found that the average age of robbery perpetrators in federal custody was around 31.[36]

TYPES OF ARMED ROBBERS

Criminologists have broken down armed robbery offenders into four general types: (1) chronic robbers, (2) professional robbers, (3) intensive robbers, and (4) occasional robbers.[37] These are profiled as follows:

- *Chronic armed robbers*–average age in committing first crime is 12, age 14 when first arrested, with the first armed robbery occurring at age 17.5. Career as armed robber usually lasts around seven or eight years, averaging 20 to 25 armed robberies, along with numerous other crimes, such as drug offenses and burglary. The chronic armed robber usually carried a loaded firearm, using it in one of every five robberies; and uses alcohol and/or drugs. On average, these offenders earn between $500 and $5,000 per robbery.
- *Professional armed robbers*–average age for first offense is 13, first arrested at sixteen, with the first armed robbery occurring at age 17. Career as an armed robber tends to last 11 to 12 years, averaging from 20 to 50 armed robberies and many other offenses, including burglary and auto theft. Often tends to be comprehensive in planning armed robberies and well armed, but only fires guns in one in ten robberies. Professional armed robbers usually earn anywhere from $1,000 to $5,000 per robbery.
- *Intensive armed robbers*–average age in first perpetrating crime and first arrest is 18, with the first armed robbery occurring at the age of 25. Career as an armed robber usually only lasts a few weeks or months, averaging five to ten armed robberies, while committing few other crimes. The intensive armed robber many carry a loaded firearm, but rarely uses it; earning around $150 to $1,400 per robbery.
- *Occasional armed robbers*–average age when committing first offense is 13, age 15.5 for first arrest, with the first armed robbery occurring at age

20.5. Career as an armed robber usually lasts anywhere from a few months to two years, with an average of one to six armed robberies. Occasional armed robbers also perpetrate many other offenses, such as drug crimes, burglary, and motor vehicle theft. On average, these offenders earn anywhere from $100 to $1,000 per armed robbery.

The majority of armed robbers are under the age of 30, with no offspring or work history, and have frequent changes of residence. Most tend to involve themselves with other criminals in adolescence and as adults, resulting in a criminal subculture that encourages perpetrating armed robberies and other antisocial behavior[38] (see also Chapter 2).

THE MALE JUVENILE ROBBER

Most robbery offenders begin committing robberies and other crimes as juveniles. In 2000 alone, 16,592 males under the age of 18 were arrested for robbery in the United States.[39] Robbery represents one of the most frequent violent and property offenses for which juveniles are arrested and referred to juvenile court.[40]

Studies show that around 96 percent of the robbery delinquency case referrals to juvenile court are made by law enforcement agencies.[41] The likelihood of detention for the juvenile offender is much greater for robbers and aggravated assaultists than other types of offenders under the age of 18.[42] In more than half of all delinquency cases of robbery disposed, secure detention was used to hold the juvenile between juvenile court referral and the disposition of the case.[43] Among prison inmates under the age of 18, more than six in ten were convicted of violent crimes such as murder, aggravated assault, forcible rape, and robbery.[44]

Violent juvenile offenders typically have backgrounds characterized by child abuse, family violence, family dysfunction, broken homes, low income, delinquent peers, and substance abuse.[45]

NOTES

1. U.S. Department of Justice, Federal Bureau of Investigation, *Crime in the United States: Uniform Crime Reports 2000* (Washington: Government Printing Office, 2001), p. 29.

2. "FYI: Robbery," http://www.ncvc.org/infolink/info40.htm. See also Sue Reid, *Crime and Criminology,* 5th ed. (Chicago: Holt, Rinehart & Winston, 1988).

3. T. Gabor, *Armed Robbery* (Springfield: Charles C Thomas, 1987); M. Banton, *Investigating Robbery* (Brookfield: Gower, 1986).

4. "FYI: Robbery." See also J. N. Gilbert, *Criminal Investigations* (Englewood: Prentice-Hall, 1998); Morton Bard and Dawn Sangrey, *The Crime Victim's Book,* 2nd ed. (Secaucus: Citadel Press, 1986).

5. Bard and Sangrey, *The Crime Victim's Book.* See also Gabor, *Armed Robbery.*

6. Federal Bureau of Investigation.

7. *Crime in the United States,* p. 29.

8. *Ibid.,* pp. 14, 25, 30.

9. *Ibid.,* p. 20.

10. U.S. Department of Justice, Bureau of Justice Statistics Special Report, *Carjackings in the United States, 1992–96* (Washington: Office of Justice Programs, 1999), p. 1.

11. Banton, *Investigating Robbery;* Correctional Service of Canada, "A Profile of Robbery Offenders in Canada," http://www.csc-scc.gc.ca/text/rsrch/briefs/b10/b10e.shtml; R. Barri Flowers, *Drugs, Alcohol and Criminality in American Society* (Jefferson: McFarland, 1999), pp. 42–43, 146–47.

12. *Crime in the United States,* p. 30.

13. Federal Bureau of Investigation.

14. *Crime in the United States,* p. 31.

15. *Ibid.,* p. 216.

16. *Ibid.,* pp. 228, 233.

17. *Ibid.,* p. 228.

18. *Ibid.,* pp. 223, 225.

19. U.S. Department of Justice, Bureau of Justice Statistics Bulletin, *Prisoners in 2000* (Washington: Office of Justice Programs, 2001), p. 11.

20. *Crime in the United States,* p. 30.

21. "FYI: Robbery;" Philip Cook, "The Technology of Personal Violence," in Michael Tonry, ed., *Crime and Justice: A Review of Research,* Vol. 14 (Chicago: University of Chicago Press, 1991).

22. Cook, "The Technology of Personal Violence."

23. See, for example, Gabor, *Armed Robbery;* Jeffrey Roth, *Firearms and Violence,* Research in Brief (Washington: National Institute of Justice, 1994); Monica Manton and Alison Talbot, "Crisis Intervention After an Armed Hold Up: Guidelines for Counselors," *Journal of Traumatic Stress 3,* 4 (1990): 507–22.

24. U.S. Department of Justice, Bureau of Justice Statistics Special Report, *Robbery Victims* (Washington: Office of Justice Programs, 1987); Ted Miller, Mark Cohen, and Brian Wiersema, *Victim Costs and Consequences: A New Look* (Washington: National Institute of Justice, 1996).

25. Banton, *Investigating Robbery;* Gilbert, *Criminal Investigations;* J. Katz, *Seductions of Crime* (New York: Basic Books, 1988); L. L. Motuik and R. L. Belcourt, *Statistical Profiles of Homicide, Sex, Robbery and Drug Offenders in Federal Corrections* (Ottawa: Correctional Service of Canada, 1995).

26. Gilbert, *Criminal Investigations;* Banton, *Investigating Robbery;* Gabor, *Armed Robbery.*

27. Banton, *Investigating Robbery;* Gilbert, *Criminal Investigations.*

28. Katz, *Seductions of Crime;* Gabor, *Armed Robbery;* Gilbert, *Criminal Investigations.*

29. "A Profile of Robbery Offenders in Canada."

30. *Ibid.;* J. Dixon and A. J. Lizotte, "Gun Ownership and the Southern Subculture of Violence," *American Journal of Sociology 93* (1987): 383–405; L. W. Kennedy and S. W. Baron, "Routine Activities and a Subculture of Violence: A Study of Violence on the Street," *Journal of Research in Crime and Delinquency 30,* 1 (1993): 88–112; R. N. Parker, "Poverty, Subculture of Violence, and Type of Homicide," *Social Forces 67* (1989): 983–1007; Marvin E. Wolfgang and Franco Ferracuti, *The Subculture of Violence: Towards an Integrated Theory in Criminology* (London: Tavistock, 1967).

31. "A Profile of Robbery Offenders in Canada."

32. Flowers, *Drugs, Alcohol and Criminality in American Society,* pp. 157–79.

33. "A Profile of Robbery Offenders in Canada;" L. L. Motiuk and F. Porporino, *The Prevalence, Nature and Severity of Mental Health Problems Among Federal Male Inmates in Canadian Penitentiaries* (Ottawa: Correctional Service of Canada, 1992); C. R. Bartol, *Criminal Behavior: A Psychosocial Approach* (Englewood: Prentice-Hall, 1991).

34. "A Profile of Robbery Offenders in Canada;" Gary Kleck and Ted Chiricos, "Unemployment and Property Crime: A Target-Specific Assessment of Opportunity and Motivation as Mediating Factors," *Criminology 40,* 3 (2002): 649–72; Thomas J. Young, "Unemployment and Property Crime: Not a Simple Relationship," *American Journal of Economics and Sociology 52* (1993): 413–15.

35. "A Profile of Robbery Offenders in Canada;" Bartol, *Criminal Behavior.*

36. Cited in "A Profile of Robbery Offenders in Canada."

37. *Ibid.; Statistical Profiles of Homicide, Sex, Robbery and Drug Offenders in Federal Corrections.*

38. "A Profile of Robbery Offenders in Canada;" Gabor, *Armed Robbery;* Banton, *Investigating Robbery.*

39. *Crime in the United States,* p. 228.

40. *Ibid.;* R. Barri Flowers, *Kids Who Commit Adult Crimes: Serious Criminality by Juvenile Offenders* (Binghamton: Haworth, 2002), pp. 156–58.

41. U.S. Department of Justice, "Juvenile Offenders and Victims: 1997 Update on Violence," http://ojjdp.ncjrs.org/pubs/juvoff/cases.html.

42. *Ibid.;* Flowers, *Kids Who Commit Adult Crimes,* pp. 158, 165–72.

43. "Juvenile Offenders and Victims."

44. Flowers, *Kids Who Commit Adult Crimes,* p. 165.

45. *Ibid.,* pp. 30–31, 127–34; R. Barri Flowers, *The Adolescent Criminal: An Examination of Today's Juvenile Offender* (Jefferson: McFarland, 1990), pp. 133–39.

Chapter 13

MOTOR VEHICLE THEFT

Motor vehicle theft affect millions of people in the United States each year, with the value of stolen vehicles estimated to be in the billions of dollars annually. The perpetrators of motor vehicle theft are predominantly young men. Motor vehicle theft involves the theft or attempted theft of a motor vehicle where no victim is present or threatened. A more serious type of motor vehicle theft is known as carjacking. While carjacking also concerns completed or attempted car theft, there is also an element of force or the threat thereof used by the offender against one or more victims present. While the majority of carjackings do not result in injury to victims, nearly two in 18 victims are injured, some seriously. Carjacking offenders are also primarily male. Arrests for thefts of motor vehicles have risen recently after being on the decline for a number of years. Overall, motor vehicle-related offenses remain a persistent problem for law enforcement.

MOTOR VEHICLE THEFT

The Federal Bureau of Investigation's Uniform Crime Reports (UCR) defines motor vehicle theft as "the theft or attempted theft of a motor vehicle [including] the stealing of automobiles, trucks, buses, motorcycles, motorscooters, snowmobiles, etc."[1] The definition includes joyriding, but excludes "the taking of a motor vehicle for temporary use by those persons having lawful access."[2]

Official data indicates that there were 1,165,559 thefts of motor vehicles in the United States in 2000.[3] These were valued at nearly $8 billion, or an average of $6,682 per vehicle. Most motor vehicle thefts involve automobiles (see Fig. 13.1). Nearly 75 percent of reported motor vehicle thefts in 2000 were of automobiles. Around 19 percent involved the theft of trucks or buses, with nearly 7 percent other kinds of motor vehicles.

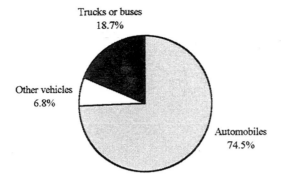

Figure 13.1. Types of Motor Vehicles Stolen, 2000. *Source:* Constructed from U.S. Department of Justice, Federal Bureau of Investigation, *Crime in the United States: Uniform Crime Reports 2000* (Washington: Government Printing Office, 2001), p. 53.

From 1960 to 2000, there were more than 44 million automobile thefts recorded in the United States, representing a significant increase over the four decade span. However, thefts of motor vehicles declined significantly during the 1990s with respect to volume and marginal rates.[4]

Between 1999 and 2000, the number of motor vehicle thefts in this country grew by just over 1 percent. It was the first year-to-year increase in motor vehicle thefts since 1990. By volume, thefts of motor vehicles declined almost 30 percent over the ten-year period from 1991 to 2000. Nationally, the rate of motor vehicle thefts per 100,000 inhabitants in 2000, was highest in metropolitan areas and lowest in rural counties.[5]

According to the National Incident-Based Reporting System (NIBRS), more than half of all stolen vehicles are recovered, with most found in a matter of days.[6]

Arrests and Motor Vehicle Theft

Arrest figures reveal that there were an estimated 148,225 arrests for motor vehicle theft in the United States in 2000.[7] Males were far more likely to be arrested for motor vehicle theft than females, constituting more than 84 percent of the arrestees. Around 66 percent of persons arrested for motor vehicle theft were under the age of 25, with almost 66 percent age 18 and over, and just over 34 percent of those arrested under 18 years of age (see Fig. 13.2).

More than half the arrestees for motor vehicle theft are white. As seen in Figure 13.3, whites made up 55.4 percent of the persons arrested for motor vehicle theft in 2000. However, blacks were disproportionately arrested for motor vehicle theft, representing 41.6 percent of total arrestees. Individuals of other races made up the remaining 3 percent of persons arrested.

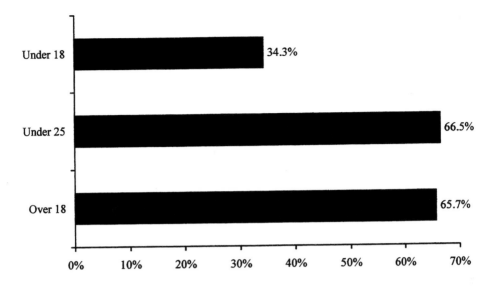

Figure 13.2. Arrests for Motor Vehicle Theft, by Age, 2000. *Source:* Derived from U.S. Department of Justice, Federal Bureau of Investigation, *Crime in the United States: Uniform Crime Reports 2000* (Washington: Government Printing Office, 2001), p. 55.

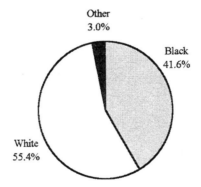

Figure 13.3. Arrests for Motor Vehicle Theft, by Race, 2000. *Source:* Derived from U.S. Department of Justice, Federal Bureau of Investigation, *Crime in the United States: Uniform Crime Reports 2000* (Washington: Government Printing Office, 2001), p. 55.
Note: Other includes American Indians or Alaskan Natives and Asians or Pacific Islanders.

There was a 14.1 percent clearance rate for motor vehicle theft in 2000, as reported by law enforcement agencies.[8] More than 81 percent of the clearances nationwide involved persons age eighteen and over.

Arrest trends show a sharp drop in male arrests for motor vehicle theft. From 1991 to 2000, arrests of males in this country for motor vehicle theft fell more than 39 percent (see Fig. 13.4).

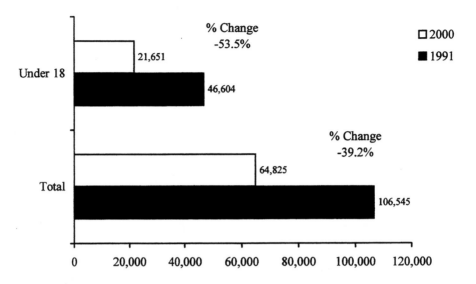

Figure 13.4. Ten-Year Male Arrest Trends for Motor Vehicle Theft, 1991–2000. *Source:* Derived from U.S. Department of Justice, Federal Bureau of Investigation, *Crime in the United States: Uniform Crime Reports 2000* (Washington: Government Printing Office, 2001), p. 221.

For males under the age of eighteen, there was a more than 53 percent drop in arrests. Although still reflecting a decrease, the decline in male arrests was not as great for five-year arrest trends for motor vehicle theft, showing a drop of nearly 21 percent, while male arrestees for auto theft increased by almost 1 percent from 1999 to 2000.[9]

WHERE MOTOR VEHICLE THEFTS OCCUR

Where do most motor vehicle thefts occur? The Justice Department reported that regionally, Western states had the highest rate of motor vehicle theft at 524.1 per 100,000 people in 1990.[10] This was followed by southern states at a rate of 417.1, midwestern states at a rate of 378.3, and northeastern states with a motor vehicle theft rate of 322.1. Three of the regions showed a decline in motor vehicle theft from the previous year, with only the rate of automobile thefts in Western states increasing.[11]

According to national victimization data, there were 1,137,940 incidents involving thefts of motor vehicles in 1998. Of these, 821,950 were completed and 315,990 were attempted motor vehicle thefts. Table 13.1 reflects the percent distribution of these incidents' place of occurrence. One-third of motor

Table 13.1
PERCENT DISTRIBUTION OF MOTOR VEHICLE THEFT INCIDENTS,
BY PLACE OF OCCURRENCE, UNITED STATES, 1998[a]

	Motor Vehicle Theft		
	Total	*Completed*	*Attempted*
Number of Incidents	1,137,940	821,950	315,990
Total	100%	100%	100%
Place of occurrence			
At respondent's home	1.9% (b)	2.1% (b)	1.3% (b)
Near home	27.6%	27.5%	27.9%
On the street near home	17.1%	15.5%	21.3%
At or near a friend's, relative's, or neighbor's home	3.4%	3.8%	2.4% (b)
Parking lot or garage	32.4%	32.1%	33.2%
On school property	1.0% (b)	1.1% (b)	0.7% (b)
In apartment yard, park, field, or playground	0.6% (b)	0.6% (b)	0.7% (b)
On street other than near own home	14.9%	15.8%	12.5%
Other	0.9% (b)	1.2% (b)	0.0% (b)

[a] Detail may not add to total because of rounding.
[b] Estimate is based on about ten or fewer sample cases.
Source: Adapted from U.S. Department of Justice, Bureau of Justice Statistics, *Sourcebook of Criminal Justice Statistics 1999* (Washington: Government Printing Office, 2000), p. 193.

vehicle thefts occurred in a parking lot or garage, while more than 27 percent of thefts occurred near home. Motor vehicle thefts were next most likely to take place on the street near home and on the street aside from near own home, at 17.1 and 14.9 percent, respectively.

Generally, the percent distribution for completed motor vehicle thefts was similar to attempted thefts. However, the percentage of attempted motor vehicle thefts tended to be higher than completed ones when occurring on the street near home, whereas the percentage of completed thefts of motor vehicles was generally higher on streets other than near own home compared to attempted motor vehicle thefts.

CARJACKINGS

Carjacking is defined by the Bureau of Justice Statistics (BJS) as "a completed or attempted theft in which a motor vehicle is taken by force or threat of force. It differs from other motor vehicle theft, which does not include incidents in which the offender used force or threats of force to obtain the vehi-

Table 13.2
TRENDS IN CARJACKINGS IN THE UNITED STATES, 1992–1996

| Annual average, 1992–96 | Carjackings | | |
	Total	Completed	Attempted
Number of Incidents	48,787	24,520	24,267
Number of victimizations	53,452	27,710	25,742
Rate per 10,000 persons	2.5	1.3	1.2
All carjackings	100%	100%	100%
No weapon	17	8 (a)	25
Total with weapon	83	92	75
Firearm	47	72	22 (a)
Knife, other, or unknown	36	20	52
Percent of carjackings			
With injury	16%	23%	10%
Reported to the police	79	100	57

[a] Based on fewer than ten sample cases.
Source: Derived from U.S. Department of Justice, Bureau of Justice Statistics Special Report, *Carjackings in the United States, 1992–96* (Washington: Office of Justice Programs, 1999), p. 1.

cle."[12] The definition relates to an offender not knowing the victim. Unlike motor vehicle theft as defined, what differentiates carjacking is that the victim is present at the time the theft occurs and the offender relies on force or the threat thereof to accomplish the motor vehicle theft, which often includes abducting or kidnapping the car driver and/or other occupants, sometimes even young children.[13]

How serious is the problem of carjacking in the United States? On average, an estimated 49,000 carjackings occur in this country every year.[14] Table 13.2 reveals the nature of carjackings, based on national data from 1992 to 1996. Completed and attempted carjackings were roughly equal during the span. Victimizations were more likely to occur in completed than attempted carjackings.

A weapon of some type was involved in 83 percent of total carjackings and 92 percent of completed carjackings. Firearms were used in 72 percent of the completed carjackings versus only 22 percent of the attempted carjackings.

Most carjackings do not result in injury. Less than one in four completed carjackings and one in ten attempted from 1992 to 1996 involved injury to the victims. Over the period, 100 percent of the completed carjackings were reported to the police, compared to 57 percent of the attempted carjackings.

The FBI reports that there are around 27 homicides committed by strangers related to motor vehicle theft each year in the United States.[15] However, according to the UCR's

Supplemental Homicide Reports, there were 272 murders committed nationally between 1992 and 1996 that were directly or indirectly related to

Table 13.3
CHARACTERISTICS OF CARJACKING OFFENDERS, 1992–1996

Characteristic of carjackers	Percent of completed or attempted and nonfatal carjackings
Total	100%
Number in incident	
1	45%
2 or more	55%
Sex[b]	
All male	97%
Both male and female	3% (a)
Race[b]	
White	19%
Black	58%
Other[c]	16%
More than one race	5% (a)

[a] Based on fewer than ten sample cases.
[b] Combines characteristics of carjackers in single-offender and multiple-offender incidents.
[c] Includes Asians and American Indians. Respondents also may have incorrectly classified Hispanic offenders as belonging to "other races."
Source: U.S. Department of Justice, Bureau of Justice Statistics Special Report, *Carjackings in the United States, 1992–96* (Washington: Office of Justice Programs, 1999), p. 3.

auto theft.[16] In 2000, motor vehicle theft was reported in official data as the murder circumstance involved in twenty-two murders in this country.[17]

Characteristics of Carjacking Offenders

Carjackings are primarily perpetrated by male minority offenders (see Table 13.3). From 1992 to 1996, 97 percent of the carjacking incidents in this country involved all male offenders, with 3 percent involving male and female offenders. Blacks were more likely than any other race to perpetrate completed, attempted, and nonfatal carjackings, accounting for nearly 60 percent of the incidents.

Almost three in four carjackings were committed by members of minority groups, as perceived by victims, compared to nearly two in ten carjackings committed by whites. Five percent of carjacking incidents were seen as involving offenders from more than one race.

In more than half the carjackings over the period, there were two or more perpetrators involved in the incident.

Although the vast majority of carjackings are committed by strangers, auto theft by force can also occur through nonstrangers to the victims. According

Table 13.4
PLACES WHERE CARJACKINGS OCCURRED, 1992–1996

Characteristic of incident	Percent of carjacking incidents		
	All	Completed	Attempted
Total	100	100	100
Place of occurrence			
At or near victim's/friends/ neighbor's home	26	25	26
Commercial place/parking lot[b]	20	16[a]	25
Open area/public transportation[c]	40	46	35
Other	13	13[a]	14
Distance from home			
At/near home	22	25	19[a]
1 mile or less	22	27[a]	18[a]
5 miles or less	21	16[a]	26
50 miles or less	30	30	29
More than 50 miles	5[a]	3[a]	8[a]

[a] Based on fewer than ten sample cases.
[b] Includes stores, gas stations, office buildings, restaurants, and other commercial places.
[c] Includes on the street (other than in front of victim's, neighbor's, or friend's home), in parks, and on public transportation, such as in a bus or train station or in an airport.
Source: U.S. Department of Justice, Bureau of Justice Statistics Special Report, *Carjackings in the United States, 1992–96* (Washington: Office of Justice Programs, 1999), p. 3.

to the National Crime Victimization Survey, between 1992 and 1996, 72 percent of carjackings involved stranger perpetrators. However, 15 percent of carjacking incidents were attributed to intimates of the victims, including spouses, ex-spouses, romantic partners, or relatives.[18] Around 14 percent of carjackings were committed by acquaintances or otherwise not described by victims.

Where Carjackings Occur

The majority of carjackings occur away from the victim's home, as shown in Table 13.4. Between 1992 and 1996, 40 percent of carjackings took place in an open area (i.e., the street) or near public transportation, such as an airport, train station, or subway. Twenty percent of the carjackings were perpetrated near commercial places such as restaurants, stores, and offices, or in parking lots.

Twenty-six percent of carjackings occurred near the victim's home or that of a friend or neighbor. The percentage of competed and attempted carjackings was roughly equal.

Table 13.5
MOTOR VEHICLE THEFT INVOLVING MULTIPLE-OFFENSE INCIDENTS, 1996

Index crime combinations for one victim, one offender	Number of incidents
Total	2,106
Violent	
Murder	5
Rape	5
Robbery	157
Assault	41
Murder, robbery	2
Rape, robbery	1
Violent and property	
Rape, burglary	1
Robbery, aggravated assault	3
Robbery, burglary	5
Robbery, larceny	1
Assault, larceny	1
Robbery, aggravated assault, burglary	1
Property	
Burglary	723
Larceny	1,101
Burglary, larceny	44
Larceny, larceny	15

Source: U.S. Department of Justice, Bureau of Justice Statistics Special Report, *Effects of NIBRS on Crime Statistics* (Washington: Office of Justice Programs, 2000), p. 8.

Carjackings occurring in open areas or near public transportation were more likely to be completed. Whereas carjacking incidents near commercial places or in parking lots were most likely to be attempted carjackings.

Around two-thirds of all carjacking incidents over the period occurred within five miles from where the victim lived. More than four in ten incidents occurred a mile or less from the victim's home. Three in ten carjackings took place within 50 miles of a victim's home, while only around one in 20 occurred more than 50 miles from the victim's home.

MOTOR VEHICLE THEFT AND OTHER OFFENSES

Aside from carjacking, many motor vehicle thefts tend to involve one or more additional offenses. Many of these are classified as serious crimes, such as robbery, burglary, and assault. This is illustrated in Table 13.5, which breaks down motor vehicle thefts in combination with other offenses in 1996, as reported by the NIBRS.

According to the data, there were 2,106 incidents in 1996 that included a single theft of a motor vehicle and at least one other Index offense. Most of these incidents involved larceny (1,162) or burglary (774). There were 44 such multiple offenses that included motor vehicle theft, burglary, and larceny. In 223 of the incidents, motor vehicle theft included one or more violent crimes, such as robbery.

Overall, the majority of motor vehicle thefts recorded by the NIBRS were classified as single-offense incidents.[19]

NOTES

1. U.S. Department of Justice, Federal Bureau of Investigation, *Crime in the United States: Uniform Crime Reports 1999* (Washington: Government Printing Office, 2000), p. 50.

2. *Ibid.*

3. *Ibid.*

4. U.S. Department of Justice, Federal Bureau of Investigation, *National Crime Information Center 2000 Operating Manual* (Washington: Office of Justice Programs, 1999).

5. *Crime in the United States,* p. 53.

6. *Ibid.*

7. *Ibid.,* p. 55.

8. *Ibid.*

9. *Ibid.,* pp. 223, 225.

10. *Ibid.,* p. 53.

11. *Ibid.*

12. U.S. Department of Justice, Bureau of Justice Statistics Special Report, *Carjackings in the United States, 1992–96* (Washington: Office of Justice Programs, 1999), p. 1.

13. *Ibid.;* N. L. Asdigian, D. Finkelhor, and G. T. Hotaling, "Varieties of Non-Family Abduction of Children and Adolescents," *Criminal Justice and Behavior 22* (1995): 215–32; D. Finkelhor and R. Ormrod, *The Characteristics of Crimes Against Children* (Washington: Office of Justice Programs, 2000); U.S. Department of Justice, *Kidnapping of Juveniles: Patterns From NIBRS* (Washington: Office of Justice Programs, 2000).

14. *Ibid.*

15. *Ibid.,* p. 4; *Crime in the United States,* p. 23.

16. *Ibid.; Carjackings in the United States.*

17. Crime in the United States, p. 23.

18. *Carjackings in the United States.*

19. U.S. Department of Justice, Bureau of Justice Statistics Special Report, *Effects of NIBRS on Crime Statistics* (Washington: Office of Justice Programs, 2000), p. 7.

Part V

MALE SEX OFFENSES

Chapter 14

INCEST

Intrafamilial sexual abuse or incestuous relations between adults and children or older children and younger ones is believed by many experts to be one of the more common and devastating forms of child sexual abuse. Although incestuous pairings can include any member of the nuclear or extended family, adult males are most often the active aggressors of incestuous contact, while female children are typically the passive victims. Older male siblings can also sexually abuse younger, more vulnerable siblings–sometimes after one of the siblings has already been sexually abused by the father. Incest offending and victimization are often seen as precursors to other forms of sexual criminality, including forcible rape, pedophilia, and prostitution. Violent crimes such as murder and assault and drug-related offenses are also typically associated with intrafamilial sexual relations and other kinds of family dysfunction.

DEFINING INCEST

What is incest? The term derives from the Latin word *incestum,* which means unchaste and low.[1] Incest is commonly defined as "sexual intercourse between relatives within the prohibited degrees of relationship defined by the law."[2] A dictionary definition of incest is "sexual relations between persons so closely related that their marriage is illegal or forbidden by custom."[3]

Today many child sexual abuse professionals have broadened the definition of incest to not only include sexual intercourse, but fondling, oral sex, anal sex, masturbation, and other forms of intrafamilial sexual contact. One such definition of incest is "any sexual contact between a child or adolescent and a person who is closely related or perceived to be related, including stepparents and live-in partners of parents."[4] While incest is usually associated with incestuous relations between blood relatives, many modern families consist of both nuclear and nonnuclear family members—any of whom can become involved incestually. Hence, incestuous pairings can generally be broken down into three groupings: (1) familial incest, (2) extended familial incest, and (3) other familial incest.

- **Familial incest** involves incestuous relations in which the active aggressor is part of the nuclear family such as a father, mother, or sibling.
- **Extended familial incest** consists of incestuous relations in which the active aggressor is a nonnuclear member of the family such as an uncle, aunt, grandfather, or cousin.
- **Other familial incest** involves incestuous relations in which the active aggressor is a stepparent, stepsibling, foster parent, foster sibling, or other perpetrator not included in other categories.[5]

Some researchers have further expanded the definition of incest to include "a violation of a trust between a caregiver and a child [involving] sexually inappropriate acts or those with sexual overtones involving a child and a person who has authority by virtue of an ongoing emotional bond."[6] The definition as such refers to child sexual abuse perpetrated by not only immediate and other members of the family, but any abusive authority figure including priests or clergy, teachers, scout leaders, camp counselors, and babysitters.

Though incest statutes and definitions thereof may vary, incest is considered a felony in nearly every state.[7] However, many intrafamilial sex offenders are never prosecuted due to nonuniform standards, unwillingness of many families to bring charges against perpetrators, and related issues.

THE MAGNITUDE OF INCEST

How widespread is the problem of incest? According to child sexual abuse expert Christine Courtois: "Incest between an adult and a related child or adolescent is now recognized as the most prevalent form of child sexual abuse and as one with great potential for damage to the child."[8] Most child sexual abuse experts agree that incest affects a significant percentage of the population in one respect or another. Estimates of incest vary from tens of thousands to well over a million cases in the United States every year.[9] One study approximated that between 11 and 33 million people are active participants in incestuous relations in this country.[10] Another study estimated that anywhere from 5 to 28 percent of females are victims of incest or sexual abuse.[11]

According to the Family Violence Research Program at the University of New Hampshire, between 5 and 15 percent of all females age 17 and younger have been victimized by intrafamilial sexual abuse and exploitation in the

United States.[12] Some researchers report that up to 10 percent of females in this country may be involved in incestuous relationships.[13] Others believe that as many as one in three people may be victims of incest prior to reaching the age of 18.[14]

These figures notwithstanding, due to the secretive and shameful nature of incestuous relationships, the vast majority of incest goes unreported. David Finkelhor estimated that 75 to 90 percent of all incest cases are never reported.[15] As one book on incest observed: "The family as a whole supports actively or passively their own incestuous equilibrium."[16]

THE NATURE OF INCEST

Incest affects people from all walks of life. According to a clinical social worker: "We know that incest cuts across every social, economic, and educational barrier."[17] Consequently, incest victims "share a common bond of betrayal and exploitation by those closest to them."[18] While incest victimization can start at any age, studies reveal that incestuous relations often begin when the victim is between age six and 11, and usually last for at least two years.[19]

Most incest tends to involve fathers and daughters, according to many experts. In fact, the study of intrafamilial child sexual abuse over the years has focused primarily on father-daughter incest.[20] A National Center for Missing and Exploited Children publication illustrates this in noting that the "vast majority of training materials, articles, and books on this topic refer to child sexual abuse only in terms of intrafamilial father-daughter incest."[21]

Researchers such as Diana Russell[22] and Finkelhor[23] have estimated that men are the active aggressors in 95 percent of the incest cases involving a girl and 80 percent of the cases involving a boy. Russell found that 4.5 percent of women reported having incestuous relations with a father or stepfather before reaching 18 years of age, while 4.9 percent of women were incestuously involved with an uncle prior to turning 18.[24]

In a *Los Angeles Times* survey, 27 percent of the women and 16 percent of the men reported being the victims of incest as children.[25] According to Mimi Silbert, two-thirds of sexually abused prostitutes were incest victims of fathers, stepfathers, or their foster fathers.[26] Other research on child sexual abuse supports the contention that the vast majority of incestuous offenders involving girl, boy, and women victims are heterosexual men.[27] This notwithstanding, incest can also involve aggressor-victim's other than adult male-child or father-daughter. A typology of such incestuous pairings has been identified by Adele Mayer as follows:

Type of Incest	*Motivations (Individual Psychopathology)*
Father-Son	Homosexual conflict
Older Sibling-Sibling	Expression of unconscious conflict
Mother-Daughter	Psychosis or infantilism
Mother-Son	Substitute appeasement for missing father
Grandfather-Granddaughter	Assertion of manhood[28]

INCESTUOUS MEN

Father-Daughter Incest

It is believed that father-daughter incest accounts for around three-quarters of all incestuous relationships in the United States. Rita Justice and Blair Justice describe the incestuous father as typically "white and middle class, has a high school education and often some college, and holds a white-collar job or skilled trade. He's most often in his late thirties, married more than ten years. His wife is slightly younger than he is."[29]

Incestuous fathers typically fall between the ages of 30 and 50. The sexual abuse of daughters can begin as early as infancy and last into the victim's adulthood. The child molestation is generally secretive and tends to involve a "misuse of power, mental duress, bribes, tricks, or misuse of parental role under the guise of sex education and threats."[30] Men who sexually abuse their daughters often use intimidation, coercion, and guilt tactics to initiate, maintain, and keep secret the incestuous relationship.

Characteristics of the typical father-perpetrator and daughter-victim of incest can be seen as follows:

Incestuous Father
- The median age of the abuser is 35.
- He is in a state of reassessing his life.
- He suffers from depression.
- Is patriarchal and emotionally immature.
- Has experienced spousal rejection.
- Abuses alcohol or drugs.
- Has diminished potency.
- A family history of abuse, abandonment, and sexual exploitation.[31]

Daughter Victim
- The median age is 8.5.
- Most victims are between five and 16 years of age.
- She is typically entering adolescence.
- She is most often the oldest daughter.[32]

Studies reveal that most men who sexually molest their daughters have "introverted personalities, an intrafamily background, and are socially isolated. Many are gradually heading towards incestuous contact with their daughters. In some cases, the wife may unwittingly aid and abet in the incestuous behavior by arranging situations that isolate the father and daughter from others."[33] Mothers in incestuous homes where the father is the aggressor against a child have been characterized as chronically depressed, chronically ill, often away from home on business trips, or having little sexual interest in their husbands.[34]

In one of the most comprehensive examinations to date of incestuous men, Finkelhor and Linda Williams identified five types of men who sexually molest their daughters:

- *Sexually preoccupied*–men with a conscious or obsessive sexual interest in their daughters.
- *Adolescent regressive*–men who are sexually attracted to their daughters as they reach puberty.
- *Instrumental self-gratifiers*–fathers who view their daughters in nonerotic terms and experience guilt over the incestuous relationship.
- *Emotionally dependent*–fathers who are emotionally needy, depressed, and/or lonely.
- *Angry retaliators*–men who sexually abuse their daughters out of anger towards them or the perpetrator's spouse, who may have neglected or abandoned them.[35]

Adolescent regressive men constituted the largest percentage of incestuous fathers, accounting for an estimated 33 percent of the sample group. They were followed by *sexually preoccupied men,* comprising more than 25 percent of the perpetrators. *Angry retaliators* represented approximately 10 percent of the father molesters. These men were also the most likely to have violent criminal records involving rape or assault.[36]

The researchers found that substance abuse was a factor in the incestuous relations for 43 percent of the molesters, with marital discord present in 43 percent of the incest cases.[37] A link was also established between fathers who molest their children and a cycle of child sexual abuse. Seventy percent of the incestuous men reported being victims of childhood sexual abuse.[38]

A high rate of father-daughter incest has been shown to involve stepfathers and stepdaughters.[39] This often reflects a "man who has married a woman with a daughter by a previous marriage. His sexual attraction to the daughter as a sex object may continue for years, though he may also [regard] her as a child dependent."[40] According to Russell, when mothers remarry, stepdaughters are over eight times more likely to be sexually abused by the stepfathers who raised them than daughters who are raised by their biological father.[41]

Father-Son Incest

Father-son incest is thought to be rare. When it does occur, it is often seen as a reflection of "interactional family disturbances and intrapsychic conflicts of the incestuous father."[42] Studies have found rates of father-son incest to range from 7 percent to 48 percent of the adult male perpetrated child sexual abuse cases.[43] In a study by R. Pierce and L. H. Pierce, stepfathers were identified as the molester in 20 percent of the cases.[44] Studies reveal that father-son incest commonly involves both individual and family pathologies, with potentially deadly implications.[45] A recent case of parricide drew national attention after two boys charged with murdering their father claimed it was due to years of incestuous relations with him.[46]

A frightening scenario of sadistic father-son incest and sibling child sexual abuse was described by a sociologist:

> Harry . . . was the victim of ritualistic and sadistic sexual abuse committed by his father as early as he could remember until about age twelve. His first memory of sex involved his father taping a crayon on his penis and making him insert it in the vagina of his younger sister. . . . He stated that his father sodomized him on several occasions, starting when Harry was five. . . . He recalled bleeding heavily . . . vomiting afterwards and thinking he was going to die. . . . For Harry, sexual contact with his father was a way of life, something that happened virtually every day.[47]

Grandfather-Granddaughter Incest

Incestuous relations between a grandfather and granddaughter have similar dynamics to father-daughter incest. This is especially true when the grandfather is young. For older grandfathers, the sexual molestation is often perpetrated to "bolster the molester's ego and help him reassert his manhood and self-esteem which have decreased due to his natural physical deterioration."[48]

Some studies have found incest to be trigenerational–involving father-daughter incest first before becoming grandfather-granddaughter incest.[49] In many instances, the grandfather was himself a victim of child sexual abuse.[50] A study of grandfather-granddaughter incest found that it constituted approximately 9 to 11 percent of all incest cases.[51]

SIBLING-SIBLING INCEST

Though much of the research on incest focuses on adult-child intrafamilial sexual relations, evidence indicates that sibling-sibling incest may be far more prevalent, with brother-sister incest seen as the most common type of incest. According to some studies, brother-sister incest may occur five times as often as father-daughter incest.[52] In such cases, the older brother is often the aggressor and the younger sister the victim.[53] In many instances, the father or another adult figure has already sexually abused her.

Studies show that the dynamics of brother-sister incest typically include circumstances in which "the brother may have coerced the sister into sexual relations after having assumed a father role in the family (usually after the biological father has abandoned the family). The idolizing sister may succumb to her brother's request while experiencing little guilt at the time."[54]

According to some researchers, just over one in four cases of sibling incest involves participants of the same sex, with 16 percent between brothers, and 10 percent involving sisters.[55] R. Longo and N. Groth found that nearly one in five of the aggressors in sibling incest were female.[56] Perpetrators of sibling incest are described as often possessing a low self-esteem, feelings of inadequacy, and tend to be loners, immature, and favor the company of young children over others.[57]

RECIDIVISM AND MULTIPLE SEX OFFENSES AMONG INCESTUOUS MEN

Men who sexually abuse their own children often commit repeat offenses. In a study of sex offenders and treatment, W. L. Marshall and H. E. Barbaree found that the rate of reoffense for untreated incestuous men varied from 4 to 10 percent.[58] Another study of incest offenders found that 21.7 percent of those untreated reoffended, compared to 8 percent of incestuous men who received treatment.[59] Some experts believe that the actual rate of recidivism among untreated and treated incestuous sex offenders may be much higher.[60]

There is evidence that many incestuous men are also involved in other sex offenses. A high percentage of male sex offenders began offending before turning 18, often involving multiple victims.[61] According to G. G. Abel and associates in a study of sex offenders committing multiple paraphilic acts, the following findings emerged:

- Almost 26 percent of incestuous sex offenders with female victims perpetrated at least two types of paraphilic acts.
- Seventeen percent of incestuous sex offenders with female victims committed at least three types of paraphilic acts.
- More than 8 percent of sex offenders with female victims committed five or more types of paraphilias.

- Almost 4 percent of incestuous offenders with female victims committed ten types of paraphilias.
- Nearly 16 percent of incestuous sex offenders with male victims perpetrated at least two paraphilic acts.
- Almost 14 percent of sex offenders with male victims committed five or more paraphilias.
- More than 9 percent of incestuous offenders that targeted male victims committed ten different paraphilas.[62]

Men who are incestuous are also guilty of committing a number of non-sexual offenses. In a survey of self-reported crimes perpetrated by incarcerated sex offenders, M. R. Weinrott and M. Saylor found that many more incestuous sex offenders admitted to also committing nonsexual crimes than previous research had suggested.[63] This was consistent with findings in the Abel and colleagues study.[64]

NOTES

1. R. Barri Flowers, *The Victimization and Exploitation of Women and Children: A Study of Physical, Mental and Sexual Maltreatment in the United States* (Jefferson: McFarland, 1994), p. 60. See also W. Maltz and B. Holman, *Incest and Sexuality* (Lexington: Lexington Books, 1987).

2. R. Barri Flowers, *Domestic Crimes, Family Violence and Child Abuse: A Study of Contemporary American Society* (Jefferson: McFarland, 2000), p. 130.

3. R. Barri Flowers, *Sex Crimes, Predators, Perpetrators, Prostitutes, and Victims: An Examination of Sexual Criminality and Victimization* (Springfield: Charles C Thomas, 2001), p. 75. See also Christine A. Courtois, *Healing the Incest Wound: Adult Survivors in Therapy* (New York: W. W. Norton, 1996).

4. "What is Incest?" http://www.travel-net.com/~pater/invis-3.htm.

5. Flowers, *Sex Crimes, Predators, Perpetrators, Prostitutes, and Victims*, pp. 74–75. See also David Finkelhor and Sharon Araji, *A Sourcebook on Child Sexual Abuse* (Thousand Oaks: Sage, 1995); John Crewdson, *By Silence Betrayed: Sexual Abuse in America* (New York: Harper & Row, 1988).

5. Flowers, *Sex Crimes, Predators, Perpetrators, Prostitutes, and Victims*, pp. 74–75.

6. "Incest and Molestation," http://www.menstuff.org/issues/byissue/incestmolest.html#incest.

7. Richard A. Posner and Katharine B. Silbaugh, *A Guide to America's Sex Laws* (Chicago: University of Chicago Press, 1996), pp. 129–42.

8. Courtois, *Healing the Incest Wound*, p. 12.

9. Flowers, *Domestic Crimes, Family Violence and Child Abuse*, p. 131.

10. Cited in *Ibid.*

11. Cited in Flowers, *Sex Crimes, Predators, Perpetrators, Prostitutes, and Victims,* p. 76. See also Diana E. Russell and Rebecca M. Bolen, *The Epidemic of Rape and Child Sexual Abuse in the United States* (Thousand Oaks: Sage, 2000).

12. Cited in Kathy McCoy, "Incest: The Most Painful Family Problem," *Seventeen 43* (June 1984), p. 18. See also Diana E. Russell, *The Secret Trauma: Incest in the Lives of Girls and Women* (New York: Basic Books, 1986).

13. Julie Howard, "Incest: Victims Speak Out," Teen (July 1985), p. 30; Russell and Bolen, *The Epidemic of Rape and Child Sexual Abuse.*

14. Heidi Vanderbilt, "Incest: A Chilling Report," *Lear's* (February 1992), p. 52. See also R. Pierce and L. H. Pierce, "The Sexually Abused Child: A Comparison of Male and Female Victims," *Child Abuse and Neglect 9,* 2 (1985): 191–99.

15. Cited in Jean Renvoize, *Incest: A Family Pattern* (London: Routledge & Kegan Paul, 1982) p. 51. See also Finkelhor and Araji, *A Sourcebook on Child Sexual Abuse.*

16. Marshall D. Schecter and Leo Roberge, "Sexual Exploitation," in Ray E. Helfer and C. Henry Kempe, eds., *Child Abuse and Neglect: The Family and the Community* (Cambridge: Ballinger, 1976), p. 129. See also Gail E. Wyatt and Gloria J. Powell, eds., *Lasting Effects of Child Sexual Abuse* (Thousand Oaks: Sage, 1988).

17. Cited in Howard, "Incest: Victims Speak Out," p. 31.

18. Flowers, *Domestic Crimes, Family Violence and Child Abuse,* p. 132.

19. *Ibid;* Courtois, *Healing the Incest Wound;* Crewdson, *By Silence Betrayed.*

20. Flowers, *Sex Crimes, Predators, Perpetrators, Prostitutes, and Victims,* p. 75; Russell, *The Secret Trauma.*

21. U.S. Department of Justice, *Child Sex Rings: A Behavioral Analysis, For Criminal Justice Professionals Handling Cases of Child Sexual Exploitation* (Alexandria: National Center for Missing & Exploited Children, 1992), p. 2.

22. Russell, *The Secret Trauma.*

23. Finkelhor and Araji, *A Sourcebook on Child Sexual Abuse;* David Finkelhor, *Sexually Victimized Children* (New York: Free Press, 1979).

24. Russell, *The Secret Trauma.*

25. Cited in Crewdson, *By Silence Betrayed.* See also T. A. Roesler and T. W. Wind, "Telling the Secret: Adult Women Describe Their Disclosures of Incest," *Journal of Interpersonal Violence 9* (1994): 327–38.

26. Mimi Silbert, "Treatment of Prostitution Victims of Sexual Abuse," in Irving R. Stuart and Joanne G. Greer, eds., *Victims of Sexual Aggression: Treatment of Children, Women, and Men* (Hoboken: John Wiley & Sons, 1984).

27. See, for example, M. A. Reinhart, "Sexually Abused Boys," *Child Abuse and Neglect 11,* 2 (1987): 229–35; A. R. De Jong, G. A. Emmett, and A. R. Hervada, "Sexual Abuse of Children: Sex-, Race-, and Age-Dependent Variations," *American Journal of Diseases of Children 136,* 2 (1982): 129–34; N. S. Ellerstein and J. W. Canavan, "Sexual Abuse of Boys," *American Journal of Diseases of Children 134* (1980): 255–57.

28. Adele Mayer, *Incest: A Treatment Manual for Therapy with Victims, Spouses, and Offenders* (Holmes Beach: Learning Publications, 1983), p. 22.

29. Quoted in Howard, "Incest: Victims Speak Out," p. 31. See also M. Gordon, "Males and Females as Victims of Childhood Sexual Abuse," *Journal of Family Violence 5,* 4 (1990): 321–33; C. C. Hartley, "How Incest Offenders Overcome Internal Inhi-

bitions Through the Use of Cognitions and Cognitive Distortions," *Journal of Interpersonal Violence 13,* 1 (1988): 25–39.

30. "Characteristics and Behavioral Indicators of Adults Who Molest Children," Minnesota Department of Corrections, http://www.doc.state.mn.us/level3/characteristics.htm.

31. R. Barri Flowers, *Children and Criminality: The Child as Victim and Perpetrator* (Westport: Greenwood, 1986), p. 79; Patricia D. McClendon, "Incest/Sexual Abuse of Children," November 1991, http://www.clinicalsocialwork.com/incest.html.

32. Flowers, *Children and Criminality,* p. 79.

33. Flowers, *Domestic Crimes, Family Violence and Child Abuse,* p. 133.

34. See http://www.childabuse.com/perp_print.htm.

35. Cited in Vanderbilt, "Incest: A Chilling Report," pp. 60–62. See also Russell, The Secret Trauma; Finkelhor and Araji, A Sourcebook on Child Sexual Abuse.

36. Cited in Vanderbilt, "Incest: A Chilling Report," pp. 60–62.

37. *Ibid.*

38. *Ibid.*

39. McClendon, "Incest/Sexual Abuse of Children;" Pierce and Pierce, "The Sexually Abused Child;" Russell, *The Secret Trauma.*

40. Flowers, *The Victimization and Exploitation of Women and Children,* p. 64.

41. Russell, *The Secret Trauma,* p. 103.

42. Flowers, *The Victimization and Exploitation of Women and Children,* p. 66.

43. Ellerstein and Canavan, "Sexual Abuse of Boys;" Pierce and Pierce," The Sexually Abused Child;" W. N. Friedrich, R. L. Beilke, and A. J. Urquiza, "Behavioral Problems in Young Sexually Abused Boys: A Comparison Study," *Journal of Interpersonal Violence 3* (1988): 21–28.

44. Pierce and Pierce," The Sexually Abused Child."

45. M. Williams, "Father-Son Incest: A Review and Analysis of Reported Incidents," *Clinical Social Work Journal 16,* 2 (1988): 165–79; Janet Baker and Trish Berry, *It Happened to Us: Men Talk About Child Sexual Abuse* (Melbourne: Victorian Government Department of Health & Community Services, 1995); M. J. Spender and P. Dunklee, "Sexual Abuse of Boys," *Pediatrics 78* (1986): 133–37.

46. R. Barri Flowers and H. Loraine Flowers, *Murders in the United States: Crimes, Killers, and Victims of the Twentieth Century* (Jefferson: McFarland, 2001), pp. 49–50, 76.

47. Douglas W. Pryor, *Unspeakable Acts: Why Men Sexually Abuse Children* (New York: New York University Press, 1996), p. 38.

48. Flowers, *Domestic Crimes, Family Violence and Child Abuse,* p. 137.

49. *Ibid.*

50. *Ibid.*

51. Jean Goodwinn, Lawrence Cormier, and John Owen, "Grandfather-Granddaughter Incest: A Trigenerational View," *Child Abuse and Neglect 7* (1983): 163–70.

52. H. Smith and E. Israel, "Sibling Incest: A Study of the Dynamics of 25 Cases," *Child Abuse and Neglect 11,* 1 (1987): 101–8; Jane M. Leder, *Brothers and Sisters: How They Shape Our Lives* (New York: St. Martin's Press, 1991); J. V. Becker, M. S. Kaplan, J. Cunningham-Rathner, and R. Kavoussi, "Characteristics of Adolescent Incest Sexual Perpetrators: Preliminary Findings," *Journal of Family Violence 1,* 1 (1986): 85–97.

53. Pierce and Pierce, "The Sexually Abused Child;" Smith and Israel, "Sibling Incest;" R. Longo and N. Groth, "Juvenile Sexual Offenses in the Histories of Adult Rapists and Child Molesters," *International Journal of Offender Therapy and Comparative Criminology 27* (1983): 155–57.

54. Flowers, *The Victimization and Exploitation of Women and Children,* p. 66; Leder, *Brothers and Sisters;* Smith and Israel, "Sibing Incest."

55. Courtois, *Healing the Incest Wound.*

56. Longo and Groth, "Juvenile Sex Offenses."

57. A. N. Groth and C. Loredo, "Juvenile Sex Offenders: Guidelines for Assessment," *International Journal of Offender Therapy and Comparative Criminology 25* (1981): 265–72.

58. W. L. Marshall and H. E. Barbaree, "Outcome of Cognitive-Behavioral Treatment," in W. L. Marshall, D. R. Laws, and H. E. Barbaree, eds., *Handbook of Sexual Assault* (New York: Plenum, 1990).

59. *Ibid.*

60. Flowers, *Sex Crimes, Predators, Perpetrators, Prostitutes, and Victims,* p. 79.

61. W. L. Marshall and A. Eccles, "Issues in Clinical Practice with Sex Offenders," *Journal of Interpersonal Violence 6* (1991): 68–93.

62. G. G. Abel, M. S. Mittleman, J. V. Becker, J. Rathner, and J. L. Rouleau, "Predicting Child Molesters' Response to Treatment," *Annals of the New York Academy of Sciences 528* (1988): 223–34.

63. M. R. Weinrott and M. Saylor, "Self-Report of Crimes Committed by Sex Offenders," *Journal of Interpersonal Violence 6,* 3 (1991): 286–300.

64. Abel, Mittleman, Becker, Rathner, and Rouleau, "Predicting Child Molesters' Response to Treatment."

Chapter 15

CHILD SEXUAL ABUSE

Along with intrafamilial child sexual abuse, many children are subjected to sexual maltreatment by offenders outside the family. Child molesters victimize children through various means including pedophilia, prostitution, pornography, child sex rings, and other means of exploitation. The vast majority of child sexual abusers are middle-aged men, though women and older children have also been known to sexually molest mostly younger children.

Victims can range from "totally accidental victimization involving little victimogenesis to seductive sexual partner with extensive victimogenesis. In many instances, the child may consent to the sexual victimization unintentionally or unwittingly, or offer only passive resistance; in other cases . . . the victim and offender are in a symbiotic relationship or form a cooperative dyad."[1] In worst case situations, child sexual abuse victims are completely powerless and vulnerable against the men who molest them.

DEFINING CHILD SEXUAL ABUSE

Child sexual abuse has been both narrowly and broadly defined, depending upon the source and parameters used. The Child Abuse Prevention and Treatment Act defines child sexual abuse as

(a) the employment, use, persuasion, inducement, enticement, or coercion of any child to engage in, or assist any other person to engage in, any sexually explicit conduct or simulation of such conduct for the purpose of producing any visual depiction of such conduct, or (b) the rape, molestation, prostitution, or other such form of sexual exploitation of children, or incest with children.[2]

In a report sponsored by the American Bar Association, the American Public Welfare Association, the Legal Resource Center for Child Advocacy and Protection, and the American Enterprise Institute, child abuse was defined as "vaginal, anal, or oral intercourse; vaginal or anal penetrations; or other forms of contact for sexual purposes."[3] The report further defined child sexual exploitation as "using a child in prostitution, pornography, or other sexually exploitative activities."[4]

Many professionals today subclassify child sexual abuse into *child molestation* and *pedophilia,* though the terms are often used interchangeably. Generally, child molestation relates to the sexual abuse of a child, usually other than incest. Pedophilia refers to a sexual preference for children instead of adults—often including fantasies—but does not necessarily result in child molestation, per se.[5] Child molesters and pedophiles are typically adult males, but may include adult females and adolescents.

THE SCOPE OF CHILD SEXUAL ABUSE

Estimates of the extent of child sexual abuse in America have varied considerably over the years, ranging from tens of thousands to well over a million victims annually.[6] The vast majority of child sexual abuse cases go unreported, according to many experts, leaving the true incidence of child sexual maltreatment unknown.[7]

What is known is that the overwhelming majority of child sex offenders are male. Studies show that 94 percent of child molesters are men.[8] Although their victims are male and female children, girls tend to be targeted and victimized more often than boys.[9] A review of nineteen studies on the prevalence of child sexual abuse found a rate of female victimization ranging from 6 percent to 62 percent, with male victimization ranging from 3 percent to 31 percent.[10] In an examination of eight random surveys of child sexual abuse, perpetrators victimized girls in 70 percent of the cases.[11] A study of 148 child molesters found that 51 percent targeted only girls, 28 percent only boys, and 21 percent sexually abused girls and boys.[12] In David Finkelhor's study on the magnitude of child sexual abuse, as many as 52 percent of adult females and 9 percent of adult males had been victims of child sexual abuse.[13]

Many believe that more boys are the targets of child molesters than studies indicate, but are less willing to report the victimization than girls.[14] In one study of male runaways, nearly four in ten were found to have been sexually abused.[15] Other research has yielded similar high rates of victimization among boys.[16]

Research on child sexual abuse further revealed the following:

- A child is the victim of sexual abuse every two minutes in the United States.
- One in four females under 18 is a victim of child sexual abuse.
- One in six to eight males under 18 is a victim of child sexual abuse.

- Two-thirds of sexual assault victims reported to law enforcement authorities are juveniles.
- One in seven victims of reported sexual assault is younger than age six.
- Fifteen to 30 percent of all females have been exposed to some type of child sexual abuse.
- Five to 15 percent of all males have been exposed to some form of child sexual abuse.
- Around 50 percent of victims of forcible rape, forcible fondling, and sodomy are children under the age of 12.[17]

THE NATURE OF CHILD SEXUAL ABUSE

Studies of child sexual abusers reveal that most have perpetrated not only multiple offenses against a child but also additional sex offenses. In a comprehensive self-report survey of 561 nonincarcerated sex offenders, Gene Abel and colleagues found that 377 of the subjects had committed a total of 48,297 acts of child molestation that was nonincestuous, consisting of 27,416 victims.[18] Another study of nonincarcerated child sexual abusers was consistent in its findings.[19]

In Abel and associates' survey of sex offenders committing multiple sex offenses, 26.8 percent of pedophiles with male victims and 23.7 percent of those with female victims had perpetrated at least two kinds of sexual offenses. Nearly 20 percent of the offenders of child victims had committed a minimum of three kinds of sex crimes. More than 2 percent had perpetrated ten different sex offenses.[20]

Studies show that many child sexual abusers were themselves victims of molestation. In T. J. Kahn and M. A. LaFond's study of adolescent sexual abusers, 60 percent of the molesters reported being sexually abused.[21] Victimization rates of 48 percent and 40 percent were reported in studies of child sexual abusers conducted by L. H. Pierce and R. L. Pierce,[22] and M. O'Brien,[23] respectively. Studies of incarcerated child molesters have reached similar results.[24]

CHILD MOLESTATION

Child molestation occurs when a child is the actual victim of sexual abuse. The dictionary definition of molestation is "to subject to unwanted or improper sexual activity." Either or both would apply where it concerns the sexual abuse of children.

Who is a child molester? According to the National Center for Missing and Exploited Children's publication, *Child Molesters: A Behavioral Analysis,* a child molester is defined as "a significantly older individual who engages in any type of sexual activity with individuals legally defined as children."[25] A child molester is typically regarded by law enforcement as one "who engages in illegal sexual activity with children," though the applicability of the term *child molester* "is more likely to conform to a legal definition of sexual molestation set forth in the penal code."[26]

Child sexual abuse expert A. Nicholas Groth defined a child molester as "having a sexual attraction toward prepubertal children (pedophilia) or sexual attraction toward pubertal children (hebephilia)."[27] He established a classification typology for child molesters, dividing them into two groups: fixated molesters and regressed molesters.

- *Fixated child molester* prefers children as sexual partners, identifying closely with them.
- *Regressed child molester* prefers sexual partners his own age, however, because of stress, diverts from his normal sexual attachment with adults.

A classification typology of child molesters was also developed by Raymond Knight and Robert Prentky, consisting of five elements:

- Social competence.
- A sexual preoccupation with children.
- Nonoffense contact with children.
- Physical harm to a child.
- Sadism.[28]

Both classification typologies are commonly used by psychologists in evaluating and treating child molesters, and by criminal justice personnel in classifying sex offenders.

TYPES OF CHILD MOLESTERS

Child molesters can be broken down into two general types: situational and preferential molesters.[29] Within these are subcategories. Some child molesters are reflected in more than one group or subgroup.

Situational Child Molester

The situational child molester typically does not have a sexual preference for children but for various reasons—such as extreme stress or self-doubt—turn to children for sexual involvement. Situational child molesters usually molest fewer children than preferential child molesters and may sexually abuse others as well, such as the elderly or disabled. Some studies have shown an over-representation of situational child molesters among the lower classes.[30]

There are four subtypes of situational child sexual molesters: (1) regressed, (2) morally indiscriminate, (3) sexually indiscriminate, and (4) inadequate.[31] The characteristics of these are described as follows:

- *Regressed child molester*–typically possesses a low self-esteem and poor coping mechanisms. He uses a child as a substitute for the more preferred adult sexual partner; often coercing the victim into sexual relations, and may also collect child pornography. The main criteria the regressed child molester has in selecting his victim is availability. His target is often his own offspring. This represents one of the more common types of child molesters.

- *Morally indiscriminate child molester*–is often abusive towards others, including their spouse and friends. He molests children largely because of a strong desire to do so, opportunity, and victim vulnerability. Coercion and manipulation are typically used to get victims, who can be strangers or family members. The morally indiscriminate child molester is without a conscience, impulsive, collects detective magazines, and adult and child pornography.

- *Sexually indiscriminate child molester*–is usually driven to molest children for sexual experimentation and out of boredom. The molester typically involves children in sexual relations with other adults, group sex, and sometimes ritual sexual abuse. He may target his own children. The sexually indiscriminate child molester is the most likely situational child molester to have multiple child victims, a higher socioeconomic background, and collect erotica and pornography.

- *Inadequate child molester*–is a social misfit and includes child sexual abusers suffering from personality disorders, psychoses, mental retardation, and senility. Inadequate child molesters are driven by insecurity, built-up impulses, and curiosity. They view child victims as nonthreatening in which to pursue sexual fantasies. The inadequate molester is capable of using violence and sexual torture on victims, which may include the elderly, and collects adult pornography.

Preferential Child Molester

The preferential child molester has a sexual preference for children, including erotic images of children and sexual fantasies. He molests not only as a reflection of situational stress, but rather due to a sexual attraction to children, seen as "safer partners who can provide adoration, have lower expectations, and are less inclined to reject the adult."[32] The preferential molester has an intense fear of rejection. Although possessing a number of character traits, the molester's sexual behavior is often "highly" predictable and seen as a "sexual ritual . . . frequently engaged in even when . . . counterproductive to getting away with the criminal activity."[33]

Preferential child molesters account for a smaller number of child sexual abusers than situational child molesters, however, they can potentially sexually molest greater numbers of victims. The preferential molester is characterized not only by "the nature of the sex drive (attraction to children) but also the quantity (need for frequent and repeated sex with children)."[34]

Studies show that preferential child molesters tend to be overrepresented among upper social and economic classes.[35] Most prefer boys over girls as victims. The true pedophile is identified as a preferential child molester.[36]

There are at least three subtypes of preferential child molesters, including: (1) seduction, (2) introverted, and (3) sadistic.[37] These are characterized as follows:

- *Seduction child molester*–manipulates child victims into participating in sexual relations by seducing through affection, kindness, and attention. The seduction child molester is often involved at the same time with multiple victims in child sex rings. His success in seducing the victim is based upon an ability to identify with the child, as well as being an adult often in an authoritative position (such as a scout master or choir director). Child victims of seduction molesters are typically also victims of child emotional and physical neglect. In order to prevent disclosure or ending the sexual abuse, the seduction child molester may resort to intimidation or violence.

- *Introverted child molester*–has a sexual preference for children, yet lacks the interpersonal skills to seduce. To compensate for this, the introverted molester relies on nonverbal communication in sexually molesting his victims. He fits the stereotypical image of the child molester who lurks around schools, parks, and playgrounds, watching his potential victims and sometimes has brief sexual contact with them. Some introverted child molesters are also exhibitionists or may engage the services of a child prostitute for satisfaction. Such molesters may even molest their own children, usually starting at infancy.

- *Sadistic child molester*–has a sexual preference for children. However, sexual arousal or gratification can only be achieved through inflicting physical or psychological pain on the child victim. The sadistic child molester often uses force to gain a victim and is more likely than other preferential child molesters to abduct or murder the child. Some seduction child molesters become sadistic child molesters. The sadistic molester is believed by authorities to represent only a small number of child sexual abusers.

PEDOPHILA

Pedophilia is believed to be the most common form of child sexual abuse. It is generally defined as "child molestation where a child is the favored sexual object of an adult through sexual fantasies and arousal or actual sexual situations."[38] Pedophilia typically consists of nonviolent adult or older child sexual contact with a child, involving "genital viewing or fondling, orogenital contact, penetration, and any other immoral or indecent behavior involving sexual activity."[39]

The American Psychiatric Association's *Diagnostic and Statistical Manual of Mental Disorders* (DSM-III-R) defines pedophilia as

> recurrent, intense, sexual urges, and sexually arousing fantasies, of at least six months' duration, involving sexual activity with a prepubescent child. The person has acted on these urges, or is markedly distressed by them. The age of the child is generally thirteen or younger. The age of the person is arbitrarily set at age sixteen years or older and at least five years older than the child.[40]

The DSM-III-R classified pedophiles as a *paraphilia,* or a psychosexual disorder. Pedophiles typically have other psychosexual or personality disorders in addition to a sexual interest in children. These include exhibitionism, voyeurism, bondage, coprophilia, and necrophilia.[41] The pedophile is regarded primarily as a preferential child molester.[42]

Dynamics of Pedophilia

Pedophilia is a widespread problem in the United States. It is estimated that anywhere from one to two million children in this country are victims of child sexual molestation every year.[43] In an 18-month examination of reported child molestation cases in Brooklyn and the Bronx, New York, the findings were as follows:

- Child molestation is statistically more prevalent than child physical abuse.
- Child molesters were male in 97 percent of the cases.
- The median age of a child molester was 31.
- The median age of a child victim was 11.

- Younger children, including infants, were also at risk for sexual molestation.
- Female victims outnumbered male victims ten to one.
- The molester was known to the molested child or the victim's family in three out of four cases.
- In more than 40 percent of the cases of molestation, the sexual abuse had occurred over a span ranging from a few weeks to seven years.
- Sixty percent of the molestation victims were molested through force or the threat thereof.
- Two-thirds of children victimized by molesters suffered some type of identifiable emotional trauma.
- Fourteen percent of victims became severely disturbed.[44]

Preferential child molester pedophiles are capable of molesting potentially thousands of children over a lifetime. In Abel and colleagues' study of sex offenders, it was reported that pedophiles who molested young boys outside the home committed the greatest number of offenses. They averaged 281.7 acts comprising of an average of 150.2 victims.[45] Almost one in four molesters perpetrated acts against victims within the family and outside it.

Kenneth Lanning identified four primary characteristics of the preferential child molester pedophile:

- A long and persistent pattern of behavior.
- A preference for children as sexual objects.
- Use of well established techniques in acquiring child victims.
- Having sexual fantasies focusing on children.[46]

Researchers have found the pedophile to often be immature, passive, and insecure in the ability to be involved in normal adult heterosexual relations.[47] According to J. M. Reinhardt, some young or middle-aged pedophiles turn to children only after an inability to achieve sexual gratification with adults.[48] Older pedophiles, usually over the age of 50, have been shown to "molest children due to diminishing physical and mental abilities brought about by the aging process."[49]

Types of Pedophiles and Pedophilia

Pedophilia can reflect different types of child molesters and pedophile acts. Three types of pedophile molesters were identified by Albert Cohen: (1) immature molester who seeks only to touch, fondle or caress the victim; (2) regressed molester, characterized by self-doubts and sexual inadequacy; and (3) aggressive molester who is often sadistic and violent in his desire for arousal and sexual excitement.[50]

In the book, *Pedophilia and Exhibitionism,* Johan Mohr, R. E. Turner, and M. B. Jerry described five types of pedophilia, including:

- *Heterosexual hebephilia*—any kind of sexual relations where the female victim is pubescent.
- *Heterosexual pedophilia*—any type of sexual relations in which the female victim has shown no pubertal changes.
- *Homosexual hebephilia*—any kind of sexual relations where the male victim is pubescent.
- *Homosexual pedophilia*—any nature of sexual relations in which the male victim of the same sex has shown no pubertal changes.
- *Undifferentiated pedophilia*—any kind of sexual relations in which the victim's gender is not differentiated.[51]

CLERGY AND CHILD SEXUAL ABUSE

The disturbing problem of child molestation and pedophilia involving Catholic priests and other members of the clergy has recently come to light. While precise figures on the magnitude of child sexual abuse perpetrated by clergy are hard to come by, given the secrecy involved and lack of cooperation by offenders and their superiors in the church, it is estimated that anywhere from 2 percent to 7 percent of priests have sexually abused a juvenile.[52] Since there are currently an estimated 60,000 active and inactive priests and brothers in the United States, this would amount to approximately 1,200 to 4,200 priests who have been involved in sexual misconduct with one or more persons under the age of 18.[53]

A similar estimated number of male clerics of Protestant and other denominations are believed to be child sexual abusers.[54] These figures are lower than the 8 percent of adult male child molesters estimated to be in the general population. However, this does not detract from the seriousness and shamefulness of child sexual abuse by members of the clergy.

It is estimated that 80 to 90 percent of priest child molesters have sexually abused adolescent boys, as opposed to prepubescent children, meaning that teenage boys are most at risk for victimization rather than young boys or girls.[55]

According to Thomas Plante, most priests who molest children perpetrate their first offense around one year following ordination. He suggested that risk factors for priests engaging in child molestation include "being sexually abused themselves as a child or adolescent, social isolation and poor social skills, impulse control problems in general, psychiatric co-morbidity with disorders such as substance abuse, mood and/or personality disorders, and brain damage."[56]

The current child sexual abuse scandal in the Catholic church demonstrates the vulnerability of child victims to not only sexual abuse by powerful spiritual leaders, but the difficulty in exposing the abuse and abuser in an institution that, until recently, was more concerned with protecting the church and offender than the victims from sexual exploitation.

CHILD SEX RINGS

Many child molesters and pedophiles are involved in child sex rings in their victimization of children. A child sex ring is defined as child sexual abuse and exploitation in which "there are one or more adult offenders and several children who are aware of each other's participation."[57] One study found at least eleven child sex rings in existence in the United States involving more than a dozen adult male and eighty-four identified sexually molested children ranging in age from eight to 15.[58]

According to Ann Burgess and Christine Grant, there are three basic types of child sex rings: (1) solo, (2) transition, and (3) syndicated.

- *Solo sex rings* involve multiple children in sexual acts with an adult, usually a male. The child molester usually has access to the victim for sexual entrapment and relies on isolation and secrecy to control the child.
- *Transition sex rings* involve multiple adults in sexual acts with children, usually adolescents. Victims are typically runaways, throwaways, or child abuse victims.
- *Syndicated sex rings* are well-structured operations involving the recruitment of children for prostitution and pornography, delivery of sexual services, and maintaining an extensive client list.[59]

Child and/or adult pornography are often an element of child sex rings. Some child sexual abusers progress from one sex ring to another in their exploitation of children.

NOTES

1. R. Barri Flowers, *Domestic Crimes, Family Violence and Child Abuse: A Study of Contemporary American Society* (Jefferson: McFarland, 2000), p. 124.
2. Child Abuse Prevention and Treatment Act, Public Law 100-294.

3. American Humane Association, *Child Abuse and Neglect Reporting and Investigation: Policy Guidelines for Decision-Making* (Denver: American Humane Association, 1987), p. 7.

4. *Ibid.*

5. R. Barri Flowers, *Sex Crimes, Predators, Perpetrators, Prostitutes, and Victims: An Examination of Sexual Criminality and Victimization* (Springfield: Charles C Thomas, 2001), p. 103.

6. *Ibid.,* p. 102; Diana E. Russell and Rebecca M. Bolen, *The Epidemic of Rape and Child Sexual Abuse in the United States* (Thousand Oaks: Sage, 2000).

7. L. Berliner and J. R. Wheeler, "Treating the Effects of Sexual Abuse on Children," *Journal of Interpersonal Violence 2* (1987): 415–24; D. Russell, *Intra-Family Child Sexual Abuse: Final Report to the National Center on Child Abuse and Neglect* (Washington: U.S. Department of Health and Human Services, 1983).

8. Cited in South Carolina Coalition Against Domestic Violence and Sexual Assault, "Child Sexual Assault," http://www.sccadvasa.org/child_sexual_assault.htm.

9. U.S. Department of Justice, *Children Traumatized in Sex Rings* (Alexandria: National Center for Missing & Exploited Children, 1988), p. 4; A. Nicholas Groth, *Men Who Rape* (New York: Plenum, 1979).

10. Cited in *Children Traumatized in Sex Rings,* p. 2.

11. David Finkelhor, *A Sourcebook on Child Sexual Abuse* (Thousand Oaks: Sage, 1986).

12. Cited in Flowers, *Sex Crimes, Predators, Perpetrators, Prostitutes, and Victims,* p. 102.

13. David Finkelhor, "How Widespread is Child Abuse?" in *Perspectives on Child Maltreatment in the Mid '80s* (Washington: National Center on Child Abuse and Neglect Information, 1984); David Finkelhor and Sharon Araji, *A Sourcebook on Child Sexual Abuse* (Thousand Oaks: Sage, 1995).

14. *Children Traumatized in Sex Rings,* p. 4; Flowers, *Sex Crimes, Predators, Perpetrators, Prostitutes, and Victims,* p. 102.

15. M. D. Janus, A. McCormack, A. W. Burgess, and C. R. Hartman, *Adolescent Runaways* (Lexington: Lexington Books, 1987).

16. See, for example, L. I. Risin and M. P. Koss, "Sexual Abuse of Boys: Prevalence and Descriptive Characteristics of the Childhood Victimizations," *Journal of Interpersonal Violence 2* (1987): 309–19; Janet Baker and Trish Berry, *It Happened To Us: Men Talk About Child Sexual Abuse* (Melbourne: Victorian Government Department of Health & Community Services, 1995).

17. "Child Sexual Assault."

18. G. G. Abel, J. V. Becker, J. Cunningham-Rathner, and J. L. Rouleau, "Self-Reported Sex Crimes of 561 Nonincarcerated Paraphiliacs," *Journal of Interpersonal Violence 2,* 6 (1987): 3–25.

19. Cited in *Children Traumatized in Sex Rings,* p. 2.

20. G. G. Abel, M. S. Mittleman, J. V. Becker, J. Rathner, and J. L. Rouleau, "Predicting Child Molesters' Responses to Treatment," *Annals of the New York Academy of Sciences 528* (1988): 223–34.

21. T. J. Kahn and M. A. LaFond, "Treatment of the Adolescent Sex Offender," *Child and Adolescent Social Work Journal 5* (1988).

22. L. H. Pierce and R. L. Pierce, "Adolescent/Sibling Incest Perpetrators," in L. Horton, B. Johnson, L. Roundy, and D. Williams, eds., *The Incest Perpetrator: A Family Member No One Wants to Treat* (Thousand Oaks: Sage, 1990).

23. M. O'Brien, "Taking Sibling Incest Seriously," in M. Quinn-Patton, ed., *Family Sexual Abuse: Frontline Research and Evaluation* (Thousand Oaks: Sage, 1991).

24. T. K. Seghorn, R. A. Prentky, and R. J. Boucher, "Childhood Sexual Abuse in the Lives of Sexually Aggressive Offenders," *Journal of the American Academy of Child and Adolescent Psychiatry 26* (1987): 262–67.

25. U.S. Department of Justice, Office of Juvenile Justice and Delinquency Prevention, *Child Molesters: A Behavioral Analysis For Law Enforcement Officers Investigating Causes of Child Sexual Exploitation* (Alexandria: National Center for Missing & Exploited Children, 1992), p. 1.

26. *Ibid.*, pp. 1–5.

27. *Ibid.*, p. 1; K. A. Danni and G. Hampe, "An Analysis of Predictors of Child Sex Offender Types Using Presentence Investigation Reports," *International Journal of Offender Therapy and Comparative Criminology 44* (2000): 490–504.

28. *Child Molesters.*

29. Flowers, *Sex Crimes, Predators, Perpetrators, Prostitutes, and Victims,* pp. 104–6; Robert E. Freeman-Longo and Geral T. Blanchard, *Sexual Abuse in America: Epidemic of the 21st Century* (Brandon: Safer Society Press, 1998), pp. 40–41.

30. *Child Molesters,* p. 6.

31. *Ibid.*, pp. 6–7; Freeman-Longo and Blanchard, *Sexual Abuse in America,* p. 40.

32. Freeman-Longo and Blanchard, *Sexual Abuse in America,* p. 40.

33. *Child Molesters,* p. 8.

34. *Ibid.*

35. *Ibid.*

36. *Ibid.*, pp. 15–21.

37. Flowers, *Sex Crimes, Predators, Perpetrators, Prostitutes, and Victims,* p. 106.

38. *Ibid.*

39. R. Barri Flowers, *The Victimization and Exploitation of Women and Children: A Study of Physical, Mental and Sexual Maltreatment in the United States* (Jefferson: McFarland, 1994), p. 73.

40. American Psychiatric Association, *Diagnostic and Statistical Manual of Mental Disorders,* 3rd ed., (Washington: American Psychiatric Association, 1987).

41. Flowers, *Sex Crimes, Predators, Perpetrators, Prostitutes, and Victims,* pp. 129–37; J. M. Reinhardt, *Sex Perversions and Sex Crimes* (Springfield: Charles C Thomas, 1957).

42. *Children Traumatized in Sex Rings,* p. 6.

43. E. P. Sarafino, "An Estimate of the National Incidence of Sexual Offenses," *Child Welfare 58,* 2 (1979): 127–34.

44. Flowers, *The Victimization and Exploitation of Women and Children,* p. 73; Susan Brownmiller, *Against Our Will: Men, Women, and Rape* (New York: Simon & Schuster, 1975), pp. 278–79.

45. Cited in Flowers, *Sex Crimes, Predators, Perpetrators, Prostitutes, and Victims,* p. 108.

46. Cited in *Child Molesters,* p. 15.

47. Flowers, *The Victimization and Exploitation of Women and Children,* p. 74.

48. Reinhardt, *Sex Perversions and Sex Crimes.*

49. Flowers, *The Victimization and Exploitation of Women and Children,* p. 74.

50. Albert K. Cohen, "The Sociology of the Deviant Act: Anomie Theory and Beyond," *American Sociological Review 2* (1965): 5–14.

51. Johan W. Mohr, R. Edward Turner, and M. B. Jerry, *Pedophilia and Exhibitionism* (Toronto: University of Toronto Press, 1964).

52. Anne A. Simpkinson, "Clergy Sexual Abuse Found in All Faiths," (March 18, 2002): http://www.beliefnet.com.

53. Thomas Plante, "A Perspective on Clergy Sexual Abuse," http://www.psy-www.com/psyrelig/plante.html.

54. *Ibid.;* R. Langevin, S. Curnoe, and J. Bain, "A Study of Clerics Who Commit Sexual Offenses: Are They Different from Other Sex Offenders?" *Child Abuse & Neglect 24* (2000): 535–45.

55. Plante, "A Perspective on Clergy Sexual Abuse."

56. *Ibid.*

57. *Children Traumatized in Sex Rings,* p. 7.

58. Cited in *Ibid.*

59. *Children Traumatized in Sex Rings,* pp. 7–14. See also U.S. Department of Justice, *Child Sex Rings: A Behavioral Analysis, for Criminal Justice Professionals Handling Cases of Child Sexual Exploitation* (Alexandria: National Center for Missing & Exploited Children, 1992), p. 11.

Chapter 16

PROSTITUTION-RELATED CRIMES

Males are actively involved in prostitution-related offenses across the country. Male pimps play a key role in the prostitution of young women and girls, recruiting as many as 90 percent of the females entering the business. Virtually all clients of prostitutes are men, including child and male prostitution. Most are habitual customers with multiple partners. Pornography and child pornography are typically interrelated to male participation in prostitution. Many johns are violent or otherwise abusive to prostitutes. Serial killers often target prostitutes for victimization. Male prostitutes cater primarily to the gay community. Their numbers are believed to be at least equal to that of female prostitutes. Overall, male perpetrators of prostitution crimes tend to be less likely than their female counterparts to face arrest or other involvement with the criminal justice system. However, law enforcement has recently begun cracking down more on the men that support the sex trade industry.

PIMPS AND PROSTITUTION

The Pimp and Runaways

Pimps are largely associated with street level prostitution. Although the role of the pimp, defined in the dictionary as "a man who procures clients for a prostitute," has lessened somewhat in recent years, pimps continue to be prominent figures in teenage female prostitution. Studies show that nine in ten girls entering prostitution were recruited by pimps or other prostitutes working for pimps.[1] According to an expert on runaways and child prostitution: "Runaway girls, scared and alone, are welcomed by pimps who watch for them as they arrive at bus and train stations. They offer them a roof over their heads, a 'caring adult,' clothes, makeup and promises of love and belonging."[2]

It is estimated that anywhere from hundreds of thousands to well over one million teenagers are selling their bodies as prostitutes in the United States.[3] Some studies suggest that as many as two-thirds of prostituted youth are female,[4] while more than two-thirds of these are believed to be runaway girls.[5] Pimps are thought to control between 80 and 95 percent of the female teen prostitution market in this country.[6]

Runaway youth, along with other troubled girls—such as those who are overweight, rebellious, drug addicted, depressed, or lonely—are typically targeted by pimps as "naïve and easy to control."[7] Most have been physically or sexually abused, some have been thrown out of the house, and all are in search of food, shelter, drugs, friendship, and companionship. Pimps take full advantage of these needs in luring such vulnerable girls into their stable. The typical process of seduction is described as follows:

> It often starts out with romance. Seduced at malls and in schoolyards, courted with restaurant meals and expensive gifts, the girls eventually find themselves cut off from their families and being asked to "return a favor." They are all, after all, very young. But the pimps also choose their targets well—girls from broken homes, girls living on the streets, girls who are just somehow troubled.[8]

In her study of teenage prostitution, Joan Johnson pointed toward two powerful emotions pimps typically use to manipulate and coerce girls into prostitution: love and fear.[9] According to the book, *Runaway Kids and Teenage Prostitution*, if the pimp "is successful in tapping into these [emotions] in taking advantage of the girl's weaknesses, she almost always will respond like the child she is and fall into the trap of believing the pimp truly has her best interests—love, support, and security—at heart."[10]

Notes a police detective on the vice squad regarding the susceptibility of girls to pimp charms and coercion: "The kids that are stable and know what their lives are about will tell these guys to hit the road. But kids who are vulnerable and hungry take up their offers of food, clothing, and a relationship and once the girls are with them, they are the pimp's property."[11]

In spite of this initial enticement, most prostituted girls will have a number of pimps over the course of their life in prostitution. Ninety percent of prostitutes leave their pimp within a year;[12] two-thirds leave within a few months.[13] In the first few years of prostituting, many streetwalkers may have "up to four pimps before settling on one, working for themselves, or leaving the business altogether in a revolving cycle of prostitute and pimp interrelations."[14]

Types of Pimps

Pimps are stereotypically portrayed as primarily African American males "wearing flashy clothes, hats, and jewelry and driving a Cadillac or other large status symbol car."[15] Yet only a relatively small portion of those pimping fit into this category. Most pimps lurking "in the shadows waiting to collect money from their stable of working girls" are white males whose operations include escort services, massage parlors, and strip clubs nationwide.[16] Some pimps are also women who may work for or with men, or operate brothels or street prostitution services independently.[17] Pimping has also been linked to other criminal activities, including drug dealing, robbery, criminal gangs, and organized crime.[18]

Researchers have identified three types of pimps: (1) the Popcorn pimp, (2) the Player pimp, and (3) the Mack pimp.[19]

Popcorn pimps are regarded as the least successful type of pimp. Working mostly with teenage girl prostitutes, Popcorn pimps tend to have little money and less roots compared to other pimps. They are highly competitive amongst themselves in the recruitment of girls, primarily runaways. These pimps are often the most violent toward the girls in their stable and have a higher turnover rate than the more successful pimps.

Player pimps are usually more successful than Popcorn pimps. They tend to have a few girls in their stable and often live with one "special" woman. The Player is less violent than his Popcorn counterparts, relying more on psychological tactics to control his prostitutes. A successful Player or "mid-range" pimp can earn as much as $200,000 a year, according to an expert on the pimp hierarchy.[20]

Mack pimps are seen as the upper class of pimps. They tend to have a much larger stable of girls working for them, with one as their "lady." Macks often combine street smarts and good business sense, investing profits from the business into legitimate investments. This enables most to maintain a comfortable suburban lifestyle while keeping a low profile, making it more difficult for law enforcement authorities to go after them.

The business of pimping is believed by some criminologists to be passed from generation to generation.[21] Many pimps also learn the trade from other pimps and prostitutes. There often exists something of a pimp fraternity among lower level pimps, encouraging sharing and cooperation.

Pimps and Violence

Pimps are often violent toward prostitutes in their stable. Studies reveal that the majority of streetwalkers are routinely physically assaulted by their pimps, ranging from beatings with "coat hangers to lashings with a six-foot bullwhip."[22] One survey found that more than two-thirds of prostitutes had been regularly assaulted by their pimps, including being hit with fists, whipped, and burned.[23] Some streetwalkers have been reported to be the victims of pimp initiated "severe violence, torture, and attempted murder."[24] According to the Justice Department, the mortality rate for female prostitutes is 40 times the national average.[25]

The relationship between a prostituted girl and her pimp has often been compared to that between a battered woman and her batterer.[26] The same dynamics of love, fear, power, psychological dominance and control tend to come into play.

Pimp violence against a prostitute can be unpredictable. Reasons for the violent behavior typically include teaching the prostitute a lesson for trying to escape or being disrespectful, or battering for not bringing in enough money. Some pimps beat one prostitute to serve as an example to others in their stable. Often a violent pimp is under the influence of alcohol or drugs, or otherwise acting out due to his own stresses and struggles in a highly competitive business.

A typical example of the pimp's psychological hold over a young prostitute can be seen as follows:

> In New York City, a girl's pimp kept her on the street six nights a week. She hated being a prostitute, but the pimp was the only person who had shown her any kindness. When she could stand it no longer and told him she had to quit, he broke her jaw. At the hospital where her jaw was wired shut, she was given pain pills and told to rest. But her pimp put her on the street the next night.
>
> Later, she tried to commit suicide using the pills, but she vomited, breaking the wires in her jaw. Her pimp would not allow her to return to the hospital and sent her back on the street. . . . She turned herself in to the police.
>
> When asked her age, she replied, "I'll be fifteen tomorrow."[27]

Relatively few pimps are ever arrested or sent to jail for assaulting prostitutes. Victims often refuse to press charges out of fear, intimidation, love, confusion, or believing justice would not be served.

MALE PROSTITUTION

Many experts on the sex trade industry believe that there are at least as many male prostitutes as an estimated up to two million female prostitutes in the United States.[28] Most male prostitutes are adult whites, though minorities and juveniles are also well represented in the male prostitution business. Male prostitutes are much more likely to face arrest in cities than rural or suburban communities.[29] The risk of HIV infection is particularly high among prostitution-involved males.[30]

Nature of Male Prostitution

Male prostitutes, similar to their female counterparts, come from all walks of life including being "delinquent school dropouts to well educated, refined college students; they come from inner city projects to middle class suburbs; from completely disintegrated families and from effective loving families."[31] Most male prostitutes are runaways or throwaways. One study found that two out of three full-time male prostitutes were runaways.[32] A high percentage of prostituted males have been victims of child physical or sexual abuse.[33] Most have also come from otherwise dysfunctional families, including incestuous and drug abusing.

Studies have shown that male prostitutes tend to be self-destructive, unstable, immature, and possess high levels of psychopathology.[34] Male prostitutes have also been found to have a high rate of sexually transmitted diseases, drug addiction, and alcoholism.[35]

Authorities contend that male prostitutes and johns have a "deep hatred" towards one another. They often "wrestle with conflicting emotions during their time together, often creating fantasies that are acted out in the course of their sexual encounter."[36]

Types of Male Prostitutes

Researchers have identified a number of types of male prostitutes. S. Caukins and N. Coombs found there to be four primary types: (1) street hustlers, (2) bar hustlers, (3) call boys, and (4) kept boys.[37] They postulated that a "gay sex market thrives in every big city . . . a profit oriented street corner college for the recruiting, training, and selling of boys and men to older, affluent homosexuals."[38]

In a study of male prostitutes and intravenous drug use, Dan Waldorf and Sheigla Murphy divided prostitution-involved males into two general categories: hustlers and call men.[39] Hustlers tended to find customer in places typically frequented by participants in male prostitution: arcades, gay bars, adult bookstores, and theaters. The researchers subcategorized hustlers into three types:

- *Trade hustlers*–heterosexual or bisexual males who trade sex for money; rarely do they acknowledge being gay or enjoying sexual relations with male johns.
- *Drag queen hustlers*–transvestites and transsexuals who specialize in oral sex; they typically operate in known gay red-light districts.
- *Youth hustlers*–young, admitted homosexual males, appearing naïve and innocent, but in fact are often well experienced in gay sexual relations.[40]

Call men "do not reflect erotic styles but rather the ways in which they locate customers," in addition to the types of services they offer.[41] Waldorf and Murphy subdivided these male prostitutes into four categories:

- *Call book men*–usually self-identified as gay or bisexual, having regular clients or acquiring them from a call book.
- *Models and escorts*–men who find customers through advertising in general or special interest publications, often establishing a network of regular johns.
- *Erotic masseurs*–men who locate new clients through advertisements while maintaining a regular client list; most are certified by licensed massage schools, combining massages with sexual services.
- *Porn industry stars*–considered the elite among male prostitutes, including erotic dancers and porn actors; clients (including female) are typically solicited on the job and serviced elsewhere.[42]

Boy Prostitution

According to the book, *For Money or Love: Boy Prostitution in America*, there are at least 300,000 male prostitutes under the age of 16 in the United States.[43] Some believe the figures may be twice as high for male prostitutes under age 18.[44] Boy prostitutes are typically referred to on the streets as *chickens*. The homosexual men that prey on them are known as *chicken hawks* or *chicken queens*. While much of the adolescent male prostitution occurs in big cities with a large gay population, many prostituted male youth ply their trade in the suburbs or rural areas.

Chicken hawks have been characterized as follows:

- Often middle aged.
- Relates to children well.
- Sees the chicken as the sexual aggressor.
- Generally nonviolent.
- Associates with other pedophiles and chicken hawks.
- Usually single, but can be married.
- Was often a victim of child sexual abuse.
- Usually a white collar or professional worker.[45]

The vast majority of boy prostitutes are streetwalkers. D. Kelly Weisberg found that 94 percent of prostitution-involved boys sell sex on the streets.[46] However, there are known boy brothels.[47] In the first national study of boy prostitutes, conducted by the Urban and Rural Systems Association of San Francisco, the following profile emerged:

- Boys prostitute themselves primarily to survive on the streets, explore their sexuality, and/or make contact with gay men.
- Money is the most important reason for male juveniles entering and remaining in prostitution.

- Most adolescent male prostitutes are runaway or throwaway children.
- Most boy prostitutes have been physically, sexually, or emotionally abused.
- Delinquency and criminal behavior are common in the life of boy prostitutes.
- Pimps are virtually nonexistent in the adolescent male prostitution subculture.
- Gay-identified young male prostitutes initially find the prostitution lifestyle to be exciting.[48]

MALE CUSTOMERS OF PROSTITUTES

The sex trade industry is predominantly supported by a male clientele. It is estimated that one-fifth of all males in the United States have solicited a prostitute at some point in their life.[49] Prostitutes' johns belong to all racial and ethnic groups, social classes, and occupational and educational levels. They are heterosexual, homosexual, and bisexual. Most are married men in their thirties, forties, and fifties but can also be younger and older.

Studies have shown that many men who solicit prostitutes are "pedophiles . . . child molesters, rapists, abusers, or substance abusers; many seek various sexual perversions such as . . . fellatio, anal sex . . . [and] triolism."[50] One study found that 75 percent of streetwalker prostitutes' services were for performing oral sex.[51] According to one expert on johns and what motivates them: "Some men crave the excitement, thrill and risk of what they perceive to be down and dirty sex."[52]

In his study of prostitutes, Richard Goodall categorized johns into eight types:

- Men deprived of sexual pleasure or regular sexual relations.
- Young men who are shy and/or sexually inexperienced.
- Lonely men.
- Men who are unattractive, deformed, or otherwise physically disadvantaged.
- Occupational johns such as those in the military.
- Sexual deviants such as sadomasochists, exhibitionists, and perverts.
- Menopausal men—spouses of menopausal women whose interest in sex has diminished.
- Castrated men—those under psychological pressure due to the modern woman's availability and ascendancy.[53]

Some clients of prostitutes have also been found to be therapeutically moti-vated johns–men who seek out prostitutes for their therapeutic needs. These johns solicit prostitutes primarily as an "outlet for venting problems or frus-trations to and receive in return a sympathetic and somewhat impersonal lis-tening ear."[54] In a four-year study of prostitutes and their customers, the most important reason johns gave for seeing prostitutes was regarding them as "paraprofessional therapists;" which raised their self-esteem and self-aware-ness and restored the confidence in the men's sexuality.[55]

Johns and Violence

Many johns are perpetrators or victims of prostitute violence. Research has shown that virtually every prostitute has experienced some form of customer violence during their career in the sex trade industry.[56] In one study, 70 per-cent of the prostitutes were found to have experienced repeated rapes by johns, for an average of 31 sexual assaults per year.[57] The study also reported that 65 percent of the prostitutes were regularly beaten or abused by clients.

Johns are also frequently victimized by female and male prostitutes. One study found that as many as half the johns were routinely robbed by prosti-tutes.[58] Some prostitutes carry guns or knives both to commit crimes against johns and for self-defense. Other research has documented the relationship between prostitution, drug addiction, and violence by a client or prostitute.[59]

MALE PROSTITUTION-RELATED OFFENSES AND THE CRIMINAL JUSTICE SYSTEM

In spite of the numbers of men involved in prostitution-related criminali-ty, relatively few are arrested or otherwise in contact with the criminal justice system. According to official data, there were only 18,542 arrests of males for prostitution and commercialized vice in the United States in 2000.[60] As shown in Figure 16.1, between 1991 and 2000, male arrests for prostitution-related offenses declined by more than 15 percent, though many experts believe that male involvement in prostitution continues to flourish in this country.[61]

Researchers have found that only two male customers of prostitutes are arrested for every eight female prostitutes arrested.[62] Similarly, prostitutes are far more likely to be arrested than pimps. For instance, in Portland, Oregon, in 1995, there were 402 arrests for prostitution, compared to only 18 arrests for pimping, and ten arrests for procuring or solicitation of a prostitute.[63]

Recent years have seen stepped up efforts by law enforcement to go after men who solicit prostitutes. These include car seizure laws that allow police

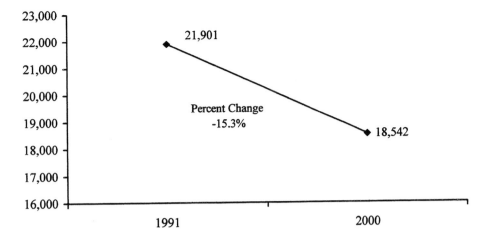

Figure 16.1. Ten-Year Male Arrest Trends for Prostitution and Commercialized Vice, 1991–2000. *Source:* Derived from U.S. Department of Justice, Federal Bureau of Investigation, *Crime in the United States: Uniform Crime Reports 2000* (Washington: Government Printing Office, 2001), p. 221.

to impound the vehicles of those arrested for solicitation,[64] and laws designed to "publicize and shame would-be johns by publishing their names or pictures," as well as increased arrests of prostitutes' clients and others involved in the sex trade industry.[65]

Male prostitutes are also less likely than their female counterparts to be involved with the criminal justice system, according to some studies. D. Sweeney estimated that 70 percent of boy prostitutes never come into contact with the police, courts, or corrections,[66] while it has been estimated that as many as 75 percent of girl prostitutes do come into contact with the criminal or juvenile justice system.[67] However, some research disputes this disparity. Weisberg found that two-thirds of her boy prostitute sample had been arrested at least once, with one-third of the arrests for prostitution-related offenses.[68]

NOTES

1. Cited in Joan J. Johnson, *Teen Prostitution* (Danbury: Franklin Watts, 1992), p. 75. See also Susanne Thorbek and Bandana Pattanaik, eds., *Prostitution in a Global Context: Changing Patterns* (London: Zed Books, 2003).

2. Patricia Hersh, "Coming of Age on City Streets," *Psychology Today* (January 1988), p. 32. See also Joanna Phoenix, *Making Sense of Prostitution* (New York: Palgrave Global, 2001).

3. R. Barri Flowers, *The Prostitution of Women and Girls* (Jefferson: McFarland, 1998), p. 71.

4. R. Barri Flowers, *The Adolescent Criminal: An Examination of Today's Juvenile Offender* (Jefferson: McFarland, 1990), p. 55.

5. Flowers, *The Adolescent Criminal,* p. 58; Clare Tattersall, *Drugs, Runaways, and Teen Prostitutes* (New York: Rosen, 1999), p. 8.

6. Kathleen Barry, *The Prostitution of Sexuality* (New York: New York University Press, 1995), p. 198. See also William W. Sanger, *History of Prostitution: Its Extent, Causes and Effects Throughout the World* (New York: Fredonia Books, 2002).

7. U.S. Department of Justice, Office of Juvenile Justice and Delinquency Prevention, *Prostitution of Children and Child-Sex Tourism: An Analysis of Domestic and International Responses* (Alexandria: National Center for Missing & Exploited Children, 1999), p. 4.

8. Deborah Jones, "Pimped," *Chatelaine 67* (November 1994), p. 111.

9. Johnson, *Teen Prostitution,* p. 79.

10. R. Barri Flowers, *Runaway Kids and Teenage Prostitution: America's Lost, Abandoned, and Sexually Exploited Children* (Westport: Greenwood, 2001), pp. 120–21.

11. Jones, "Pimped," p. 111.

12. Cited in Johnson, *Teen Prostitution,* p. 83.

13. *Ibid*; Phoenix, *Making Sense of Prostitution.*

14. Flowers, *Runaway Kids and Teenage Prostitution,* p. 125.

15. Flowers, *The Prostitution of Women and Girls,* p. 100.

16. Flowers, *Runaway Kids and Teenage Prostitution,* p. 121.

17. *Ibid*; Alexa Albert, *Mustang Ranch and Its Women* (New York: Ballantine, 2002).

18. Flowers, *Runaway Kids and Teenage Prostitution,* pp. 121–22.

19. Johnson, *Teen Prostitution,* p. 77; Sanger, *History of Prostitution.*

20. *Ibid.*

21. *Ibid.*

22. *Ibid.,* p. 86.

23. Flowers, *The Prostitution of Women and Girls,* p. 103.

24. Anastasia Volkonsky, "Legalizing the 'Profession' Would Sanction the Abuse," *Insight on the News 11* (1995): 20.

25. Cited in *Ibid.*

26. Evelina Giobbe, "An Analysis of Individual, Institutional and Cultural Pimping," *Michigan Journal of Gender and Law 1* (1993): 33, 46.

27. John G. Hubbell, "Child Prostitution: How It Can Be Stopped," *Reader's Digest* (June 1984), pp. 202, 205.

28. Flowers, *The Prostitution of Women and Girls,* p. 15.

29. *Ibid.,* p. 135.

30. *Ibid.,* p. 143. See also Martin A. Plant, ed., *AIDS, Drugs, and Prostitution* (London: Routledge, 1990).

31. Donald M. Allen, "Young Male Prostitutes: A Psychosocial Study," *Archives of Sexual Behavior 9* (1980): 418.

32. *Ibid.,* pp. 409–18.

33. Flowers, *The Prostitution of Women and Girls,* pp. 136–41.

34. See, for example, *Ibid.*, p. 138; D. MacNamara, "Male Prostitution in American Cities: A Socioeconomic or Pathological Phenomenon?" *American Journal of Orthopsychiatry 35* (1965): 204.

35. Flowers, *The Prostitution of Women and Girls*, p. 138.

36. *Ibid.*

37. S. Caukins and N. Coombs, "The Psychodynamics of Male Prostitution," *American Journal of Psychotherapy 30* (1976): 441–51.

38. *Ibid.*, p. 441.

39. Dan Waldorf and Sheigla Murphy, "Intravenous Drug Use and Syringe-Sharing Practices of Call Men and Hustlers," in Martin A. Plant, ed., *AIDS, Drugs, and Prostitution* (London: Routledge, 1990), pp. 109–31.

40. *Ibid.*

41. Flowers, *The Prostitution of Women and Girls*, p. 137; Thorbek and Pattanaik, *Prostitution in a Global Context.*

42. Waldorf and Murphy, "Intravenous Drug Use and Syringe-Sharing Practices of Call Men and Hustlers," pp. 109–31.

43. Robin Lloyd, *For Money or Love: Boy Prostitution in America* (New York: Ballantine, 1976), p. 211. See also Flowers, *The Prostitution of Women and Girls*; Sanger, *History of Prostitution.*

44. Flowers, *Runaway Kids and Teenage Prostitution*, p. 130.

45. *Ibid.*, p. 131.

46. D. Kelly Weisberg, *Children of the Night: A Study of Adolescent Prostitution* (Lexington: Lexington Books, 1985), p. 61.

47. Johnson, *Teen Prostitution*, p. 100.

48. Cited in Hilary Abramson, "Sociologists Try to Reach Young Hustlers," *Sacramento Bee* (September 3, 1984), p. A8.

49. Jennifer James, "The Prostitute as Victim," in Jane R. Chapman and Margaret Gates, eds., *The Victimization of Women* (Thousand Oaks: Sage, 1978), p. 176.

50. Flowers, *The Prostitution of Women and Girls*, p. 128.

51. Cited in Barbara Goldsmith, "Women on the Edge: A Reporter at Large," *New Yorker 69* (April 26, 1993), p. 216.

52. Quoted in Susan Bakos, "The Hugh Grant Syndrome: Why Nice Guys Go to Hookers," *McCall's 123* (November 1995), p. 106.

53. Richard Goodall, *The Comfort of Sin: Prostitutes and Prostitution in the 1990s* (Kent: Renaissance Books, 1995), pp. 69–79.

54. Flowers, *The Prostitution of Women and Girls*, p. 129.

55. M. Stein, *Lovers, Friends, Slaves . . .* (New York: Berkeley, 1974), pp. 1–2.

56. Cited in Johnson, *Teen Prostitution*, p. 131.

57. Cited in Volkonsky, "Legalizing the 'Profession' Would Sanction the Abuse," p. 20.

58. "The Enablers," *Juvenile Prostitution in Minnesota: The Report of a Research Project* (St. Paul: The Enablers, 1978), p. 75.

59. Flowers, *The Prostitution of Women and Girls*, pp. 127–30.

60. U.S. Department of Justice, Federal Bureau of Investigation, *Crime in the United States: Uniform Crime Reports 2000* (Washington: Government Printing Office, 2001), p. 221.

61. Flowers, *The Prostitution of Women and Girls*, pp. 100–4, 126–44; R. Barri Flowers, *Sex Crimes, Predators, Perpetrators, Prostitutes and Victims: An Examination of Sexual Criminality and Victimization* (Springfield: Charles C Thomas, 2001), pp. 169–79.

62. R. Barri Flowers, *Women and Criminality: The Woman as Victim, Offender, and Practitioner* (Westport: Greenwood, 1987), p. 129.

63. Laura Trujillo, "Escort Services Thriving Industry in Portland Area," *Oregonian* (June 7, 1996), p. B1.

64. Flowers, *The Prostitution of Women and Girls*, pp. 131–32.

65. Volkonsky, "Legalizing the 'Profession' Would Sanction the Abuse," p. 22.

66. Cited in Tamara Stieber, "The Boys Who Sell Sex to Men in San Francisco," *Sacramento Bee* (March 4, 1984), p. A22. See also Thorbek and Pattanaik, *Prostitution in a Global Context.*

67. Weisberg, *Children of the Night*, pp. 124–28.

68. *Ibid.*, p. 75.

Chapter 17

PORNOGRAPHY, SEX CRIMES, AND VIOLENCE

The correlation between pornography and male criminality has been clearly demonstrated in the literature. Use of pornographic materials are linked to male aggression, violence, sex offenses, domestic violence, and other antisocial behavior. Most disturbing with respect to men and pornography is the sexual misuse and exploitation of children by child molesters and pedophiles through child pornography.

Millions of children are potentially at risk for victimization by pornographers and pedophiles through child porn films, magazines, books, child sex rings, and the Internet. Online child pornography is the most recent assault on the innocence of children and perhaps the most challenging for law enforcement authorities to combat. Nevertheless, child pornography laws exist and new ones are being enacted on both the federal and state level in efforts to protect children in cyberspace and elsewhere, and to go after their sexual exploiters.

WHAT IS PORNOGRAPHY?

The term *pornography* comes from the Greek word *pornographos*. This derives from *porne*, which refers to a prostitute or female captive, and *graphein*, meaning to write–thus writings concerning prostitution and prostitutes.[1] Pornography is defined in the dictionary as "writings, pictures, films, or other materials that are meant to stimulate erotic feelings by describing or portraying sexual activity."[2] According to philosopher Helen Longino, pornography is material that "explicitly represents or describes degrading and abusive sexual behavior so as to endorse and/or recommend the behavior as described."[3]

A broader definition of pornography is given in the book, *The Prostitution of Women and Girls,* as

> any sexually explicit and/or titillating, arousing, written, photographic, pictorial, computer, or live depiction of women or children as objects for commercial exploitation, including acts of prostitution or other illicit sexual performances; or which depicts sexual abuse, degradation, or humiliation of subjects; and is offensive in its sexual content or acts to the public at large.[4]

What is clear is that pornography is a big business, bringing in an estimated $7 to $10 billion in the United States annually.[5] In 1992 alone, an estimated 1,600 new pornographic videos were produced in this country, resulting in 500 million rentals.[6] Females represent the primary participants in pornography, with males being the primary users.

Pornography is viewed by many experts on violent behavior by its very nature as "systematically eroticizing violence against women by producing and marketing images of men humiliating, battering, and murdering women for sexual pleasure."[7] According to Francis Patai, the organizer for Women Against Pornography, "pornography objectifies women by caricaturing and reducing them to a sum of their sexual parts and functions—devoid of sensibilities and intelligence. . . . Objectifying the sexual anatomy of women renders them inferior and nonhuman, thus providing the psychological foundation for committing violence against them."[8]

PORNOGRAPHY AND ANTISOCIAL BEHAVIOR

The relationship between pornography and antisocial behavior has been studied by government commissions with varying results. In 1970, a Presidential Commission on Obscenity and Pornography found no evidence that "exposure to explicit sexual materials plays a significant role in the causation of delinquency or criminal behavior among youths or adults."[9] However, in 1985, the Attorney General's Commission on Pornography came to a different conclusion, finding that there was a "correlation between certain types of pornography and sexual violence and abuse toward women," adding that "exposure to even nonviolent sexually explicit material 'bears some causal relationship to the level of sexual violence.'"[10]

According to the commission's report:

> When clinical and experimental research has focused particularly on sexually violent material, the conclusion has been nearly unanimous. In both clinical and experimental settings, exposure to sexually violent material has indicated an increase in the likelihood of aggression. . . . The research . . . shows a causal relationship between exposure to material of this type and aggressive behavior

towards women. . . . The assumption that increased aggressive behavior toward women is casually related . . . to increased sexual violence is significantly supported by the clinical evidence, as well as by much of the less scientific evidence.[11]

In spite of the differing conclusions by the commissions' reports, many experts on sexual violence concur that at least some cause and effect relationship exists between the pornography industry and women's victimization.[12]

PORNOGRAPHY AND VIOLENCE TOWARD FEMALES

Researchers have found a strong association between the use of pornography by men and violence against women.[13] In *Take Back the Night: Women on Pornography*, Laura Lederer asserts that "pornography is the ideology of a culture which promotes and condones rape, woman battering, and other crimes against women."[14] A study of battered wives found that 15 percent believed their spouse batterers experienced sexual arousal after watching hard-core pornography, "since the demand for sexual intercourse immediately followed the assault."[15]

A number of studies have examined the role pornography may play in sex crimes. After studying pornography and rape victims, Pauline Bart stated: "I didn't start out being against pornography; but if you're a rape researcher, it becomes clear that there is a direct link. . . . Men are not born thinking women enjoy rape and torture. . . . They learn from pornography."[16] In a study of mass-circulation sex magazines and the incidence of rape, Larry Baron and Murray Straus reported that "rape increases in direct proportion to the readership of sex magazines."[17] According to Neil Malamuth, co-editor of *Pornography and Sexual Aggression*: "In a culture that celebrates rape, the lives of millions of women will be affected."[18]

In a public lecture titled "Does Pornographic Literature Incite Sexual Assault?", the correlation between pornography and sex offenses is further supported. The speaker, a Michigan State Police detective, cited

> numerous cases where the assailants had immersed themselves in pornographic films or pictures and then gone out and committed sex crimes. These crimes included rape, sodomy, and even the bizarre erotic crime of piquerism (piercing with a knife till blood flows, a kind of sexual torture). In some cases the attacker admitted that the urge to rape or torture erotically came over him while reading an obscene picture magazine or attending a movie showing rape and erotic torture.[19]

Other studies have noted the relationship between pornography and prostitution—as part of the sex trade and exploitation industry—and physical and sexual assaults of prostitutes by pimps, johns, and strangers.[20]

CHILD PORNOGRAPHY

Defining Child Pornography

Child pornography has been referred to by experts on child sexual abuse as "the most inhuman of crimes. For pleasure and profit, pornographers have murdered the childhood of a million girls and boys, victims who must live with the dreadful memories of their experience."[21] Often referred to as "kiddie porn" and "chicken porn," child pornography is generally defined as "photographs, videos, books, magazines, and motion pictures that depict children in sexually explicit acts with other children, adults, animals, and/or foreign objects."[22] Other definitions of child pornography include that of the International Criminal Police Organization (INTERPOL), which defines it as "the visual depiction of the sexual exploitation of a child, focusing on the child's sexual behavior or genitals;"[23] and the Council of Europe's definition of child pornography as "any audiovisual material which uses children in a sexual context."[24]

According to the U.S. Department of Justice publication, *Child Molesters: A Behavioral Analysis*, a legal definition of child pornography is

> the sexually explicit reproduction of a child's image—including sexually explicit photographs, negatives, slides, magazines, movies, videotapes, and computer disks. In essence, it is the permanent record of the sexual abuse or exploitation of an actual child. In order to be legally considered child pornography, it must be a visual depiction (not the written word), of a minor (as defined by statute), which is sexually explicit (not necessarily obscene, unless required by state law).[25]

The definition of child pornography today includes the use and creation of or spreading such materials via the Internet and online communication.

Child pornography victims are subjected to virtually every kind of sexual abuse, misuse, and exploitation including rape, molestation, sadism, bestiality, torture, and murder. One magazine vividly depicts adults in various sexual acts with toddlers.[26] At least one audiotape, accompanied by a graphic narrative description, has been discovered that recorded the cries of a young girl being raped.[27]

Though child pornography is illegal in the United States, most experts agree that current laws and manpower makes it difficult to enforce. With the emergence of child pornography on the Internet, the task has become that much harder.

The Extent of Child Pornography

Similar to adult pornography, child pornography is a multibillion dollar international enterprise. The United States has the biggest market for child pornography, taking in an estimated $6 billion dollars a year.[28] Eighty-five percent of worldwide sales of child porn materials occurs in this country.[29] In Los Angeles alone, an estimated 30,000 children are sexually exploited by child pornographers and consumers annually.[30] Child pornography represents approximately 7 percent of the total pornography market in the United States.[31]

Many of the kiddie porn films and magazines come from abroad from countries such as Sweden, Germany, Denmark, and Switzerland. A recent study found that at least 264 different magazines showing children involved in sexual acts are produced and distributed every month in the United States.[32] A magazine of sexually explicit images of children can be produced for as little as fifty cents and sold for 20 times as much.[33] The profit margin is believed to be even higher for child pornography sold on the Internet.

Recently, a number of high-profile law enforcement operations have resulted in scores of arrests of suspected child pornographers and other sexual exploiters of children nationwide, as well as in other countries.[34]

In spite of these successes and tough antipornography laws in this country, according to researchers Margaret Hyde and Elizabeth Forsyth "several hundred magazines, international mailing lists, videotapes, and other forms of child pornography are still being sold. Producers find a steady supply of [children] for their 'kiddie porn' on the streets . . . [searching] for money . . . food and shelter."[35] Child pornographers have little trouble recruiting willing participants. The pool of susceptible, vulnerable child victims includes runaways, throwaways, homeless youth, teenage prostitutes, young drug addicts, neighborhood youth, and sometimes family members. Most of these children are looking for quick and easy money, drugs, excitement, and adventure. They are usually brought into the child porn business through money, food, drugs, gifts, shelter, trips, and camaraderie. On occasion, some children are forced into child porn through white slavery, kidnapping, threats, intimidation, and blackmail.[36]

Although child pornography is unquestionably a global profit making business, and has been linked to organized crime, experts on child sexual exploitation believe that "the majority of child pornography disseminated internationally is, in fact, exchanged between pedophiles and child molesters without any commercial motive."[37] Similarly, a recent U.S. Senate Report stated: "The overwhelming majority of child pornography seized in the United States has not been produced or distributed for profit. . . . [Rather], the cost must be measured in terms of the sexual exploitation of children represented by child pornography, and the sexual abuse of children to which child pornography is a central contributing factor."[38]

Types of Child Pornography

There are four subtypes of child pornography: (1) commercial, (2) homemade, (3) technical, and (4) simulated.[39] Each of these represent different aspects of the child porn industry in understanding the sexual exploitation of children.

- *Commercial child pornography*–produced primarily by child molesters and pedophiles and meant for commercial sale.
- *Homemade child pornography*–not originally produced for commercial sale by molesters and pedophiles, usually swapped and traded with other molesters and pedophiles.
- *Technical child pornography*–pornography involving persons age 17 and under, as legally defined. It is typically produced, distributed, and purchased by adult pedophiles and molesters.
- *Simulated child pornography*–consists of persons age 18 and over in pornographic depictions designed to simulate child pornography.

Sometimes homemade child pornography becomes commercial. For example, some homemade child porn is sold or otherwise winds up in commercial child pornography publications, pictures, or videos.

Child pornography is often exchanged, sold, and purchased through child sex rings. These have been broken down into *historical child sex rings* and *multidimensional child sex rings*.[40] The former refers to traditional child sex rings including solo, transition, and syndicated. The latter involves multiple victims and offenders, fear as an instrument of control, and often bizarre, satanic, and/or ritual activity. See Chapter 15 for more discussion on child sex rings.

Child pornography is commonly confused with *child erotica*, defined as "any material, relating to children, that serves a sexual purpose for a given individual."[41] Child erotica, also referred to as *pedophile paraphernalia*, includes drawings, diaries, books, games, toys, manuals, sexual aids, and souvenirs that are related to children. The possession and distribution of child erotica is not illegal, so long as it does not violate child pornography laws, by legal definition.

The Victims of Child Pornography

Who are the children being exploited by child pornographers? Children of all ages, races, ethnicities, nationalities, and backgrounds are targeted and victimized in the worldwide production of child pornography. It is estimated that hundreds of thousands of children may be victims of child pornographic material.[42]

Boys are generally viewed as being more represented in child porn than girls. According to the Federal Bureau of Investigation (FBI), more than half the child pornography confiscated in the United States depicts male children.[43] Three-quarters of the child pornography seized in Canada has been found to feature boys instead of girls.[44] This differs from general child sexual abuse studies which show higher rates of victimization for girls.[45]

Both boys and girls are equally vulnerable to child pornographers and sexual exploiters. This is especially true today with the growing presence of child pornography on the Internet.

The Producers and Consumers of Child Pornography

Child pornographers and consumers of child porn are predominantly adult males. These sexual exploiters of children come from all walks of life. Many also sexually molest children or exploit them through child prostitution. While many pornographers, purveyors, and consumers of child pornography are strangers to the victims, some are family members or otherwise known to those targeted.

In a recent 20/20 news story on ABC involving a U.S. Postal Service sting operation known as "Operation Special Delivery," many of the child pornography distributors and consumers were described as "respected members of the community."[46] Confiscated were videotapes and photographs of children crying, sexually or physically mistreated, and tortured. According to the book, *Children and Criminality,*

> The men who support this industry do so to rationalize and seek justification for their perverted and deviant mentality, whereas the pornographers who bring children into this seedy world are primarily interested in capitalizing monetarily from the sickness of disturbed, immature pedophiles who receive their only sexual satisfaction [through] children.[47]

Pedophiles represent a high percentage of the sexual exploiters of children through involvement with child porn and child molestation. According to the American Psychiatric Association's *Diagnostic and Statistical Manual of Mental Disorders*, pedophilia is defined as "a disorder in which an adult's primary sexual attraction is to prepubescent children, generally age 13 and under."[48] However, many law enforcement agencies tend to be broader in their definition of pedophilia as adults having a sexual preference for children as defined legally, which is typically age 17 and under.[49]

Although some pedophiles' sexual attraction is to children of the same gender, most pedophiles are heterosexual. Child pornographers and exploiters are described in the FBI's pedophile profile as men who are "intelligent enough to recognize they have a problem," yet are able to rationalize that "what they're doing is right."[50] An FBI agent, in explaining the mindset of pedophiles, noted that for most "pedophilia is a way of life. They believe there's nothing wrong with it, so naturally they're looking for other individuals who support their thinking."[51]

While the terms "pedophile" and "child molester" are often used interchangeably, they are not necessarily synonymous. A child molester is one who actually sexually abuses a child, whereas a pedophile may fantasize about molesting a child but not follow through on it. A *preferential child molester* refers to the pedophile who does act on his sexual attraction to children and sexually molests a child.

According to child sexual exploitation expert Margaret Healy, child pornography is the common element of pedophiles and child molesters:

> Child pornography serves significant purposes for both paedophiles and child molesters. Preferential child molesters often possess large collections of child pornography that are meticulously catalogued and carefully guarded. They, however, are not the only ones who produce or consume child pornography. A much broader segment of the population is interested in pornography featuring pubescent children in their teens. . . . With the emergence of the use of computers to traffic in child pornography, a new and growing segment of producers and consumers is being identified. They are individuals who may not have a sexual preference for children, but who have seen the gamut of adult pornography and who are searching for more bizarre material.[52]

Pedophiles and child molesters often find support for their sexual exploitation of children through child sex rings and powerful organizations that advocate sexual activity between adults and children such as the North American Man-Boy Love Association (NAMBLA), the Rene Guyon Society, and the Paedophilia Information Exchange (PIE).[53]

Child Pornography and the Internet

The creation, exchange, and use of child pornography on the Internet have exploded in recent years. According to the government, for pornographers, pedophiles, and other sexual predators of children, "the Internet is a new, effective, and more anonymous way to seek out and groom children for criminal purposes such as producing and distributing child pornography . . . and exploiting children for sexual tourism [and] personal and commercial purposes."[54]

Because online sexual exploiters of children are not limited geographically, they can easily and simultaneously victimize multiple youths across the country and the world. A recent survey of online victimization found that:

- One in four children were victims of undesired exposure to sexually explicit material online in the past year.
- One in five children were solicited for sexual purposes over the Internet within the past year.
- One in 33 children was the victim of an aggressive sexual solicitation in the last year.
- Few such incidents were reported to law enforcement, a hotline, or Internet service provider.
- Less than four in ten youths who reported being exposed to undesired sexual material online disclosed this to a parent.
- Less than one in five child victims of online sexual exploitation knew in specific an authority to whom they could report Internet crime such as the FBI, police, or their service provider.
- Online sexual predators were diverse in offenses perpetrated, background, and other dynamics.
- Around half of all online child sexual victimizers were young, while more than three-quarters of those targeted were 14 years of age and older.[55]

Federal law enforcement authorities have begun cracking down on Internet child pornographers in a number of highly publicized sweeps. For example, in March 2002, the FBI, in an investigation known as Operation Candyman, reported breaking up a major child pornography ring based online at Yahoo.com.[56] It initially led to the arrests of more than 90 people covering 20 states. Suspects ranged from age 17 to 70, and included clergy, Little League coaches, and others. The FBI vowed to continued to be aggressive in going after Internet child pornographers. However, given the vast nature and complexities of the world wide web, online child exploiters, pornographers, and pedophiles continue to thrive while circumventing the law.

Child Pornography and the Law

Prior to 1978, there was little legislation on the federal or state front that specifically addressed the sexual exploitation of children. The Protection of

Children Against Sexual Exploitation Act of 1978 was designed to curb the production and dissemination of child pornography by prohibiting the transportation of children across state lines for the purpose of sexual exploitation.[57] The act provided punishment and stiff penalties against those who "use, employ, or persuade minors . . . to participate in sexually explicit print materials or visual productions."[58] Penalties included up to ten years in prison and a fine of up to $10,000 for a first offense.

Other federal laws related to child pornography include the Child Protection, Restoration and Penalties Enhancement Act of 1990,[59] increasing prohibitions against pornographers, and the Child Protection and Obscenity Enforcement Act,[60] requiring producers of pornography to have and maintain proof of performers' ages.

Some federal laws have addressed child pornography in cyberspace. The Child Pornography Prevention Act of 1996's definitions of child pornography includes "situations in which a visual depiction, or what appears to be, of a minor engaging in sexually explicit conduct."[61] The Protection of Children from Sexual Predators Act of 1998 "added a jurisdictional basis for prosecution of the visual depiction using materials that were mailed, shipped, or transported in interstate or foreign commerce, including by computer."[62]

The Communications Decency Act of 1996[63] sought to protect children from pornography and "patently offensive" material on the Internet, but was later declared unconstitutional by the Supreme Court.[64] In 2002, the Supreme Court upheld part of the 1998 Child Online Protection Act, designed to protect children from exposure to pornography on the Internet. The Act required that those operating online commercial sites must use credit cards or another form of screening for adults only, so that children are unable to access material viewed as harmful or inappropriate.[65]

On the state level, child pornography has also resulted in improved or new statutes. Since 1978, at least 48 states have adopted legislation aimed at combating child pornography and sexual exploitation.[66]

NOTES

1. R. Barri Flowers, *Women and Criminality: The Woman as Victim, Offender, and Practitioner* (Westport: Greenwood, 1987), pp. 47–48.

2. R. Barri Flowers, *The Prostitution of Women and Girls* (Jefferson: McFarland, 1999), p. 116.

3. Helen E. Longino, "Pornography, Oppression, and Freedom: A Closer Look," in Laura Lederer, ed., *Take Back the Night: Women on Pornography* (New York: William Morrow, 1980), p. 44.

4. Flowers, *The Prostitution of Women and Girls*.

5. Cited in Flowers, *Women and Criminality*, p. 48.

6. Cited in Richard Goodall, *The Comfort of Sin: Prostitutes and Prostitution in the 1990s* (Kent: Renaissance Books, 1995), p. 186.

7. Frances Patai, "Pornography and Woman Battering: Dynamic Similarities," in Maria Roy, ed., *The Abusive Partner: An Analysis of Domestic Battering* (New York: Van Nostrand Reinhold, 1982), pp. 91–92.

8. *Ibid.*, pp. 93–94.

9. Flowers, *The Prostitution of Women and Girls*, p. 117.

10. *Ibid.*, pp. 117–18.

11. U.S. Department of Justice, *Attorney General's Commission on Pornography: Final Report*, Vol. 1, (Washington: Government Printing Office, 1986), pp. 324–25.

12. Flowers, *Women and Criminality*, p. 53.

13. *Ibid.*, pp. 53–56; Flowers, *The Prostitution of Women and Girls*, pp. 118–19.

14. Laura Lederer, ed., *Take Back the Night: Women on Pornography* (New York: William Morrow, 1980), p. 19–20.

15. Kathleen Barry, *Female Sexual Slavery* (Englewood Cliffs: Prentice-Hall, 1979), p. 145.

16. Quoted in Hillary Johnson, "Violence Against Women: Is Porn to Blame?" *Vogue 175* (September 1985), p. 678.

17. Larry Baron and Murray A. Straus, "Sexual Stratification, Pornography, and Rape in the United States," in Neil Malamuth and Edward Donnerstein, eds., *Pornography and Sexual Aggression* (Orlando: Academic Press, 1984), p. 206.

18. Quoted in Johnson, "Violence Against Women," p. 678.

19. Quoted in William A. Stanmeyer, *The Seduction of Society* (Ann Arbor: Servant Books, 1984), pp. 29–30.

20. *Ibid.*, p. 49; Flowers, *The Prostitution of Women and Girls*, pp. 119–20; R. Barri Flowers, *Female Crime, Criminals and Cellmates: An Exploration of Female Criminality and Delinquency* (Jefferson: McFarland, 1995), pp. 108–11.

21. Rita Rooney, "Children for Sale: Pornography's Dark New World," *Reader's Digest* (July 1983), p. 53.

22. Reay Tannahill, *Sex in History* (New York: Stein and Day, 1980), p. 90.

23. Quoted in Margaret A. Healy, "Child Pornography: An International Perspective," http://www.usis.usemb.se/children/csec/child_pornography.html.

24. *Ibid.*

25. U.S. Department of Justice, Office of Juvenile Justice and Delinquency Prevention, *Child Molesters: A Behavioral Analysis, For Law Enforcement Officers Investigating Cases of Child Sexual Exploitation* (Alexandria: National Center for Missing & Exploited Children, 1992), p. 24.

26. Cited in R. Barri Flowers, *Sex Crimes, Predators, Perpetrators, Prostitutes, and Victims: An Examination of Sexual Criminality and Victimization* (Springfield: Charles C Thomas, 2001), p. 121.

27. Tannahill, *Sex in History*, p. 90.

28. Cited in Flowers, *The Prostitution of Women and Girls*, p. 122.

29. Cited in Joan J. Johnson, *Teen Prostitution* (Danbury: Franklin Watts, 1992), p. 90.

30. R. Barri Flowers, *The Adolescent Criminal: An Examination of Today's Juvenile Offender* (Jefferson: McFarland, 1990), p. 64.

31. Shirley O'Brien, *Child Pornography* (Dubuque: Kendall/Hunt, 1983), p. 19; M. Guio, A. Burgess, and R. Kelly, "Child Victimization: Pornography and Prostitution," *Journal of Crime and Justice 3* (1980): 65–81.

32. Cited in Flowers, *Sex Crimes, Predators, Perpetrators, Prostitutes, and Victims*, p. 121.

33. *Ibid.*, p. 122.

34. Ted Bridis, "FBI Says It Has Shut Down Worldwide Child Pornography Ring," *Newsday* (March 19, 2002); http://www.crimelibrary.com/criminal_mind/psychology/pedophiles/bibliography.htm.

35. Margaret O. Hyde and Elizabeth H. Forsyth, *The Sexual Abuse of Children and Adolescents* (Brookfield: Milbrook Press, 1997), p. 18.

36. Flowers, *The Prostitution of Women and Girls*, pp. 122–23.

37. Healy, "Child Pornography: An International Perspective."

38. Quoted in *Ibid.*

39. *Child Molesters*, pp. 24–26.

40. U.S. Department of Justice, *Child Sex Rings: A Behavioral Analysis, For Criminal Justice Professionals Handling Cases of Child Sexual Exploitation* (Alexandria: National Center for Missing & Exploited Children, 1992), pp. 10–30.

41. *Ibid.*, p. 12.

42. Cited in Healy, "Child Pornography: An International Perspective."

43. *Ibid.*

44. *Ibid.*

45. *Ibid.*; Flowers, *Sex Crimes, Predators, Perpetrators, Prostitutes, and Victims*, pp. 129–41; David Finkelhor and Sharon Ardji, *A Sourcebook on Child Sexual Abuse* (Thousand Oaks: Sage, 1995).

46. Cited in Robert E. Freeman-Longo and Geral T. Blanchard, *Sexual Abuse in America: Epidemic of the 21st Century* (Brandon: Safer Society Press, 1998), p. 99.

47. R. Barri Flowers, *Children and Criminality: The Child as Victim and Perpetrator* (Westport: Greenwood, 1986), pp. 82–83.

48. Healy, "Child Pornography: An International Perspective." See also *Diagnostic and Statistical Manual of Mental Disorders* (DSM-IV) (Washington: American Psychiatric Association, 1994), pp. 527–28.

49. *Child Molesters.*

50. "Child Pornography on the Rise Despite Tougher Laws," *Sacramento Union* (April 7, 1984), p. E6.

51. Quoted in *Ibid.*

52. Healy, "Child Pornography: An International Perspective."

53. Flowers, *The Prostitution of Women and Girls*, p. 123; Flowers, *Sex Crimes, Predators, Perpetrators, Prostitutes and Victims*, p. 110.

54. "Internet Crimes Against Children," http://www.ojp.usdoj.gov/ovc/publications/bulletins/internet_2_internet_2_01_2.html. See also Philip Jenkins, *Beyond Tolerance: Child Pornography Online* (New York: New York University Press, 2001).

55. David Finkelhor, Kimberly J. Mitchell, and Janis Wolak, *Online Victimization: A Report on the Nation's Youth* (Alexandria: National Center for Missing & Exploited Children, 2000).

56. *Ibid.*; Bridis, "Feds Break Computer-Porn Ring."

57. 18 U.S.C. §§2251, 2253–54 (1978).

58. Flowers, *The Prostitution of Women and Girls*, p. 124.

59. P.L. No. 101-647, §323, 104 Stat. 4789, 4818 (1990).

60. 33 F. 3d 78 (D.C.C. 1994), rehearing denied, 47 F. 3d 1215 (1995), cert denied, 515 U.S. 1158 (1995).

61. P.L. No. 104-208, §121, 110 Stat. 3009, 3009–26 (1996); U.S. Department of Justice, Office of Juvenile Delinquency Prevention, *Prostitution of Children and Child-Sex Tourism: An Analysis of Domestic and International Response* (Alexandria: National Center for Missing & Exploited Children, 1999), p. 22.

62. 18 U.S.C. §2251 (a), as amended by the Protection of Children from Sexual Predators Act, §201; *Prostitution of Children and Child-Sex Tourism*, p. 22.

63. Communications Decency Act (1996); American Civil Liberties Union, http://www.ac/u.org/.

64. Flowers, *The Prostitution of Women and Girls*, p. 125.

65. *Ashcroft v. American Civil Liberties Union*, 217 F 3d 162 (2002). See also The American Center for Law and Justice, http://www.aclj.org/new/pressrelease/020513_online_porn.asp.

66. R. Barri Flowers, *The Victimization and Exploitation of Women and Children: A Study of Physical, Mental and Sexual Maltreatment in the United States* (Jefferson: McFarland, 1994), pp. 92–93.

Part VI

JUVENILE MALE CRIME AND DELINQUENCY

Chapter 18

YOUTH GANGS, CRIME, AND VIOLENCE

Youth involvement in criminal, delinquent, and violent gangs has prolif-erated in the United States since 1980. Law enforcement has been con-fronted with gang migration, a growing diversity in gang membership, and the racial, ethnic and general makeup of gangs along with a greater relation-ship between gangs, possession of firearms, homicide, school crime and vio-lence, and drug offenses. The vast majority of youth gang members are male. Most juvenile gangs are only loosely organized. Many are associated with adult or prison gangs. Experts believe that youth participation in gangs is one of the most serious concerns in identifying, recognizing, and preventing juve-nile crime, violence, and delinquency.

WHAT IS A YOUTH GANG?

Various definitions have been applied to describing the youth gang. In gen-eral, such gangs are differentiated from youth groups by their involvement in antisocial or deviant behavior. Most of these gangs consist of juvenile mem-bers, though it is not uncommon to have young adult membership and some-times older adults in leadership positions. Frederic Thrasher was among the first to define the juvenile gang in the 1920s as

> an interstitial group originally formed spontaneously and then integrated through conflict. It is characterized by . . . meeting face to face, milling, move-ment through space as a unit, conflict, and planning. The result of this collective behavior is the development of tradition, unreflective internal structure, espirit de corps, solidarity, morale, group awareness, and attachment to local territory.[1]

More recently, Walter Miller, an expert on youth gangs, defined the delin-quent gang as

> a group of recurrently associating individuals with identifiable leadership and internal organization, identifying with or claiming control over territory in the

community, and engaging either individually or collectively in violent and other forms of illegal behavior.[2]

In an overview of youth gangs, the term was defined as a group that "must be involved in a pattern of criminal acts to be considered a youth gang. These groups are typically composed only of juveniles, but may include young adults in their membership."[3]

THE EXTENT OF YOUTH GANGS AND MEMBERSHIP

Much of the empirical research on youth gangs in the United States took place during the 1950s, 1960s, and 1970s. Recent studies have focused more on exploring youth antisocial behavior in general. However, there has been some current research on the problem of youth gangs that has shown rapid growth since the 1980s. Miller's study of youth gangs in 1980 estimated a membership of almost 100,000 and over 2,000 gangs from nearly 300 jurisdictions.[4] By comparison, in 1996, there were an estimated 31,000 gangs with nearly 846,000 members in 4,800 jurisdictions across the country.[5]

In a survey of eighth grade students in eleven cities, 9 percent were presently members of a gang, while nearly one in five had ever been part of a gang.[6] Youth gangs present a problem mostly in big cities. According to the National Youth Gang Center, in 1996 law enforcement agencies reported the highest incidence of gang activity in large cities, followed by suburban counties, small cities, and rural counties.[7] The level of activity in large cities was reported at 74 percent, compared to 57 percent in the suburbs, 34 percent in small cities, and 25 percent in rural counties. Nearly three-quarters of cities with populations of at least 25,000 reported the presence of youth gangs.

Youth gangs are particularly prevalent in cities with serious gang problems such as Los Angeles and Chicago. It is estimated that there are more than 58,000 gang members in Los Angeles, the most of any city in the United States.[8] Chicago is believed to have approximately 132 gangs with some 30,000 to 50,000 hardcore members.[9] The four largest gangs and most deviant constitute around 19,000 members, including gangs such as the Black Gangster Disciples Nation and the Latin Kings.

CHARACTERISTICS OF YOUTH GANGS

Gender and Gang Membership

Youth gangs are predominantly composed of male members. Miller found that 90 percent of those in youth gangs were male.[10] In a survey of law enforcement agencies, it was reported that an estimated 94 percent of gangs were composed of males.[11] There have been some studies that suggest an active role of females in youth gangs. F. Esbensen and D. W. Osgood's survey of eighth graders revealed that 38 percent of those claiming to belong to gangs were females.[12] Another study suggested that the involvement of females in gangs may be rising proportionately to that of male participation in youth gangs.[13] Nevertheless, criminal youth gangs continue to be dominated and occupied by males.

Age and Gang Membership

Most members of youth gangs tend to fall between ten and 24 years of age. The average age of a gang member is believed to be around 17 to 18 years old.[14] Members appear to be older in cities with a longer history of gang membership such as Chicago and Los Angeles.[15] Miller found that more than eight in ten gang members arrested in the four cities with the largest gang problem fell between the ages of 14 and 19.[16] Just over 4 percent of the members were under the age of 14. Studies show that while the membership of younger persons is becoming more prevalent in gangs, a greater increase has been shown in the gang membership of older persons.[17]

Race, Ethnicity, and Gang Involvement

Minority youth are disproportionately involved in gangs. Miller reported that black youths comprised 47.6 percent of gang membership, with Hispanic representation at 36.1 percent, non-Hispanic whites at 8.8 percent, and Asian youths constituting 7.5 percent of gangs.[18] A recent law enforcement survey indicated a similar overrepresentation of African American and Hispanic involvement in youth gangs (see Fig. 18.1). Forty-eight percent of gangs were composed of African Americans, 43 percent Hispanic, 5 percent white, and 4 percent Asian youths.

Other studies indicate a greater representation of white youths in gangs. Esbensen and Osgood found that 25 percent of gang members were white, 31 percent African American, 25 percent Hispanic, 5 percent Asian, and 15 percent belong to other racial or ethnic backgrounds.[19] Miller cited seven white youth gangs in a large metropolitan area.[20] The most criminally active, the Senior bandits, was composed mainly of Irish Catholic youths between 16 and 18 years of age. Members of this gang were frequently convicted and incarcerated.

According to R. J. Bursik, Jr. and H. G. Grasmick, the disproportionate involvement of certain minority youths in gangs compared to white youths is not a reflection of a particular predisposition of such groups to gang involve-

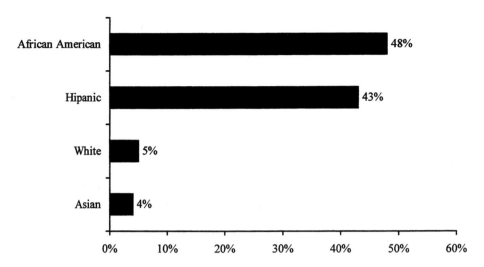

Figure 18.1. Racial and Ethnic Breakdown of Youth Gangs in the United States. *Source:* Derived from U.S. Department of Justice, *Youth Gangs: An Overview* (Washington: Office of Juvenile and Delinquency Prevention, 1998), p. 2.

ment, but an indication of overrepresentation in jurisdictions most prone to gang membership and participation.[21]

Various types of offenses have been associated more often with particular racial or ethnic youth gangs. For example, African American gangs have been shown to be more likely to engage in drug offenses, while Hispanic gangs are more related to turf violence, and Asian and white youth gangs are commonly associated with property offenses.[22] The kind of gang involvement may be related to other gang dynamics such as territory, culture, socialization process, and other factors.[23]

Class and Youth Gangs

Much of the research on criminal and delinquent youth gangs has found an overrepresentation within the urban lower class.[24] Miller found a correlation between the greater prevalence of populations in the lower class and more gang involvement.[25] While this conclusion was supported by I. A. Spergel, the researcher noted that "it is not clear that either class, poverty, culture, race or ethnicity, or social change per se primarily accounts for gang problems."[26]

Some studies indicate that gang involvement amongst the middle class of rural and suburban America has become more common in recent years. In a study of middle class gangs, Howard Myerhoff and Barbara Myerhoff documented not only their existence but also their similarities to urban youth gangs in terms of objectives such as status, protection, and belonging.[27] Similarly, Dale Hardman's study of small town youth gangs revealed much the same in their goals and motivations.[28] He noted that members' criminal activities ranged from petty crimes to crimes of violence, including rape and murder.

YOUTH GANG VIOLENCE

The relationship between youth gangs and violent activity has been well documented in the literature. Miller contended that gang members were responsible for one-third of all violent crimes, the terrorizing of entire communities, and maintaining a state of siege in many of the inner city schools.[29] According to the Program of Research on the Causes and Correlates of Delinquency, 30 percent of the sample group of gang members reported perpetrating 68 percent of violent crimes.[30] Another self-report survey found that 14 percent of juvenile gang members committed 89 percent of total serious violent crimes.[31]

Other research has supported findings that youth gang members are responsible for a disproportionate share of crimes of violence as well as property and drug offenses.[32] In a Rochester study, gang members were found to commit seven times as many serious and violent crimes as nongang youths.[33] Similarly, in Seattle, gang youth were found in a self-report survey to have perpetrated five times the violent crimes as youth who were not in gangs.[34]

Gang norms have been shown to be a significant factor in the increased amount of violence among youth gangs. According to S. H. Decker and B. Van Winkle, "Violence that is internal to the gang, especially during group functions such as an initiation, serves to intensify the bonds among members."[35] James Howell notes from an examination of research on youth gangs that "most gangs are governed by norms supporting the expressive use of violence to settle disputes and to achieve group goals associated with member recruitment, defense of one's identity as a gang member, turf protection and expansion, and defense of the gang's honor."[36]

Studies further indicate that gang adoption and support of violence is a reflection of the gang code of honor that "stresses the inviolability of one's manhood and defines breaches of etiquette."[37] Violence has also been shown to be a way of showing toughness, the ability to fight, and to gain gang status. Researchers have found that the willingness to engage in violent conduct is a primary characteristic that distinguishes youth gangs from other youth groups.[38]

YOUTH GANGS, GUNS, AND HOMICIDES

The interrelationship between youth gangs, guns, and homicides has been established through a number of studies. Most violent gang members possess illegal firearms.[39] In turn, the lethal use of such weapons appears on the rise, in part due to the greater availability of more potent weapons.[40] The proliferation of lethal weapons among gang members and gang-related shootings has succeeded in intensifying and perpetuating violence among youth gangs and their rivals who believe they must keep pace with one another in maintaining balance, power, and control.[41] For example, drive-by shootings, which have been on the increase in some cities, are perpetrated primarily to promote fear and intimidate rival gangs, with murder being a secondary objective.[42]

Youth gang homicides, defined as homicides involving gang members as victims and/or perpetrators, have shown an overall decline through the 1990s. Between 1991 and 1996, gang homicides dropped by almost 15 percent in more than 400 cities in the United States (see Fig. 18.2). However, while 32 percent of cities reported a drop in the numbers of homicides, 29 percent of cities reported an increase. In all, there were 1,492 youth gang homicides perpetrated in 1996, according to the study.

In a study utilizing findings from 237 cities with populations of more than 25,000 and gang problems and gang homicides, there was nearly an 18 percent drop in gang homicides between 1996 and 1998 (see Fig. 18.3). Almost half the states reported a decrease and 36 percent an increase. There were a total of 1,061 gang homicides in 1998.

Los Angeles and Chicago had the highest rate of gang homicides during the three-year span. Studies show that the growing use of high caliber, automatic, and semiautomatic firearms are significantly related to gang homicides.[43]

Characteristics of gang homicides tend to distinguish them from homicides by those who are not gang affiliated. Gang homicides are more likely to occur in public settings such as on the street, involve strangers, multiple parties, automobiles, and fear of reprisal.[44]

YOUTH GANGS AND DRUG CRIMES

Youth gangs are commonly involved in various drug-related offenses, including drug trafficking, drug use, and drug violence. Some studies have identified gangs specializing in drug trafficking and drug distribution.[45] Other findings have related gang drug trafficking to gang migration.[46] The use of

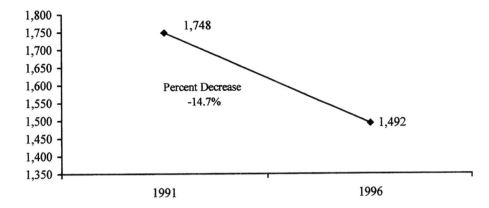

Figure 18.2. Youth Gang Homicide Trends from 408 American Cities, 1991–1996. *Source:* Derived from U.S. Department of Justice, *Youth Gang Homicides in the 1990s* (Washington: Office of Juvenile and Delinquency Prevention, 2001), pp. 1–2.

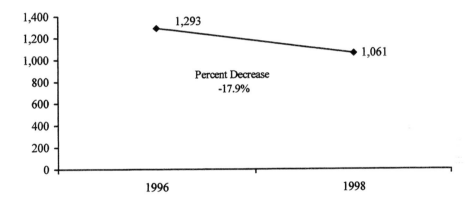

Figure 18.3. Youth Gang Homicide Trends from 237 American Cities, 1996–1998. *Source:* Derived from U.S. Department of Justice, *Youth Gang Homicides in the 1990s* (Washington: Office of Juvenile Justice and Delinquency Prevention, 2001), pp. 1–2.

drugs among youth gangs has also been strongly related to drug trafficking, use of firearms, and other crimes of violence and serious offenses.[47]

Homicide violence by youth gangs appears to be associated with an epidemic in crack cocaine in the United States. Some researchers have found that gangs played an important role in the rise in sales of crack cocaine and that drug trafficking by youth gangs led to an increase in youth homicides and other violence.[48]

ORGANIZED CRIMINAL GANGS

There is evidence that some youth criminal gangs become organized to some degree in their activities, especially as it relates to drug trafficking.[49] Minority gangs, in particular, have combined traditional gang activities with nontraditional organized crime structure and operations. According to Robert Ruchhoft, an expert on youth gangs, black gangs have moved from turf wars and knife fights to drug distribution and murder, in what was described as "disorganized crime on the threshold of organized crime."[50] Similarly, Asian youth gangs appear to be expanding their activities into such organized criminality as extortion and robbery. Ruchhoft suggests that Asian gangs are "the closest thing we've got to real organized crime in Los Angeles."[51]

Youth gangs have also been shown to demonstrate some loosely organized capacity in other criminal pursuits such as robbery, prostitution, larceny-theft, burglary, and con games. A common element among many of today's more violent and sophisticated youth gangs is the stockpiling of lethal and more powerful firearms.

EXPLAINING YOUTH GANG CRIME AND VIOLENCE

General theories on male crime and delinquency can be found in Part I. However, a number of criminologists have offered theoretical perspectives on youth gangs, criminality, and violent behavior. Amongst the most influential theories are reaction-formation theory, opportunity theory, and lower class culture theory.

Reaction-Formation Theory

Reaction-formation theory was first put forth by Albert Cohen in his 1955 book, *Delinquent Boys: The Culture of the Gang*.[52] The theory advanced that lower-class youths turn to gang delinquency as a reaction or group response to a failure to acquire middle-class status and values. According to Cohen, the goals and values of the middle class (such as success as a result of hard work, and using a person's skills to progress) are desired by lower-class youth. However, these youths are generally disadvantaged in institutional settings such as school, where they are measured by middle-class standards, or otherwise deprived of approved opportunities to attain culturally prescribed goals.

As a result of these blocked opportunities and conflicts with social institution of the middle class, Cohen theorized that lower-class youth undergo a delinquent response to their limitations which he refers to as "status frustration" or a "reaction-formation against a middle class organized status dilemma in which the lower class boy suffers status frustrations in competition with middle class boys."[53] This status frustration causes many of these youths to band together in juvenile gangs or a delinquent subculture where they engage in nonutilitarian, negativistic, malicious, and hedonistic behavior.

The theory posits that the values of the delinquent subculture are opposite of those of the middle class. Due to an emotional attachment to unachievable middle-class goals, these youths must reject such goals and develop standards of their own in which success can be achieved, along with status, self-esteem, and solidarity.

Reaction-formation theory has been criticized on a number of fronts. The primary reason is that the premise has not been validated empirically. There is also little evidence supporting the notion that lower class youths repudiate middle-class values.

Finally, Cohen puts too much value on the rejection of middle-class standards in explaining delinquent gangs, while giving little attention to such factors as family, race or ethnicity, and other demographic characteristics in delinquency formation.

In responding to criticisms, Cohen, collaborating with James Short, Jr., later expanded upon his original theory by suggesting there was more than one kind of lower-class gang subculture. They held that a *parent subculture* was the primary type with other gang orientations offshoots, such as a middle-class gang subculture and drug addict subculture.[54]

Opportunity Theory

An opportunity theory of gang delinquency was introduced by Richard Cloward and Lloyd Ohlin in their 1960 work, *Delinquency and Opportunity: A Theory of Delinquent Gangs.*[55] The theory proposed that one's access to legitimate and illegitimate means is greatly influenced by the social structure. As such, while differential opportunity exists in obtaining culturally prescribed goals through legitimate means, it also exists in using illegitimate means for acquiring socially approved goals.

Opportunity theory explains gang delinquency in terms of a discrepancy between lower-class youth aspirations and what they have access to, assuming that "discrepancies between aspirations and legitimate chances of achievement increase as one descends in the class structure."[56] According to Cloward and Ohlin, there are two types of opportunities which are distributed unequally: access to "learning structures" or the "appropriate environments for the acquisition of the values and skills associated with the performance of a particular role," and access to "performance structures," or the opportunity to organize with those who also have a problem with adjustment and the opportunity to receive peer approval for one's behavior.[57] Thus the kind of youth gang and delinquent subculture varies largely by the social structure or environment within a community.

The researchers identified three primary types of lower class juvenile gangs, or subcultural responses to blocked legitimate or illegitimate opportunities for success: (1) criminal gangs, (2) conflict gangs, and (3) retreatist gangs:

- *Criminal gangs*–youth gangs who acquire criminal values and skills from adult and organized criminals. These gangs are driven primarily through illegitimate means such as larceny-theft and extortion in gaining power, prestige, and material items.
- *Conflict gangs*–youth gangs formed under conditions in which both legitimate and illegitimate opportunities are blocked. Membership in conflict gangs allows juveniles and young adults to gain status, prestige, and/or a reputation of toughness among their peers. The principles of youth conflict gangs often include fighting, violence, and rival gang conflict.
- *Retreatist gangs*–youth gangs who emerge when young people are denied or reject success through legitimate and illegitimate means. Retreatist youths often delve into a world of drug and alcohol abuse and take on secondary criminal activities to support habits such as drug dealing and prostitution.

Opportunity theory's major drawback lies in its concentration on lower-class gang delinquency, while inadequately taking into account individual delinquency or criminality or gang delinquency among other classes. The theory has also been criticized for its failure to explain why some communities have different types of delinquent or criminal gangs at the same time. Some critics further question whether or not lower-class youth actually aspire to middle-class values. These criticisms notwithstanding, Cloward and Ohlin's theory of differential opportunity is credited with being a significant contribution to sociological theory on criminal youth gangs and juvenile delinquency.

Lower-Class Culture Theory

A lower-class culture theory of gang delinquency was offered by Walter Miller.[58] Contrary to Cohen's, Cloward's, and Ohlin's beliefs that lower-class gang delinquency is a reflection of a rejection of middle-class values, Miller held that gang delinquency of the lower class results from positive attempts by youths to attain goals determined by values or focal concerns of the lower class culture.

According to Miller, there are six such lower-class focal concerns, or areas representing the primary concerns of lower-class youths: (1) trouble, (2) toughness, (3) smartness, (4) excitement, (5) fate, and (6) autonomy, described as follows:

- *Trouble* refers to circumstances resulting in unwanted involvement with law enforcement.
- *Toughness* relates to masculinity, physical superiority, daring, and bravery.
- *Smartness* refers to the capacity to outsmart, outwit, or con others, while avoiding being deceived or duped.
- *Excitement* relates to the desire for thrills, taking risks, and to avoid boredom.
- *Fate* concerns beliefs or interests having to do with luck, fortunes, and jinxes.
- *Autonomy* is closely associated with fate and refers to a desire to control one's own destiny or life.

Lower-class culture theory posits that the delinquent gang serves as a social setting through which youths can achieve prestige from actions in relation to focal concerns of the lower class.

Although Miller's theory of lower-class culture does succeed in relating differential lower-class values to gang criminality and delinquency, some critics dismiss the notion that lower-class youths fail to adhere to the larger norms and values of society. The theory also does not explain how these focal concerns originated or distinguish between lower-class offenders and law abiders as it relates to focal concerns and values of the lower class.[59]

Other cultural deviance theories on juvenile gang delinquency and youth violence show similar theoretical weaknesses, including that related to reliable measurement and flaws in logic.[60] However, there are some who continue to focus primarily on lower-class subcultures in explaining gang criminality and violence.[61]

NOTES

1. Frederic M. Thrasher, *The Gang* (Chicago: University of Chicago Press, 1927), p. 57.

2. Walter B. Miller, *Violence by Youth Gangs and Youth Groups as a Crime Problem in Major American Cities* (Washington: Government Printing Office, 1975).

3. U.S. Department of Justice, *Youth Gangs: An Overview* (Washington: Office of Juvenile Justice and Delinquency Prevention, 1998), p. 1.

4. Walter B. Miller, *Crime by Youth Gangs and Groups in the United States* (Washington: Office of Justice Programs, 1992).

5. Cited in *Youth Gangs: An Overview*, p. 1.

6. F. Esbensen and D. W. Osgood, *National Evaluation of G.R.E.A.T.* Research in Brief. (Washington: National Institute of Justice, 1997).

7. Cited in *Youth Gangs: An Overview*, p. 4.

8. National Youth Gang Center, 1995 *National Youth Gang Survey* (Washington: Office of Juvenile Justice and Delinquency Prevention, 1997).

9. C. R. Block, A. Christakos, A. Jacob, and R. Przybylski, *Street Gangs and Crime: Patterns and Trends in Chicago.* Research Bulletin (Chicago: Criminal Justice Information Authority, 1996).

10. Miller, *Violence by Youth Gangs and Youth Groups,* pp. 21–23.

11. Cited in *Youth Gangs: An Overview,* p. 3.

12. Esbensen and Osgood, *National Evaluation of G.R.E.A.T.*

13. M. W. Klein, *The American Street Gang* (New York: Oxford University Press, 1995).

14. G. D. Curry and S. H. Decker, *Confronting Gangs: Crime and Community* (Los Angeles: Roxbury, 1998).

15. Klein, *The American Street Gang;* I. A. Spergel, *The Youth Gang Problem* (New York: Oxford University Press, 1995).

16. Miller, *Violence by Youth Gangs and Youth Groups,* pp. 21–23.

17. Spergel, *The Youth Gang Problem;* J. J. Hagedorn, *People and Folks: Gangs, Crime and the Underclass in a Rustbelt City* (Chicago: Lakeview Press, 1988).

18. Miller, *Violence by Youth Gangs and Youth Groups,* p. 26.

19. Esbensen and Osgood, *National Evaluation of G.R.E.A.T.*

20. Walter B. Miller, "White Gangs," in James F. Short, Jr., ed., *Modern Criminals* (Chicago: Aldine, 1970), pp. 57, 60, 64.

21. R. J. Bursik, Jr. and H. G. Grasmick, *Neighborhoods and Crime: The Dimensions of Effective Community Control* (New York: Lexington Books, 1993).

22. Block, Christakos, Jacob, and Przybylski, *Street Gangs and Crime;* I. A. Spergel, "Youth Gangs: Continuity and Change," in M. Tonry and N. Morris, eds., *Crime and Justice: A Review of Research,* Vol. 12 (Chicago: University of Chicago Press, 1990), pp. 171–275.

23. See E. Anderson, *Streetwise: Race, Class, and Change in an Urban Community* (Chicago: University of Chicago Press, 1990); J. W. Moore, *Homeboys: Gangs, Drugs and Prison in the Barrios of Los Angeles* (Philadelphia: Temple University Press, 1978).

24. R. Barri Flowers, *The Adolescent Criminal: An Examination of Today's Juvenile Offender* (Jefferson: McFarland, 1990), pp. 102–3.

25. Walter B. Miller, "American Youth Gangs: Past and Present," in A. Blumberg, ed., *Current Perspectives in Criminal Behavior* (New York: Knopf, 1974), pp. 410–20.

26. Spergel, *The Youth Gang Problem,* p. 60; *Youth Gangs: An Overview,* p. 3.

27. Howard L. Myerhoff and Barbara G. Myerhoff, "Field Observation of Middle Class 'Gangs'," *Social Forces* 42 (1964): 328–36.

28. Dale G. Hardman, "Small Town Gangs," *Journal of Criminal Law, Criminology and Police Science 60,* 2 (1969): 176–77.

29. Miller, *Violence by Youth Gangs and Youth Groups.*

30. T. P. Thornberry, "Membership in Youth Gangs and Involvement in Serious and Violent Offending," in R. Loeber and D. P. Farrington, eds., *Serious and Violent Offenders: Risk Factors and Successful Interventions* (Thousand Oaks: Sage, 1998), pp. 147–66.

31. D. Huizinga, "The Volume of Crime by Gang and Nongang Members," paper presented at the Annual Meeting of the American Society of Criminology, San Diego, 1997.

32. See, for example, S. R. Battin, K G. Hill, R. D. Abbott, R. F. Catalano, and J. D. Hawkins, "The Contribution of Gang Membership to Delinquency Beyond Delinquent Friends," *Criminology 36* (1998): 93–115.

33. B. Bjerregaard and C. Smith, "Gender Differences in Gang Participation, Delinquency, and Substance Use," *Journal of Quantitative Criminology 9* (1993): 329–55.

34. Cited in *Youth Gangs: An Overview,* p. 9.

35. *Ibid.;* S. H. Decker and B. Van Winkle, *Life in the Gang: Family, Friends, and Violence* (New York: Cambridge University Press, 1996), p. 270.

36. *Youth Gangs: An Overview,* p. 9.

37. *Ibid.* See also M. S. Sanchez-Jankowski, *Islands in the Street: Gangs and American Urban Society* (Berkeley: University of California Press, 1991).

38. J. F. Short, Jr. and F. L. Strodtbeck, *Group Process and Gang Delinquency* (Chicago: University of Chicago Press, 1965); R. Horowitz, *Honor and the American Dream: Culture and Identity in a Chicano Community* (New Brunswick: Rutgers University Press, 1983).

39. J. F. Sheley and J. D. Wright, *In the Line of Fire: Youth, Guns and Violence in Urban America* (Hawthorne: Aldine De Gruyter, 1995).

40. *Youth Gangs: An Overview,* p. 10.

41. Decker and Van Winkle, *Life in the Gang,* p. 23; Horowitz, *Honor and the American Dream.*

42. H. R. Hutson, D. Anglin, and M. Eckstein, "Drive-by Shootings by Violent Street Gangs in Los Angeles: A Five-Year Review from 1989 to 1993," *Academic Emergency Medicine 3* (1996): 300–3.

43. *Youth Gangs: An Overview,* p. 10.

44. *Ibid.*

45. *Ibid.,* p. 11; Decker and Van Winkle, *Life in the Gang; C. S. Taylor, Dangerous Society* (East Lansing: Michigan State University Press, 1989).

46. See, for example, C. L. Maxson, K. Woods, and M. W. Klein, "Street Gang Migration: How Big A Threat?" *National Institute of Justice Journal 2* (1996): 26–31.

47. *Youth Gangs: An Overview,* p. 11; R. Barri Flowers, *Drugs, Alcohol and Criminality in American Society* (Jefferson: McFarland, 1999), pp. 132–33.

48. See, for example, D. W. Hayeslip, Jr., *Local-Level Drug Enforcement: New Strategies* (Washington: National Institute of Justice, 1980); K. C. McKinney, *Juvenile Gangs: Crime and Drug Trafficking Bulletin* (Washington: Office of Justice Programs, 1988).

49. Sanchez-Jankowski, *Islands in the Street; Taylor, Dangerous Society.*

50. Quoted in Jim Morris, "Gangs at War in L.A. Streets," *Sacramento Bee* (October 19, 1986), p. A1.

51. *Ibid.*

52. Albert K. Cohen, *Delinquent Boys: The Culture of the Gang* (New York: Free Press, 1955).

53. *Ibid.*, pp. 36–44.

54. Albert K. Cohen and James F. Short, Jr., "Research on Delinquent Subcultures," *Journal of Social Issues 14,* 3 (1958): 20–37.

55. Richard A. Cloward and Lloyd E. Ohlin, *Delinquency and Opportunity: A Theory of Delinquent Gangs* (New York: Free Press, 1960).

56. *Ibid.*, p. 80.

57. *Ibid.*, p. 148.

58. Walter B. Miller, "Lower-Class Culture as a Generating Milieu of Gang Delinquency," *Journal of Social Issues 14* (1958): 5–19.

59. R. Barri Flowers, *Kids Who Commit Adult Crimes: Serious Criminality by Juvenile Offenders* (Binghamton: Haworth, 2002), pp. 66–73; Barbara Costello, "On the Logical Adequacy of Cultural Deviance Theories," *Theoretical Criminology 1* (1997): 403–28.

60. Ross Matsueda, "Cultural Deviance Theory: The Remarkable Persistence of a Flawed Term," *Theoretical Criminology 1* (1997): 429–52.

61. Flowers, *Kids Who Commit Adult Crimes;* Thornberry, "Membership in Gangs and Involvement in Serious and Violent Offending," pp. 147–66; L. W. Kennedy and S. W. Baron, "Routine Activities and a Subculture of Violence: A Study of Violence on the Street," *Journal of Research in Crime and Delinquency 30,* 1 (1993): 88–112.

Chapter 19

SCHOOL CRIME AND VIOLENCE

Crime and violence on and around school campuses has long been a problem. However, the recent surge in fatal school shootings and mass murders at schools across the United States has focused more attention on youth violence at school, its precursors, and ways to identify and prevent it. Both perpetrators and victims of serious school crime and violence are typically male. School criminality has often been linked to family issues such as domestic violence and child abuse, substance abuse, a gang presence at school, and school problems including learning difficulties, dropping out of school, and behavioral issues. Researchers are now closely examining bullying in school as a major factor in the onset of school crime and victimization in relation to the aforementioned correlates. Most experts agree that seriously reducing school crime and violence will require more effectively recognizing at risk youths, early intervention, and preventative measures both at school and outside of it.

THE SCOPE OF SCHOOL CRIME AND VIOLENCE

The seriousness and extent of school crime and violence in the United States has been illustrated through a number of studies. In a recent National School Boards Association study over a five-year period, 78 percent of school districts reported student assaults against other students, 60 percent student assaults against teachers, and 61 percent reported school violence that involved weapons.[1] Eighty-two percent of districts reported an increase in school violence during the span.

As shown in Table 19.1, the *National Crime Victimization Survey Report* estimated that in 1995 there were more than 1.2 million crimes of violence inside school buildings or on school property in the United States. This represented 14.2 percent of all reported violent crimes. There were more than 956,000 attempted or threatened incidents of violence at school.

Table 19.1
SCHOOL CRIMES OF VIOLENCE, BY TYPE OF CRIME, 1995

Type of Crime	Number of incidents	Inside school building/ on school property
Crimes of violence	8,727,230	14.2%
Completed violence	2,515,470	11.1%
Attempted/threatened violence	6,211,770	15.4%
Rape/sexual assault[b]	355,450	4.0% (a)
Robbery	1,039,490	5.7%
Completed/property taken	673,440	5.1%
With injury	196,880	0.0%(a)
Without injury	476,560	7.2%
Attempted to take property	366,050	6.7%
With injury	87,610	12.8% (a)
Without injury	278,440	4.8% (a)
Assault	7,352,290	15.8%
Aggravated	1,622,360	6.4%
Simple	5,729,920	18.5%
Purse snatching/pocket picking	362,100	14.2%
Motor vehicle theft	1,653,820	2.0%
Completed	1,098,280	1.9% (a)
Attempted	555,540	2.2% (a)
Theft	22,006,050	13.3%

[a] Estimate is based on about ten or fewer sample cases.
[b] Includes verbal threats of rape and threats of sexual assault.
Source: Derived from U.S. Department of Justice, *Criminal Victimization in the United States, 1995: A National Crime Victimization Survey Report* (Washington: Office of Justice Programs, 2000), p. 71.

A more comprehensive picture of school crime and violence can be seen in the annual National Center for Education and Statistics and Bureau of Justice Statistics *Indicators of School Crime and Safety* (see Table 19.2). According to the report, in 1998 an estimated 2,715,600 school crimes occurred in the United States, involving students between the ages of 12 and 18. Of these, nearly 253,000 incidents were classified as serious crimes, including rape, sexual assault, robbery, and aggravated assault.

Overall, victims of school crimes were most likely to be male, younger students, white, non-Hispanic, suburban, with a household income of $50,000 or more. However, student characteristics varied for specific types of crime. For instance, older students were more likely to be victims of theft than younger students, while urban students were the most likely to be victimized by serious violent crimes.

Table 19.2
SCHOOL CRIMES[a] AGAINST STUDENTS 12 TO 18 YEARS OLD, BY TYPE OF
CRIME AND STUDENT CHARACTERISTICS, 1998

Student characteristics	Total[b]	Theft	Violent[c]	Serious violent[d]
Total	2,715,600	1,562,300	1,153,200	252,700
Gender				
Male	1,536,100	814,900	721,300	144,200
Female	1,179,400	747,500	431,900	108,400
Age				
12–14	1,475,100	769,300	705,800	162,200
15–18	1,240,500	793,000	447,400	90,500
Race/ethnicity				
White, non-Hispanic	1,824,300	1,038,800	785,500	157,100
Black, non-Hispanic	464,000	265,700	198,200	48,100
Hispanic	315,100	185,900	129,200	42,600
Other, non-Hispanic	105,700	67,600	38,100	4,900 (e)
Urbanicity				
Urban	865,000	503,600	361,400	99,100
Suburban	1,319,500	771,000	548,400	91,700
Rural	531,100	287,700	243,400	61,900
Household income				
Less than $7,500	136,500	69,900	66,700	21,100 (e)
$7,500–14,999	242,600	95,700	146,900	30,400 (e)
$15,000–24,999	428,700	218,300	210,400	35,400
$25,000–34,999	351,100	173,000	178,200	52,100
$35,000–49,999	361,500	239,100	122,400	27,200 (e)
$50,000–74,999	497,400	306,700	190,600	45,000
$75,000 or more	453,000	303,500	149,500	23,800 (e)

[a] Includes crimes occurring inside or on school property, as well as on the way to or from school.

[b] Includes violent crimes and theft. Due to rounding, totals may not add up.

[c] Includes serious violent crimes and simple assault.

[d] Includes rape, sexual assault, robbery, and aggravated assault.

[e] Estimate based on fewer than ten cases.

Source: Derived from U.S. Department of Education and Justice, *Indicators of School Crime and Safety 2000* (Washington: Offices of Educational Research and Improvement and Justice Programs, 2000), p. 49.

Data from the Centers for Disease Control and Prevention's Youth Risk Behavior Survey on school crime and violence further puts it in perspective as follows:

- Almost four in ten high school students were in a physical fight within the last year.
- Nearly half of male students were in a school fight within the last year.

- Nationwide, 15 percent of high school students fought on school property within the past year.
- More than twice the number of male students were likely to have been in a fight as female students within the past year.
- Minority students were more likely than white students to be in school fights and to suffer injuries.
- Almost two in ten high school students carried a weapon to school in the last month.
- Nearly 6 percent of students carried a gun in the past month.
- Seven percent of high school students were either threatened or injured at school with a weapon.
- Four in ten high school students stayed out of school at least once during the past month for fear of crime or victimization.
- One in three high school students was the victim of property crime or vandalism within the last year.
- Over half the middle and high schools across the country reported at least one incident of fighting or unarmed assault during the past year.
- About one in five middle and high schools reported at least one serious violent crime during the last year.
- Violent and school crime is more than twice as likely to occur in cities as rural areas, and more than three times as likely to take place than in small towns.[2]

School Crimes Against Teachers

Teachers are also prone to crime and violence victimization at school. As shown in Table 19.3, between 1994 and 1998, teachers were victims of an estimated 1,755,300 nonfatal crimes at school. Of these, 668,400 were classified as violent crimes and 1,086,900 crimes of theft. Nearly 80,000 of the victimizations were considered serious violent crimes, for an average of 16,000 such crimes per year.

While elementary school teachers were more likely to suffer theft crimes, middle and high school teachers were the most likely to be victimized by crimes of violence. Teacher victims of all school crimes were far more likely to be female than male, white, non-Hispanic, and urban. On average, there were 83 total criminal victimizations per 1,000 teachers annually.

SCHOOL SHOOTINGS AND VIOLENT DEATHS

A number of school shootings and school related violent deaths in recent years have put the spotlight on school violence and school safety, or lack of.

Table 19.3
NONFATAL CRIMES AGAINST TEACHERS AT SCHOOL[a], BY TYPE OF CRIME
AND TEACHER CHARACTERISTICS, 1994–1998

Teacher characteristics	Total[b]	Theft	Violent[c]	Serious violent[d]
Total	1,755,300	1,086,900	668,400	79,800
Instructional level				
Elementary	630,800	434,000	196,800	51,800
Middle/junior high	531,700	281,400	250,300	15,400
Senior high	592,900	371,500	221,300	12,600
Gender				
Male	514,400	238,100	276,300	29,700
Female	1,241,000	848,900	392,100	50,100
Race/ethnicity				
White, non-Hispanic	1,488,900	913,500	575,400	67,000
Black, non-Hispanic	130,100	82,100	48,000	10,500
Hispanic	104,800	66,400	38,400 (e)	
Other, non-Hispanic	16,200 (f)	11,800 (f)	4,400 (f)	2,300 (f)
Urbanicity[g]				
Urban	999,300	612,200	387,100	48,300
Suburban	469,600	308,700	160,900	21,800
Rural	213,700	120,700	93,000	9,800

[a] Includes crimes occurring inside or on school property.
[b] Includes violent crimes and theft. Due to rounding, totals may not add up.
[c] Includes serious violent crimes and simple assault.
[d] Includes rape, sexual assault, robbery, and aggravated assault.
[e] No cases were reported.
[f] Estimate based on fewer than ten cases.
[g] Teachers teaching in more than one school in different locales are not included.
Source: Derived from U.S. Department of Education and Justice, *Indicators of School Crime and Safety 2000* (Washington: Offices of Educational Research and Improvement and Justice Programs, 2000), p. 76.

For various reasons, some students, virtually all male, have been driven to commit lethal and often dramatic school violence at primarily suburban and rural schools throughout the country. Between 1992 and 2001, there were 13 shootings with multiple victims in rural and suburban schools in the United States.[3] The following examples illustrate this disturbing trend:

- On March 2, 1987, 12-year-old Nathan Ferris, an overweight honor student, took his father's .45 caliber pistol to school in Missouri and shot and killed a classmate who teased him, before killing himself.
- On February 19, 1997, 16-year-old Evan Ramsey brought a shotgun to Bethel Regional School in Bethel, Alaska. He shot to death the principal and a student, wounding two others.
- On December 1, 1997, 14-year-old Michael Carneal went on a shooting spree at Heath High School in West Paducah, Kentucky, killing three

students and wounding five. He was reportedly inspired by the movie, "The Basketball Diaries," in which the main character dreamed of entering a classroom and shooting five classmates.

- On March 24, 1998, Mitchell Johnson and Andrew Golden, 14 and 12, respectively, were dressed in camouflage as they entered a middle school in Jonesboro, Arkansas. They opened fire on students and teachers, killing five and wounding ten.
- On April 24, 1998, 14-year-old Andrew Wurst, armed with a .25 caliber handgun, entered the banquet hall at James W. Parker Middle School in Edinboro, Pennsylvania where he shot to death a science teacher.
- On May 21, 1998, 15-year-old Kip Kinkel, heavily armed, went on a shooting rampage at Thurston High School in Springfield, Oregon. He killed two students and wounded 25. Earlier he had shot to death his mother and father at home.
- On April 21, 1999, Eric Harris, 18, and Dyland Klebold, 17, armed with semiautomatic weapons and dressed in long trench coats, entered Columbine High School in Littleton, Colorado. They went on a shooting spree that took 13 lives and injured 25 before they killed themselves. It was the worst school mass murder in U.S. history.
- On February 29, 2000, a six-year-old boy used a .32 caliber handgun to shoot to death a six-year-old student at Buell Elementary School near Flint, Michigan.
- On May 26, 2000, 13-year-old Nate Brazil used a .25 caliber semiautomatic pistol to kill a teacher at Lake Worth Middle School in Lake Worth, Florida.
- On November 12, 2001, Chris Buschbacher, 17 years old, took two people hostage at the Caro Learning center in Caro, Michigan, before committing suicide.[4]

These tragic school shootings notwithstanding, relatively few youth homicides are perpetrated at school. As seen in Figure 19.1, from 1997 to 1998, there were a total of 2,752 murders of persons between five and 19 years of age in the United States. However, only 35 of these were school related homicides.

Studies show that lethal violence at school is closely related to students carrying or having easy access to guns.[5] According to the Youth Risk Behavior Survey, 61 percent of students said they knew other students who could bring a gun to school if they wanted to.[6] One in four respondents claimed they could easily obtain a gun, while one in five students had heard rumors that another student at school planned to shoot someone.

Experts on school violence have identified warning signs for youth at risk for demonstrating violent and deadly behavior, including:

- Depression.
- History of temper tantrums.

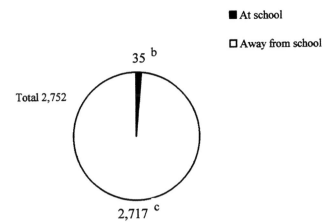

Figure 19.1. Murders of Students at School[a] and of Youths 5 to 19 Years of Age Away from School, 1997–1998. *Source:* Derived from U.S. Department of Education and Justice, *Indicators of School Crime and Safety 2000* (Washington: Offices of Educational Research and Improvement and Justice Programs, 2000), p. 2.
[a] "At School" includes on school property, on the way to or from school, and while attending or traveling to or from a school-sponsored event.
[b] Student murders at school, July 1, 1997 to June 30, 1998.
[c] Murders of youth ages 5 through 19 away from school, July 1, 1997 to June 30, 1998.

- History of disciplinary problems.
- A victim of child abuse or witness to family violence.
- History of drug or alcohol abuse.
- Frequent problems with truancy, school suspensions, or being expelled.
- A preoccupation with firearms or explosives.
- Exhibits cruelty to animals.
- Obsessed with hate groups or antigovernment organizations.
- Belongs to a gang or antisocial group.
- A bully or victim of bullying.
- Involved with a satanic cult.
- Has a fascination with violence in movies, games, books, or other entertainment.
- Is suicidal.
- Blames others for their problems.[7]

A DECLINE IN SCHOOL CRIME AND VIOLENCE

Though school crime and violence continues to be a source of concern for teachers, students, parents, and the public, recent years have shown such criminality to be on the decline, if only slightly. According to *Indicators*, from

1992 to 1998, the victimization rate for violent crimes at school went from 48 per 1,000 to 43 per 1,000 students between the ages of 12 and 18.[8] Theft crimes have also been less prevalent at school, going from 7 percent reported victimizations in 1995 to around 6 percent of students who reported being victims of theft in 1999.[9]

The percentage of high school students involved in physical fights on school property in the last year—often a precursor to additional crimes and violence—dropped from 16.2 percent of students in 1993 to 14.8 percent in 1997 (see Table 19.4). Among male students in grades nine to 12, around two in ten engaged in physical fights at school in 1997. This compares to less than one in ten female students who reported school fighting.

About two in ten black, non-Hispanic, and Hispanic students were involved in fighting on school property in 1997. The percentage of Hispanic ninth through twelfth graders reporting fighting at school increased between 1993 and 1997, yet declined from 1995 to 1997.

Other trends support the reduction in school crime and victimization, as follows:

- From 1993 to 1997, the percentage of high school students who reported bringing a weapon onto school property decreased from 12 percent to 9 percent.
- From 1995 to 1999, the percentage of students who reported a gang presence at school dropped from around 29 percent to just over 17 percent.
- From 1995 to 1999, the percent of 12- to 18-year-old students who avoided places at school declined from 9 to 5 percent.[10]

CORRELATES OF SCHOOL CRIME AND VIOLENCE

Weapons and School Crime

The research indicates that there is s strong relationship between students, possession of weapons, and violence on and off school property.[11] As shown in Table 19.5, in 1997, more than 18 percent of students in grades nine to twelve reported carrying a weapon such as a gun, knife, or club at some time within the last 30 days. Nearly 9 percent of students said they had taken a weapon onto school property at least one day during the past 30 days.

Males were far more likely than females to have carried a weapon to school or at any time in the last 30 days. More than three times as many male high school students reported carrying a weapon on school property as female

Table 19.4

PERCENTAGE OF STUDENTS, GRADES 9 THROUGH 12, WHO REPORTED
HAVING BEEN IN A PHYSICAL FIGHT ON SCHOOL PROPERTY IN THE LAST
12 MONTHS, BY STUDENT CHARACTERISTICS, 1993, 1995, AND 1997

Student characteristics	*1993*	*1995*[a]	*1997*[a]
Total	16.2	15.5	14.8
Gender			
Male	23.5	21.0	20.0
Female	8.6	9.5	8.6
Race/ethnicity			
White, non-Hispanic	15.0	12.9	13.3
Black, non-Hispanic	22.0	20.3	20.7
Hispanic	17.9	21.1	19.0
Asian/Pacific Islander	11.7	18.3	8.3
Other, non-Hispanic	18.8	23.0	14.8
Grade			
9th	23.1	21.6	21.3
10th	17.2	16.5	17.0
11th	13.8	13.6	12.5
12th	11.4	10.6	9.5

[a] The response rate for this survey was less than 70 percent and a full non-response bias analysis has not been done to date.

Source: Adapted from U.S. Department of Education and Justice, *Indicators of School Crime and Safety 2000* (Washington: Offices of Educational Research and Improvement and Justice Programs, 2000), p. 61.

high school students; while nearly four times as many male students had possessed a weapon anywhere in the past month.

Hispanic and black, non-Hispanic ninth through twelfth grade students were more likely than white, non-Hispanic and Asian-Pacific Islander students to bring weapons to school in the past 30 days. Ninth and eleventh grade students had a higher percentage of bringing weapons on school property than tenth and twelfth grade students.

Generally, high school students were more than twice as likely to carry weapons at any time within the past 30 days than onto school property.

Gangs at School

The presence of youth gangs at school has been shown to be significantly interrelated to school crime, violence, and drug activity.[12] As seen in Table 19.6, in 1994, more than 17 percent of students ages twelve to eighteen reported that street gangs could be found at school. This represented a 2 percent increase since 1989. Gangs were more than four times as likely to be reported in public schools as private schools in 1999.

Table 19.5
PERCENTAGE OF STUDENTS, GRADES 9 THROUGH 12, WHO REPORTED
CARRYING A WEAPON ON SCHOOL PROPERTY DURING THE PAST 30 DAYS,
BY STUDENT CHARACTERISTICS, 1997

Student characteristics	At any time[a]	On school property[a]
Total	18.3	8.5
Gender		
Male	27.7	12.5
Female	7.0	3.7
Race/ethnicity		
White, non-Hispanic	17.0	7.8
Black, non-Hispanic	21.7	9.2
Hispanic	23.3	10.4
Asian/Pacific Islander	9.2	4.0
Other, non-Hispanic	19.2	10.9
Grade		
9th	22.6	10.2
10th	17.4	7.7
11th	18.2	9.4
12th	15.4	7.0
Ungraded or other	16.7	16.2

[a] The response rate for this survey was less than 70 percent and a full non-response bias analysis has not been done to date.

Source: Adapted from U.S. Department of Education and Justice, *Indicators of School Crime and Safety 2000* (Washington: Offices of Educational Research and Improvement and Justice Programs, 2000), p. 78.

Street gangs were most likely to be reported by urban students to be present at school. Around one in four students at urban schools said gangs were at their school in 1999. Hispanic and black, non-Hispanic students were much more likely than other students to report a gang presence at school in 1999. Older students tended to believe that street gangs were at their schools more than younger students, whereas the percentage of males and females were roughly equal in their perception of a gang presence at school.

School Bullying

Bullying or being bullied at school is an important at-risk factor for school crime and violence.[13] A bully is defined as a person "who directs physical, verbal, or psychological aggression or harassment toward others, with the goal of gaining power over or dominating another individual.[14] The act of bullying has proven to be a common problem at school and in neighborhoods. It is

Table 19.6
PERCENTAGE OF STUDENTS, 12 TO 18 YEARS OF AGE, REPORTING THE
PRESENCE OF STREET GANGS AT SCHOOL DURING THE PAST SIX MONTHS,
BY STUDENT CHARACTERISTICS, 1989–1999

Student characteristics	1989[a]	1999
Total	15.3	17.3
Gender		
Male	15.8	17.5
Female	14.8	17.1
Race/ethnicity		
White, non-Hispanic	11.7	13.1
Black, non-Hispanic	19.8	24.7
Hispanic	31.6	28.3
Other, non-Hispanic	25.4	17.9
Grade		
6th	10.3	9.2
7th	16.6	12.0
8th	13.6	12.9
9th	19.6	22.7
10th	16.0	22.1
11th	15.3	19.6
12th	14.2	20.0
Urbanicity		
Urban	24.8	25.1
Suburban	14.0	15.8
Rural	7.8	11.1
Control		
Public	16.4	18.6
Private	4.4	4.4

[a] Includes students ages 12 through 19.

Source: Adapted from U.S. Department of Education and Justice, *Indicators of School Crime and Safety 2000* (Washington: Offices of Educational Research and Improvement and Justice Programs, 2000), p. 83.

estimated that between 15 and 30 percent of all students are bullies or their victims.[15] A report by the American Medical Association estimated that some 3.7 million youths bully other youths, while more than 3.2 million persons are victims of some form of bullying every year in the United States.[16]

Boys are more likely to be the perpetrators of bullying than girls, according to research.[17] This is particularly true for physical bullying. The victims of bullying tend to be boys more than girls, younger students, and persons who are physically or socially disadvantaged. Most have few friends or other social confidants and often exhibit poor social skills and have academic problems.

Studies show that physical bullying tends to increase in elementary school, while peaking in junior high, and decreasing in high school, whereas verbal bullying remains steadfast throughout. The lack of serious concern by schools about bullying is seen as part of the problem in combating it. More than two-thirds of students surveyed feel that school response to bullying has been weak, whereas around one-fourth of teachers fail to take action against bullying incidents.[18]

Experts believe that bullying is a reflection of a number of family, school, peer, environmental, and mental factors. These include child abuse, family violence, emotional problems, indifference by school personnel, and lack of a peer support group or involvement with one that encourages the practice of bullying. The rate of fighting by bullies and their victims is higher than among other children.[19]

The frustrations and pent up anger felt by many victims of bullying can often manifest itself in a violent response, as the recent rash of school shootings attest to. Of more than 250 school-related violent deaths involving multiple victims in this country since 1992, bullying played a role in almost every incident. In the wake of these tragedies, many schools are now implementing antibullying programs as an important means to prevent school violence.[20]

Substance Abuse

Students' use of alcohol or drugs is seen as a major factor in school crime and violence.[21] Studies show that more than half of all junior high and high school students in the United States have had at least one drink within the past year, while nearly half of all high school seniors have ever used one or more illicit drugs.[22]

Male students are significantly more likely to have at some point used alcohol or drugs than their female counterparts.[23] The same is true for alcohol or drug use at school. According to the book, *Drugs, Alcohol and Criminality in American Society*, male students were more than twice as likely as female students to have used marijuana on school property, and were more likely to have used alcohol at school.[24]

The availability of drugs at school has also been shown to be related to school crime, youth gangs, drug dealing, and other antisocial behavior.[25] Figure 19.2 shows that in 1997, nearly one-third of ninth through twelfth grade students in this country reported that illegal drugs were offered, sold, or given to them on school property within the past year. Males were more likely to report the availability of drugs than females. Thirty-seven percent of male students said they had been offered, given, or sold an illicit drug at school, compared to 25 percent of female students. Alcohol or drugs have proven to be a factor in many of the recent school shootings and related violence.

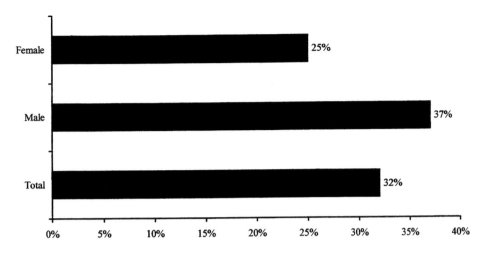

Figure 19.2. Percentage of Students, Grades 9 through 12, Reporting Drugs Were Made Available to Them on School Property During the Past 12 Months, by Sex, 1997. *Source:* Adapted from U.S. Department of Education and Justice, *Indicators of School Crime and Safety 2000* (Washington: Offices of Educational Research and Improvement and Justice Programs, 2000), p. 42.

NOTES

1. Cited in R. Barri Flowers, *The Victimization and Exploitation of Women and Children: A Study of Physical, Mental and Sexual Maltreatment in the United States* (Jefferson: McFarland, 1994), p. 111.

2. R. Barri Flowers, *Kids Who Commit Adult Crimes: A Study of Serious Juvenile Criminality and Delinquency* (Binghamton: Haworth, 2002).

3. Cited in Darcia H. Bowman, "Lethal School Shootings Resemble Workplace Rampages, Report Says," http://www.edweek.org/ew/newstory.cfm?slug=37safety.h21.

4. R. Barri Flowers and H. Loraine Flowers, *Murders in the United States: Crimes, Killers and Victims of the Twentieth Century* (Jefferson: McFarland, 2001), pp. 183–87; "A Time Line of Recent Worldwide School Shootings," http://www.infoplease.com/ipd/A0777958.html.

5. *Ibid.*; U.S. Department of Health and Human Services, *Youth Violence: A Report of the Surgeon General* (Rockville: National Institute of Health and Mental Health, 2001).

6. Youth Risk Behavior Survey, http://www.Alfred.edu/teenviolence/potential_violence.html.

7. Flowers, *Kids Who Commit Adult Crimes.*

8. U.S. Department of Education and Justice, *Indicators of School Crime and Safety* (Washington: Offices of Educational Research and Imprisonment and Justice Programs, 2000), p. 4.

9. *Ibid.*, p. 59.

10. *Ibid.*, pp. 28, 35.

11. Flowers, *Kids Who Commit Adult Crimes*; Flowers and Flowers, *Murders in the United States.*

12. *Indicators of School Crime and Safety,* pp. 28, 35; U.S. Department of Justice, *Youth Gangs: An Overview* (Washington: Office of Juvenile Justice and Delinquency Prevention, 1998).

13. Flowers, *Kids Who Commit Adult Crimes*; D. Olweus, "Bully/Victim Problems Among School Children: Basic Facts and Effects of a School Based Intervention Program," in D. J. Pepler and K. H. Rubin, eds., *The Development and Treatment of Childhood Aggression* (Hillsdale: Erlbaum, 1991).

14. Andrea Cohn and Andrea Carter, "Bullying: What Schools and Parents Can Do," National Association of School Psychologists, http://www.guideancechannel.com/details.asp?index=508&cat=1.

15. Cited in *Ibid.*

16. *Ibid.*

17. *Ibid.*

18. *Ibid.*

19. *Ibid.*

20. Jessica Garrison and Erika Hayasaki, "Schools Roll Out Plans to Get Tough on Bullies," (September 6, 2001): http://latimes.com.

21. R. Barri Flowers, Drugs, *Alcohol and Criminality in American Society* (Jefferson: McFarland, 1999), pp. 99–111.

22. *Ibid.*, pp. 100, 104.

23. *Ibid.*, p. 108; *Indicators of School Crime and Safety,* pp. 38–42.

24. Flowers, *Drugs, Alcohol and Criminality in American Society,* pp. 104–10.

25. Flowers, *Kids Who Commit Adult Crimes*; R. Barri Flowers, *The Adolescent Criminal: An Examination of Today's Juvenile Offender* (Jefferson: McFarland, 1990), pp. 94–97.

Part VII

RESPONDING TO MALE CRIME AND DEVIANCE

Chapter 20

COMBATING MALE CRIMINALITY AND DEVIANCE

In the wake of recent school shootings, mass murders, and deadly terrorist attacks in the United States, stronger laws have been enacted and policy initiatives proposed and implemented to respond to this predominantly male crime and violence. Legislation at the federal level has led to increased law enforcement, prohibitions against the sale and possession of firearms, and stiffer penalties against those committing federal crimes, crimes of violence and against women and children, gang-related crimes, terrorist acts, sex crimes, and drug offenses.

State and local governments have followed the federal government's lead in passing tough measures aimed at cracking down on dangerous, violent, and habitual criminals; crime control; and crime prevention. The results of these collective efforts has been the apprehension and longer incarceration of more offenders, more funding provided for law enforcement, construction of prisons, and crime prevention, along with a greater societal awareness of serious criminality and its potential implications.

What follows is some key anticrime legislation to impact American society, male crime, and violence.

VIOLENT CRIME CONTROL AND LAW ENFORCEMENT ACT

The Violent Crime Control and Law Enforcement Act (the Federal Crime Bill) was enacted into law in 1994.[1] As the largest crime bill in United States' history, the Act contained a number of provisions including providing for 100,000 new police officers, nearly $10 billion for prison construction, over $6 billion for crime prevention programs, and $2.6 billion for new federal law enforcement. Penalties were also increased for many types of offenses, including federal crimes, violent crimes, sex crimes, gang criminality, and white-collar offenses. Highlights of the Act's provisions include:

- Banning the manufacture of nineteen military assault weapons and those with certain combat features.
- Expanding the death penalty to include around 60 offenses, such as terrorist-related homicides, murder of a federal officer of the law, carjackings and drive-by shootings that result in death, and large drug trafficking operations.
- New and stronger penalties for gang-related violent crimes and drug trafficking.
- Strengthened federal licensing requirements for firearm dealers.
- Prohibiting the sale to or possession of firearms by persons who have domestic violence restraining orders against them.
- Requiring the registration of sexually violent criminals with state law enforcement agencies.
- Doubling the penalties for repeat sex offenders convicted of federal sex crimes.
- A mandatory life sentence with no chance of parole for federal offenders with three or more serious violent felony or drug trafficking convictions.
- Authorizing the prosecution in adult court of persons age 13 and older charged with certain types of serious violent offenses.
- Creating new crimes or enhancing penalties for such offenses as use of semiautomatic weapons, drive-by shootings, sex crimes, hate crimes, crimes against the elderly, interstate domestic violence, and interstate trafficking of firearms.

VIOLENCE AGAINST WOMEN ACT

The Violence Against Women Act (VAWA) was signed into law in 2000, reauthorizing provisions of the VAWA first passed in 1994 and merging with the Victims of Trafficking and Violence Protection Act of 2000.[2] The VAWA 2000 called for more than $3 billion in federal funding for more police officers, prosecutors, battered women's shelters, and a National Domestic Violence Hotline. Specifically, the Act included:

- **STOP grants** (Services and Training for Officers and Prosecutors) totaling $925 to go to states to distribute among law enforcement, prosecutors, courts, and victims services agencies at state and local levels.
- **Battered women's shelters** funding of $875 million to assist communities in providing services for battered women and their children staying in shelters.

- ***Battered immigrant women*** legislation that addresses the needs of immigrant women victims of domestic violence.
- ***Disabled and older women*** services with funding of $25 million for grants to train police and develop policies to address the needs of older and disabled battered women or those victimized through sexual violence.
- ***Dating violence,*** defining of and enabling grants to be awarded to programs addressing issues surrounding dating violence.

ANTITERRORISM AND EFFECTIVE DEATH PENALTY ACT

The Antiterrorism and Effective Death Penalty Act was signed into law in 1996 in response to the Oklahoma City and World Trade Center terrorist attacks.[3] The Act includes habeas corpus reform, mandatory restitution for victims of terrorism, and provisions related to stopping the financing of terrorists and immigration-deportation of alien terrorists. These are summarized as follows:

- Habeas corpus law amendments, applicable to all state and federal prisoners, include a one year statute of limitation for filing habeas petitions, a six-month deadline in death penalty cases, and required appellate court approval for repetitious habeas petitions.
- Restitution for victims provisions defines circumstances in which foreign governments supporting terrorism can be sued as a result of injuries and increases compensation for victims of terrorism.
- Financing of terrorist activities provisions includes regulating of fundraising by those foreign organizations that support terrorists, and isolates countries associated with terrorists and strengthening counter-errorism efforts.
- Alien terrorists and related immigration issues are addressed in establishing or expediting means to bar or deport criminal aliens from the United States, and to limit asylum measures that prevent or thwart efforts at barring or removing terrorists.

RACKETEER INFLUENCED AND CORRUPT ORGANIZATIONS ACT

The Racketeer Influenced and Corrupt Organizations Act (RICO) as part of the Organized Crime Control Act enacted in 1970, focused on controlling organized criminal activities and stiffening penalties against those convicted of racketeering, defined as the participation in at least two acts prohibited by existing federal and state statutes.[4] These offenses included such federal crimes as white slavery, bribery, counterfeiting, loan sharking, wire fraud, mail fraud, and drug violations; and state crimes such as murder, kidnapping, extortion, bribery, and gambling.

The Act specifically states,

(a) It shall be unlawful for any person who has received any income derived, directly or indirectly, from a pattern of racketeering activity or through collection of an unlawful debt in which such person has participated as a principal . . . ; (b) it shall be unlawful for any person through a pattern of racketeering activity or through collection of an unlawful debt to acquire or maintain, directly or indirectly, an interest in or control of any enterprise which is engaged in, or the activities which affect, interstate and foreign commerce; (c) it shall be unlawful for any person employed by or associated with any enterprise engaged in, or the activities of which affect, interstate or foreign commerce, to conduct or participate, directly or indirectly, in the conduct of such enterprise's affairs through a pattern of activity or collection of unlawful debt.[5]

Amendments to RICO over the years have strengthened or added prohibitions against such criminality as the sexual exploitation of children, fraudulent activities, money laundering, and witness tampering.[6]

LAWS AGAINST HATE CRIMES

Hate Crimes Prevention Act

The Hate Crimes Prevention Act of 1999 prohibits interfering with a person's federal right through violence or threat of due to the individual's race, ethnicity, gender, religion, national origin, or sexual orientation.[7] The Act gives federal prosecutors greater authority to investigate and prosecute perpetrators of hate crimes.

Church Arson Prevention Act

The Church Arson Prevention Act of 1996 created the National Church Arson Task Force (NCATF) whose purpose is to overlook the investigation and prosecution of arson committed at houses of worship across the United States.[8] The Act also allows for wider federal jurisdiction for such criminal activity and a rebuilding recovery fund.

Hate Crime Sentencing Enhancement Act

The Hate Crimes Sentencing Act is part of the Violent Crime Control and Law Enforcement Act of 1994.[9] The Act allows for longer sentences for crimes deemed to be hate crimes, or motivated by a victim's race, ethnicity, gender, color, sexual orientation, or disability.

Hate Crimes Statistics Act

The Hate Crimes Statistics Act of 1990 requires the Justice Department, through the Federal Bureau of Investigation, to collect data pertaining to hate crimes, or crimes based on prejudice due to race, ethnicity, religion, or sexual orientation.[10] The Crime Bill of 1994 required the FBI to include statistics on disability-related hate crimes.[11]

CHILD ABUSE PREVENTION AND TREATMENT ACT

The Child Abuse Prevention and Treatment Act, enacted in 1974 and amended in 1978, came in response to a growing problem of abused, neglected, and sexually exploited children in the United States.[12] The Act defined child abuse and neglect, and provided for several programs to combat the maltreatment of children, including:

(1) the establishment of a National Center on Child Abuse and Neglect, (2) increasing public awareness on child maltreatment, detection, and reporting, (3) assisting states and local communities in developing more effective mechanisms for delivery of services to families, (4) providing training and technical assistance to state and local communities in dealing with the problems of child abuse and neglect, and (5) supporting research into causal and preventative measures in child victimization.[13]

To qualify for federal funding, states were required to meet certain criteria such as a uniform and comprehensive definition of child abuse and neglect, investigating reports of child abuse, and the confidentiality of records.

PROTECTION OF CHILDREN AGAINST SEXUAL EXPLOITATION ACT

The Protection of Children Against Sexual Exploitation Act was signed into law in 1978.[14] Its purpose was to close gaps existing in federal statutes for protecting children from sexual maltreatment and commercial sexual exploitation by sexual predators, such as through juvenile prostitution and child pornography. The Act sought to stop the production and dissemination of child pornography by prohibiting the interstate transporting of underage persons for purposes of sexual exploitation. Additionally, the legislation increased the federal government's power to prosecute producers and distributors of child pornographic materials.

Specifically,

> the law provides punishment for persons who use, employ, or persuade minors (defined as any persons under sixteen) to become involved in the production of visual or print materials that depict sexually explicit conduct if the producers know or have reason to know that the materials will be transported in interstate or foreign commerce or mailed. Punishment is also specifically provided for parents, legal guardians, or other persons having custody or control of minors and who knowingly permit a minor to participate in the production of such material.[15]

Other important related recent federal statutes designed to protect juveniles from sexual exploiters include the Protection of Children from Sexual Predators Act of 1998;[16] the Child Pornography Prevention Act of 1996;[17] and the Child Protection, Restoration and Penalties Enhancement Act of 1990.[18]

JUVENILE JUSTICE AND DELINQUENCY PREVENTION ACT

The Juvenile Justice and Delinquency Prevention Act was enacted into law in 1974 and amended in 1980.[19] The Act addressed the problem and implications of housing status offenders or dependent children in juvenile detention or correctional facilities with serious juvenile or adult offenders. It sought to divert nondelinquents from facilities that detained delinquents and adult criminals, requiring: (1) a comprehensive assessment of the current juvenile justice system's effectiveness, and (2) the development and implementation of innovative alternatives in preventing delinquency and diverting status offenders from the juvenile justice system to more effectively deal with juvenile offenders.

> The Act mandated that for states to receive federal funds, juveniles who are charged with or who have committed offenses that would not be criminal if committed by an adult or offenses which do not constitute violations of valid court orders, or alien juveniles in custody, or such nonoffenders as dependent or neglected children, shall not be placed in secure detention facilities or secure correctional facilities, but must be placed in shelter facilities.[20]

A sight and sound separation provision further required that juveniles who are alleged or adjudicated delinquent, along with status offenders and nonoffenders, "shall not be detained or confined in any institution in which they have contact with adult persons incarcerated because they have been convicted of a crime or are awaiting trial on criminal charges."[21]

DRUG CONTROL LAWS

A number of federal laws have been enacted in recent years aimed at fighting drug abuse and increasing penalties against drug dealers, drug traffickers, and other drug-related offenders. The Comprehensive Methamphetamine Control Act was enacted into law in 1996.[22] This enabled law enforcement to seize the chemicals used to manufacture methamphetamine and strengthen penalties for the trafficking of the chemicals and possession of equipment used to manufacture the drug.

Other federal laws combating illegal drugs, drug use, and drug-related crimes include the Anti-Drug Abuse Act of 1986,[23] and the Crime Control Act of 1990,[24] as well as the Money Laundering Act of 1986, which prohibited certain financial transactions associated with drug trafficking and concealment of funds used in illegal activities.[25]

New laws on the state level have also been created to battle the drug problem in the country's war on drugs. In 1990, changes in the Uniform Controlled Substances Act (UCSA), a prototype law designed to make state laws more uniform as well as compatibility between federal and state Controlled Substances Acts, led to the enactment of more than 450 new drug laws.[26] These included laws:

- Protecting minors from drug sales and exploiting by using in drug distribution.
- Increasing penalties for drug traffickers.
- Facilitating seizure of drug profits.
- Channeling forfeited assets into drug law enforcement.
- Making drug users more accountable in penalties as a deterrence against future drug use.

U.S.A. PATRIOT ACT

Following the devastating terrorist attacks on America in September 2001, the Uniting and Strengthening America by Providing Appropriate Tools

Required to Intercept and Obstruct Terrorism Act (U.S.A. Patriot Act) was enacted into law in October 2001.[27] The Act extended the federal government's power to go after terrorists—both abroad and domestically—and those who support them. It also established a new cooperative relationship between domestic criminal investigations pertaining to foreign intelligence. Specifically, the law contained provisions that:

- Enhances the Department of Justice's ability to gather intelligence in fighting global terrorism, including increased wiretapping capabilities.
- Enhances the Immigration and Naturalization Service's authority to detain and deport suspected terrorists by broadening the definition of terrorists to include those supporting terrorist organizations and activities.
- Strengthens prosecutors' efforts in using the legal system to cripple terrorist organizations, as well as increase penalties for persons convicted of committing terrorist acts.
- Focus on the financial infrastructure of terrorist organizations by allowing for criminal and civil forfeiture of assets used by terrorist groups to finance their illegal activities, as well as making those who knowingly engage in financial transactions related to the proceeds of terrorist acts criminally liable.
- Authorizes emergency operations as a response to the terrorist attacks of September 11, 2001, and aids the Attorney General in providing relief to victims, as well as giving greater authority to offer rewards in relation to terrorist offenses.

NOTES

1. P.L. 103–322 (1994).
2. P.L. 106–386 (2000).
3. P.L. 104–132 (1996).
4. P.L. 91–452, Title IX, 84 Stat. 941 (1970).
5. 18 U.S.C. §1962 (1982).
6. P.L. 101–647 (1990); P.L. 99–646 (1986); P.L. 99–570 (1984); P.L. 100–690 (1986).
7. 18 U.S.C. 245; as amended by H.R. 1082 (1999).
8. 18 U.S.C. 247 (1996).
9. P.L. 103–322, Sec. 280003 (1994).
10. 28 U.S.C. 534 (1990).
11. P.L. 103–322 (1994).
12. 42 U.S.C. §5101–5106 (1974); as amended by P.L. 95–266, 92 Stat. 205 (1978).
13. *Ibid.*

14. 18 U.S.C. §2251, 2253–2254 (1978).
15. *Ibid.*
16. P.L. 105–314, §101, 112 Stat. 2974 (1998).
17. P.L. 104–208, §121, 110 Stat. 3009, 3009–3026 (1996).
18. P.L. 101–647, §323, 104 Stat. 4789, 4818 (1990).
19. P.L. 93–415 (1974); as amended in P.L. 96–509 (1980).
20. P.L. 93–415.
21. *Ibid.*
22. P.L. 104–237 (1996).
23. P.L. 99–570, H.R. 5484 (1986).
24. P.L. 101–647 (1990).
25. P.L. 99–570 (1986).
26. Uniform Controlled Substances Act (1990).
27. P.L. 107–56 (2001).

REFERENCES

Abel, E. L. (1987) "Drugs and Homicide in Erie County, New York." *International Journal of the Addictions 22*: 195–200.

Abel, G. G., J. V. Becker, J. Cunningham-Rathner, & J. L. Rouleau. (1987) "Self-Reported Sex Crimes of 561 Nonincarcerated Paraphiliacs." *Journal of Interpersonal Violence 2*, 6: 3–25.

——, M. S. Mittleman, J. V. Becker, J. Rathner, & J. L. Rouleau. (1988) "Predicting Child Molesters' Response to Treatment." *Annals of the New York Academy of Sciences 528*: 223–34.

Abrahamsen, D. (1970) *Our Violent Society*. New York: Funk and Wagnalls.

Abramson, Hilary. "Sociologists Try to Reach Young Hustlers." *Sacramento Bee* (September 3, 1984), p. A8.

Acoca, L. (1998) "Defusing the Time Bomb: Understanding and Meeting the Growing Health Care Needs of Incarcerated Women in America." *Crime & Delinquency 44*, 1: 44–69.

Adams, D. E., H. A. Ishizula, & K. S. Ishizula. (1977) The Child Abuse Delinquents: An Exploratory/Descriptive Study. Unpublished MSW thesis. University of South Carolina, South Carolina.

Adler, Freda. (1975) *Sisters in Crime: The Rise of the New Female Criminal*. New York: McGraw-Hill.

Agnew, Robert. (1992) "Foundation for a General Strain Theory." *Criminology 30*, 1: 47–87.

——, Timothy Brezina, John P. Wright, & Francis T. Cullen. (2002) "Strain, Personality Traits, and Delinquency: Extending General Strain Theory." *Criminology 40*, 1: 43–70.

Aichorn, August. (1935) *Wayward Youth*. New York: Viking Press.

Akers, Ronald L., Marvin D. Krohn, Lonn Lanza-Kaduce, & Marcia Radosevich. (1979) "Social Learning and Deviant Behavior: A Specific Test of a General Theory." *American Sociological Review 44*: 636–55.

——, Marvin D. Krohn, Lonn Lanza-Kaduce, & Marcia Radosevich. (1996) "Social Learning and Deviant Behavior: A Specific Test of a General Theory." In Dean G. Rojek & Gary F. Jensen, eds. *Exploring Delinquency: Causes and Control*. Los Angeles: Roxbury.

Albert, Alexa. (2002) *Mustang Ranch and Its Women*. New York: Ballantine.

Aldarondo, E., & D. B. Sugarman. (1996) "Risk Marker Analysis of the Cessation and Persistence of Wife Assault." *Journal of Consulting and Clinical Psychology 64*, 5: 1010–19.

Allen, Donald M. "Young Male Prostitutes: A Psychosocial Study." (1980) *Archives of Sexual Behavior 9*: 409–418.

Allen, Ralph C. (1996) "Socioeconomic Conditions and Property Crime: A Comprehensive Review and Test of the Professional Literature." *American Journal of Economics and Sociology 55*: 293–308.

American Humane Association. (1987) *Child Abuse and Neglect Reporting and Investigation: Policy Guidelines for Decision-Making.* Denver: American Humane Association.

American Psychiatric Association. (1987) *Diagnostic and Statistical Manual of Mental Disorders.* 3rd ed. Washington: American Psychiatric Association.

American Psychological Association. (1998) http://www.apa.org/pubinfo/hate/ #who.

——. (1993) Commission on Violence and Youth. *Violence and Youth: Psychology's Response.* Washington: American Psychological Association.

Amir, Menachem. (1971) *Patterns in Forcible Rape.* Chicago: University of Chicago Press.

Anderson, E. (1990) *Streetwise: Race, Class, and Change in an Urban Community.* Chicago: University of Chicago Press.

Anderson, James F., & Laronistine Dyson. (2002) *Criminological Theories: Understanding Crime in America.* Lanham: University Press of America.

Andry, Robert G. (1962) "Paternal Affection and Delinquency." In Marvin F. Wolfgang, Leonard Savitz, & Norman Johnson, eds. *The Sociology of Crime and Delinquency.* New York: John Wiley & Sons.

Archer, J. (1991) "The Influence of Testosterone on Human Aggression." *British Journal of Psychology 82*: 1–28.

Arriaga, Ximena B., & Stuart Oskamp, eds. (1999) *Violence in Intimate Relationships.* Thousand Oaks: Sage.

Asdigian, N. L., D. Finkelhor, & G. T. Hotaling. (1995) "Varieties of Non-Family Abduction of Children and Adolescents." *Criminal Justice and Behavior 22*: 215–32.

Ashcroft v. American Civil Liberties Union. (2002) 217 F 3d 162.

"Attention Deficit Hyperactivity Disorder." (1997) Commonwealth of Australia. http://www.health.gov.au/nhmrc/publications/adhd/contents.htm.

Auerhahn, Kathleen, & Robert N. Parker. (1999) "Drugs, Alcohol, and Homicide." In M. Dwayne Smith & Margaret A. Zahn, eds. *Studying and Preventing Homicide: Issues and Challenges.* Thousand Oaks: Sage.

Azar, Sandra, & David Wolfe. (1998) "Child Physical Abuse and Neglect." In Eric J. Mash & Russell A. Barkley, eds. *Treatment of Childhood Disorders.* 2nd ed. New York: Guilford Press.

Bachman, R. (1991) "The Social Causes of American Indian Homicide as Revealed by the Life Experiences of Thirty Offenders." *American Indian Quarterly 15*: 468–92.

Bain, J., R. Langevin, R. Dickey, & M. Ben-Aron. (1987) "Sex Hormones in Murderers and Assaulters." *Behavioral Science and the Law 5*: 95–101.

Baker, Janet, & Trish Berry. (1995) *It Happened To Us: Men Talk About Child Sexual Abuse*. Melbourne: Victorian Government Department of Health & Community Services.

Bakos, Susan. "The Hugh Grant Syndrome: Why Nice Guys Go to Hookers." *McCall's 123* (November 1995), p. 106.

Bandura, Albert. (1977) *Social Learning Theory*. Englewood Cliffs: Prentice-Hall.

——, & Richard H. Walters. (1958) "Dependency Conflicts in Aggressive Delinquents." *Journal of Social Issues 4*: 52–65.

Banton, M. (1986) *Investigating Robbery*. Brookfield: Gower.

Barash, D., & J. Lipton. (2001) "Making Sense of Sex." In D. Barash, ed. *Understanding Violence*. Boston: Allyn & Bacon.

Bard, Morton, & Dawn Sangrey. (1986) *The Crime Victim's Book*. 2nd ed. Secaucus: Citadel Press.

Baron, Larry, & Murray A. Straus. (1984) "Sexual Stratification, Pornography, and Rape in the United States." In Neil Malamuth & Edward Donnerstein, eds. *Pornography and Sexual Aggression*. Orlando: Academic Press.

Barry, Kathleen. (1979) *Female Sexual Slavery*. Englewood Cliffs: Prentice-Hall, 1979.

——. (1995) *The Prostitution of Sexuality*. New York: New York University Press.

Bartol, C. R. (1991) *Criminal Behavior: A Psychosocial Approach*. Englewood: Prentice-Hall.

Battelle Law and Justice Study Center Report. (1977) *Forcible Rape: An Analysis of Legal Issues*. Washington: Government Printing Office.

Battin, S. R., K G. Hill, R. D. Abbott, R. F. Catalano, & J. D. Hawkins. (1998) "The Contribution of Gang Membership to Delinquency Beyond Delinquent Friends." *Criminology 36*: 93–115.

Bean, Philip. (2002) *Critical Concepts in Sociology*. London: Routledge.

Becker, J. V., M. S. Kaplan, J. Cunningham-Rathner, & R. Kavoussi. (1986) "Characteristics of Adolescent Incest Sexual Perpetrators: Preliminary Findings." *Journal of Family Violence 1*, 1: 85–97.

Belknap, Joanne (2001) *The Invisible Woman: Gender, Crime, and Justice*. Belmont: Wadsworth.

——, & Edna Erez. (1995) "The Victimization of Women on College Campuses: Courtship Violence, Date Rape, and Sexual Harassment." In Bonnie S. Fisher & John J. Sloan III, eds. *Campus Crime: Legal, Social and Policy Perspectives*. Springfield: Charles C Thomas.

Bell, Jeannine. (2002) *Policing Hatred: Law Enforcement, Civil Rights, and Hate Crime*. New York: New York University Press.

Benedict, J. R. (1998) *Athletes and Acquaintance Rape*. Thousand Oaks: Sage.

Bennett, James. "Clinton Backs Expanding Definition of a Hate Crime." *New York Times* (November 11, 1997), p. A20.

Bergen, R. K. (1996) *Wife Rape: Understanding Responses of Survivors and Service Providers*. Thousand Oaks: Sage.

Berliner, L., & J. R. Wheeler. (1987) "Treating the Effects of Sexual Abuse on Children." *Journal of Interpersonal Violence 2*: 415–24.

Bernard, J. L., S. L. Bernard, & M. L. Bernard. (1985) "Courtship Violence and Sex-Typing." *Family Relations 34*: 573–76.

Bernard, Thomas. (1981) "The Distinction Between Conflict and Radical Criminology." *Journal of Criminal Law and Criminology 72*: 366–70.

Bettin, Rebecca. Young Women's Resource Center. Testimony at Iowa House of Representatives Public Hearing on Dating Violence. March 31, 1992.

Bjerregaard, B., & C. Smith. (1993) "Gender Differences in Gang Participation, Delinquency, and Substance Use." *Journal of Quantitative Criminology 9*: 329–55.

Block, C. R., A. Christakos, A. Jacob, & R. Przybylski. (1996) *Street Gangs and Crime: Patterns and Trends in Chicago.* Research Bulletin. Chicago: Criminal Justice Information Authority.

Bourgis, P. (1996) "In Search of Masculinity: Violence, Respect and Sexuality Among Puerto Rican Crack Dealers in East Harlem." *British Journal of Criminology 36*, 3: 412–27.

Bowlby, J. (1951) *Maternal Care and Mental Health.* Geneva: World Health Organization.

Bowman, Darcia H. "Lethal School Shootings Resemble Workplace Rampages, Report Says." http://www.edweek.org/ew/newstory.cfm?slug=37safety.h21.

Boyle, D. J., & D. Vivian. (1996) "Generalized versus Spouse-Specific Anger/Hostility and Men's Violence Against Intimates." *Violence and Victims 11*: 293–317.

Brain, P. (1993) "Hormonal Aspects of Aggression and Violence." In A. Reiss & J. Roth, eds. *Understanding and Preventing Violence.* Washington: National Academy Press.

Breslau, N., N. Klein, & L. Allen. (1988) "Very Low Birthweight: Behavioral Sequelae at Nine Years of Age." *Journal of the American Academy of Child and Adolescent Psychiatry 27*: 605–12

Bridis, Ted. "FBI Says It Has Shut Down Worldwide Child Pornography Ring." *Newsday* (March 19, 2002).

Brodsky, Stanley L., & Susan C. Hobart. (1978) "Blame Models and Assailant Research." *Criminal Justice and Behavior 5*: 379–88.

Broidy, Lisa. (2001) "A Test of General Strain Theory." *Criminology 39*: 9–36.

Brooke, Jim. "Feminism in Foreign Lands: Two Perspectives: Macho Killing in Brazil Spurs Protesters." *Boston Globe* (January 2, 1982): A23.

Brooks, J. H., & J. R. Reddon. (1996) "Serum Testosterone in Violent and Nonviolent Young Offenders." *Journal of Clinical Psychology 52*: 475–83.

Brown, S. A. (1993) "Drug Effect Expectancies and Addictive Behavior Change." *Experimental and Clinical Psychopharmacology 1*: 55–67.

Browne, Angela. (1987) *When Battered Women Kill.* New York: Free Press.

——, Kirk R. Williams, & Donald G. Dutton. (1999) "Homicide Between Intimate Partners." In M. Dwayne Smith & Margaret A. Zahn, eds. *Studying and Preventing Homicide: Issues and Challenges.* Thousand Oaks: Sage.

Browne, K., & M. Herbert. (1997) *Preventing Family Violence.* Chichester: Wiley & Sons.

Browning, Charles J. (1960) "Differential Impact of Family Disorganization on Male Adolescents." *Social Forces 8*: 37–44.

Brownmiller, Susan. (1975) *Against Our Will: Men, Women, and Rape.* New York: Simon & Schuster.

Buchanan, Ann. (1996) *Cycles of Child Maltreatment: Facts, Fallacies, and Interventions.* Hoboken: John Wiley & Sons.

Burgess, Robert L., & Ronald L. Akers. (1966) "A Differential Association-Reinforcement Theory of Criminal Behavior." *Social Problems 14*: 128–47.

Bursik, R. J., Jr., & H. G. Grasmick. (1993) *Neighborhoods and Crime: The Dimensions of Effective Community Control.* New York: Lexington Books.

Burt, Cyril. (1938) *The Young Delinquent.* London: University of London Press.

Burt, Martha R. (1980) "Cultural Myths and Support for Rape." *Journal of Personality and Social Psychology 38*: 217–30.

Buttons, A. (1973) "Some Antecedents of Felonious and Delinquent Behavior." *Journal of Child Clinical Psychology 2*: 35–37.

Campbell, Anne. (1999) "Staying Alive: Evolution, Culture, and Women's Intrasexual Aggression." *Behavioral and Brain Sciences 22*: 203–15.

——, S. Muncer, & J. Odber. (1997) "Aggression and Testosterone: Testing a Bio-Social Model." *Aggressive Behavior 23*: 229–38.

Campbell, Beatrix. (1993) *Goliath: Britain's Dangerous Places.* London: Metheun.

Campbell, Jacquelyn C. (1992) "If I Can't Have You, No One Can: Issues of Power and Control in Homicide of Female Partners." In J. Radford & D. E. Russell, eds. *Femicide: The Politics of Women Killing.* Boston: Twayne.

——. (1995) "Prediction of Homicide of and by Battered Women." In J. Campbell & J. Milner, eds. *Assessing Dangerousness: Potential for Further Violence of Sexual Offenders, Batterers, and Child Abusers.* Thousand Oaks: Sage.

——, & P. Alford. (1989) "The Dark Consequences of Marital Rape." *American Journal of Nursing 1*: 946–49.

Carter, Keith. (1996) "Masculinity in Prison." In Jane Pilcher & Amada Coffey, eds. *Gender and Qualitative Research.* Aldershot: Avebury.

Cashdan, E. (1995) "Hormones, Sex, and Status in Women." *Hormones and Behavior 29*: 354–66.

Caukins, S., & N. Coombs. (1976) "The Psychodynamics of Male Prostitution." *American Journal of Psychotherapy 30*: 441–51.

Chadwick-Jones, J. K. (1976) *Social Exchange Theory: Its Structure and Influence in Social Psychology.* New York: Academic Press.

Chesney-Lind, M., & R. G. Shelden. (1998) *Girls, Delinquency, and Juvenile Justice.* Belmont: West/Wadsworth.

"Child Pornography on the Rise Despite Tougher Laws." *Sacramento Union* (April 7, 1984), p. E6.

Chimbos, P. D. (1978) *Marital Violence: A Study of Interspousal Homicide.* San Francisco: R & E Research Associates.

Chodorow, Nancy. (1989) *Feminism and Psychoanalytic Theory.* New Haven: Yale University Press.

Christiansen, Karl O. (1977) "Seriousness of Criminality and Concordance Among Danish Twins." In R. Hood, ed. *Crime, Criminology and Public Policy.* London: Heinemann.

Clare, Anthony. (2000) *On Men: Masculinity and Crises.* London: Chatto and Windus.

Clark, Lorenne M., & Debra J. Lewis. (1977) *Rape: The Price of Coercive Sexuality.* Toronto: Canadian Women's Educational Press.

Cloward, Richard A., & Lloyd E. Ohlin. (1960) *Delinquency and Opportunity: A Theory of Delinquent Gangs*. New York: Free Press.

Cohen, Albert K. (1955) *Delinquent Boys: The Culture of the Gang*. New York: Free Press.

——. (1965) "The Sociology of the Deviant Act: Anomie Theory and Beyond." *American Sociological Review 2*: 5–14.

——, & James F. Short, Jr. (1958) "Research on Delinquent Subcultures." *Journal of Social Issues 14*, 3: 20–37.

Coleman, F. L. (1997) "Stalking Behaviour and the Cycle of Domestic Violence." *Journal of Interpersonal Violence 12*, 3: 420–32.

Cohn, Andrea, & Andrea Carter. "Bullying: What Schools and Parents Can Do." National Association of School Psychologists. http://www.guideancechannel .com/details.asp?index=508&cat=1.

Collier, Richard. (1997) *Masculinities, Crime, and Criminology: Men, Corporeality, and the Criminal(ized) Body*. Thousand Oaks: Sage.

Collinson, M. (1996) "In Search of the High Life: Drugs, Crime, Masculinities and Consumption." *British Journal of Criminology 36*, 3: 428–33.

Commonwealth Fund, The. *First Comprehensive National Health Survey of American Women*. July 1993.

Conger, Rand D. (1976) "Social Control and Social Learning Models of Delinquent Behavior–A Synthesis." *Criminology 14*: 17–40.

Connell, Robert. (1995) *Masculinities*. Berkeley: University of California Press.

Constantino, J. D., D. Grosz, P. Saenger, D. Chandler, R. Nandi, & F. Earls. (1993) "Testosterone and Aggression in Children." *Journal of the American Academy of Child & Adolescent Psychiatry 32*: 1217–22.

Cook, Philip. (1991) "The Technology of Personal Violence." In Michael Tonry, ed. *Crime and Justice: A Review of Research*. Vol. 14. Chicago: University of Chicago Press.

Corrado, R., C. Odgers, & I. M. Cohen. (2000) "The Incarceration of Female Young Offenders: Protection for Whom?" *Canadian Journal of Criminology 42*, 2: 189–207.

Cortes, J. B., & F. M. Gatti. (1972) *Delinquency and Crime: A Biopsychosocial Approach*. New York: Seminar Press.

Costello, Barbara. (1997) "On the Logical Adequacy of Cultural Deviance Theories." *Theoretical Criminology 1*: 403–28.

Courtois, Christine A. (1996) *Healing the Incest Wound: Adult Survivors in Therapy*. New York: W. W. Norton.

Crew, Keith A. (1991) "Sex Differences in Criminal Sentencing: Chivalry or Patriarchy?" *Justice Quarterly 8*: 59–83.

Crewdson, John. (1988) *By Silence Betrayed: Sexual Abuse in America*. New York: Harper & Row.

Crowell, Nancy A., & Ann W. Burgess, eds. (1996) *Understanding Violence Against Women*. Washington: National Academy Press.

Curry, G. D., & S. H. Decker. (1998) *Confronting Gangs: Crime and Community*. Los Angeles: Roxbury.

Cyriaque, Jeanne. "The Chronic Serious Offender: How Illinois Juveniles 'Match Up.'" *Illinois* (February 1982): 4–5.

Dabbs, J. M., R. L. Frady, T. S. Carr, & N. F. Besch. (1987) "Saliva Testosterone and Criminal Violence in Young Adult Prison Inmates." *Psychosomatic Medicine 49*: 74–182.

——, R. B. Ruback, R. Frady, C. H. Hopper, & D. S. Sgoutas. (1988) "Saliva Testosterone and Criminal Violence Among Women." *Personality and Individual Differences 9*: 269–75.

——, T. S. Carr, R. L. Frady, & J. K. Riad. (1995) "Testosterone, Crime, and Misbehavior Among 692 Prison Inmates." *Personality and Individual Differences 18*: 627–33.

Dalgaard, Odd S., & Einar Kringler. (1976) "A Norwegian Twin Study of Criminality." *British Journal of Criminology 16*: 213–33.

Daly, K. (1992) "Women's Pathways to Felony Court: Feminist Theories of Lawbreaking and Problems of Representation." *Review of Law and Women's Studies 2*: 11–52.

——. (1997) "Different Ways of Conceptualizing Sex/Gender in Feminist Theory and Their Implications for Criminology." *Theoretical Criminology 1*, 1.

Daly, M., & M. Wilson. (1988) *Homicide.* New York: Aldine de Gruyter.

Damrin, Dora E. (1949) "Family Size and Sibling Age, Sex, and Position as Related to Certain Aspects of Adjustment." *Journal of Social Psychology 29*: 93–102.

Danni, K. A., & G. Hampe. (2000) "An Analysis of Predictors of Child Sex Offender Types Using Presentence Investigation Reports." *International Journal of Offender Therapy and Comparative Criminology 44*: 490–504.

Davids, Leo. (1977) "Delinquency Prevention through Father Training: Some Observations and Proposals." In Paul C. Friday & V. Lorne Stewart, eds. *Youth, Crime and Juvenile Justice: International Perspectives.* New York: Holt, Rinehart & Winston.

Davidson, Terry. (1979) *Conjugal Crime: Understanding and Changing the Wife-Beating Pattern.* New York: Hawthorne.

Davidson, Theodore. (1974) *Chicano Prisoners: The Key to San Quentin.* New York: Holt, Rinehart & Winston.

Davis, A. (1998) "Masked Racism: Reflections on the Prison Industrial Complex." *ColorLines 1*, 2: 11–17.

De Jong, A. R., G. A. Emmett, & A. R. Hervada. (1982) "Sexual Abuse of Children: Sex-, Race-, and Age-Dependent Variations." *American Journal of Diseases of Children 136*, 2: 129–34.

De Keseredy, Walter. (1988) "Women Abuse in Dating Relationships: The Relevance of Social Support Theory." *Journal of Family Violence 3*, 1: 1–14.

——, & Katharine Kelly. (1993) "The Incidence and Prevalence of Women Abuse in Canadian University and College Dating Relationships." *Canadian Journal of Sociology 18*: 137–59.

Decker, S. H., & B. Van Winkle. (1996) *Life in the Gang: Family, Friends, and Violence.* New York: Cambridge University Press.

DeMott, Kathryn. (1999) "Personality Disorders May Be Genetic." *Clinical Psychiatry News 27*, 12: 27.

Denno, D. W. (1990) *Biology and Violence.* Cambridge: Cambridge University Press.

Developmental Crime Prevention Consortium, Pathways to Prevention: Developmental and Early Intervention Approaches to Crime in Australia (Full Report). (1999) Canberra: National Crime Prevention.

Deykin, E. Y. (1971) "Life Functioning in Families of Delinquent Boys: An Assessment Model." *Social Services Review 46*, 1: 90–91.

Diagnostic and Statistical Manual of Mental Disorders (DSM-IV). (1994) Washington: American Psychiatric Association.

Dietz, Park. (1986) "Mass, Serial, and Sensational Homicides." *Bulletin of the New York Academy of Medicine 62*: 477–91.

——, & Daniell Martell. (1991) "Threatening and Otherwise Inappropriate Letters to Members of the United States Congress." *Journal of Forensic Sciences 36*, 5.

DiLalla, L. F., & I. I. Gottesman. (1991) "Biological and Genetic Contributors to Violence–Widom's Untold Tale." *Psychological Bulletin 109*: 125–29.

Dixon, J., & A. J. Lizotte. (1987) "Gun Ownership and the Southern Subculture of Violence." *American Journal of Sociology 93*: 383–405.

Dobash, R. E., & R. P. Dobash. (1979) *Violence Against Wives*. New York: Free Press.

Donat, Patricia L., & John D'Emilio. (1998) "A Feminist Redefinition of Rape and Sexual Assault: Historical Foundations and Change." In Mary E. Odem & Jody Clay-Warner, eds. *Confronting Rape and Sexual Assault*. Wilmington: Scholarly Resources Inc.

Donziger, S., ed. (1996) *The Real War on War: The Report of the National Criminal Justice Commission*. New York: Harper Collins.

Dowds, Lizanne, & Carol Hedderman. (1997) "The Sentencing of Men and Women." In C. Hedderman & L. Gelsthorpe, eds. *Understanding the Sentencing of Women*. London: Home Office.

Dugdale, Richard L. (1877) *The Jukes: A Study in Crime, Pauperism, and Heredity*. New York: Putnam.

Durkheim, Emile. (1933) *The Division of Labor in Society*. New York: Free Press.

Dusky, Lorraine. (1996) *Still Unequal: The Shameful Truth About Women and Justice in America*. New York: Crown.

Eagly, A. H., & V. J. Steffen. (1986) "Gender and Aggressive Behavior: A Meta-Analytic Review of the Social Psychological Literature." *Psychological Bulletin 100*: 309–30.

Eggen, Dan. "FBI: U.S. Crime Rate is on Rise–Increase in Incidents of Major Violence Ends 10-Year Decline." http://www.detnews.com/2002/nation/0206/24/nation-522429.htm.

Ehlers, C. L., K. C. Rickler, & J. E. Hovey. (1980) "A Possible Relationship Between Plasma Testosterone and Aggressive Behavior in a Female Outpatient Population." In M. Girgis & L. G. Kiloh, eds. *Limbic Epilepsy and Dyscontrol Syndrome*. Amsterdam: Elsevier/North Holland Biomedical Press.

Eide, Ingrid, Ingeborg Breines, & Robert Connell, eds. (2000) *Male Roles, Masculinities and Violence: A Culture of Peace Perspective*. Paris: UNESCO.

Einstadter, W., & S. Henry. (1995) *Criminological Theory*. Fort Worth: Harcourt Brace.

Eley, Thalia C., Paul Lichtenstein, & Jim Stevenson. (1999) "Sex Differences in the Etiology of Aggressive and Nonaggressive Antisocial Behavior: Results From Two Twin Studies." *Child Development 70*, 1: 155–68.

Ellerstein, N. S., & J. W. Canavan. (1980) "Sexual Abuse of Boys." *American Journal of Diseases of Children 134*: 255–57.

Elliott, Delbert S., Beatrix A. Hamburg, & Kirk R. Williams, eds. (1998) *Violence in American Schools*. New York: Cambridge University Press.

——, D. Huizinga, & S. S. Ageton. (1985) *Explaining Delinquency and Drug Use*. Thousand Oaks: Sage.

Ellison, C. G. (1991) "An Eye for an Eye? A Note on the Southern Subculture of Violence Thesis." *Social Forces 69*: 1223–39.

"Enablers, The." (1978) *Juvenile Prostitution in Minnesota: The Report of a Research Project*. St. Paul: The Enablers.

Erikson, Kirstan G., Robert Crosnoe, & Sanford M. Dornbusch. (2000) "A Social Process Model of Adolescent Deviance: Combining Social Control and Differential Association Perspectives." *Journal of Youth and Adolescence 29*: 395–99.

Erlander, H. S. (1974) "The Empirical Status of the Sub-Cultures of Violence Thesis." *Social Problems 22*: 280–92.

Esbensen, F., & D. W. Osgood. (1997) *National Evaluation of G.R.E.A.T.* Research in Brief. Washington: National Institute of Justice.

Eysench, Hans J. (1973) *The Inequality of Man*. San Diego: Edits Publishers.

Family Violence Prevention Fund. San Francisco, http://www.fvpf.org.

Farrington, David P. (1987) "Epidemiology." In H. C. Quay, ed. *Handbook of Juvenile Delinquency*. New York: Wiley.

——. (1992) "Juvenile Delinquency." In J. C. Coleman, ed. *The School Years*. 2nd ed. London: Routledge.

——. (1996) "The Explanation and Prevention of Youthful Offending." In J. David Hawkins, ed. *Delinquency and Crime: Current Theories*. New York: Cambridge University Press.

——, & D. J. West. (1990) "The Cambridge Study in Delinquent Development: A Long-Term Follow-Up of 411 London Males." In H. J. Kerner & G. Kauser, eds. *Criminality: Personality, Behavior, Life History*. Berlin: Springer-Verlag.

Feldman, M. P. (1977) *Criminal Behavior: A Psychological Analysis*. London: Wiley.

Felson, Richard B. (2001) "Arrest for Domestic and Other Assaults." *Criminology 39*: 501–21.

——, A. E. Liska, S. J. South, & T. L. McNulty. (1994) "The Subculture of Violence and Delinquency: Individual vs. School Context Effects." *Social Forces 73*, 1: 155–73.

——, Steven F. Mesner, Anthony W. Hoskin, & Glenn Deane. (2002) "Reasons for Reporting and Not Reporting Domestic Violence to the Police." *Criminology 40*, 3: 617–46.

Ferrante, A., F. Morgan, D. Indermaur, & R. Harding. (1996) *Measuring the Extent of Domestic Violence*. Sydney: Hawkins Press.

"Final Report of the Supreme Court Task Force on Courts' and Communities' Response to Domestic Abuse." Submitted to the Supreme Court of Iowa. August 1994, p. 13.

Finkelhor, David. (1979) *Sexually Victimized Children*. New York: Free Press.

——. (1984) "How Widespread is Child Abuse?" In *Perspectives on Child Maltreatment in the Mid '80s*. Washington: National Center on Child Abuse and Neglect Information.

——. (1986) *A Sourcebook on Child Sexual Abuse.* Thousand Oaks: Sage.

——. (1995) "The Victimization of Children: A Developmental Perspective." *American Journal of Orthopsychiatry 65*: 177–93.

——, & J. Dziuba-Leatherman. (1994) "Victimization of Children." *American Psychologist 49*, 3: 173–83.

——, & Kersti Yllo. (1985) *License to Rape: Sexual Abuse of Wives.* New York: Holt, Rinehart & Winston.

——, & R. Ormrod. (2000) *The Characteristics of Crimes Against Children.* Washington: Office of Justice Programs.

——, & Sharon Araji. (1995) *A Sourcebook on Child Sexual Abuse.* Thousand Oaks: Sage.

——, Kimberly J. Mitchell, & Janis Wolak. (2000) *Online Victimization: A Report on the Nation's Youth.* Alexandria: National Center for Missing & Exploited Children.

Fishbein, D. (1990) "Biological Perspectives in Criminology." *Criminology 28*, 1: 27–72.

Fisher, Bonnie S., & Elaine Gunnison. (2001) "Violence in the Workplace Gender Similarities and Differences." *Journal of Criminal Justice 29*: 145–55.

——, Francis T. Cullen, & Michael G. Turner. (2000) *The Sexual Victimization of College Women.* Washington: National Institute of Justice.

——, Francis T. Cullen, & Michael G. Turner. (2002) "Being Pursued: Stalking Victimization in a National Study of College Women." *Criminology & Public Policy 1*, 2: 257–308.

Flannery, D. J. (1997) *School Violence: Risk, Preventive Intervention, and Policy.* New York: Teachers College, ERIC Clearinghouse on Urban Education.

——, & C. R. Huff, eds. (1999) *Youth Violence: Prevention, Intervention, and Social Policy.* Washington: American Psychiatric Press.

Flowers, R. Barri. (1986) *Children and Criminality: The Child as Victim and Perpetrator.* Westport: Greenwood.

——. (1987) *Women and Criminality: The Woman as Victim, Offender, and Practitioner.* Westport: Greenwood.

——. (1989) *Demographics and Criminality: The Characteristics of Crime in America.* Westport: Greenwood.

——. (1990) *The Adolescent Criminal: An Examination of Today's Juvenile Offender.* Jefferson: McFarland.

——. (1990) *Minorities and Criminality.* Westport: Greenwood.

——. (1994) *The Victimization and Exploitation of Women and Children: A Study of Physical, Mental and Sexual Maltreatment in the United States.* Jefferson: McFarland.

——. (1995) *Female Crime, Criminals and Cellmates: An Exploration of Female Criminality and Delinquency.* Jefferson: McFarland.

——. (1999) *Drugs, Alcohol and Criminality in American Society.* Jefferson: McFarland.

——. (1999) *The Prostitution of Women and Girls.* Jefferson: McFarland.

——. (2000) *Domestic Crimes, Family Violence and Child Abuse: A Study of Contemporary American Society.* Jefferson: McFarland.

——. (2001) *Runaway Kids and Teenage Prostitution: America's Lost, Abandoned, and Sexually Exploited Children.* Westport: Greenwood.

——. (2001) *Sex Crimes, Predators, Perpetrators, Prostitutes, and Victims: An Examination of Sexual Criminality and Victimization.* Springfield: Charles C Thomas.

——. (2002) *Kids Who Commit Adult Crimes: A Study of Serious Juvenile Criminality and Delinquency.* Binghamton: Haworth.

——. (2002) *Murder, At the End of the Day and Night: A Study of Criminal Homicide Offenders, Victims, and Circumstances.* Springfield: Charles C Thomas.

——, & H. Loraine Flowers. (2001) *Murders in the United States: Crimes, Killers, and Victims of the Twentieth Century.* Jefferson: McFarland.

Fontana, Vincent J. (1964) *The Maltreated Child: The Maltreatment Syndrome in Children.* Springfield: Charles C Thomas.

——, & Douglas J. Besharov. (1995) *The Maltreated Child.* Springfield: Charles C Thomas.

Frazier, Charles E. (1976) *Theoretical Approaches to Deviance: An Evaluation.* Columbus: Charles E. Merrill.

Freeman, Beatrice, George Savastano, & J. J. Tobias. (1970) "The Affluent Suburban Male Delinquent." *Crime and Delinquency 16*: 274–72.

Freeman-Longo, Robert E., & Geral T. Blanchard. (1998) *Sexual Abuse in America: Epidemic of the 21st Century.* Brandon: Safer Society Press.

Freud, Sigmund. (1933) *New Introductory Lectures on Psychoanalysis.* New York: W. W. Norton.

Friedrich, W. N., R. L. Beilke, & A. J. Urquiza. (1988) "Behavioral Problems in Young Sexually Abused Boys: A Comparison Study." *Journal of Interpersonal Violence 3*: 21–28.

Gaarder, Emily, & Joanne Belknap. (2002) "Tenuous Borders: Girls Transferred to Adult Court." *Criminology 40*, 3: 481–517.

Gabor, T. (1987) *Armed Robbery.* Springfield: Charles C Thomas.

Gager, Nancy, & Cathleen Schurr. (1976) *Sexual Assault: Confronting Rape in America.* New York: Grosset and Dunlap.

Gallup, George, Jr., & Alec Gallup. (1999) *The Gallup Monthly.* No. 401. Princeton: The Gallup Poll.

——, & Alec Gallup. (1999) *The Gallup Poll Monthly.* No. 410. Princeton: The Gallup Poll.

Ganley, Anne L. "Understanding Domestic Violence." Family Violence Prevention Fund. http://www.fvpf.org.

Garbarino, James. (1981) "Child Abuse and Delinquency: The Developmental Impact of Social Isolation." In Robert J. Hunner & Yvonne E. Walker, eds. *Exploring the Relationship Between Child Abuse and Delinquency.* Montclair: Allanheld, Osmun and Co.

Garrison, Jessica, & Erika Hayasaki. "Schools Roll Out Plans to Get Tough on Bullies." (September 6, 2001): http://latimes.com.

Geary, D. (2000) "Evolution and Proximate Expression of Human Paternal Investment." *Psychological Bulletin 126*: 55–77.

Geberth, Vernon J. (1996) *Practical Homicide Investigation: Tactics, Procedures and Forensic Techniques.* Boca Raton: CRC Press.

Gebhard, Paul H., John H. Gagnon, Wardell B. Pomeroy, & Cornelia V. Christenson. (1965) *Sex Offenders: An Analysis of Types.* New York: Harper & Row.

Gelles, Richard J. (1975) "Violence and Pregnancy: A Note on the Extent of the Problem and Needed Services." *Family Coordinator 24*: 81–86.

——. (1978) "Violence Toward Children in the United States." *American Journal of Orthopsychiatry 48*, 4: 580–92.

——. *The Violent Home.* (1985) Thousand Oaks: Sage.

——, & Claire P. Cornell. (1990) *Intimate Violence in Families.* Thousand Oaks: Sage.

——, & Murray A. Straus. (1988) *Intimate Violence.* New York: Simon & Schuster.

Gil, David G. (1970) *Violence Against Children: Physical Child Abuse in the United States.* Cambridge: Harvard University Press.

——. (1978) "Societal Violence in Families." In J. M. Eekelaar & S. N. Katz, eds. *Family Violence.* Toronto: Butterworths.

Gilbert, Evelyn. (1999) "Crime, Sex, and Justice; African-American Women." In Sandy Cook & Susanne Davies, eds. *Harsh Punishment: International Experience of Women's Imprisonment.* Boston: Northeastern University Press.

Gilbert, J. N. (1998) *Criminal Investigations.* Englewood: Prentice-Hall.

Gilfus, Mary E. (1992) "From Victims to Survivors to Offenders: Women's Routes of Entry and Immersion into Street Crime." *Women & Criminal Justice 4*, 1: 63–89.

Gill, Martin, Bonnie Fisher, & Vaughan Bowie, eds. (2001) *Violence at Work.* Devon: Willan Publishing.

Gillespie, Cynthia. (1989) *Justifiable Homicide: Battered Women, Self-Defense, and the Law.* Columbus: Ohio State University Press.

Gilligan, James. (1997) *Violence: Reflections on a National Epidemic.* New York: Vintage.

Gilmore, David D. (1991) *Manhood in the Making: Cultural Concepts of Masculinity.* New Haven: Yale University Press.

Giobbe, Evelina. (1993) "An Analysis of Individual, Institutional and Cultural Pimping." *Michigan Journal of Gender and Law 1*: 33, 46.

Girls Incorporated. (1996) *Prevention and Parity: Girls in Juvenile Justice.* Indianapolis: Girls Incorporated National Resource Center.

Glueck, Sheldon, & Eleanor T. Glueck. (1950) *Unraveling Juvenile Delinquency.* New York: Commonwealth Press.

——, & Eleanor T. Glueck. (1956) *Physique and Delinquency.* New York: Harper and Row.

——, & Eleanor T. Glueck. (1962) *Family Environment and Delinquency.* Boston: Houghton Mifflin.

——, & Eleanor T. Glueck. (1968) *Delinquents and Non-Delinquents in Perspective.* Cambridge: Harvard University Press.

Goddard, Henry H. (1914) *Feeblemindedness, Its Causes and Consequences.* New York: Macmillan.

Goetting, A. (1987) "Homicidal Wives: A Profile." *Journal of Family Issues 8*: 332–41.

Goldsmith, Barbara. "Women on the Edge: A Reporter at Large." *New Yorker 69* (April 26, 1993), p. 216.

Goldstein, P., H. H. Brownstein, P. J. Ryan, & P. A. Bellucci. (1989) "Crack and Homicide in New York City, 1988: A Conceptually Based Event Analysis." *Contemporary Drug Problems 16*: 651–87.

Gondolf, E. W. (1988) "Who Are Those Guys? Toward A Behavioral Typology of Batterers." *Violence and Victims 3*: 187–203.

Gonzalez-Bono, E., A. Salvador, J. Ricarte, M. A. Serrano, & M. Arnedo. (2000) "Testosterone and Attribution of Successful Competition." *Aggressive Behavior 26*: 235–40.

Goodall, Richard. (1995) *The Comfort of Sin: Prostitutes and Prostitution in the 1990s.* Kent: Renaissance Books.

Goode, W. (1969) "Violence Among Intimates." *Crimes and Violence 13*: 941–77.

Goodwinn, Jean, Lawrence Cormier, & John Owen. (1983) "Grandfather-Granddaughter Incest: A Trigenerational View." *Child Abuse and Neglect 7*: 163–70.

Gordon, M. (1990) "Males and Females as Victims of Childhood Sexual Abuse." *Journal of Family Violence 5*, 4: 321–33.

Gove, Walter R., Michael Hughes, & Michael Geerken. (1985) "Are Uniform Crime Reports a Valid Indicator of the Index Crimes? An Affirmative Answer with Minor Qualifications." *Criminology 23*: 451–500.

Graney, Dawn J., & Bruce A. Arrigo. (2002) *Power Serial Rapist: A Criminology-Victimology Typology of Female Victim Selection.* Springfield: Charles C Thomas.

Greenberg, David F. (1977) "Delinquency and the Age Structure of Society." *Contemporary Crises 1*: 189–224.

Gregorie, Trudy M. "Cyberstalking: Dangers on the Information Superhighway." http://www.ncvc.org/src/help/cyberstalking.html.

Gross, Andrea. "A Question of Rape." *Ladies Home Journal 110*, 11 (November 1993), p. 170.

Groth, A. Nicholas. (1979) *Men Who Rape.* New York: Plenum.

——, & C. Loredo. (1981) "Juvenile Sex Offenders: Guidelines for Assessment." *International Journal of Offender Therapy and Comparative Criminology 25*: 265–72.

——, & H. Jean Birnbaum. (2001) *Men Who Rape: The Psychology of the Offender.* Cambridge: Perseus.

Guio, M., A. Burgess, & R. Kelly. (1980) "Child Victimization: Pornography and Prostitution." *Journal of Crime and Justice 3*: 65–81.

Hagan, John, John Simpson, & A. R. Gillis. (1987) "Class in the Household: A Power-Control Theory of Gender and Delinquency." *American Journal of Sociology 92*: 788–816.

Hagedorn, J. J. (1988) *People and Folks: Gangs, Crime and the Underclass in a Rustbelt City.* Chicago: Lakeview Press.

Hakeem, Michael. (1958) "A Critique of the Psychiatric Approach." In Joseph S. Roucek, ed. *Juvenile Delinquency.* New York: Philosophical Library.

Hamberger, K. L., & J. E. Hastings. (1988) "Characteristics of Male Spouse Abusers Consistent with Personality Disorders." *Hospital and Community Psychiatry 39*: 763–70.

Hanson, Victor D. (2002) *An Autumn of War: What America Learned from September 11 and the War on Terrorism.* New York: Vintage Books.

Harding, Sandra, ed. (1987) *Feminism and Methodology.* Milton Keyes: Open University Press.

Hardman, Dale G. (1969) "Small Town Gangs." *Journal of Criminal Law, Criminology and Police Science 60*, 2: 176–77.

Harmon, R. B., R. Rosner, & H. Owen. (1995) "Obsessional Harassment and Eroto-mania in a Criminal Court Population." *Journal of Forensic Sciences 40*, 2: 188–96.

Harris, Ian. (1995) *Messages Men Hear: Constructing Masculinities.* Bristol: Taylor and Francis.

Harris, J. A., J. P. Rushton, E. Hampson, & D. Jackson. (1996) "Salivary Testosterone and Self-Report Aggressive and Prosocial Personality Characteristics in Men and Women." *Aggressive Behavior 22*: 321–31.

Hartley, C. C. (1988) "How Incest Offenders Overcome Internal Inhibitions Through the Use of Cognitions and Cognitive Distortions." *Journal of Interpersonal Violence 13*, 1: 25–39.

Haskell, Martin R., & Lewis Yablonsky. (1974) *Crime and Delinquency.* 2nd ed. Chica-go: Rand McNally.

——, & Lewis Yablonsky. (1978) *Juvenile Delinquency.* 2nd ed. Chicago: Rand McNally.

Haslanger, Sally. Gender and the Events of 9/11." http://web.mit.edu/cms/recon-structions/interpretations/gender.html.

Hayeslip, D. W., Jr. (1980) *Local-Level Drug Enforcement: New Strategies.* Washington: National Institute of Justice.

Hazelwood, R. R., P. E. Dietz, & J. Warren. (1992) "The Criminal Sexual Sadist." *FBI Law Enforcement Bulletin 61*: 477–91.

Healy, Margaret A. "Child Pornography: An International Perspective," http://www.usis.usemb.se/children/csec/child_pornography.html.

Healy, William, & Augusta F. Bronner. (1926) *Delinquency and Criminals: Their Making and Unmaking.* New York: Macmillan.

——, & Augusta F. Bronner. (1936) *New Light on Delinquency and Its Treatment.* New Haven: Yale University Press.

Helton, A. S., M. S. McFarlane, & E. T. Anderson. (1987) "Battered and Pregnant: A Prevalence Study." *American Journal of Public Health 77*: 10.

Henderson, Helene. (1999) *Domestic Violence and Child Abuse Sourcebook.* Detroit: Omn-igraphics, Inc.

Henggeler, S. W. (1989) *Delinquency in Adolescence.* Thousand Oaks: Sage.

Herbert, T. W. (2002) *Sexual Violence and American Manhood.* Cambridge: Harvard University Press.

Herek, Gregory M., ed. (1998) *Stigma and Sexual Orientation: Understanding Prejudice Against Lesbians, Gay Men, and Bisexuals.* Thousand Oaks: Sage.

Hersh, Patricia. "Coming of Age on City Streets." *Psychology Today* (January 1988), p. 32.

Herzberger, Sharon D. (1996) *Violence Within the Family: Social Psychological Perspectives.* Boulder: Westview Press.

Hilberman, E., & L. Munson. (1978) "Sixty Battered Women." *Victimology 2*, 3–4: 460–71.

Hirschi, Travis. (1969) *Causes of Delinquency.* Berkeley: University of California.

——, & Michael J. Hindelang. (1977) "Intelligence and Delinquency: A Revisionist Review." *American Sociological Review 42*: 571–86.

Hofeller, Kathleen H. (1982) *Social, Psychological and Situational Factors in Wife Abuse.* Palo Alto: R. & E Research Associates.

Holland, Sally, & Jonathan B. Scourfield. (2000) "Managing Marginalized Masculinities: Men and Probation." *Journal of Gender Studies 9*, 2: 7.

Holmes, R. M., & J. DeBurger. (1988) *Serial Murder*. Thousand Oaks: Sage.

——, & S. T. Holmes. (1992) "Understanding Mass Murder." *Federal Probation 56*, 1: 53–61.

Holtzworth-Munroe, A. (1992) "Social Skill Deficits in Maritally Violent Men: Interpreting the Data Using a Social Information Processing Model." *Clinical Psychology Review 12*: 605–17.

——, & G. L. Stuart. (1994) "Typologies of Male Batterers: Three Subtypes and the Differences Among Them." *Psychological Bulletin 116*, 3: 476–97.

Holzman, Harold R. (1979) "Learning Disabilities and Juvenile Delinquency: Biological and Sociological Theories." In C. R. Jeffrey, ed. *Biology and Crime*. Thousand Oaks: Sage.

Homans, George C. (1961) *Social Behavior: Its Elementary Forms*. New York: Harcourt Brace Jovanovich.

Hood-Williams, J. (2001) "Gender, Masculinities and Crime: From Structures to Psyches." *Theoretical Criminology 5*, 1: 37–60.

Hooten, Ernest A. (1939) *The American Criminal: An Anthropological Study*. Cambridge: Harvard University Press.

——. (1939) *Crime and the Man*. Cambridge: Harvard University Press.

Horowitz, R. (1983) *Honor and the American Dream: Culture and Identity in a Chicano Community*. New Brunswick: Rutgers University Press.

Horrocks, Roger. (1996) *Masculinity in Crisis*. London: Macmillan.

Howard, Julie. "Incest: Victims Speak Out." *Teen* (July 1985), pp. 30–31.

Hubbell, John G. "Child Prostitution: How It Can Be Stopped." *Reader's Digest* (June 1984), pp. 202, 205.

Hudziak, James J., Lawrence P. Rudiger, Michael C. Neale, Andrew C. Heath, & Richard D. Todd. (2000) "A Twin Study of Inattentive, Aggressive, and Anxious/Depressed Behaviors." *Journal of the American Academy of Child and Adolescent Psychiatry 39*: 469–76.

Huizinga, D. (1997) "The Volume of Crime by Gang and Nongang Members." Paper presented at the Annual Meeting of the American Society of Criminology. San Diego.

Hunzeker, Donna. (1992) "Stalking Laws." *State Legislative Report 17*, 19: 1–6.

Hurley, Jennifer A. (1999) *Child Abuse*. San Diego: Greenhaven Press.

Hutchings, Bernard, & Sarnoff A. Mednick. (1975) "Registered Criminality in the Adoptive and Biological Parents of Registered Male Criminal Adoptees." In R. R. Fiene, D. Rosenthal, & H. Brill, eds. *Genetic Research in Psychiatry*. Baltimore: John Hopkins University Press.

Hutson, H. R., D. Anglin, & M. Eckstein. (1996) "Drive-by Shootings by Violent Street Gangs in Los Angeles: A Five-Year Review from 1989 to 1993." *Academic Emergency Medicine 3*: 300–3.

Hyde, Margaret O., & Elizabeth H. Forsyth. (1997) *The Sexual Abuse of Children and Adolescents*. Brookfield: Milbrook Press.

Ilfeld, F., Jr. (1970) "Environmental Theories of Violence." In D. Danield, M. Gilula & F. Ochberg, eds. *Violence and the Struggle for Existence.* Boston: Little Brown.

Ireland, Timothy O., Carolyn A. Smith, & Terrence P. Thornberry. (2002) "Developmental Issues in the Impact of Child Maltreatment on Later Delinquency and Drug Use." *Criminology 40*, 2: 359–95.

Jaffe, Lester D. (1963) "Delinquency Proneness and Family Anomie." *Journal of Criminal Law, Criminology and Police Science 54*: 146–54.

James, Jennifer. (1978) "The Prostitute as Victim." In Jane R. Chapman & Margaret Gates, eds. *The Victimization of Women.* Thousand Oaks: Sage.

Jang, Sung J., & Carolyn A. Smith. (1997) "A Test of Reciprocal Causal Relationships Among Parental Supervision, Affective Ties, and Delinquency." *Journal of Research in Crime and Delinquency 344*: 307–36.

Janus, M. D., A. McCormack, A. W. Burgess, & C. R. Hartman. (1987) *Adolescent Runaways.* Lexington: Lexington Books.

Jenkins, Philip. (2001) *Beyond Tolerance: Child Pornography Online.* New York: New York University Press.

Jensen, Gary F. (1973) "Inner Containment and Delinquency." *Journal of Criminal Law and Criminology 64*: 464–70.

Johnson, Hillary. "Violence Against Women: Is Porn to Blame?" *Vogue 175* (September 1985), p. 678.

Johnson, Joan J. (1992) *Teen Prostitution.* Danbury: Franklin Watts.

Johnson, Robert. (1976) *Culture and Crisis in Confinement.* Lexington: D. C. Heath.

Jones, Deborah. "Pimped." *Chatelaine 67* (November 1994), p. 111.

Jurik, Nancy C., & Susan E. Martin. (2001) "Femininities, Masculinities, and Organizational Conflict: Women in Criminal Justice Occupations." In Claire M. Renzetti & Lynne Goodstein, eds. *Women, Crime and Criminal Justice.* Los Angeles: Roxbury.

Justice, Blair, & Rita Justice. (1976) *The Abusing Family.* New York: Human Sciences Press.

Kahn, T. J., & M. A. LaFond. (1988) "Treatment of the Adolescent Sex Offender." *Child and Adolescent Social Work Journal 5.*

Kakar, Suman. (1996) *Child Abuse and Delinquency.* New York: University Press of America.

Kandel, E., S. A. Mednick, L. Kirkegaard-Sorenson, B. Hutchings, J. Knop, R. Rosenberg, & F. Schulsinger. (1988) "IQ as a Protective Factor for Subjects at High Risk for Antisocial Behavior." *Journal of Consulting and Clinical Psychology 56*: 224–26.

Kanin, E. J., & S. R. Parcell. (1977) "Sexual Aggression: A Second Look at the Offended Female." *Archives of Sexual Behavior 6*: 67–76.

Kapoor, Sushma. (2000) *Domestic Violence Against Women and Girls.* UNICEF: Innocenti Research Center. http://www.sccadvasa.org/Domestic%20Violence.htm.

Karjane, Heather M., Bonnie S. Fisher, & Francis T. Cullen. (2001) *Campus Sexual Assault: How America's Institutions of Higher Education Respond. Final Report.* Washington: National Institute of Justice.

Katz, Jack. (1988) *Seductions of Crime.* New York: Basic Books.

———. (1990) *Seductions of Crime: Moral and Sensual Attractions in Doing Evil.* New York: Basic Books.

Kellerman, A. L., & J. A. Mercy. (1992) "Men, Women, and Murder: Gender-Specific Differences in Rates of Fatal Violence and Victimization." *Journal of Trauma 33*: 1–5.

Kelly, Liz. (1987) "Continuum of Sexual Violence." In Jalna Hanmer & Mary Maynard, eds. *Women, Violence and Social Control.* London: Macmillan.

Kempf-Leonard, K., & L. L. Sample. (2000) "Disparity Based on Sex: Is Gender-Specific Treatment Warranted?" *Justice Quarterly 17*, 1: 89–128.

Kennedy, L. W., & S. W. Baron. (1993) "Routine Activities and a Subculture of Violence: A Study of Violence on the Street." *Journal of Research in Crime and Delinquency 30*, 1: 88–112.

Kerner, H. J., E. G. Weitekamp, & J. Thomas. (1997) "Patterns of Criminality and Alcohol Abuse: Results of the Tuebinger Criminal Behavior Development Study." *Criminal Behavior & Mental Health 7*, 4: 401–20.

Kersten, Joachim. (1996) "Culture, Masculinities and Violence Against Women." *British Journal of Criminology 36*, 3: 381–95.

Kilpatrick, D. G., C. N. Edmunds, & A. K. Seymour. (1992) *Rape in America: A Report to the Nation.* Charleston: Medical University of South Carolina, Crime Victims Research and Treatment Center.

Kimmel, Michael S. "Gender, Class, and Terrorism." http://www.xyonline.net/terror.shtml.

———. (2001) *The Gendered Society.* Oxford: Oxford University Press.

Kleck, Gary, & Ted Chiricos. (2002) "Unemployment and Property Crime: A Target-Specific Assessment of Opportunity and Motivation as Mediating Factors." *Criminology 40*, 3: 649–72.

Klein, M. W. (1995) *The American Street Gang.* New York: Oxford University Press.

———, C. L. Maxson, & L. C. Cunningham. (1991) "Crack, Street Gangs, and Violence." *Criminology 29*: 623–50.

Klemmack, Susan H., & David L. Klemmack. (1976) "The Social Definition of Rape." In Marcy J. Walker & Stanley L. Brodsky, eds. *Sexual Assault.* Lexington: Lexington Books.

Kletschka, H. D. (1966) "Violent Behavior Associated with Brain Tumors." *Minnesota Medicine 49*: 1835–55.

Knox, G. W. (1991) *An Introduction to Gangs.* Berrien Springs: Vande Vere Publishing.

Kolvin, I., F. W. Miller, M. Fleeting, & P. A. Kolvin. (1988) "Social and Parenting Factors Affecting Criminal-Offense Rates: Findings from the Newcastle Thousand Family Study (1947–198). *British Journal of Psychiatry 152*: 80–90.

Koons-Witt, Barbara A. (2002) "The Effect of Gender on the Decision to Incarcerate Before and After the Introduction of Sentencing Guidelines." *Criminology 40*, 2: 297–327.

Koss, Mary P. (1988) "Hidden Rape: Sexual Aggression and Victimization in a National Sample of Students in Higher Education." In Ann W. Burgess, ed. *Rape and Sexual Assault II.* New York: Garland.

——. (1992) "The Undetection of Rape: Methodological Choices Influence Incidence Estimates." *Journal of Social Issues 48*: 61–75.

Kovandzic, Tomislav V., John J. Sloan III, & Lynne M. Vieraitis. (2002) "Unintended Consequences of Politically Popular Sentencing Policy: The Homicide Promoting Effects of 'Three Strikes' in U.S. Cities (1980–1999)." *Criminology 1*, 3: 399–424.

Kreuz, L. E., & R. M. Rose. (1972) "Assessment of Aggressive Behavior and Plasma Testosterone in a Young Criminal Population." *Journal of Psychosomatic Medicine 34*: 321–32.

Kuehe, S. (1998) "Legal Remedies for Teen Dating Violence." In Barrie Levy, ed. *Dating Violence: Young Women in Danger*. Seattle: Seal Press.

Kushner, Harvey W. (2002) *Encyclopedia of Terrorism*. Thousand Oaks: Sage.

Labouvie, Erich. (1996) "Maturing Out of Substance Use: Selection and Self-Correction." *Journal of Drug Issues 26*, 2: 457–76.

Lange, Johannes. (1931) *Crime as Destiny*. London: George Allen and Unwin.

Langevin, R., S. Curnoe, & J. Bain. (2000) "A Study of Clerics Who Commit Sexual Offenses: Are They Different From Other Sex Offenders?" *Child Abuse & Neglect 24*: 535–45.

Langley, Robert, & Richard C. Levy. (1977) *Wife Beating: The Silent Crisis*. New York: Dutton.

Lawrence, Frederick M. (2002) *Punishing Hate: Bias Crimes and American Law*. Cambridge: Harvard University Press.

Leder, Jane M. (1991) *Brothers and Sisters: How They Shape Our Lives*. New York: St. Martin's Press.

Lederer, Laura, ed. (1980) *Take Back the Night: Women on Pornography*. New York: William Morrow.

Leibling, A. (1994) "Suicide Among Women Prisoners." *Howard Journal 33*, 1: 1–9.

Lemmon, John H. (1999) "How Child Maltreatment Affects Dimensions of Juvenile Delinquency in a Cohort of Low-Income Urban Youths." *Justice Quarterly 16*: 357–76.

Leonard, K. E., & S. P. Taylor. (1983) "Exposure to Pornography, Permissive and Nonpermissive Cues, and Male Aggression Toward Females." *Motivation and Emotion 7*: 291–99.

Lester, David. (1995) *Serial Killers: The Insatiable Passion*. Philadelphia: The Charles Press.

Levin, J., & J. A. Fox. (1985) *Mass Murder*. New York: Plenum.

Levinger, G. (1966) "Sources of Marital Dissatisfaction Among Applicants for Divorce." *American Journal of Orthopsychiatry 36*, 5: 803–7.

Levit, Nancy. (1996) "Feminism for Men: Legal Ideology and the Construction of Maleness." *UCLA Law Review 43*, 4: 1037–1116.

Levy, Barrie, ed. (1998) *Dating Violence: Young Women in Danger*. Seattle: Seal Press.

Lieberman Research, Inc. *Domestic Violence Advertising Campaign Tracking Survey*. Conducted for the Advertising Council and Family Violence Prevention Fund. July–October 1996.

Lin, William. (1997) "Perpetrators of Hate." *Yale Political Quarterly 19*, 2: 12.

Lindman, R., P. Jarvinen, & J. Vidjeskog. (1987) "Verbal Interactions of Aggressively and Nonaggressively Predisposed Males in a Drinking Situation." *Aggressive Behavior 13*: 187–96.

Lindquist, R. (1991) "Homicides Committed by Abusers of Alcohol and Illicit Drugs." *British Journal of Addiction 86*: 321–26.

Liverant, S. (1959) "MMPI Differences Between Parents of Disturbed and Non-Disturbed Children." *Journal of Consulting Psychology 23*: 256–60.

Lloyd, A. (1995) *Doubly Deviant, Doubly Damned*. Sydney: Penguin.

Lloyd, Robin. (1976) *For Money or Love: Boy Prostitution in America*. New York: Ballantine.

Lloyd-Goldstein, R. (1998) "De Clerembault On-Line: A Survey of Erotomania and Stalking from the Old World to the World Wide Web." In J. R. Meloy, ed. *The Psychology of Stalking: Clinical and Forensic Perspectives*. San Diego: Academic Press.

Loeber, R., & T. Dishion. (1983) "Early Predictors of Male Delinquency: A Review." *Psychological Bulletin 94*: 68–99.

Logan, T. K., Carl Leukefeld, & Bob Walker. (2000) "Stalking as a Variant of Intimate Violence: Implications From a Young Adult Sample." *Violence and Victims 15*: 91–111.

Lombroso, Cesare. (1981) *Crime, Its Causes and Remedies*. Boston: Little, Brown.

——, & William Ferrero. (1972) *Criminal Man*. Montclair: Patterson Smith. Originally titled *L 'Uomo Delinquente* in its 1876 publication.

Longino, Helen E. (1980) "Pornography, Oppression, and Freedom: A Closer Look." In Laura Lederer, ed. *Take Back the Night: Women on Pornography*. New York: William Morrow.

Longo, R., & N. Groth. (1983) "Juvenile Sexual Offenses in the Histories of Adult Rapists and Child Molesters." *International Journal of Offender Therapy and Comparative Criminology 27*: 155–57.

Lunde, D. T. (1979) *Murder and Madness*. New York: Norton.

Lytton, H., & D. Romney. (1991) "Parents' Differential Socialization of Boys and Girls: A Metaanalysis." *Psychological Bulletin 109*: 267–96.

MacLeun, Brian D., & Dragon Milovanovic. (1997) *Thinking Critically About Crime*. Richmond: Collective Press.

MacNamara, D. (1965) "Male Prostitution in American Cities: A Socioeconomic or Pathological Phenomenon?" *American Journal of Orthopsychiatry 35*: 204.

Mahoney, Patricia, & Linda M. Williams. (1998)"Sexual Assault in Marriage: Prevalence, Consequences, and Treatment of Wife Rape." In Jana L. Jasinski & Linda M. Williams, eds. *Partner Violence: A Comprehensive Review of 20 Years of Research*. Thousand Oaks: Sage.

Maltz, W., & B. Holman. (1987) *Incest and Sexuality*. Lexington: Lexington Books.

Manton, Monica, & Alison Talbot. (1990) "Crisis Intervention After an Armed Hold Up: Guidelines for Counselors." *Journal of Traumatic Stress 3*, 4: 507–22.

Marshall, W. L., & A. Eccles. (1991) "Issues in Clinical Practice with Sex Offenders." *Journal of Interpersonal Violence 6*: 68–93.

——, & H. E. Barbaree. (1990) "Outcome of Cognitive-Behavioral Treatment." In W. L. Marshall, D. R. Laws, & H. E. Barbaree, eds. *Handbook of Sexual Assault*. New York: Plenum.

Martinez, R. (1996) "Latinos and Lethal Violence: The Impact of Poverty and Inequality." *Social Problems 43*: 131–46.

Marvell, Thomas B., & Carlisle E. Moody. (2001) "The Lethal Effects of Three Strikes Laws." *Journal of Legal Studies 30*: 89–106.

Matsueda, Ross. (1997) "Cultural Deviance Theory: The Remarkable Persistence of Flawed Term." *Theoretical Criminology 1*: 429–52.

Mattman, Jurg W. "Preventing Violence in the Workplace." http://www.noworkviolence.com/articles/preventing_violence.htm.

Mattsson, A., D. Schalling, D. Olweus, H. Low, & J. Stevenson. (1980) "Plasma Testosterone, Aggressive Behavior, and Personality Dimensions in Young Male Delinquents." *Journal of the American Academy of Child Psychiatry 19*: 476–90.

Mawby, R. (1980) "Sex and Crime: The Results of a Self-Report Study." *British Criminology of Sociology 31*, 4: 537–43.

Maxson, C. L., K. Woods, & M. W. Klein. (1996) "Street Gang Migration: How Big A Threat?" *National Institute of Justice Journal 2*: 26–31.

Maxwell, Christopher, Joel Garner, & Jeffrey Fagan. (2001) *The Effects of Arrest on Intimate Partner Violence: New Evidence from the Spouse Assault Replication Program.* Washington: National Institute of Justice.

Mayer, Adele. (1983) *Incest: A Treatment Manual for Therapy with Victims, Spouses, and Offenders.* Holmes Beach: Learning Publications.

Mazur, A., & A. Booth. "Testosterone and Dominance in Men," http://www.thehormoneshop.com/testosteroneanddominanceinmen.htm.

McClendon, Patricia D. "Incest/Sexual Abuse of Children." (November 1991) http://www.clinicalsocialwork.com/incest.html.

McCord Joan. (1977) "A Comparative Study of Two Generations of Native Americans." In R. F. Meier, ed. *Theory in Criminology.* Thousand Oaks: Sage.

——. (1979) "Some Child-Rearing Antecedents of Criminal Behavior in Adult Men." *Journal of Personality and Social Psychology 37*: 1477–86.

——. (1982) "A Longitudinal View of the Relationship between Paternal Absence and Crime." In J. Gunn & D. P. Farrington, eds. *Abnormal Offenders, Delinquency, and the Criminal Justice System.* New York: John Wiley & Sons.

McCord, William. (1958) "The Biological Bases of Juvenile Delinquency." In J. S. Roucek, ed. *Juvenile Delinquency.* Freeport: Philosophical Library.

——, & Joan McCord. (1964) *The Psychopath.* Princeton: Van Nostrand.

——, Joan McCord, & Irving K. Zola. (1959) *Origins of Crime.* New York: Columbia University Press.

McCoy, Kathy. "Incest: The Most Painful Family Problem." *Seventeen 43* (June 1984), p. 18.

McDill, S. Rutherford, & Linda McDill. (1998) *Dangerous Marriage: Breaking the Cycle of Domestic Violence.* Grand Rapids; Baker Books.

McGuffin, Peter, & Anita Thapar. (1997) "Genetic Basis of Bad Behavior in Adolescents." *The Lancet 350*: 411–412.

McKinney, K. C. (1988) *Juvenile Gangs: Crime and Drug Trafficking Bulletin.* Washington: Office of Justice Programs.

McLaughlin, Barry. (1971) *Learning and Social Behavior.* New York: Free Press.

Mednick, S. A., W. F. Gabrielli, & B. Hutchings. (1984) "Genetic Influences in Criminal Convictions: Evidence from an Adoption Cohort." *Science 234*: 891–94.

Megargee, E. I. (1966) "Uncontrolled and Overcontrolled Personality Types in Extreme Antisocial Aggression." *Psychological Monographs 80*, 3: 611.

Meloy, J. R. (1996) "Stalking (Obsessional Following): A Review of Some Preliminary Studies." *Aggression and Violent Behavior 1*, 2: 147–62.

——, & S. Gothard. (1995) "Demographic and Clinical Comparison of Obsessional Followers and Offenders with Mental Disorders." *American Journal of Psychiatry 152*, 2: 258–62.

Merton, Robert K. (1938) "Social Structure and Anomie." *American Sociological Review 3*: 672–82.

——. (1957) *Social Theory and Social Structure*. Glencoe: Free Press.

Messerschmidt, James W. (1986) *Capitalism, Patriarchy, and Crime: Towards a Socialist Feminist Criminology*. Totowa: Rowman and Littlefield.

——. (1993) *Masculinities and Crime: Critique and Reconceptualization of Theory*. Lanham: Rowman and Littlefield.

——. (1995) "From Patriarchy to Gender: Feminist Theory, Criminology and the Challenge of Diversity." In N. Rafter & F. Heidensohn, eds. *International Feminist Perspectives in Criminology*. Milton Keyes: Open University Press.

Messner, S. (1988) "Merton's Anomie: The Road Not Taken." *Deviant Behavior 9*: 33–53.

——, & R. Rosenfeld. (1994) *Crime and the American Dream*. Belmont: Wadsworth.

Michael, R. T., J. H. Gagnon, E. O. Lauman, & G. Kolata. (1994) *Sex in America: A Definitive Survey*. New York: Warner.

Miedzian, M. (1992) *Boys Will Be Boys: Breaking the Link Between Masculinity and Violence*. London: Virago Press.

Miethe, Terance D., & Robert F. Meier. (1994) *Crime and Its Social Context: Toward an Integrated Theory of Offenders, Victims, and Situations*. Albany: State University of New York Press.

Miller, Ted, Mark Cohen, & Brian Wiersema. (1996) *Victim Costs and Consequences: A New Look*. Washington: National Institute of Justice.

Miller, Walter B. (1958) "Lower-Class Culture as a Generating Milieu of Gang Delinquency." *Journal of Social Issues 14*: 5–19.

——. (1966) "Violent Crimes in City Gangs." *Annals of the American Academy of Political and Social Science 364*: 96–112.

——. (1970) "White Gangs." In James F. Short, Jr., ed. *Modern Criminals*. Chicago: Aldine.

——. (1974) "American Youth Gangs: Past and Present." In A. Blumberg, ed. *Current Perspectives in Criminal Behavior*. New York: Knopf.

——. (1975) *Violence by Youth Gangs and Youth Groups as a Crime Problem in Major American Cities*. Washington: Government Printing Office.

——. (1992) *Crime by Youth Gangs and Groups in the United States*. Washington: Office of Justice Programs.

Miller-Perrin, Cindy L., & Robin D. Perrin. (2001) *Child Maltreatment: An Introduction*. Thousand Oaks: Sage.

Moffit, T. E., & P. A. Silva. (1988) "Neuropsychological Deficit and Self-reported Delinquency in an Unselected Birth Cohort." *Journal of the American Academy of Child and Adolescent Psychiatry 27*: 233–40.

Mohr, Johan W., R. Edward Turner, & M. B. Jerry. (1964) *Pedophilia and Exhibitionism.* Toronto: University of Toronto Press.

Moore, J. W. (1978) *Homeboys: Gangs, Drugs and Prison in the Barrios of Los Angeles.* Philadelphia: Temple University Press.

——, & R. Pinderhughes, eds. (1993) *In the Barrios: Latinos and the Underclass Debate.* New York: Russell Sage.

——, D. Vigil, & R. Garcia. (1983) "Residence and Territoriality in Chicano Gangs." *Social Problems 31*: 182–94.

Morris, Jim. "Gangs at War in L.A. Streets." *Sacramento Bee* (October 19, 1986), p. A1.

Motiuk, L. L., & F. Porporino. (1992) *The Prevalence, Nature and Severity of Mental Health Problems Among Federal Male Inmates in Canadian Penitentiaries.* Ottawa: Correctional Service of Canada.

——, & R. L. Belcourt. (1995) *Statistical Profiles of Homicide, Sex, Robbery and Drug Offenders in Federal Corrections.* Ottawa: Correctional Service of Canada.

Moyer, Imogene L. (2001) *Criminological Theories: Traditional and Nontraditional Voices and Themes.* Thousand Oaks: Sage.

Muehlenhard, Charlene L., & Melaney A. Linton. (1987) "Date Rape and Sexual Aggression in Dating Situations: Incidence and Risk Factors." *Journal of Consulting Psychology 34*: 186–96.

Mugford, J., & S. Mugford. (1992) "Policing Domestic Violence." In P. Moir & H. Eijkman, eds. *Policing Australia: Old Issues, New Perspectives.* South Melbourne: MacMillan.

Mullen, P. E., & M. Pathe. (1994) "The Pathological Extensions of Love." *British Journal of Psychiatry 165*: 614–23.

——, M. Pathe, R. Purcell, & G. W. Stuart. (1999) "A Study of Stalkers." *American Journal of Psychiatry 156*: 1244–49.

"Murderous Obsession: Can New Laws Deter Spurned Lovers and Fans From 'Stalking' or Worse?" *Newsweek 120* (July 13, 1992), p. 61.

Murray, Charles A. (1976) *The Link Between Learning Disabilities and Juvenile Delinquency.* Washington: Government Printing Office.

Mustaine, Elizabeth E., & Richard Tewksbury. (1999) "A Routine Activity Theory Explanation of Women's Stalking Victimizations." *Violence Against Women 5*, 1: 43–62.

Myerhoff, Howard L., & Barbara G. Myerhoff. (1964) "Field Observation of Middle Class 'Gangs'." *Social Forces 42*: 328–36.

Naffine, Ngaire. (1996) *Feminism and Criminology.* Philadelphia: Temple University Press.

Nancarrow, H. (1998) "Crime Prevention and Social Justice: Preventing Domestic Violence." Unpublished MA paper. Griffith University: Queensland.

National Center for Policy Analysis. "Suicide Terrorists." http://www.ncpd.org/pi/congress/pd091201e.html.

——. (2000) *Crime and Punishment in America: 1999.* U.S. Department of Justice. http://www.ncpd.org/studies/s229/s229.html.

National Crime Prevention. *Working With Adolescents to Prevent Domestic Violence-Rural Town Model.* http://www.ncavac.gov.au/ncp/publications/no3/no3_6sec.2.htm.

National Criminal Justice Association. (1993) *Project to Develop a Model Anti-Stalking Code for States.* Washington: National Institute of Justice.

National Institute of Justice and Centers for Disease Control and Prevention. (1998) *Prevalence, Incidence, and Consequences of Violence Against Women: Findings from the National Violence Against Women Survey.* (November)

National Youth Gang Center. (1997) *1995 National Youth Gang Survey.* Washington: Office of Juvenile Justice and Delinquency Prevention.

Newburn, Tim, & Elizabeth A. Stanko. (1994) *Just Boys Doing Business? Men, Masculinities and Crime.* London: Routledge.

Newson, J., E. Newson, & M. Adams. (1993) "The Social Origins of Delinquency." *Criminal Behavior and Mental Health 3*: 19–29.

Noblit, George W., & Janie M. Burcart. (1976) "Women and Crime: 1960–1970." *Social Science Quarterly 56*: 656–57.

Nye, F. Ivan. (1958) *Family Relationships and Delinquent Behavior.* New York: John Wiley & Sons.

——, & James F. Short. (1958) "Scaling Delinquent Behavior." *American Sociological Review 22*: 326–32.

O'Brien, M. (1991) "Taking Sibling Incest Seriously." In M. Quinn-Patton, ed. *Family Sexual Abuse: Frontline Research and Evaluation.* Thousand Oaks: Sage.

O'Brien, Shirley. (1983) *Child Pornography.* Dubuque: Kendall/Hunt.

Odem, Mary E., & Jody Clay-Warner. (1998) *Confronting Rape and Sexual Assault.* Wilmington: Scholarly Resources, Inc.

Offord, D. R., M. H. Boyle, & Y. Racine. (1989) "Ontario Child Health Study: Correlates of Disorder." *Journal of the American Academy of Child and Adolescent Psychiatry 28*: 856–60.

Ogilvie, Emma. (1996) "Masculine Obsessions: An Examination of Criminology, Criminality and Gender." *Australian and New Zealand Journal of Criminology 29*, 3: 62–70.

Olweus, D. (1991) "Bully/Victim Problems Among School Children: Basic Facts and Effects of a School Based Intervention Program." In D. J. Pepler & K. H. Rubin, eds. *The Development and Treatment of Childhood Aggression.* Hillsdale: Erlbaum.

Orion, Doreen. (1997) *I Know You Really Love Me: A Psychiatrist's Journal of Erotomania, Stalking, and Obsessive Love.* New York: Macmillan.

Ounsted, Christopher, Rhoda Oppenheimer, & Janet Lindsay. (1975) "The Psychopathology and Psychotherapy of the Families, Aspects Bounding Failure." In A. Franklin, ed. *Concerning Child Abuse.* London: Churchill Livingston.

Ouston, J. (1984) "Delinquency, Family Background, and Educational Attainment." *British Journal of Criminology 24*: 2–26.

"Overview of Subculture Theories." http://home.attbi.com/~ddemelo/crime/subculture.html.

Owen, B., & B. Bloom. (1995) "Profiling Women Prisoners: Findings from National Surveys and a California Sample." *Prison Journal 75*, 2: 165–85.

Palmer, S. (1960) *A Study of Murder.* New York: Thomas Y. Crowell.

Panksepp, J. (1986) "The Psychobiology of Prosocial Behaviors: Separation Distress, Play, and Altruism." In C. Zahn-Wazler, E. Cummings, & R. Ianotti, eds. *Altruism and Aggression: Biological and Social Origins.* Cambridge: Cambridge University Press.

Park, Robert E., & Ernest W. Burgess. (1925) *The City.* Chicago: University of Chicago Press.

Parker, R. N. (1989) "Poverty, Subculture of Violence, and Type of Homicide." *Social Forces 67*: 983–1007.

Patai, Frances. (1982) "Pornography and Woman Battering: Dynamic Similarities." In Maria Roy, ed. *The Abusive Partner: An Analysis of Domestic Battering.* New York: Van Nostrand Reinhold.

Payne, S. (1996) "Masculinity and the Redundant Male: Explaining the Increasing Incarceration of Young Men." *Social & Legal Studies 5,* 2: 5–14.

Pearson, P. (1997) *When She Was Bad: Violent Women and the Myth of Innocence.* Toronto: Random House.

Peters, Warwick T. "Phrenology Biological Theories of Crime Criminology." http://members.ozemail.com.au/~wtmp/misc/phrenology.html.

Phoenix, Joanna. (2001) *Making Sense of Prostitution.* New York: Palgrave Global.

Pierce, L. H., & R. L. Pierce. (1990) "Adolescent/Sibling Incest Perpetrators." In L. Horton, B. Johnson, L. Roundy, & D. Williams, eds. *The Incest Perpetrator: A Family Member No One Wants to Treat.* Thousand Oaks: Sage.

Pierce, R., & L. H. Pierce. (1985) "The Sexually Abused Child: A Comparison of Male and Female Victims." *Child Abuse and Neglect 9,* 2: 191–99.

Piquero, Nicole L., & Miriam D. Sealock. (2000) "Generalizing General Strain Theory: An Examination of an Offending Population." *Justice Quarterly 17*: 449–84.

Plant, Martin A., ed. (1990) *AIDS, Drugs, and Prostitution.* London: Routledge.

Plante, Thomas. "A Perspective on Clergy Sexual Abuse." http://www.psywww.com/psyrelig/plante.html.

Polansky, Norman A., Christine De Souix, & Shlomo A. Sharlin. (1972) *Child Neglect: Understanding and Reaching the Parents.* New York: Child Welfare League of America.

Polk, Kenneth. (1994) *Why Men Kill: Scenarios of Masculine Violence.* Cambridge: Cambridge University Press.

——, C. Alder, G. Bazemore, G. Blake, S. Cordray, G. Coventry, J. Galvin, & M. Temple. (1981) *Becoming Adult.* Washington: National Institute of Mental Health.

Pollock, Vicki, Sarnoff A. Mednick, & William F. Gabrielli, Jr. (1983) "Crime Causation: Biological Theories." In Sanford H. Kadish, ed. *Encyclopedia of Crime and Justice.* Vol. 1. New York: Free Press.

Pollock-Byrne, J. M. (1990) *Women, Prison, and Crime.* Pacific Grove: Brooks/Cole.

Pope, H. G., & D. L. Katz. (1989) "Homicide and Near-Homicide by Anabolic Steroid Users." *Journal of Clinical Psychiatry 51*: 28–31.

Posner, Richard A., & Katharine B. Silbaugh. (1996) *A Guide to America's Sex Laws.* Chicago: University of Chicago Press.

Prescott, Carol A., & Kenneth S. Kendler. (1999) "Genetic and Environmental Contributions to Alcohol Abuse and Dependence in a Population Based Sample of Male Twins." *American Journal of Psychiatry 156,* 1: 34–40.

Pryor, Douglas W. (1996) *Unspeakable Acts: Why Men Sexually Abuse Children*. New York: New York University Press.

Puzzanchera, C. M. (2000) *Self-Reported Delinquency by 12-Year-Olds, 1997*. OJJDP Fact Sheet. Washington: Office of Juvenile Justice and Delinquency Prevention.

Quay, Herbert C. (1983) "Crime Causation: Psychological Theories." In S. H. Kadish, ed. *Encyclopedia of Crime and Justice*. Vol. 1. New York: Free Press.

Quintero, G., & A. L. Estrada. (1998) "Machismo, Drugs and Street Survival in a US-Mexican Border Community." *Free Inquiry in Creative Sociology 26*, 1: 3–10.

Rada, Richard T. (1978) *Clinical Aspects of the Rapist*. New York: Grune and Stratton.

——, D. R. Laws, & R. Kellner. (1976) "Plasma Testosterone Levels in the Rapist." *Psychosomatic Medicine 38*: 257–68.

Rafter, Nicole. (1990) *Pretrial Justice: Women, Prisons, and Social Control*. New Brunswick: Transaction Publishers.

Ralph, P., R. J. Hunter, J. W. Marquart, S. J. Cuvelier, & D. Merianos. (1996) "Exploring the Differences Between Gang and Non-Gang Prisoners." In C. R. Huff, ed. *Gangs in America*. 2nd ed. Thousand Oaks: Sage.

Rape, Abuse & Incest National Network (RAINN) Statistics. http://www.rain.org/statistics.html.

Ray, M. C., & R. L. Simons. (1987) "Convicted Murderers' Accounts of Their Crimes: A Study of Homicide in Small Communities." *Symbolic Interaction 10*: 57–70.

Rebellion, Cesar J. (2002) "Reconsidering the Broken Homes/Delinquency Relationship and Exploring Its Mediating Mechanism(s)." *Criminology 40*, 1: 103–33.

Reckless, Walter C. (1973) *The Crime Problem*. 5th ed. Santa Monica: Goodyear.

——, Simon Dinitz, & Ellen Murray. (1970) "Self-Concept as an Insulator Against Delinquency." In James E. Teele, ed. *Juvenile Delinquency: A Reader*. Itasca: Peacock.

Reid, Sue. (1988) *Crime and Criminology*. 5th ed. Chicago: Holt, Rinehart & Winston.

Reinhardt, J. M. (1957) *Sex Perversions and Sex Crimes*. Springfield: Charles C Thomas.

Reinhart, M. A. (1987) "Sexually Abused Boys." *Child Abuse and Neglect 11*, 2: 229–35.

Reiss, Albert J. (1961) "Social Correlates of Psychological Types of Delinquency." *American Sociological Review 17*: 710–18.

——, & Albert J. Rhodes. (1961) "The Distribution of Juvenile Delinquency in the Social Class Structure." *American Sociological Review 26*: 720–32.

Reitsma-Street, M. (1999) "Justice for Canadian Girls: A 1990s Update." *Canadian Journal of Criminology 41*, 3: 335–63.

Rennison, Callie M. (2001) *Intimate Partner Violence and Age of Victim, 1993–1999*. Washington: U.S. Department of Justice.

Renvoize, Jean. (1982) *Incest: A Family Pattern*. London: Routledge & Kegan Paul.

Risin, L. I., & M. P. Koss. (1987) "Sexual Abuse of Boys: Prevalence and Descriptive Characteristics of the Childhood Victimizations." *Journal of Interpersonal Violence 2*: 309–19.

Rivera, B., & C. S. Widom. (1990) "Childhood Victimization and Violent Offending." *Violence & Victims 5*, 1: 19–35.

Rivinus, Timothy M., & Mary E. Larimer. (1993) "Violence, Alcohol, Other Drugs, and the College Student." In Leighton C. Whitaker & Jeffrey W. Pollard, eds. *Campus Violence: Kinds, Causes, and Cures*. Binghamton: Haworth.

Robertson, S. (2001) "Separating the Men from the Boys: Masculinity, Psychosexual Development, and Sex Crime in the United States, 1930s–1960s." *Journal of the History of Medicine & Allied Sciences 56*, 1: 3–35.

Robins, Lee N. (1966) *Deviant Children Grown Up*. Baltimore: Williams and Wilkins.

——. (1979) "Study Childhood Predictors of Adult Outcomes: Replications from Longitudinal Studies." In J. E. Barrett, R. M. Rose, & G. L. Klerman, eds. *Stress and Mental Disorder*. New York: Raven Press.

——, P. J. West, & B. L. Herjanic. (1975) "Arrests and Delinquency in Two Generations: A Study of Black Urban Families and Their Children." *Journal of Child Psychology and Psychiatry 16*: 125–40.

Roesler, T. A., & T. W. Wind. (1994) "Telling the Secret: Adult Women Describe Their Disclosures of Incest." *Journal of Interpersonal Violence 9*: 327–38.

Rojek, Dean G., & Gary F. Jensen. (1996) *Exploring Delinquency: Causes and Control*. Los Angeles: Roxbury.

Rooney, Rita. "Children for Sale: Pornography's Dark New World." *Reader's Digest* (July 1983), p. 53.

Rose, David. (2001) "Masculinity, Offending and Prison-Based Work." In Bob Pease & Peter Camilleri, eds. *Working With Men in the Human Services*. Sydney: Allen & Unwin.

Roth, Jeffrey. (1994) *Firearms and Violence*. Research in Brief. Washington: National Institute of Justice.

Roy, Maria. (1982) "Four Thousand Partners in Violence: A Trend Analysis." In Maria Roy, ed. *The Abusive Partner: An Analysis of Domestic Battering*. New York: Van Nostrand Reinhold.

Russell, Diana E. (1982) *Rape in Marriage*. New York: Macmillan.

——. (1983) *Intra-Family Child Sexual Abuse: Final Report to the National Center on Child Abuse and Neglect*. Washington: U.S. Department of Health and Human Services.

——. (1984) *Sexual Exploitation: Rape, Child abuse, and Workplace Harassment*. Thousand Oaks: Sage.

——. (1986) *The Secret Trauma: Incest in the Lives of Girls and Women*. New York: Basic Books.

——, & Rebecca M. Bolen. (2000) *The Epidemic of Rape and Child Sexual Abuse in the United States*. Thousand Oaks: Sage.

Rutter, M. (1971) "Parent-Child Separation: Psychological Effects on the Children." *Journal of Child Psychology and Psychiatry 12*: 233–60.

——, B. Maughan, P. Mortimore, & J. Ouston. (1979) *Fifteen Thousand Hours*. London: Open Books.

Saltzman, Linda, & James Mercy. (1993) "Assaults Between Intimates: The Range of Relationships Involved." In Anna Wilson, ed. *Homicide: The Victim/Offender Connection*. Cincinnati: Anderson.

Samenow, Stanton E. (1984) *Inside the Criminal Mind*. New York: Time Books.

Sanchez-Jankowski, M. S. (1991) *Islands in the Street: Gangs and American Urban Society*. Berkeley: University of California Press.

Sandberg, A. A., G. F. Koepf, T. Ishiara, & T. S. Hanschka. (1961) "An XYY Human Male." *Lancet 262*: 488–89.

Sanger, William W. (2002) *History of Prostitution: Its Extent, Causes and Effects Throughout the World.* New York: Fredonia Books.

Sarafino, E. P. (1979) "An Estimate of the National Incidence of Sexual Offenses." *Child Welfare 58*, 2: 127–34.

Saunders, D. G. (1992) "A Typology of Men Who Batter Women: Three Types Derived From Cluster Analysis." *American Orthopsychiatry 62*: 264–75.

Schecter, Marshall D., & Leo Roberge. (1976) "Sexual Exploitation." In Ray E. Helfer & C. Henry Kempe, eds. *Child Abuse and Neglect: The Family and the Community.* Cambridge: Ballinger.

Schoenfeld, C. G. (1975) "A Psychoanalytic Theory of Juvenile Delinquency." In Edward E. Peoples, ed. *Readings in Correctional Casework and Counseling.* Pacific Palisades: Goodyear.

Schulsinger, F. (1972) "Psychopathy: Heredity and Environment." *International Journal of Mental Health 1*: 190–206.

Schwartz, Martin D. (1996) "Study of Masculinities and Crime." *Criminologist 21*, 1: 1–5.

——, & Victoria L. Pitts. (1995) "Exploring a Feminist Routine Activities Approach to Explaining Sexual Assault." *Justice Quarterly 12*: 9–31.

Schwartz-Watts, D., & D. W. Morgan. (1998) "Violent versus Nonviolent Stalkers." *Journal of the American Academy of Psychiatry Law 26*: 241–45.

Schwendinger, Julia R., & Herman Schwendinger. (1983) *Rape and Inequality.* Thousand Oaks: Sage.

Scottish Office. (1998) *Women Offenders–A Safer Way: A Review of Community Disposals and the Use of Custody for Women Offenders in Scotland.* Edinburgh: The Stationery Office.

Seghorn, T. K., R. A. Prentky, & R. J. Boucher. (1987) "Childhood Sexual Abuse in the Lives of Sexually Aggressive Offenders." *Journal of the American Academy of Child and Adolescent Psychiatry 26*: 262–67.

Serant, Claire. "Stalked: Any Woman Can Become a Victim of This Heinous Crime." *Essence* (October, 1993), pp. 73–76.

Shaw, Clifford R., & Henry D. McKay. (1932) "Are Broken Homes a Causative Factor in Juvenile Delinquency?" *Social Forces 10*: 514–24.

——, & Henry D. McKay. (1969) *Juvenile Delinquency and Urban Areas.* Chicago: University of Chicago Press.

Sheffield, Carole J. (1984) "Sexual Terrorism." In Jo Freeman, ed. *Women: A Feminist Perspective.* 4th ed. Mountain View: Mayfield.

Shelden, R. G. (1998) "Gender Bias in the Juvenile Justice System." *Juvenile and Family Court Journal 49*, 1: 11–26.

Sheldon, William H. (1942) *Varieties of Temperament.* New York: Harper and Row.

Sheley, J. F. (1985) *America's "Crime Problem": An Introduction to Criminology.* Belmont: Wadsworth.

——, & J. D. Wright. (1995) *In the Line of Fire: Youth, Guns and Violence in Urban America.* Hawthorne: Aldine De Gruyter.

Shihadeh, E., & D. J. Steffensmeir. (1994) "Economic Inequality, Family Disruption, and Urban Black Violence: Cities as Units of Stratification and Social Control." *Social Forces 73*, 1: 729–51.

Shore, M. F. (1971) "Psychological Theories of the Causes of Antisocial Behavior." *Crime and Delinquency 17*, 4: 456–58.

Short, J. F., Jr. (1964) "Gang Delinquency and Anomie." In Marshall B. Clinard, ed. *Anomie and Deviant Behavior.* New York: Free Press.

——, & F. L. Strodtbeck. (1965) *Group Process and Gang Delinquency.* Chicago: University of Chicago Press.

Silbert, Mimi. (1984) "Treatment of Prostitution Victims of Sexual Abuse." In Irving R. Stuart & Joanne G. Greer, eds. *Victims of Sexual Aggression: Treatment of Children, Women, and Men.* Hoboken: John Wiley & Sons.

Simmons, H. E. (1970) *Protective Services for Children.* 2nd ed. Sacramento: Citadel Press.

Simon, Rita J. (1975) *Women and Crime.* Lexington: D.C. Heath.

——, & J. Landis. (1991) *The Crimes Women Commit, The Punishments They Receive.* Lexington: Lexington Books.

Simpkinson, Anne A. "Clergy Sexual Abuse Found in All Faiths." (March 18, 2002) http://www.beliefnet.com.

Simpson, Sally. "Gendered Theory and Single Sex Research." http://www.ou.edu/soc/dwc/simpson2.htm.

Slocum, Walter, & Carol L. Stone. (1963) "Family Culture Patterns and Delinquent-Type Behavior." *Marriage and Family Living 25*: 202–8.

Slutske, Wendy, Andrew Heath, Stephen Dinwiddie, Pamela Madden, Kathleen Bucholz, Michael Dunne, Dixie Statham, & Nicholas Martin. (1977) "Modeling Genetic and Environmental Influences in the Etiology of Conduct Disorder: A Study of 2,682 Adult Twin Pairs." *Journal of Abnormal Psychology 106*, 2: 266–79.

Smart, Carol. (1979) "The New Female Criminal: Reality or Myth." *British Journal of Criminology 19*: 50–59.

——. (1995) *Law, Crime and Sexuality: Essays in Feminism.* Thousand Oaks: Sage.

Smith, Brent L., Kelly R. Damphouse, Freedom Jackson, & Amy Sellers. (2002) "The Prosecution and Punishment of International Terrorists in Federal Courts: 1980–1988." *Criminology 1*, 3: 311–37.

Smith, D. (1988) *The Everyday World as Problematic.* Milton Keyes: Open University Press.

Smith, H., & E. Israel. (1987) "Sibling Incest: A Study of the Dynamics of 25 Cases." *Child Abuse and Neglect 11*, 1: 101–8.

Smith, Merril D. (2002) *Sex Without Consent: Rape and Sexual Coercion in America.* New York: New York University Press.

Sohn, Ellen. (1994) "Antistalking Statutes: Do They Actually Protect Victims?" *Criminal Law Bulletin 30*, 3: 203–41.

Sokil-Katz, Jan, Roger Dunham, & Rick Zimmerman. (1997) "Family Structure Versus Parental Attachment in Controlling Adolescent Deviant Behavior: A Social Control Model." *Adolescence 32*: 199–215.

South Carolina Coalition Against Domestic Violence and Sexual Assault. "Child Sexual Assault." http://www.sccadvasa.org/child_sexual_assault.htm.

Spender, M. J., & P. Dunklee. (1986) "Sexual Abuse of Boys." *Pediatrics 78*: 133–37.

Spergel, I. A. (1990) "Youth Gangs: Continuity and Change." In M. Tonry & N. Morris, eds. *Crime and Justice: A Review of Research*, Vol. 12. Chicago: University of Chicago Press.

——. (1995) *The Youth Gang Problem*. New York: Oxford University Press.

Sprich, Susan, Joseph Biederman, Margaret H. Crawford, Elizabeth Mundy, & Stephen V. Fardone. (2000) "Adoptive and Biological Families of Children and Adolescents with ADHD." *Journal of the American Academy of Child and Adolescent Psychiatry 39*, 11: 1432–37.

Spunt, B., H. H. Brownstein, P. Goldstein, M. Fendrich, & H. J. Liberty. (1995) "Drug Use by Homicide Offenders." *Journal of Psychoactive Drugs 27*: 125–34.

"Stalking and Domestic Violence Report to Congress." May 2001. Office of Justice Programs. http://www.ojp.usdoj.gov.

Stanmeyer, William A. (1984) *The Seduction of Society*. Ann Arbor: Servant Books.

Steele, B. F. (1976) "Violence Without the Family." In Ray E. Helfer & C. Henry Kempe, eds. *Child Abuse and Neglect: The Family and the Community*. Cambridge: Ballinger.

——, & C. Pollock. (1968) "A Psychiatric Study of Parents Who Abuse Infants and Small Children." In R. E. Helfer & C. H. Kempe, eds. *The Battered Child*. Chicago: University of Chicago Press.

Steffensmeir, Darrell J. (1980) "Sex Differences in Patterns of Adult Crime, 1965–77: A Review and Assessment." *Social Forces 58*: 1098–99.

——, & Dana Haynie. (2000) "Gender, Structural Disadvantages and Urban Crime: Do Macrosocial Variables also Explain Female Offending Rates." *Criminology 38*, 2: 403–38.

——, & E. Allan. (1996) "Gender and Crime: Toward a Gendered Theory of Female Offending." *Annual Review of Sociology 22*: 459–87.

Stein, M. (1974) *Lovers, Friends, Slaves . . .* New York: Berkeley.

Steinmetz, Suzanne K. (1977) *The Cycle of Violence: Assertive, Aggressive, and Abusive Family Interaction*. New York: Praeger.

——. (1978) "The Battered Husband Syndrome." *Victimology 2*: 507.

Stieber, Tamara. "The Boys Who Sell Sex to Men in San Francisco." *Sacramento Bee* (March 4, 1984), p. A22.

Stratton, Peter, Helga Hanks, & Kevin D. Browne, eds. (2002) *Early Prediction and Prevention of Child Abuse: A Handbook*. Hoboken: John Wiley & Sons.

Straus, Murray A. (1973) "A General System Theory Approach to a Theory of Violence Between Family Members." *Social Science Information 12*, 3: 101–25.

——. (1993) "Physical Assaults by Wives: A Major Social Problem." In Richard J. Gelles & Denise R. Loseke, eds. *Current Controversies on Family Violence*. Thousand Oaks: Sage.

——, & Richard J. Gelles. (1990) *Physical Violence in American Families: Risk Factors and Adaptations to Violence in 8,145 Families*. New Brunswick: Transaction Publishers.

——, Richard J. Gelles, & Suzanne K. Steinmetz. (1980) *Behind Closed Doors: Violence in the American Family*. New York: Anchor Books.

Streshinsky, Shirley. "The Stalker and Her Prey." *Glamour* (August 1992), p. 238.

Sugarman, D., & G. Hotaling. (1998) "Dating Violence: A Review of Contextual and Risk Factors." In Barrie Levy, ed. *Dating Violence: Young Women in Danger.* Seattle: Seal Press.

Susman, E. J., G. Inhoff-Germain, E. D. Nottleman, D. L. Loriaux, G. B. Cutler, & G. P. Chrousos. (1987) "Hormones, Emotional Dispositions, and Aggressive Attributes in Young Adolescents." *Child Development 58*: 114–34.

Sutherland, Edwin H. (1939) *Principles of Criminology.* Philadelphia: Lippincott.

Sykes, Gresham M. (1974) "The Rise and Fall of Critical Criminology." *Journal of Criminal Law and Criminology 65*: 206–13.

——, & David Matza. (1957) "Techniques of Neutralization: A Theory of Delinquency." *American Sociological Review 22*: 664–70.

Szatmari, P., D. R. Offord, & M. H. Boyle. (1989) "Correlates, Associated Impairments and Patterns of Service Utilization of Children with Attention Deficit Disorder: Findings from the Ontario Child Health Study." *Journal of Child Psychology and Psychiatry 30*: 205–17.

Tannahill, Reay. (1980) *Sex in History.* New York; Stein and Day.

Tattersall, Clare. (1999) *Drugs, Runaways, and Teen Prostitutes.* New York: Rosen.

Taylor, C. S. (1989) *Dangerous Society.* East Lansing: Michigan State University Press.

Taylor, Jeanette, William G. Iacono, & Matt McGue. (2000) "Evidence for a Genetic Etiology of Early-Onset Delinquency." *Journal of Abnormal Psychology 109*, 4: 634–43.

Thomas, Mark. "A Study on the Psychospiritual Rehabilitation of the American Nation: The Patterns and Processes in Transforming a Culture of Crime and Violence." http://www.neteze.com/mkthomas/proposal.htm.

Thorbek, Susanne, & Bandana Pattanaik, eds. (2003) *Prostitution in a Global Context: Changing Patterns.* London: Zed Books.

Thornberry, T. P. (1998) "Membership in Youth Gangs and Involvement in Serious and Violent Offending." In R. Loeber & D. P. Farrington, eds. *Serious and Violent Offenders: Risk Factors and Successful Interventions.* Thousand Oaks: Sage.

Thrasher, Frederic M. (1927) *The Gang.* Chicago: University of Chicago Press.

Tjaden, Patricia, & Nancy Thoennes. (1998) *Stalking in America: Findings From The National Violence Against Women Survey.* Research in Brief. National Institute of Justice. Centers for Disease Control and Prevention. Washington: National Institute of Justice.

——, N. Thoennes, & C. J. Allison. (2000) "Comparing Stalking Victimization From Legal and Victim Perspectives." *Violence and Victims 15*: 7–22.

Torres, J. B. (1998) "Masculinity and Gender Roles Among Puerto Rican Men: Machismo on the U.S. Mainland." *American Journal of Orthopsychiatry 68*, 1: 16–26.

Totaling, G. T., & D. B. Sugarman. (1986) "An Analysis of Risk Markers in Husband to Wife Violence: The Current State of Knowledge." *Violence and Victims 1*: 101–24.

Tower, Cynthia C. (1998) *Understanding Child Abuse and Neglect.* Needham Heights: Allyn & Bacon.

Tremblay, R. E., B. Boulerice, P. W. Harden, P. McDuff, D. Perusse, R. O. Pihl, & M. Zoccolillo. (1996) *Do Children in Canada Become More Aggressive As They Approach*

Adolescence? Growing Up in Canada: National Longitudinal Survey of Children and Youth. Ottawa: Human Resources Development Canada and Statistics Canada.

Trujillo, Laura. "Escort Services Thriving Industry in Portland Area." *Oregonian* (June 7, 1996), p. B1.

U.S. Department of Education and Justice. (2000) *Indicators of School Crime and Safety.* Washington: Offices of Educational Research and Imprisonment and Justice Programs.

U.S. Department of Health and Human Services. (2001) *Child Maltreatment 1999.* Washington: Government Printing Office.

———. (2001) *Youth Violence: A Report of the Surgeon General.* Rockville: National Institute of Health and Mental Health.

———. Children's Bureau. (1998) *Child Maltreatment 1996: Reports From The States to the National Child Abuse and Neglect Data System.* Washington: Government Printing Office.

———. Substance Abuse and Mental Health Services Administration. (1996) *National Household Survey on Drug Abuse: Population Estimates 1995.* Rockville: U.S. Department of Health and Human Services.

U.S. Department of Justice. *An Analysis of National Data on the Prevalence of Alcohol Involvement in Crime.* http://www.ojp.usdoj.gov/bjs/.

———. "Juvenile Offenders and Victims: 1997 Update on Violence." http://ojjdp.ncjrs.org/pubs/juvoff/cases.html.

———. (1986) *Attorney General's Commission on Pornography: Final Report.* Vol. 1. Washington: Government Printing Office.

———. (1988) *Children Traumatized in Sex Rings.* Alexandria: National Center for Missing & Exploited Children.

———. (1992) *Child Sex Rings: A Behavioral Analysis, For Criminal Justice Professionals Handling Cases of Child Sexual Exploitation.* Alexandria: National Center for Missing & Exploited Children.

———. (1996) *Domestic Violence, Stalking, and Antistalking Legislation: An Annual Report to Congress Under the Violence Against Women Act.* Washington: National Institute of Justice.

———. (1998) *Youth Gangs: An Overview.* Washington: Office of Juvenile Justice and Delinquency Prevention.

———. (1999) *Cyberstalking: A New Challenge for Law Enforcement and Industry.* Attorney General's Report to the Vice President. Washington: U.S. Department of Justice.

———. (1999) *Juvenile Offenders and Victims: 1999 National Report.* Washington: Office of Juvenile Justice and Delinquency Prevention.

———. (2000) *Firearm Injury and Death From Crime, 1993–97.* Washington: Office of Justice Programs.

———. (2000) *Full Report of the Prevalence, Incidence, and Consequences of Violence Against Women: Findings From the National Violence Against Women Survey.* Washington: National Institute of Justice.

———. (2000) *Kidnapping of Juveniles: Patterns From NIBRS.* Washington: Office of Justice Programs.

———. Bureau of Justice Statistics. (1983) *Report to the Nation on Crime and Justice: The Data.* Washington: Government Printing Office.

——. Bureau of Justice Statistics. (1991) *Female Victims of Violent Crime.* Washington: Government Printing Office.

——. Bureau of Justice Statistics. (1992) *Drugs, Crime, and the Justice System.* Washington: Government Printing Office.

——. Bureau of Justice Statistics. (1993) *Highlights from 20 Years of Surveying Crime Victims: The National Crime Victimization Survey, 1973–92.* Washington: Government Printing Office.

——. Bureau of Justice Statistics. (1994) *Child Rape Victims, 1992.* Washington: Office of Justice Programs.

——. Bureau of Justice Statistics. (1995) *Drugs and Crime Facts, 1994.* Washington: Government Printing Office.

——. Bureau of Justice Statistics. (1997) *Sex Offenses and Offenders: An Analysis of Data on Rape and Sexual Assault.* Washington: Office of Justice Programs.

——. Bureau of Justice Statistics. (1999) *Mental Health and Treatment of Inmates and Probationers.* Washington: Office of Justice Programs.

——. Bureau of Justice Statistics. (1999) *Substance Abuse and Treatment, State and Federal Prisoners, 1997.* Washington: Office of Justice Programs.

——. Bureau of Justice Statistics. (2000) *Drug Use, Testing, and Treatment in Jails.* Washington: Office of Justice Programs.

——. Bureau of Justice Statistics. (2000) *Incarcerated Parents and Their Children.* Washington: Office of Justice Programs.

——. Bureau of Justice Statistics Bulletin. (2001) *Capital Punishment 2000.* Washington: Office of Justice Programs.

——. Bureau of Justice Statistics Bulletin. (2001) *HIV in Prisons and Jails, 1999.* Washington: Office of Justice Programs.

——. Bureau of Justice Statistics Bulletin. (2001) *Prison and Jail Inmates at Midyear 2000.* Washington: Office of Justice Programs.

——. Bureau of Justice Statistics Bulletin. (2001) *Prisoners in 2000.* Washington: Office of Justice Programs.

——. Bureau of Justice Statistics Crime Data Brief. (2000) *Homicide Trends in the United States: 1998 Update.* Washington: Office of Justice Programs.

——. Bureau of Justice Statistics Factbook. (1998) *Violence by Intimates: Analysis of Data on Crimes by Current or Former Spouses, Boyfriends, and Girlfriends.* Washington: Government Printing Office.

——. Bureau of Justice Statistics Special Report. (1987) *Robbery Victims.* Washington: Office of Justice Programs.

——. Bureau of Justice Statistics Special Report. (1998) *Workplace Violence, 1992–96.* Washington: Office of Justice Programs.

——. Bureau of Justice Statistics Special Report. (1999) *Carjackings in the United States, 1992–96.* Washington: Office of Justice Programs.

——. Bureau of Justice Statistics Special Report. (2000) *Effects of NIBRS on Crime Statistics.* Washington: Government Printing Office.

——. Bureau of Justice Statistics Special Report (2001) *Sourcebook of Criminal Justice Statistics 2000.* Washington: Government Printing Office.

——. Bureau of Justice Statistics Special Report. (2001) *Violence in the Workplace, 1993–99*. Washington: Office of Justice Programs.

——. Federal Bureau of Investigation. (2000) *National Crime Information Center 2000 Operating Manual*. Washington: Office of Justice Programs.

——. Federal Bureau of Investigation. (2001) *Crime in the United States: Uniform Crime Reports 2000*. Washington: Government Printing Office.

——. Office of Juvenile Justice and Delinquency Prevention. (1992) *Child Molesters: A Behavioral Analysis For Law Enforcement Officers Investigating Causes of Child Sexual Exploitation*. Alexandria: National Center for Missing & Exploited Children.

——. Office of Juvenile Justice and Delinquency Prevention. (1999) *Prostitution of Children and Child-Sex Tourism: An Analysis of Domestic and International Response*. Alexandria: National Center for Missing & Exploited Children.

van den Oord, Edwin, J. G., Dorret I. Boomsma, & Frank C. Verhulst. (1994) "A Study of Problem Behaviors in 10- to 15-Year Old Biologically Related and Unrelated International Adoptees." *Behavior Genetics 24*, 3.

Vander Mey, Brenda J., & Ronald L. Neff. (1986) *Incest as Child Abuse: Research and Applications*. New York: Praeger.

Vanderbilt, Heidi. "Incest: A Chilling Report." *Lear's* (February 1992), pp. 52–60.

"The Varieties of Strain Theory." http://faculty.ncwc.edu/toconnor/301/301lect09.htm.

VAWnet Applied Research Forum. National Electronic Network on Violence Against Women. (1999) "Marital Rape." National Resource Center on Domestic Violence, San Francisco.

Volkonsky, Anastasia. (1995) "Legalizing the 'Profession' Would Sanction the Abuse." *Insight on the News 11*: 20–22.

Wadsworth, M. (1979) *Roots of Delinquency*. London: Martin Robertson.

Waldfogel, Jane. (2001) *The Future of Child Protection: How to Break the Cycle of Abuse and Neglect*. Cambridge: Harvard University Press.

Waldo, Gordon, & Simon Dinitz. (1967) "Personality Attributes of the Criminal: An Analysis of Research Studies, 1950–1965." *Journal of Research in Crime and Delinquency 4*: 185–202.

Waldorf, Dan, & Sheigla Murphy. (1990) "Intravenous Drug Use and Syringe-Sharing Practices of Call Men and Hustlers." In Martin A. Plant, ed. *AIDS, Drugs, and Prostitution*. London: Routledge.

Walker, Lenore E. (1976) "Treatment Alternatives for Battered Women." In Jane R. Chapman & Margaret Gates, eds. *Women into Wives: The Legal and Economic Impact of Marriage*. Thousand Oaks: Sage.

——. (1979) *The Battered Woman*. New York: Harper & Row.

——. (1984) *The Battered Woman Syndrome*. New York: Springer.

Walklate, S. (1998) *Understanding Criminology: Current Theoretical Debates*. Philadelphia: Open University Press.

Walsh, Anthony. "Companions in Crime: A Biosocial Perspective." http://human-nature.com/nibbs/02/walsh.html.

Ward, Sally K., Kathy Chapman, Ellen Cohn, Susan White, & Kirk Williams. (1991) "Acquaintance Rape and the College Social Scene." *Family Relations 40*: 65–71.

Warr, Mark. (2002) *Companions in Crime: The Social Aspects of Criminal Conduct.* New York: Cambridge University Press.

Watson, Jennifer, Michele Cascardi, & Daniel O'Leary. (2001) "High School Students' Responses to Dating Aggression." *Violence and Victims 16*, 3: 339–43.

Webster, D. W., P. S. Gainer, & H. R. Champion. (1993) "Weapon Carrying Among Inner-City Junior High School Students: Defensive Behavior versus Aggressive Delinquency." *American Journal of Public Health 83*: 1604–08.

Weeks, H. Ashley, & Margaret G. Smith. (1939) "Juvenile Delinquency and Broken Homes in Spokane, Washington." *Social Forces 18*: 48–49.

Weinberg, S. Kirson. (1958) "Sociological Processes and Factors in Juvenile Delinquency." In Joseph S. Roucek, ed. *Juvenile Delinquency.* New York: Philosophical Library.

Weinrott, M. R., & M. Saylor. (1991) "Self-Report of Crimes Committed by Sex Offenders." *Journal of Interpersonal Violence 6*, 3: 286–300.

Weisberg, D. Kelly. (1985) *Children of the Night: A Study of Adolescent Prostitution.* Lexington: Lexington Books.

Wells, L. Edward, & Joseph H. Rankin. (1986) "The Broken Homes Model of Delinquency: Analytic Issues." *Journal of Research in Crime and Delinquency 23*: 68–93.

——, & Joseph H. Rankin. (1991) "Families and Delinquency: A Meta-Analysis of the Impact of Broken Homes." *Social Problems* 38: 73–93.

Williams, M. (1988) "Father-Son Incest: A Review and Analysis of Reported Incidents." *Clinical Social Work Journal 16*, 2: 165–79.

West, D. J., & D. P. Farrington. (1973) *Who Becomes Delinquent?* London: Heinemann.

White, J. L., T. E. Moffit, & P. A. Silva. (1989) "A Prospective Replication of the Protective Effects of IQ in Subjects at High Risk for Juvenile Delinquency." *Journal of Consulting and Clinical Psychology* 57: 719–24.

Whitehurst, R. (1971) "Violently Jealous Husbands." *Sexual Behavior 1*, 4: 32–38, 40–41.

Widom, Cathy S. (1989) "The Cycle of Violence." *Science 244*: 160–66.

Wieczorek, W., J. Welte, & E. Abel. (1990) "Alcohol, Drugs, and Murder: A Study of Convicted Homicide Offenders." *Journal of Criminal Justice 18*: 217–27.

Wilson, H. (1987) "Parental Supervision Re-examined." *British Journal of Criminology* 27: 275–301.

Witkin, H., S. Mednick, F. Schulsinger, E. Bakkestrom, K. Christiansen, D. Goodenough, K. Hirschorn, C. Lundsteen, D. Owen, J. Philip, D. Rubin, & M. Stocking. (1977) "Criminality, Aggression, and Intelligence Among XYY and XXY Men." In S. Mednick & K. O. Christiansen, eds. *Biosocial Bases of Criminal Behavior.* New York: Gardner.

Wolfgang, Marvin E. (1958) *Patterns in Criminal Homicide.* Philadelphia: University of Pennsylvania Press.

——, & Franco Ferracuti. (1967) *The Subculture of Violence; Toward an Integrated Theory in Criminology.* London: Tavistock.

——, & R. B. Strohm. (1956) "The Relationship Between Alcohol and Criminal Homicide." *Quarterly Journal of Studies on Alcoholism 17*: 411–26.

Wolman, Benjamin B. (1999) *Antisocial Behavior.* Amherst: Prometheus Books.

Wong, Sui K. (1999) "Acculturation, Peer Relations, and Delinquent Behavior of Chinese-Canadian Youth." *Adolescence 34*, 1: 107.

Worrall, A. (1995) "Gender, Criminal Justice and Probation." In G. McIvor, ed. *Working With Offenders: Research Highlights in Social Work 26.* London: Jessica Kingsley.

Wright, J. A., A. G. Burgess, A. W. Burgess, A. T. Laszlo, G. O. McCrary, & J. E. Douglas. (1996) "A Typology of Interpersonal Stalking." *Journal of Interpersonal Violence 11*, 4: 487–503.

Wyatt, Gail E., & Gloria J. Powell, eds. (1988) *Lasting Effects of Child Sexual Abuse.* Thousand Oaks: Sage.

Yiaoru, L., & H. B. Kaplan. (1999) "Explaining the Gender Differences in Adolescent Delinquent Behavior: A Longitudinal Test of Mediating Mechanisms." *Criminology 37*, 1: 195–215.

Yllo, Kersti, & David Finkelhor. (1985) *License to Rape: Sexual Abuse of Wives.* New York: Free Press.

Yochelson, Samuel, & Stanton E. Samenow. (1976) *The Criminal Personality.* Vol. 1. New York: Jason Arsonson.

Young, Thomas J. (1993) "Unemployment and Property Crime: Not a Simple Relationship." *American Journal of Economics and Sociology 52*: 413–15.

Youth Risk Behavior Survey. http://www.Alfred.edu/teenviolence/potential_violence.html.

Zalba, S. (1971) "Battered Children." *Trans-Action 8*: 58–61.

Zimring, F. E. (1981) "Kids, Groups and Crime: Some Implications of a Well-Known Secret." *Journal of Criminal Law and Criminology 72*: 867–85.

Zona, M. A., K. K. Sharma, & M. D. Lane. (1993) "A Comparative Study of Erotomanic and Obsessional Subjects in a Forensic Sample." *Journal of Forensic Sciences 38*: 894–903.

——, R. E. Palarea, & J. C. Lane. (1998) "Psychiatric Diagnosis and the Offender-Victim Typology of Stalking." In J. R. Meloy, ed. *The Psychology of Stalking: Clinical and Forensic Perspectives.* San Diego: Academic Press.

INDEX